Bertrand Russell
Public Intellectual

BERTRAND RUSSELL
Public Intellectual

Tim Madigan and Peter Stone, Editors

SPOKESMAN

Copyright © 2021 by Tim Madigan and Peter Stone. All rights reserved. No part of this work may be reproduced in any technology or format without written permission from the publisher, except by a reviewer.

First and second editions published in the USA by Tiger Bark Press, 2021
This edition published in Britain in 2022 by Spokesman Books, 5 Churchill Park, Nottingham, NG4 2HF, England. www.spokesmanbooks.org

Tiger Bark Press books are published by Steven Huff, and designed by Philip Memmer.

The cover image is a public domain drawing by J.F. Horrabin.

This book was made possible with the support of the Trinity College Dublin Association and Trust.

The editors wish to thank *The Journal of Bertrand Russell Studies* for allowing use of the previously published "Six Degrees of Separation" and "Chomsky and Russell Revisited" and *Free Inquiry* magazine for allowing use of the previously published "A Chair of Indecency: The Bertrand Russell/City College Case," all of which have been revised for this volume.

ISBN: 978 0 85124 910 0

Printed and bound in Britain

Contents

PETER STONE	Preface to the New Edition	i
MICHAEL RUSE	*Foreword* Bertrand Russell as Public Intellectual: A Personal Reflection	7
PETER STONE	Introduction: Who Was Bertrand Russell?	13
TIM MADIGAN	Six Degrees of Bertrand Russell	25
JOHN LENZ	How Bertrand Russell Became a New Kind of Intellectual during World War I	31
TIM MADIGAN	Russell and Dewey on Education: Similarities and Differences	51
CARA RICE	Somewhere in England: Voluntary Education at Beacon Hill and Summerhill	61
DAVID E. WHITE	Russell in the Jazz Age	75
THOM WEIDLICH	A Chair of Indecency: The Bertrand Russell/City College Case	91
PETER STONE	Russell the Political Activist	99
DAVID BLITZ	A Public Intellectual on War and Peace: Russell's "Little Books" During the Great War and the Cold War	135
TIM MADIGAN	Russell in Popular Culture	167
ROBERT HEINEMAN	*The World as I Found It:* Twentieth Century British Philosophy through a Literary Prism	175
CHAD TRAINER	Would Russell Have Used E-Mail? A Continuing Perplexity	187

PETER STONE	The Logic of Storytelling and the Storytelling of Logic	213
TIM MADIGAN	Russell and *The Conquest of Happiness*	241
LANDON D.C. ELKIND	Russell on the Ethical Value of Logic	251
TONY SIMPSON	Bertrand Russell's Long Pursuit of Peace	269
ALAN SCHWERIN	Did Russell Experience an Epiphany in 1911?	279
PETER STONE	Chomsky and Russell Revisited	299
"BUT THERE ARE ALWAYS EXCEPTIONS": An Interview with Noam Chomsky by Peter Stone		321
ABOUT THE CONTRIBUTORS		335

Preface to the Second Edition

Peter Stone

I AM DELIGHTED TO SEE A NEW EDITION of *Bertrand Russell: Public Intellectual* appear in print, as is my co-editor, Tim Madigan. By way of a foreword to this new edition, I would like to say a few words as to how Tim and I came to produce this book.

Tim and I had been in conversation for some time about writing a book on Russell—something that would help introduce people to Russell, his life, work, and legacy. We had both been members of the Bertrand Russell Society (BRS) for quite some time, but we knew that Russell had been dead and gone for decades, and so public awareness of him was fading. As enthusiastic Russellians, we hoped to share our enthusiasm for a new generation concerned with philosophy, science, humanism, and peace—all causes near and dear to Russell's heart.

And so we worked on the book, off and on, here and there, for several years, under the working title *So You Want to Read Bertrand Russell*. (The title might have been a bit presumptuous—after all, its whole point was to make people want to read Bertrand Russell!) To that end, I wrote two chapters for the book, one on Russell's politics and one on "Who Was Bertrand Russell?" (Both these essays are included in this volume.) Our mutual friend, David White, also wrote a chapter on Russell's relationship with Horace Liveright, the maverick publisher (also included in this volume). But Tim and I struggled to come up with a structure for the book, one that would make it work as a truly serviceable introduction to the many sides of Russell.

Eventually, we realized that the book would work better as a collection of essays, each dealing with Russell from a different angle. It became easy to conceive of a unifying theme to the anthology—Russell as public intellectual. The book would not, therefore, delve into the details of Russell's philosophy, except insofar as he presented his philosophy to the general public, through such books as *The Problems of Philosophy* (1912) and *A History of Western Philosophy* (1945). This theme, in turn, made it easy to recruit authors from a wide variety of disciplines to contribute papers to the volume.

    The resulting book explores Russell the public intellectual from a wide variety of perspectives. The first edition examines Russell's long career of political activism (chapter 8), including his specific interventions during the First World War (chapters 3 and 9) and the Cold War (chapter 9). It considers Russell's connections to other leading public figures (chapter 2), such as Horace Liveright (chapter 6), and John Dewey (chapters 3 and 4). It examines his views on education (chapter 4), including his experience running the Beacon Hill school (chapter 5). It looks at the price Russell paid for his public life during the infamous CCNY affair (chapter 7). And it looks at Russell's continuing presence in our public sphere (chapter 10), including his appearances in novels (chapter 11) and graphic novels (chapter 13). It even takes up what must surely be a most pressing question to any Russellian—would a man of letters like Russell have used e-mail (chapter 12)? And the introductory essay provides everything a complete beginner to Russell might need to know about him—hopefully enough to pique some curiosity!

    The first edition of this book received a reception that was most gratifying to us. It won the 2017 BRS Book Award. It also received favourable reviews in places like *Russell,* the leading journal of Russell studies, and *Free Inquiry* magazine, a well-known resource for freethinkers (Andersson 2017-2018; Flynn 2018/2019). The reception was such that a new edition seemed clearly warranted. We think the new contributions add much value to the collection. They include two papers on Russell's philosophy— one on the *Conquest of Happiness* (1930), one of Russell's most famous popular books (chapter 14), and one on the ethical value of Russell's logic (chapter 15). They also include a paper on Russell the peace activist (chapter 16), Russell's search for certainty in his popular book *The Problems of Philosophy* (chapter 17), and a comparison of Russell with another leading public intellectual, Noam Chomsky (chapter 18). I had the good fortune of interviewing Chomsky about Russell as well, and this interview forms the final chapter of this volume.

All in all, we think the new edition provides an even better introduction to Russell as public intellectual. We very much hope it will bring a new generation of readers to Russell. In the current crazy world, Russell still has a lot to say. I'll conclude this introduction with one of his more astute pieces of advice to the reading public: "Remember your humanity and forget the rest. If you can do so, the way lies open for a new paradise; if you cannot, there lies before you the risk of universal death." In the age of COVID-19, climate change, and the continuing danger of nuclear Armageddon, these words could not be more timely.

We dedicate this second edition to the late Michael Berumen (1952-2020), a stalwart Russellian.

Bibliography

Andersson, Stefan. 2017-2018. Review of *Bertrand Russell: Public Intellectual* edited by Tim Madigan and Peter Stone. *Russell* n.s. 37 (2): 348-360.

Flynn, Tom. 2018/2019. "A Worthy Introduction to Russell." *Free Inquiry,* December/January.

Foreword

BERTRAND RUSSELL AS PUBLIC INTELLECTUAL: A PERSONAL REFLECTION

Michael Ruse

THE ONLY TIME I EVER SAW BERTRAND RUSSELL IN THE FLESH, as it were—although it was at a long distance and he was then very old, so how much flesh there was to be seen is perhaps another matter—was on Easter Monday in 1961 in Trafalgar Square in the heart of London, at the conclusion of an Aldermaston March. I should explain that then, as now, Britain had the H-Bomb and there was a vigorous (and obviously in the end unsuccessful) drive to get rid of it. The Campaign for Nuclear Disarmament (CND) was the organization leading the fight and every Easter it used to sponsor a walk from Aldermaston in Berkshire, where the Bomb was designed and made, to Trafalgar Square, taking four days (about fifty miles or so), and ending as a kind of climax with speeches given from the plinth of Nelson's column, the towering monument to the great naval hero, Admiral Horatio Nelson, victor over the fleet of Napoleon at the battle of Trafalgar in 1805. Russell who (I presume) had only joined the march in the last stages (he would have been about ninety then) was one of the speakers and I still remember his rather high-pitched aristocratic voice sounding out across the crowds in the square. At the end of the speeches, he and other leaders went up Whitehall to the home of the Prime Minister (Harold Macmillan) on Downing Street (less than half a mile), where they sat on the pavement and were promptly arrested. I went off to Green Park with a rather pretty girl I had met on the March, where we lay in the grass and kissed. I had never met her before and I never met her again, but the Aldermaston Marches were those sorts of occasions.

That I should have been there that day was almost predetermined. My family were Quakers, so inclined to pacifism generally, and the opposition to nuclear weaponry was part and parcel of this attitude. I was an undergraduate so of an age where spending four nights sleeping on the floors of schoolrooms with a crowd of strangers was almost inviting, especially if (as was the case) in those far off (pre-pill) days virtually uniquely half of the crowd was of the opposite sex. Marching along through the suburbs of London chanting our hymns and songs was so much fun.

> Don't you hear the H-bomb's thunder
> Echo like the crack of doom?
> While they rend the skies asunder
> Fall-out makes the earth a tomb
> Do you want your homes to tumble
> Rise in smoke towards the sky?
> Will you let your cities crumble
> Will you see your children die?
>
> *Chorus:*
> Men and women, stand together
> Do not heed the men of war
> Make your minds up now or never
> Ban the bomb for evermore

Bliss was it in that dawn to be alive.

A privilege and thrill it was to be part of the same group as Bertrand Russell, even though he was so high and I so low. As was usual for Quakers in England in the 1950s my family was fairly middle-class, fairly left-wing, with some pretentions to being intellectuals. To be honest, they were pretentions. The radio—in those days only the government-run BBC—had three channels: the Home Service, with lots of local news and middle-brow programs; the Light Programme, for the working classes and what you would hear in factories during the day; and the Third Programme, for eggheads. It might broadcast a reading of T. S. Eliot's *Murder in the Cathedral* followed by a few snappy, twelve-tone tunes by Arnold Schoenberg. I am sure my father was not alone in listening to the Third Programme until the family had closed the front door, at which point he would turn to the "Goon Show" (with Peter Sellers, Spike Milligan, and Harry Secombe) on the Home Service. But to be fair, my father did try and my mother (who was a more formidable intellect) did support the attempt to live the life of the mind, and Bertrand Russell—along with a number of other figures of whom I remember particularly Julian Huxley the biologist and Alan Bullock the historian—were significant contributors to that world to which my parents aspired.

Russell was certainly the leader of the group and particularly cherished was a radio debate on the nature and existence of God in which he had engaged with Father Frederick Copleston S. J.. You might think that as Quakers my parents' sympathies would have been with Father Copleston, but that is to discount the fact of their being both British and Protestant. Anyone against Jesuits had the tide flowing with them, although Russell, to be fair, needed no such help. Recently, while writing a book on atheism, I had occasion to return to the encounter and found that (although it is true that many of the arguments were hardly new) Russell had gone after the priest under full sail with all colors flying. Going back to it after many years, I am hardly surprised to find how seriously technical the debate was with detailed discussions about the nature of necessary existence and so forth. Although the flesh was sometimes weak, my father had the right ideals. I am interested to reflect—and rather proud both of my parents and of the culture from which we all came—that being a public intellectual as Russell was (and to be fair, in his way, Copleston also) did not mean compromise on the level of debate. Serious subjects required serious discussion and one was expected to keep up to the mark. Russell may have been the professional in the public marketplace, but that did not mean he was going to dumb down his thinking or his expectations of and demands on his audience.

In fact, it was thanks to Bertrand Russell that I had my first exposure to philosophy. I must have been about fourteen (the summer of 1954), home for the holidays from boarding school, and my father plonked down in my lap the very large volume by Russell on the *History of Western Philosophy*. Again, I suspect that the aspirations were greater than the realities, because I don't think my father himself had read it, but he thought that I should! Well, it certainly was a change from Nicholas Monserrat's *The Cruel Sea* and Neville Shute's *A Town Like Alice*, which was my kind of reading in those days. I think, although I cannot swear to it, that I got to about page one hundred out of what seemed in those days about fifteen thousand pages. (I find on checking that it was less than four hundred pages. I am now beginning to wonder if my memory plays other tricks and that my headmaster was not in fact twenty-five feet tall.) Many years later, just after McMaster University had bought the Russell Papers—something that has personal resonance because, having come to North America in 1962, it was at Mac that I started graduate school and so it is an institution that I love perhaps above all others—I remember going to the library and being shown the manuscript for that book. I am still incredibly impressed that there was no more than about one correction a page and that the text flowed fluently as the ideas came out in perfectly formed sentences. I know that for Russell it was something of a money-making pot boiler, but still.

I am afraid however that it was all a bit beyond me, although I still remember the poem about Bishop George Berkeley, by Ronald Knox, "God in the Quad."

> There was a young man who said, "God
> Must find it exceedingly odd
> If he finds that this tree
> Continues to be
> When there's no one about in the Quad."
>
> *Reply*
> Dear Sir:
> "Your astonishment's odd:
> I am always about in the Quad.
> And that's why the tree
> Will continue to be,
> Since observed by,
> Yours faithfully,
> God."

Perhaps somewhat unkindly, those limericks have stayed with me. In fact they are the only thing about Berkeley that has stayed with me, and to be frank I am untroubled by this. He has always struck me as a very minor stop along the way from Locke to Hume. Although I grant you that his thinking about tar water probably merits reexamination.

Speaking now a bit more seriously—it is hard to be entirely serious about Berkeley—although I may have failed in my adolescent Russell reading, he did then and for the rest of my life fill me with the conviction that intellectuals have a duty to the public. I don't say all intellectuals all of the time to all of the public. I have had worthy colleagues who would make a description of oral sex with a giraffe boring. Not everyone is so *gifted*, if I might make use of the term fully realizing that a lot of academics think that any approach to the public is prostitution of one's talents and status. But some of us are. I like to pride myself that I am one such. This has led me into such activities as being an expert witness on the philosophy of science for the American Civil Liberties Union in 1981 in a successful attempt in the State of Arkansas to overthrow a law making the teaching of biblical literalism mandatory in the publicly financed schools in the state. Making an effort to speak to regular people about serious things, as Russell did through my childhood and on to my young manhood—I realize he had been doing it long before I was born (in 1940)—seems to me to be not just a socially good thing but a morally good thing. I have no more religious belief than did Russell, but I (obviously like he) take very seriously the parable of the talents. We are not put on this earth just to have a good time, but to take seriously our lives and to use that with which we are blessed for the good of others.

That is what I got from Bertrand Russell. As a professional philosopher—despite reading the *History of Western Philosophy*!—I owe a great deal to Russell's pioneering work on logic and mathematics at the beginning of the century. Like most people I suspect I don't think the logicism program—deriving mathematics from the principles of logic—works, but I am almost daily aware of how much we owe Russell in the attempt to show this. However, for me overall, it has always been Russell the public intellectual that counts most. The aristocrat who went to prison in the Great War to protest against the insane slaughter in Belgium and Northern France. The man who was so appalled at the dreadful system of education in Britain that he founded and ran his own alternative school. The atheist who not only gave trenchant arguments against the existence of the deity, but who showed through his own life how a belief in God is not only unneeded to be a full human being, but in some respects a great hindrance. And then, towards the end of his life, the protester against the obscenity of nuclear weapons, even though there were times when one suspects that his fellow travelers used a rather frail old man to their own ends. (My professor, Stephan Körner, who worshiped the ground on which Russell walked, would get incandescent on this subject.)

I once had the very great privilege of writing a new introduction to a book Russell had penned on the topic of science and religion. I am not given to hero worship. Since apparently Jesus is a man that is one of the reasons why I am not a Christian. But if I were, then along with Johann Sebastian Bach, René Descartes—the man whose *Meditations* convinced me within five minutes that I could never be anything but a philosopher—and Charles Dickens, there would be a place in my Pantheon for Bertrand Arthur William Russell.

Introduction

WHO WAS BERTRAND RUSSELL?*

Peter Stone

BERTRAND ARTHUR WILLIAM RUSSELL ENTERED THE WORLD on May 18, 1872 in the village of Trelleck, now part of Wales. The youngest of three children born to John and Katharine Russell, Bertie (as he was known to his family) was definitely a child of the aristocracy; his grandfather, also named John Russell, had twice served as prime minister, and was made an earl by Queen Victoria in 1861. Bertie's childhood was marred by tragedy. When he was two, his sister Rachel contracted diphtheria, which subsequently infected their mother as well. Both mother and sister died in 1874, leaving Bertie's father devastated. He never recovered from these losses, and succumbed to bronchitis only two years later. By 1876, Bertie and his brother, Frank, were alone.

Well, not completely alone. Russell's grandparents were still alive, and moved quickly to take custody of the two children. This meant going against the will of Russell's parents. John and Katharine had lived an eccentric, bohemian lifestyle, and had named Douglas Spalding (the children's tutor) and T.J. Cobden-Sanderson as guardians of their children. But Spalding and Cobden-Sanderson, like Bertie's parents, were freethinkers, and not at all suitable in the eyes of Russell's devoutly religious grandparents. More importantly, Spalding had engaged in a sexual affair with Bertie's mother, apparently with her husband's consent. (Spalding suffered from consumption, and so never married. Apparently, Bertie's parents did not think it fair that he should be denied a sexual relationship.) Bertie's grandparents learned of the affair by reading his mother's journals, and took Spalding and Cobden-Sanderson to court. The two guardians were well aware of

---

* I would like to thank the Bay Area Russell Set (BARS), a local chapter of the Bertrand Russell Society (BRS), for a stimulating discussion of an early draft of this short introduction to Russell. Emma Pease offered particularly detailed criticism, which has benefited this work.

their chances in court against a former prime minister, and so surrendered custody without a fight. Bertie and Frank were quickly taken to Pembroke Lodge, an estate given to Lord Russell and his wife by Queen Victoria to occupy for the rest of their lives.

Lord Russell died in 1878, when Bertie was only six, and so he and Frank were brought up primarily by their grandmother, Frances. Both Bertie and Frank found life at Pembroke Lodge dour and depressing. Frank became very rebellious, but Bertie retreated into introspection, unable to accept the outlook of his grandmother but unwilling to act out or cause his relatives pain. This led him, for example, to conceal his growing doubts as an adolescent regarding God and religion. (His grandmother, who had shocked the British aristocracy by becoming a Unitarian at age 70, was uninterested in details of theology, and didn't care what sort of religion one practiced so long as one had a religion.) He developed his doubts—dismissing the existence of free will, an afterlife, and finally God—keeping them secret by writing them out in Greek letters, in a notebook he labeled "Greek Exercises."

Russell never attended an elementary school or high school, but was educated by private tutors. His first exposure to school came in 1888, at the age of 16, when he enrolled at B.A. Green's University and Army Tutors in Southgate, London. The school was a "crammer," designed to prepare the young and well-placed as quickly as possible for the various examinations they would need to pass. Russell's grandmother wanted him to be well-prepared for the entrance examination at Cambridge University, and indeed he had no trouble passing the exam, winning a minor scholarship in mathematics. Russell arrived at Trinity College, Cambridge in 1890, and found the experience immensely liberating. Here, unlike at Pembroke Lodge, Russell was free to explore ideas in the company of likeminded truth-seekers. He quickly became close to a number of people, including a fellow student named G.E. Moore and a professor named Alfred North Whitehead. It was Whitehead who had read Russell's entrance examination, and had been very impressed. Whitehead belonged to a secret academic society at Cambridge called the Conversazione Society, but more famously known as the "Apostles." The Apostles prided themselves on being the intellectual elite of Cambridge, and were very secretive regarding their membership and their activities. Whitehead quietly recommended Russell to the group, and by 1892 he was accepted. Russell would gain great intellectual pleasure from his association with the group over the decades to come.

Russell studied a variety of subjects, including economics and politics, but he quickly gravitated toward philosophy and mathematics. He took his first tripos (a set of exams) in math, and scored seventh in his class ("seventh wrangler"). He then took his second tripos, and got a First in Moral Philosophy in 1894. The successful completion of the first and second tripos led to Russell receiving a BA from Cambridge that year. He subsequently received an MA from Cambridge in January 1897, and his first major work in philosophy, *An Essay on the Foundations of Geometry*, won him a Prize Fellowship at Trinity in 1895. (This work was published as a book in 1897.) Russell then worked as a lecturer at Trinity until the First World War.

While Russell had always been fascinated by mathematics, and the certainty it seemed to promise in the realm of knowledge, he was deeply unsatisfied with the mathematics he learned at Cambridge. To him, it seemed to be nothing more than a toolkit of technical tricks used to solve problems. It functioned with only a vague and intuitive understanding of some of the central concepts that lay at its core, such as "number," "limit," and "infinity." He was therefore delighted to learn that there were mathematicians elsewhere in the world—great minds like Georg Cantor, Karl Weierstrass, and Richard Dedekind—who were actively tackling these difficult questions. This led Russell into the area of work in which he would establish his intellectual reputation—the philosophy of mathematics.

With his friend G.E. Moore, Russell became one of the founders of a movement in philosophy called analytic philosophy. This movement was inspired by the idea that many concepts of ordinary language are vague, and that the purpose of philosophy is to make them more precise, and thereby advance our ability to establish which ideas are true and which are false. This attitude is clearly visible in Russell's attitude towards mathematics, and his desire to define more rigorously the central concepts of the discipline. This project gained decisive direction when Russell became acquainted in 1900 with the work of Giuseppe Peano, an Italian mathematician who had provided a set of axioms for the natural numbers suitable for deriving the results of traditional arithmetic. Russell was inspired by this work, and believed that it could be extended to show that all of mathematics could be derived from a few foundational concepts of logic. (In philosophy, the belief that such a derivation is possible is known as *logicism*.) He had already been tinkering with the idea of writing a book on the foundations of mathematics; his encounter with Peano gave this work a definite direction.

To this end, Russell wrote a book entitled *The Principles of Mathematics* (1903). He hoped to write a sequel to advance the ideas in this book further and to tie up a number of philosophical "loose ends." He teamed up with his old mentor at Cambridge, Alfred North Whitehead. Whitehead had also written a book on the foundations of mathematics entitled *A Treatise on Universal Algebra* (1898), and wished to publish a sequel to his own book. Russell and Whitehead began collaborating on a work that eventually became the three-volume *Principia Mathematica* (published in 1910, 1912, and 1913). It is a long and difficult work, and no one can doubt its level of rigor; it is not until midway through the second volume that Russell and Whitehead are able to establish that $1 + 1 = 2$. (Immediately after proving this result in the book, Russell quips, "The above proposition is occasionally useful.") Unfortunately, this work, while impressive, did not accomplish what Russell had hoped it would—place all of mathematics on the secure foundation of the fundamental concepts of logic. Indeed, his work uncovered a number of deep and difficult philosophical problems, one of the most important of which would become known as the "Russell Paradox."[1] These problems suggest that the project motivating Russell might well be impossible to achieve. (Indeed, Gödel's famous theorem is often interpreted as proving precisely that.)

Russell derived a great deal of pleasure from his work on *Principia Mathematica*, even if he was somewhat let down by the final result. His personal life at this time, however, was much less of a source for happiness. Russell had married Alys Pearsall Smith, an American and a Quaker, in 1894. It had been a difficult courtship; Russell's family, especially his grandmother, vehemently opposed the marriage. But in the end the couple enjoyed a number of happy years together before problems started to emerge. Alys was five years older than Russell, who was only 22 when they married. Russell had led a very sheltered life with little real-world experience, especially with women; in short, he had a lot of growing up to do. Sadly, as he matured he became less and less interested in her, while she remained deeply in love with him. These difficulties came to a head in 1902,

---

[1] Briefly, the paradox results when one considers classes of objects, some of which might be other classes. Some classes are members of themselves; the class of all classes is itself a class. Other classes are not members of themselves; the class of all shoes is not itself a shoe. But suppose one considers the class of all classes that do not belong to themselves. Does this class belong to itself? If it does belong to itself, then it cannot belong to itself. But if it does not belong to itself, then it must belong to itself.

when Russell took an infamous bike ride, at the end of which he decided that he no longer loved Alys. She refused to accept a divorce, and so they remained married for almost two more decades, even though they shared hardly any life together from that point on.

Around the time he completed *Principia Mathematica*, Russell became involved with two individuals who would have a tremendous influence on the rest of his life. The first was Lady Ottoline Morrell, with whom Russell began a passionate affair in 1911 that resulted in what must surely be one of the largest collection of letters ever produced between a man and a woman. Morrell was fascinated by brilliant and profound men, and served as muse for a number of them, both inside the bedroom and out. (She was married at the time to Philip Morrell, a prominent Liberal politician.) The relationship lost its intensity after a few short years; Ottoline was never as keen on the sexual side of their relationship as Russell, and she had a deep mystical streak which Russell the freethinker and agnostic found difficult to accept.[2] Ottoline remained, however, a friend and confidante to Russell throughout her life. She would be the first (but most important) of a series of lovers Russell would entertain during that decade, the most famous of whom were the writer and actress Lady Constance Malleson (usually known by her stage name, "Colette"), and Vivienne Eliot, T.S. Eliot's wife.

The other major influence was an Austrian student named Ludwig Wittgenstein, who would ultimately become one of the most famous philosophers of the twentieth century. Wittgenstein was studying engineering at the University of Manchester, but had become more and more interested in the foundations of mathematics. Naturally, he sought out Russell, and Russell quickly began to see the Austrian as his successor, the man who would make the next big breakthroughs in the field. (Wittgenstein also convinced Russell that he was getting too old for major projects on the scope of *Principia Mathematica*.) Unfortunately, Wittgenstein was a difficult individual with whom to work, and his own ideas and interests took him in directions that Russell found strange and unhelpful. While Russell wrote an introduction for Wittgenstein's first book, *Tractatus Logico-Philosophicus* (1921)—an introduction without which the book would never have been published (Russell was a "big name" in philosophy, while Wittgenstein was

---

[2] This is not to say that Russell didn't try. In 1912 he wrote a rather turgid short story with her in mind entitled "The Perplexities of John Forstice" in which he tried to reconcile the rational and the mystical outlooks on life. It was a position he would later repudiate, and "John Forstice" was not published until after Russell's death.

still an unknown)—he never embraced the path Wittgenstein was charting for analytic philosophy.

The onset of World War I was a turning point in Russell's life. Russell was shocked and disheartened by Britain's entry into the war, and he quickly threw himself into antiwar work. He focused his energies on supporting the conscientious objectors who resisted being drawn into Britain's war effort. He paid a considerable price for his efforts, however. He lost his position at Cambridge, alienated numerous friends (notably his mentor, Alfred North Whitehead, whose son perished fighting in the war), was arrested twice, and finally spent six months in prison. (The chapters by John Lenz and David Blitz discuss Russell's activism in World War I in more detail.)

During the war, Russell met Dora Black, a graduate student studying French literature at University College London. Though she was over twenty years younger than Russell, they became lovers shortly after the war. Each of them paid a visit to the newly-created Soviet Union in 1920. Russell was accompanying a delegation of labor representatives interested in learning more about the conditions in Russia under the Bolsheviks. Dora wanted to accompany him, but he thought the conditions too dangerous. Far too headstrong to take "no" for an answer, Dora traveled to Russia on her own. She was very excited and encouraged by what she saw—unlike Russell, who was suspicious of the Bolsheviks from the start.

In 1920, Bertie and Dora traveled to China together. While there Russell taught philosophy at the University of Peking, and both gave public lectures on liberal values. The very presence of the (very publicly) unmarried couple had an impact on the country; the Christian missionaries from the West were scandalized, while many Chinese students, energized and excited by the prospect of adopting modern values, began contemplating "Russell marriages." Russell greatly enjoyed his time in China, except for a bout of double pneumonia that almost killed him. (A number of newspapers, notably in Japan, printed stories indicating that he had in fact died. When word of this reached Russell's brother, Frank, he reportedly replied that his brother would never do something like die without telling him first.) While in China, Dora became pregnant. Russell was anxious to get married, so as to ensure the child's legitimacy. Dora cared little for such things, for reasons which would come back to haunt Russell later, but she went along with Russell's wishes. Before Russell had left for China, Alys had finally consented to grant Russell a divorce (although it required an elaborate charade, as Bertie staged a night of "official" adultery, and Alys pretended to discover the affair via a private detective.) Russell and Dora were married on September 27, 1921, and on November 16, John Conrad Russell was born. (Russell named both of his sons after Joseph Conrad, a writer that Russell had met and greatly admired.)

By the time he returned to Britain, Russell had given up on the idea of returning to academia. He had enjoyed success during the war and in China as a popular speaker and writer, and he now aspired to earn a living as a popularizer of philosophy and as an apostle of liberal causes. (This did not stop him, however, from writing a new introduction for the second edition of *Principia Mathematica*, published in 1925.) He took very seriously his responsibilities as a father, writing numerous popular books and articles and undertaking a public lecture tour of the United States in 1924. These responsibilities had grown by the time he left for America; Dora had born him a daughter, Katherine Jane Russell, the previous year. With two children to raise, Russell and Dora were anxious to find the most appropriate school for them. Concerned that existing schools were havens for mindless religious dogma and equally mindless jingoism—the second of which Russell blamed for World War I—Russell and Dora resolved to found their own school, a new progressive option in the spirit of A.S. Neill's Summerhill and Maria Montessori's schools. They opened Beacon Hill in 1927. (For more on this school, see the essays by Cara Rice and Tim Madigan in this volume.)

The school, however, caused a huge strain in Russell's relationship with both his children and his wife. While Beacon Hill must have sounded like a great opportunity for John and Katherine, in fact it deprived them of much of their parents' time and attention. Russell and Dora tried not to show favoritism towards their own children at the school—a move that was probably the best available but that still left the two children feeling isolated and without proper support. Moreover, the school was constantly short of money, and so Russell had to undertake three more lecture tours of the United States (1927, 1929, and 1931) and take on even more writing for hire in order to make ends meet. (David White's essay discusses Russell's writing and speaking tours.) From 1931 to 1935, he even wrote a regular newspaper column for the yellow tabloids of William Randolph Hearst. (His best title in that series? "Who Should Use Lipstick?")

But it was the very different opinions of Bertie and Dora regarding sex and marriage that ultimately caused their marriage to collapse. Neither Russell nor Dora was committed to sexual monogamy, and the couple practiced an open marriage from the very start. For Russell, however, casual sex was one thing, and children were quite another. Russell believed that children should only be had within a stable relationship, for the sake of both the parents and the children. (He expressed this position in one of his most popular and controversial books, *Marriage and Morals* (1929).) Dora, however, thought that children were really nobody's business but the mother's, and so women should be able to sleep and have children with whom they will.[3] She was not afraid to act upon her beliefs. While carrying on an affair with journalist Griffin Barry, she became pregnant with his child. Russell, while deeply hurt by this, concealed his true feelings and tried to make the best of the situation. As a result, Harriet Ruth Barry Russell was born in 1930. (Russell agreed to be the official father of record.) The emotional wound Russell suffered was left to fester until 1932, when Dora bore Barry a son named Roderick. Russell was deeply proud of his family name and legacy; while far from the typical pompous aristocrat, his noble heritage meant a lot to him. (He had inherited the title of Earl Russell upon his brother's death in 1931.) The prospect of another man's son being raised as a Russell—and possibly even inheriting the title—was more than he could bear. He broke with Dora, and began divorce proceedings, an ugly affair that lasted several years and caused all concerned much heartache.

In January 1936, Russell married Patricia Helen Spence (known as "Peter" to her friends), who had served as a governess of John and Kate during the Beacon Hill days. (When they met, Russell was almost exactly triple her age.) She would bear him a son—his third and last, a boy named Conrad Sebastian Robert Russell—in 1937. By now Russell had tired of relying purely upon frenzied rounds of public lectures and the constant demands of popular writing, and sought to return to some sort of academic appointment. (He was already in his late 60s, but with a young wife and newborn, plus two other children who would soon be ready for university, he was in no position to retire.) After a number of failed attempts, he managed to secure a visiting position at the University of Chicago. In September 1938, Russell and his family sailed for America. He spent a year at Chicago, then took up another visiting position at the University of California. In 1940, he was offered an appointment at the City College of New York. The faculty and students at CCNY were generally very anxious to attract a philosopher of

---

[3] Dora had expressed this position to Russell before they became involved. Russell's reaction, ironically enough, was to declare, "Well, whoever I have children with, it won't be you!"

Russell's standing. Unfortunately, a large coalition of religious zealots, led by Bishop Manning of the Episcopal Diocese of New York, fought to have the appointment denied because of Russell's outspoken defense of atheism and liberal views regarding sex. (Ironically, this campaign was fueled by William Randolph Hearst, Russell's former employer.) In one of the United States' first major battles regarding academic freedom at the university level, the anti-Russell forces prevailed through a highly questionable lawsuit that annulled the appointment. (Thom Weidlich's chapter contains a more detailed discussion of the CCNY affair.)

Russell was thus left stranded in the United States without a job. (World War II had already begun in Europe, although the U.S. had not yet entered it. This made it difficult to get back to Britain, not that Russell had employment prospects there.) The American philosopher John Dewey came to his rescue. Dewey disagreed strongly with Russell's philosophical topics, and disliked Russell personally (as much as he disliked anyone—Dewey was a very easygoing guy). Nevertheless, he was appalled by the entire CCNY affair, and so prevailed upon a close friend, the eccentric millionaire art collector Dr. Albert Barnes, to help Russell. Barnes offered Russell a five-year job teaching the history of philosophy at the Barnes Foundation, which Barnes had established to instruct the masses in art appreciation using his world-renowned collection of impressionist and other artworks.[4] But Barnes was a very headstrong and stubborn man, and he ran the Foundation as his personal fiefdom. He soon had a falling-out with Russell, and fired him after only two years. Russell sued, and won most of the salary to which he was entitled from his contract with Barnes. Even better, however, was the fact that Russell was able to turn the lectures he had prepared for Barnes into a book. *A History of Western Philosophy* (1945) quickly became one of Russell's best-selling books, and the money it made put Russell on a secure financial footing for the first time in decades.

Russell returned to Britain in 1944. In an effort to make up for its earlier treatment of him during World War II, Trinity College offered him a full-fledged Fellowship that year. He received the Order of Merit in 1949, and won the Nobel Prize for Literature in 1950. He conducted highly successful lecture tours of America in 1950 and 1951 and of Australia in 1950. His personal life at this time, however, was much less satisfying. His mar-

---

[4] The collection, which can still be seen at the Foundation in Philadelphia, houses an impressive collection of Renoirs, Cézannes, and Matisses.

riage to Peter had been terribly unhappy since the early 1940s, although the couple did not divorce until 1952.[5] Later that year Russell married Edith Finch, a longtime friend. It would be his fourth, last, and by all accounts happiest marriage; he would remain utterly devoted to Edith until his death.[6]

Even worse was the situation with John, Russell's eldest son. John had married Susan Lindsay, daughter of the poet Vachel Lindsay, in 1946. Their daughter Sarah was born in 1947, and another daughter, Lucy, was born the following year. (John also adopted Anne, Susan's daughter by a previous relationship.) John began to suffer from some form of mental illness—most likely schizophrenia. Unable to support his family (despite the generous trust that Russell had set up for him), he, Susan, and their three daughters moved in with Russell in 1950. Russell, and later, Edith, became increasingly intolerant of the erratic and irresponsible behavior of the young couple. The situation came to a head at Christmas 1953, when John and Susan abruptly left, leaving the three young girls in the care of their grandparents. Russell subsequently fought both to have John committed (out of concern for his welfare), and to maintain custody of his three granddaughters (out of concern for *their* welfare). He largely succeeded in the latter effort, but whatever demons haunted John continued to plague the family.

---

[5] The breakup of the marriage took a serious toll on their son, Conrad. Peter demanded that Conrad have no contact with his father at all; if he did, she threatened to cut off her own contact with her son. After several years, Conrad felt he could not in good conscience continue to avoid his father, and wrote to him. Peter kept her word, and never spoke to him again.

[6] His *Autobiography* begins with the following poem, entitled "To Edith":

> Through the long years
> I sought peace.
> I found ecstasy, I found anguish,
> I found madness,
> I found loneliness,
> I found the solitary pain
> that gnaws the heart,
> but peace I did not find.
>
> Now, old & near my end,
> I have known you,
> and, knowing you,
> I have found both ecstasy & peace.
> I know rest.
> After so many lonely years,
> I know what life & love may be.
> Now, if I sleep,
> I shall sleep fulfilled.

Years later, on April 11, 1975, Lucy Russell entered a churchyard, doused herself with paraffin, and immolated herself.

Although Russell turned 80 in 1952, he remained active and engaged right up to the end of his life. In the 1950s, he became more and more involved with the movement against the atomic bomb. Unlike many peace activists, Russell did not believe in the slogan, "Ban the bomb." Instead, he thought it was war itself that must be abolished in the atomic age. It was this position he advanced through a variety of activities—through his famous "Man's Peril" radio broadcast at Christmas 1954; through the release of the Russell-Einstein Manifesto in 1955; through the founding of the Pugwash Conferences in 1957; through his public exchange of letters with Nikita Khrushchev and John Foster Dulles in 1957-1958; through his book *Common Sense and Nuclear Warfare* (1959); and through his activism with the Campaign for Nuclear Disarmament and with the Committee for 100. By the 1960s, Russell had become extremely critical of the role the United States was playing in world affairs. This led him to intervene publicly during the Cuban Missile Crisis of 1962. It also led him to establish, with the help of French philosopher Jean-Paul Sartre, an International War Crimes Tribunal to investigate the U.S. war in Vietnam. (All of these activities will be discussed more fully in David Blitz's chapter.)

Over the last few decades of his life, Russell would periodically work on his autobiography. It was not until the War Crimes Tribunal needed money, however, that he would finally complete this monumental work and see it through to publication. It appeared, in 3 volumes, in 1967, 1968, and 1969. His timing was excellent; on February 2, 1970, Russell died at the age of 97.

This short biographical sketch should give some sense of the immense richness of Russell's life—his many accomplishments and disappointments, triumphs and tragedies. It should give some sense of how many people Russell knew; of the many places Russell visited; and of the sheer number of events in which Russell played an influential role. And hopefully it will make you want to check out a book by this interesting and engaging man. Yet it only scratches the surface of reasons for reading Russell. There are a lot of questions left to be answered. Just what sort of ideas did Russell defend, and why? What was his outlook on life? And how did he express this outlook in print? The next chapters will endeavor to answer these questions. Hopefully, they will give you solid answers to the question—should *you* be reading Bertrand Russell?

SIX DEGREES OF BERTRAND RUSSELL

Tim Madigan

ONE OF THE MOST QUOTED PHRASES in current popular culture is "six degrees of separation." It expresses the idea that, on average, any human being is connected with any other human being by at most six acquaintances. While there is much debate as to whether this is literally true, it is an interesting thought-experiment, as well as the basis for many fun parlor games. One of these is entitled "Six Degrees of Kevin Bacon," in which film fans try to connect the aforementioned actor with any other movie star with as few links as possible.

I have been thinking of launching a similar parlor game called "Six Degrees of Bertrand Russell," in which any figure from the past two hundred years or so could be connected with BR in as few steps as possible. Why BR rather than, say, Ludwig Wittgenstein (who, after all, had a stated interest in games)? I have two reasons. First, Russell lived to the ripe old age of ninety-seven, and thus had the time to interact with a wider variety of people; and second, he was for most of that long life a celebrity, who rubbed elbows with all manner of individuals, many of whom were either celebrities themselves at the time or else came to be celebrated later. As is often pointed out, Russell's list of acquaintances stretched from Lenin (V.I.) to Lennon (John), from the Bloomsbury Group to the Doomsday Prophets, from William Gladstone to Harold Wilson. Russell's grandfather, Lord John Russell, had as a young man visited Napoleon on the island of Elba and shaken his hand. When I shake the hand of Russell Emeritus Archivist Kenneth Blackwell, who knew and worked closely with BR, I often think that I am only six degrees of separation from shaking Napoleon's hand as well. And as for Napoleon—well, who really knows where *that* hand had been?

Given this strong connection to history, it is not surprising that Russell himself wrote an essay entitled "How to Read and Understand History"

(1957), first published in 1943. In his autobiography and other works such as *Portraits from Memory* (1956), Russell made it quite clear that his aristocratic and privileged background gave him access to many of the most important movers and shakers in twentieth century politics, literature, and academia, areas in which he himself excelled. He was aware that—unlike many of his fellow philosophers, who were known only to a small coterie of fellow deep thinkers—he was an historic figure, one who could interact on a personal level with cabinet ministers, Nobel Prize winners in all fields, press barons, movie stars, presidents, and premiers. During the Cuban Missile Crisis, for instance, many concerned individuals tried to reach Kennedy and Krushchev to give them advice, but Russell was one of the few outsiders whose letters actually got through, as he no doubt knew they would.

For all of his concern with history, both personal and impersonal, Russell did not really have a philosophy of history. He was scornful of writers such as Saint Augustine, G.W.F. Hegel, Karl Marx, and Oswald Spengler, who devised grandiose schemes that sought to explain all historical phenomena under the rubric of some grand plan, either celestial or bestial. He makes it clear in "How to Read and Understand History" that he does not consider himself to be a specialist. For him, reading history was a leisure activity, one which gave him pleasure. He therefore proposes a kind of utilitarian defense of reading history. In effect, he offers a how-to guide on getting people to delve into history and enjoy doing so. Much of the essay consists of friendly advice and comments about the nature of history sure to make professional historians grit their teeth. One wonders what Russell's own son Conrad (who became one of the best-known historians of the English Civil War) made of this essay.

Basically, Russell argues that one should make history as entertaining as possible. This is what he himself did with his *A History of Western Philosophy* (1945), which is subtitled, *And Its Connection with Political and Social Circumstances from the Earliest Times to the Present Day*. He places the various philosophers he discusses within their historical contexts, and cannot resist telling various anecdotes about them, the more scurrilous the better. While one may debate the accuracy of his presentations, one cannot deny that the book itself is incredibly entertaining, something one might not suspect given the topic.

In "How to Read and Understand History," Russell raises the question, can history be studied scientifically? In a nutshell, he answers "no." Too much depends on chance and the whims of individuals to make accurate predictions, which any scientific theory should be able to do. "Some of those who write in the large are actuated by a desire to demonstrate some 'philosophy' of history," Russell writes. "They think they have discovered some formula according to which human events develop" (Russell 1957, 15; all subsequent references will be to this text). They think they know the end result long before it occurs. Of course, in his post-World War II writings, Russell himself often predicted the likely outcome of the human species—complete and utter annihilation. But he did not claim that this was a scientific prediction, as it was not inevitable, but only very likely given current circumstances. He was willing to grant that human attitudes could change, thereby changing the likely outcome, something that philosophers of history such as Hegel, Marx or Spengler would never admit.

Still, for all his criticisms, Russell was willing to grant that it is possible to look at history from a scientific standpoint, in the sense of examining trends, recurring events and human behavior. One can learn from history, but not by using simple formulae. Two services which the study of history can provide are:

1. Modest and humble generalizations, which can constitute steps toward a scientific approach;
2. The study of individuals, which offers a combination of drama and truth (something which Aristotle had advocated as well).

"Scientific history is a modern invention," Russell notes (18). And while it is certainly an area which interested him, Russell's primary concern in the essay remains the examination of the pleasures found in reading history. What can be gained, he asks, by reading historians of the past? Herodotus, "the Father of History," gives us amusing stories in which the respect for fact does not cause him to abstain from drama. Such mixtures of legends and truth would appall Russell when he is wearing his philosopher's cap, but when engaged in reading Herodotus and Thucydides he is much more charitable. The latter shares with Plutarch a concern for moral tales, but, unlike the severe Thucydides, Plutarch "is an easy-going gossipy writer, who cannot resist a good story, and except in a few instances is quite willing to relate and even exaggerate the weaknesses of his heroes" (21). No doubt it is this iconoclasm which appealed particularly to Russell, who throughout his life remained skeptical about the virtues of those in power. (As the grandson of a Prime Minister he knew better than most what goes on behind the closed doors of state.)

Finally, while Russell admits that Gibbon has grave defects as a writer ("Everyone, even barbarians, sound like Eighteenth Century Gentlemen"), one senses that he is Russell's personal favorite among the historians of old (21). Gibbon's "wit and irony—particularly when he uses them to contemn superstition—are inimitable" (21-2). Sound familiar? It is surprising that Russell doesn't also discuss Gibbon's friend and fellow historian David Hume, who was no slouch in the superstition-contemning field himself. Perhaps Hume's pro-Tory sympathies did not appeal to the much more Whiggish Russell.

In the remainder of the essay, Russell shows his hand by following in Gibbon's footsteps, presenting "the march of great events" as basically the history of the warfare between superstition (primarily religious superstition) and science. This view, while certainly agreeable to freethinkers, is itself a contentious one, and Russell's sweeping assertions are no more scientifically grounded than the very sort of sweeping assertions by Hegel, Marx or Spengler at which he sneers. Still, Russell is careful to add that all theories of history are misleading if accepted as dogma, but valuable if used as means of suggesting hypotheses (34).

It is clear from reading "How to Read and Understand History" that Russell had little sympathy for grand abstract theories of history. For him, the benefit of studying history is to get a sense of what makes human beings act the way that they do. For instance, reading about the meetings of eminent men, particularly those from different areas, can be both amusing and surprising. Who would have thought that the socialist and atheist inventor Robert Owen would have hit it off so well with the autocratic and ferocious Czar Nicholas I of Russia? Much knowledge can be gained from reading biographies and memoirs. "The professionals," Russell writes, "must not prevent us from realizing that history is full of fun, and that the most bizarre things really happen....Until one knows much intimate detail about a prominent man, it is impossible to judge whether he was really as great as he appeared or not" (22).

Russell, of course, wrote his memoirs as one way of describing the intimate details of his life. But surely he could not have imagined that so *much* of his long life— thanks in large part to the retrieval by the Russell archives of the myriad letters he exchanged with lovers and friends—would become available for perusal by scholars. Perhaps there's such a thing as knowing *too much* about the intimate details of a person's life.

That being said, there remains the question of Russell's own continuing historical importance. To what extent does he remain a significant influence on modern times? Almost two generations have passed since Russell's death, and the number of people who knew him by direct acquaintance is dwindling. I can remember a time when Russell was a symbol of the public-engaged intellectual, in the same way that Einstein was a symbol for scientific learning. But I'm not so sure this is still the case. Recently, for instance, I received a call from a woman who had seen a listing for the Bertrand Russell Society in which my phone number was given. "Are you Bertrand Russell?" she asked me. I was rather taken aback (albeit flattered) that someone could even ask such a question. But then I remembered the ending of Russell's essay, in which he talks about the importance of organizations, a department of history he claims is too little studied. "Some organizations," he writes, "succeed throughout a long period in fulfilling their original object; others soon fail" (49-50). Time will tell whether the Bertrand Russell Society will fulfill its original object of helping to keep alive the memory of this eminent person. And while I can't in good faith claim to be Bertrand Russell, I can honestly say I've shaken the hand of a man who shook his hand. One degree of separation!

Bibliography

Russell, Bertrand. 1957. "How to Read and Understand History." *Understanding History and Other Essays*. New York: Philosophical Library.

HOW BERTRAND RUSSELL BECAME A NEW KIND OF INTELLECTUAL DURING WORLD WAR I*

John Lenz

I. INTRODUCTION—TWO TYPES OF PUBLIC INTELLECTUALS

Bertrand Russell became an iconic public intellectual, one of the enduring public intellectuals of the twentieth century, during World War I, by dissenting both from the war and from other intellectuals' war efforts. This paper discusses the ideas behind Russell's courageous act of resistance, by contrast with the war writings of other intellectuals, especially John Dewey.

Russell's resistance to World War I took place close in time to the creation of the modern public intellectual. The term "intellectual," as a noun designating a class of people, was a new one at that time. It is thought to have been coined in the Dreyfus affair, when intellectuals, first so-called, rallied in independent dissent (Collini 2007, 20-25).[1] In fact, an earlier use of the word to refer to a social class can be found in the French utopian socialist Henri de Saint-Simon (1760-1825), who imagines a different relation of intellectuals to society. Saint-Simon's intellectuals, in contrast to the type of the dissenting intellectual, were experts who could improve society with their expertise. One could call them the first social scientists, in fact.[2] In these two earliest uses of the word "intellectual"—both, significantly, defined in relation to public issues—we thus have two different models: dissent (a Socratic model), or involvement as citizen or social-scientific expert.

---

* I presented an earlier version of this paper at the European Conference on Public Intellectuals at the Luso-American Foundation in Lisbon, Portugal in October, 2013. I would like to thank them, as well as Tim Madigan for decades of friendship and humanistic leadership.
[1] Russell himself in 1916 linked his "new career" with this earlier defining episode, calling his work "a rallying-ground for the intellectuals...who...are being driven to action, as they were in France by the Dreyfus case" (quoted in Russell 1988, xxxvii, 340; see also lvi).
[2] The word "sociology" was coined in the circle of Saint-Simon and his followers, notably his one-time secretary, Auguste Comte.

Intellectuals may or may not be experts in social-scientific areas themselves, yet they offer something valuable. A key point of difference between these two broad types is whether intellectuals operate from without or from within, and whether they reinforce the dominant ideology or offer alternatives to it. While social-scientific expertise is often contributed with progressive intent for utopian improvement (as with Saint-Simon and indeed with both Dewey and Russell), it may also all-too-often be allied, less positively, with power, influence and success in society. I will call this the first type of public intellectual, and the dissenter the second type.

These two kinds exemplify a difference of opinion about the relation of ideas to life (particularly politics). Russell himself commented on the rise of technicians: "Unfortunately, the more civilized the world becomes the less it wants to listen to the sages" (Russell 1939, 495-6). Russell was a prophet (disobedient to power) and not a priest (part of the system), as Erich Fromm framed the dichotomy (Fromm 1967, 68).

At the hundredth anniversary of the start of World War I, it is appropriate to consider the role of intellectuals in that conflict. Opposing the war propelled Bertrand Russell into his long careeer as perhaps the foremost English-speaking public intellectual of the twentieth century. Russell believed that his life's work was more important to humanity than his technical work in mathematical logic. While he displayed political interests earlier, it was the onset of war between the supposedly most civilized countries on earth that raised Russell's awareness to a higher level. From being an occasional political activist, furthering the causes of one party versus another, he became a critic on a higher plane of the self-interested behavior of states, and a decades-long advocate of an international perspective. This set him against most intellectuals at the time, such as John Dewey (the case studied here). His message is just as important today as ever. What was at stake was the role of the intellectual in improving the world.

Opposing war is virtually regarded as part of the job description of a public intellectual, and if we widen that job description to "speak truth to power,"[3] few would disagree. But this has not always been the case in history and in the present. Intellectuals often take sides in national disputes.

---

[3] This is a theme of Edward Said's book, *Representations of the Intellectual* (1994). The phrase originated with Quakers, possibly in the eighteenth century. Quakers adopted this slogan in the 1950s and retrospectively used it to describe George Fox (seventeenth century). Russell, by the way, engaged in some political work before the war with his Quaker first wife, Alys Pearsall Smith.

They often provide ammunition for a ruling ideology and justify the status quo. That is common for many reasons. They want success and power. That is the theme of Julien Benda's brilliant polemic, *Le trahison des clercs* (1927). I'll end with a word about that, because I found that Benda himself was not above the kind of hypocrisy that I am going to talk about here.

This paper illustrates two different types of public intellectuals as well as an interesting historical example of intellectuals fighting a war—*or not*—on the plane of ideas. Behind this dispute lies an important philosophical difference about the relation of ideas to life—in this case, Dewey's Pragmatism versus Russell's philosophy of detachment.

First I will talk about John Dewey's book *German Philosophy and Politics* (1915), as well as a similar book by Santayana. Then I will present Bertrand Russell's more high-minded and international or cosmopolitan point of view, a view which had much influence through the century. I will conclude with a brief word about two Frenchmen, Romain Rolland and Benda, and Russell's legacy.

II. DEWEY AND SANTAYANA IN WORLD WAR I—INTELLECTUAL NATIONALISM

Although he serves as a foil for the views favored in this paper, John Dewey (1859-1952) was a great public intellectual (although not personally charismatic), and a noble figure (Menand 2001, 235-6). He is certainly a hero to professors: on January 1, 1915, he delivered the first presidential address of the American Association of University Professors (AAUP), a new organization that he cofounded. The AAUP championed academic freedom and tenure, on the grounds that professors work for the public good (*ibid.*, 413).[4] *(Thank you!)*

The month after inaugurating the AAUP, February 1915, Dewey began a series of lectures on German philosophy at the University of North Carolina. They were published soon after by a mass-market publisher (Henry Holt). In this work, *German Philosophy and Politics*, he used his

---

[4] The AAUP was founded, not initially to defend academic freedom, but to promote scholarship to the American public. (At first membership was restricted to prominent scholars.) When academic freedom became a big issue in its first year, the AAUP defended it on the ground that professors are responsible to the public rather than to their employers—that is, to "their moral employer—society as a whole" (Dewey quoted in Menand 2001, 415-6). Dewey scornfully wrote in one case that "this college is nothing but a factory" (*ibid.*, 420), where employees could be fired at will.

academic freedom to attack German thought and implicate it in what he did not like about German politics.

German Philosophy and Politics is a war book (Ryan 1995, 169).[5] It pretends to be a study of philosophy but the pretense is thin. Dewey denies any connection with the war, stating disingenuously up front, "Somewhat arbitrarily I have...selected some aspects of classic German thought for my illustrative material" (Dewey 1915, 14). Sure, the United States had not entered the war yet, but how can anyone pretend that a book about German militarism at that time was just academic? Of course he was well aware of the war; at one point he refers to "the present European situation." What he says there shows that this book is in fact a contest pitting Germans against Americans on an intellectual battleground. He writes: "the present European situation forces home upon us the need for constructive planning....it does encourage us to believe that a philosophy which should articulate and consolidate the ideas to which our social practice commits us would clarify and guide our future endeavor" (129-30). In other words, our philosophy is (or will be) better than theirs because our "social practice" is better. While he believes the present crisis demonstrates "the breakdown of the whole philosophy of Nationalism" (whose evils he apparently attributes to Germans) and calls for an international solution (130-1), his work can be seen as part of the competition of nations.

Of interest here is the close connection of ideas to life. In Dewey's philosophy of Pragmatism, ideas cannot be separated from social practice. Dewey represents one type of public intellectual: he holds an extreme view of the relation of ideas to life. Philosophy is all public and practical, or it is worthless. Russell and others became public intellectuals of a different kind.

About the Germans (both German thinkers and the nation as a whole), Dewey's 1915 book is harsh. The book's main theme is, "The nature of the influence of general ideas upon practical affairs" (Dewey 1915, 3). Dewey accuses German philosophy of being a cover for military conquest. How are the two related? Dewey does not argue that ideas cause action in the real world (7, 130). He knew they did not: politics, especially German politics, is harsh *Realpolitik*, and political Realism presents an extreme case *against* ideas in politics.

So Dewey argues as follows. Ideas arise from the society. German philosophers such as Fichte, Kant, Hegel, and Nietzsche have really offen-

---

[5] Ryan describes it as "a wartime tract" and (to be fair) a book on education.

sive ideas. Therefore, they spring from bad soil; they reflect a bad national character. In particular, they promote the idea that Germans have absolute truth and must spread this to the world. These pedants show Germans to be would-be world-conquerors. Watch out.[6]

We are familiar with this general attack on German thought because it is very familiar and has been commonplace since the 1930s. But it goes back to World War I, when it was less justified, unless you happened to be fighting Germany. Nietzsche was already taking a beating in England (Martin 2003). Dewey makes a point of saying he doesn't think Nietzsche started this supposed German militarism; instead, he relates it back to Kant and others. Kant, the cosmopolitan advocate of "perpetual peace"? In other words, Dewey shows that he is following up on British propaganda and *reinforcing* it.

The reference to British propaganda is no coincidence. The modern theory of propaganda originated in this same period in both Britain and the U.S. "Leading public intellectuals" were behind this social-scientific work on public opinion in the U.S. This again exemplifies one type of public intellectual, a potentially negative one (Chomsky 2003, 6; 2005, 19-24).[7] Chomsky writes, "People in the John Dewey circle...took pride in the fact that for the first time in history, as they saw it, a wartime fervor was created not by military leaders and politicians but by the more responsible, serious members of the community—namely, thoughtful intellectuals...turning a relatively pacifist population into raving anti-German fanatics" (2005, 19-20).[8]

---

[6] Interestingly, Dewey clarified his position in his reply to a critical review. In doing so, he proferred a seemingly different explanation of the relation between ideas and politics. He explained that he held that German idealistic philosophy serves as a false ideology to disguise the *Realpolitik* from the masses. "[I]t is dangerous to maintain a philosophy which is at odds with the facts of action"; their supposed "immutable principles" conceal actual class stratification (Dewey 1979, 419-20). This Marxist line differs from that in his book.

[7] *Manufacturing Consent* (Herman and Chomsky 2002) is an extended treatment of this theme. Chomsky, interestingly, has said that his criticisms of the media are but a subset of his criticism of intellectual culture generally (Chomsky 2005, 142). Some relevant history: the references are to the British Department and then Ministry of Information (c. 1917-1919) and President Woodrow Wilson's Committee on Public Information. Incidentally, Columbia University's famed "great books" course, Contemporary Civilization, originated in World War I as a so-called "war issues" course developed in cooperation with the U.S. Army, to teach Americans about the European civilization they were fighting for.

[8] Chomsky writes with the Iraq war in mind. He called the Bush circle "radical nationalists" (Chomsky 2005, 4); this linkage between nationalism and violence is Russellian.

But German thought was just so persistently all-embracing, always talking about ultimate truth. Dewey called it "a self-conscious assertion of nationalism" beginning with Luther (Dewey 1915, 91).[9] Rather incredibly, he accuses German philosophy from Kant on as being inherently part of a warlike and imperialistic culture that America must defend against using its own best philosophy. When you oppose one nationalism, the best response is not another nationalism. Of course Dewey's vision is a very American one. He ends with a call for more international cooperation, explaining that the American way has to be the future way of the world.

Dewey was a gentle man, but take a look at the military metaphors he uses to promote American philosophy. Talking about the virtues of experimental philosophy, he says it has to be done in the proper way, "by bringing to bear all the resources of inquiry upon locating the target, constructing propulsive machinery and figuring out the curve of the trajectory" (1915, 128). His philosophy is like a missile aimed at an enemy! He also says America should take what it does at home and bring the American way to the world.[10] While his values are fine ones, the claim that the American way is and should be the international way, and the ending of his attack on German Idealist ambitions with American ones, are ironic.

Dewey expresses noble values, but his conduct raises questions about public intellectuals. His work is a salvo in a competition of nationalisms; it wages the Great War on the battleground of philosophy. Perhaps the problem lies in the theory of ideas expressed here. American Pragmatism is a philosophy of practice, and opposed to theory. This is often socially useful, admirably democratic, and inclusive. But it is limiting. All ideas are social and not separated from practical politics. This makes it hard to rise above partisan politics.[11] In short, what is an intellectual?

To be fair, I am talking about a single book and not all of Dewey's life and work. He did become a pacifist after the war. He reprinted this war book during World War II, maintaining his thesis about "essential continuity" of German thought from Luther *et al.* to Hitler (Ryan 1995, 379, n.

---

[9] The contrast is with French cosmopolitanism.
[10] "We are," he writes, "actually interracial and international." American values promote "furtherance of the depth and width of human intercourse" and "intelligent coöperative experimentation" (Dewey 1915, 130-2).
[11] One bad misreading will make the point. Dewey says that Plato "defined philosophy as the science of the State" (Dewey 1915, 13). No. Even in the Republic, philosophy transcends politics.

33).¹² By then that was much easier to do, and we now take it for granted. But this conceals how unjust it was in World War I.

George Santayana (1863-1952) provides another example of the type of intellectual under consideration here. Santayana, a Spaniard long associated with Harvard, had been a student of the Pragmatist William James. In 1916 he published the book *Egotism in German Philosophy*. He admits (unlike Dewey) that the book fits in the context of the war; long study has convinced him of "something sinister...at once hollow and aggressive" in German thought, something which is "now...evident to the whole world" (5, 7). Like Dewey, he is careful not to argue that philosophy caused the war (but he too seems not to doubt that blame for the war lies with Germany). Rather, again, philosophy reveals the shared German character (7).¹³ You, his reader, may feel badly about fighting the Germans because we admire gentle souls like Goethe. But no, he argues, Goethe is not like that, he is really egotistic; you may think he's cosmopolitan, but he gave the Germans the obnoxious idea of Absolute Will (Santayana 1915)! It is embarrassing when intellectuals fight national wars like this.

It is unfortunate, but still too very commonplace today, for academics to reduce intellectual life to taking political sides. In other words, the battle is just as much about education. Education is also the solution. Russell knew this. This view of intellectual politics is what Bertrand Russell and others objected to.

III. BERTRAND RUSSELL—BEING ENGAGED BY BECOMING DETACHED

The war made Russell (1872-1970) a public intellectual, a model one for the rest of the century. He campaigned and wrote tirelessly and went to prison for his efforts. The war changed his life.

Russell had been involved in politics earlier. His first book was *German Social Democracy* (1896). He ran for political office twice. In 1907, when a Liberal, he ran for Parliament in the Wimbledon by-election as the first candidate of the National Union of Women's Suffrage Societies. His opponents released rats in the meeting-hall to disperse the ladies. In 1922 and

---

¹² Ryan unfortunately misstates the title of Dewey's book.
¹³ "Self-assertion" is one of the alleged sins.

1923, he ran for Parliament in Chelsea as a Socialist.[14] But these examples of an intellectual engaging in politics, while praiseworthy, are different from the type of intellectual he became after 1914. In running for office or writing on public policy (e.g., free trade was an early cause of his), an intellectual acts as a concerned citizen. Sometimes this means one is a citizen like any other; sometimes it means that an intellectual brings some expertise to bear on public issues. The idea of social science expertise, after all, increased in the twentieth century (but this is not entirely a positive story—as discussed above, expertise can be used to reinforce the status quo). In other words, intellectuals do what everyone else does, or sometimes they do it better and get more rewards—or mess things up. That's what I will call the first type of public intellectual. Apart from the strengths and pitfalls of engaging in that kind of political activity, there is another intellectual stance which criticizes politics and power structures from outside. Russell became this second type, a dissenting public intellectual. This type relies on a different idea of the relation between intellectual life and real life. It implies that there is something in being an engaged intellectual that is more than being a citizen of the existing state of affairs.[15] Socrates is a model of this type, and Russell became one.

Russell called for intellectuals to rise above nationalism; winning a short-term conflict was no solution for anyone. His long-term hope was to improve humanity. He describes becoming a public intellectual, which involved putting aside his now world-famous work in mathematical logic, in the following terms:

> I was making a very difficult renunciation. Nevertheless, I never had a moment's doubt as to what I must do. I have at times been paralyzed by skepticism, at times I have been cynical, at other times indifferent, but when the War came I felt as if I heard the voice of God. I knew that it was my business to protest, however futile protest might be. My whole nature was involved. As a lover of truth, the national propaganda of all the belligerent nations sickened me. As a lover of civilization, the return to barbarism ap-

---

[14] Russell remained a socialist for life, although Alan Ryan downplays this to some extent (Ryan 1988).
[15] "One of the difficulties in discussing the duty of a philosopher is to find some difference between his duty and that of every other human being" (Russell 1997, 457).

> palled me....the massacre of the young wrung my heart. (Russell 1968, 7)[16]
>
> The War of 1914-1918 changed everything for me. I ceased to be academic and took to writing a new kind of books. I changed my whole conception of human nature. (*ibid.*, 36)
>
> My life before 1910 and my life after 1914 were as sharply separated as Faust's life before and after he met Mephistopheles. (*ibid.*, 3)

Intellectuals disappointed him: "I had supposed that intellectuals frequently loved truth, but I found here again that not ten per cent of them prefer truth to popularity" (6). Almost all the other Cambridge dons, even the liberals, turned against him; he eventually lost his Trinity College lectureship despite having a few brave supporters (Hardy 1949).[17] Liberals were the worst, because the most disappointing. Of one friend he wrote, "If she had known Christ before he delivered the Sermon on the Mount she would have begged him to keep silent for fear of injuring his social position in Nazareth" (Russell 1988, xxxvii).[18] But of course reasons for silence were more nefarious and dangerous. Twenty-five English writers worked with the new war propaganda bureau in a literary campaign against the German "Huns." Most people, in short, celebrated divisiveness; that is part of the definition of nationalism (Grosby 2005, 98, cp. Ch. 7), but that was exactly what contributed to the war.

Authority and respectability are often enemies of truth, a point Russell illustrated with some satirical definitions:

> Liberty: The right to obey the police;
> Holy: Maintained by fools for centuries;
> Knowledge: What Archbishops do not doubt. (Russell 1953

---

[16] Russell's first biographer, Alan Wood, called him a "passionate skeptic."
[17] A note on two of Russell's notable intellectual rivals at this time. Russell wrote a response to H.G. Wells who coined the term "the war that will end war" (Russell 1988, 10-5). Wells, although generally an admirer of Russell, attacked him during the war (Russell 2001, 282-3). Russell also engaged in lengthy polemics with Gilbert Murray.
[18] Russell says this in the same letter in which he compares himself to the Dreyfusards (noted above). The target is American Helen Flexner. Her husband Abraham later blocked (for other personal reasons) Russell's proposed appointment to the Institute for Advanced Study in Princeton—just another reminder of everyday academic politics (Clark 1975, 455).

Most scientists, Russell thought, are no better. Scientists are immersed in technique at the expense of the bigger picture. They do not consider the ends of knowledge and of human life. They can make a bomb but don't ask them how to use it. They serve the status quo "in their capacity of good citizens, anxious to defend virtue and property" (Russell 1949, 105).

Intellectuals, Russell thought, had known better before the war. They had been holding international congresses to work for the common progress of civilization. Truth is an international, universal goal. But once the war came, some of the worst offenders were the intellectuals. They ceased being intellectuals, Russell complained. "Suddenly...all this [cooperation] is forgotten: German scholars repudiate English honours, English scholars maintain that Germany has done nothing of importance in learning" (Russell 1988, 177). Why? Russell explains:

> Nationalism, the greatest curse of the modern world, as religious bigotry was the curse of former ages....there is no remedy except the recognition, through reason, of the absurdity and limitation of the national ideal. In this work, no help is to be expected from the intellectuals, who are everywhere the slaves of the State, in spirit if not in pocket. (*ibid.*, 111-2)

Russell believed intellectuals should have a more universal outlook. He knew that propaganda was not truth but myth. Lovers of truth should criticize the propaganda of their own side, and not just buy into the demonizing of the enemy (e.g., Germans).

In 1915 Russell published in neutral Switzerland a long essay entitled, "On Justice in War-Time: An Appeal to the Intellectuals of Europe." The subtitle deliberately evokes the Dreyfus-era dissenters. In that and numerous other wartime writings filling several volumes today, Russell based his arguments on three broad grounds: the nature of reason, human compassion, and the special duty of intellectuals to a higher truth.

Reason made Russell doubt the propaganda of all sides. "The truth, whatever it may be, is the same in England, France, and Germany, in Russia and in Austria. It will not adapt itself to national needs: it is in its essence neutral. It stands outside the clash of passions and hatreds" (Russell 1988, 170). He does not mean only scientific truth; that is part of it, but not all. More importantly, Russell stresses human truths, political truths. These truths include the fact that most people think their own group is better. But people think things like this for emotional, not rational, reasons, and it is obvious that not every group can be right about this. (This is similar to Russell's criticism of the claims of different religions.)

As truth is universal, so is humanity. He appeals to our "common humanity" (Russell 1988, 4), as he did again famously in 1954 to oppose nuclear warfare: "the enemy are men, like ourselves, neither better nor worse" (*ibid.*, 6).[19] "All nations," Russell wrote, "at all times, are egoistic.... until it is recognized that all the nations engaged in the war are equally and wholly selfish, no true thought about the issues involved is possible" (*ibid.*, 171). This realist view of politics, of which he was proud and which he expounded in his book *Power: A New Social Analysis* (1938), means that solutions cannot be sought within this type of divisive politics, i.e., the politics of competing self-interest classically criticized by Thucydides and by Plato's Socrates.

In other words, intellectuals should know better, by virtue of being intellectuals; they have a duty to all of humanity. Although Russell is known as a logician, it is important to note that this is an emotional appeal, not only a logical one. Reason is not enough. He is talking about a truth of the world, the application of reason in the world, rather than, say, objective scientific facts. Not all humanists are humane, as anyone in a university knows. For many people, intellect only provides a rationale for their desires; this is instrumental reason, a means to an end—he faulted Pragmatists like Dewey for holding this view—rather than universal, compassionate and humane.[20] Most academics, he says, "hardly have any spiritual life"—a most interesting complaint, coming from an atheist (quoted in Atkins 2002, 74, n. 29)![21] By "spiritual" Russell meant inner conscience.

---

[19] As I write this, President Obama expressed the same sentiment in a live broadcast statement (July 18, 2014): "In this world today we shouldn't forget that in the midst of conflict and killing, there are people like these, people who are focused on what can be built rather than what can be destroyed, people who are focused on how they can help people that they've never met, people that define themselves not by what makes them different from other people but by the humanity that we hold in common."

[20] "There is no reason to expect an unusual degree of humane feeling from professors" (Russell 1988, 176). This is particularly a problem given the way that nations engage in "artifical rationalizing of instinctive actions and passions" (*ibid.*, 178).

[21] While many Russellians explain this kind of talk away as pandering to his mistress, Ottoline Morrell, I disagree. By "spiritual" Russell means inner conscience and non-material values. Consider the following words by Russell:

> Men inspired by faith and freed from the domination of fear are unconquerable. The noblest thing in a man is the spiritual force which enables him to stand firm against the whole world in obedience to his sense of right; and I will never acquiesce in silence while men in whom spiritual force is strong are treated as a danger to the community

Thus, impartial truth, meaning human truth, combined with compassion, is Russell's hallmark. It is not an obvious combination for one whose work had been on abstract, perhaps eternal, mathematical, scientific truths. Still, his notion of the duty of an intellectual relies on an idea of universal, almost transcendent truth. Russell passionately advocates intellectual detachment. Spinoza was one of his heroes (Blackwell 1985).[22] A universal view is ethically superior because all humans are part of something larger, the cosmos. He ends one appeal to intellectuals with a call for this broader perspective:

> Men of learning should be the guardians of one of the sacred fires that illumine the darkness…upon them depends the ideal of just thought, of disinterested pursuit of truth, which, if it had existed more widely, would have sufficed alone to prevent the present horror. To serve this ideal, to keep alive a purpose remote from strife, is more worthy of the intellectual leaders of Europe than to help Governments in stimulating hatred and slaughtering more…young men… It is time to forget our supposed separate duty towards Germany, Austria, Russia, France, or England, and remember that higher duty to mankind in which we can still be at one. (Russell 1988, 180)

Russell became engaged by being detached: his detachment from national self-interest went hand-in-hand with a detached view of universal truth and humanity. This high-minded ideal carried an important political consequence: cosmopolitanism. Being detached gives one a larger perspective and therefore such an intellectual is able to engage at a higher level (in a different way than a public intellectual of my first type). This is a Socratic position; it can be summed up in the motto that the intellectual, having become enlightened, "returns to the cave" (i.e., the world). In this way intellectualism improves the world. Though all this is open to suspicions of intellectual elitism, the interesting point here is the value of the intellectual life in itself and its contribution to the public good. In other words, we do

---

rather than as its most precious heritage….You cannot defeat such men…. all the material force the world contains is powerless against the spirit of indomitable love. (Russell 1988, 407)

This is a Socratic position (apart from the addition of quasi-Christian "love"). Russell wrote those words for his own criminal trial in June 1916.

[22] For Russell's praises of contemplation, see Russell (1912, ch. xv).

not just have intellectuals working in the fields or doing public service; they bring something to the real world that would otherwise be lost. Initially at odds with the state, like Socrates, they work for utopian improvement.

Russell's hopes, his criticism of the present state of affairs combined with his vision of progress towards an ideal—this is a classic recipe for utopianism. His internationalism led him to propose various forms of world government from 1915 until at least 1964. Education was the best hope. If (as the realist holds) people have always behaved this way, human beings must (the utopian thinks) act differently than they have in all of history. History teaching itself must be reformed to combat nationalism. He proposed, somewhat fancifully, schools "controlled by neutrals" and "an international news agency" (Russell 1988, 112, 303). "Teaching of history ought to be internationalized, not taught in each country so as to produce false beliefs favouring that country. This would be done if men [human beings] wished to diminish strife and hatred" (*ibid.*, 342; see also 105). (But do they?) This empiricist was idealistic.

IV. RUSSELL'S POSITION QUALIFIED: CHANGE AFTER THE WAR

Of course Russell was not perfect on these issues. He admitted that Germany might be more militaristic, but not for racial reasons (Russell 1988, 141, 301).[23] He praises the English as special and different.[24] However, at that time, recognition of these supposed differences serves only to highlight his plea to transcend them. Russell did not then have a pro-British agenda; but, with a more critical reading, we can see today that he did, only that he wished to include Germany: he possessed a European bias that lay behind his desire for Britain and Germany to reconcile. He assumed that Germany and England should not fight each other because as two civilized countries they are really on the same side, the side of civilization. They might combine to create one international navy, just about his first proposal of this nature in Russell's lifelong advocacy of world government (Russell

---

[23] Here Russell downplays the racial position with the liberal argument that is "accidents of history and geography, rather than innate wickedness, which have produced German aggressiveness" (Russell 1988, 141, cp. 177 on German traits).
[24] "The English people is, I believe, the most humane, generous, and peace-loving in the world…The interests of the British democracy do not conflict at any point with the interests of mankind." (265, 266) However, he often reserved criticism for the government.

1988, 76). Rusell later overcame in a major way the imperialist, colonialist assumptions of his early years, but they are present at this time.[25] Indeed, historians of the League of Nations and the United Nations argue that such movements arose from a desire of the powers to maintain control (Mazower 2012).

More troubling for our topic of the unfortunate vilification of foreign intellectuals in World War I, and Russell's courageous opposition to this, is that Russell reversed his position in the 1930s. If Dewey became a pacifist, Russell, the famous pacifist, supported the war against fascism. At that time he did blame fascism on the usual suspects: German philosophers, Romanticism, Fichte, Hegel, Nietzsche, *et al.* (Russell 1935; Russell 1997, 367-70).[26] Ironically, Russell (or his assistant) mined Santayana's 1916 book (discussed above) for notes to use against Fichte, a villain in his new schema.[27] Indeed, Russell went even further in his vilification. Among the ancestors of fascism in a proposed study of "irrationalism in philosophy... and its connection to violence in politics," he even included William James and John Dewey (Lintott 2008, 42, 60)! In *A History of Western Philosophy and Its Connection with Political and Social Circumstances*, he claims that Dewey's Pragmatism is a philosophy of "social power"—all practical, promoting technological manipulation, lacking higher ideals (Russell 1946, 855; see also 854). (It is worth remembering that Russell always advocated both technological and contemplative notions of science; by "contemplative," I mean the higher cosmic perspective discussed in this paper.) This involves a new understanding of the relation between ideas (or some ideas) and history; bad ideas have bad social causes and effects. Russell, as a political realist, was skeptical about the importance of ideas in social life as a rule, but evidently he came to regard some trends in the history of thought as uncivilized by his criteria (Russell 1939, 491-3).

---

[25] A letter of 1900 to Louis Couturat is embarrassing today: "the fewer states there are, the fewer the borders and the less militarism. I despise patriotism …it is the small states which ought to disappear…. I wish that every part of the world were governed by a European race…." (Russell 1992, 200)

[26] See Lintott (2008) for Russell's aborted plans for an anti-fascist book, *The Revolt against Reason*, consisting of a history of irrational philosophies. I thank Kenneth Blackwell for this reference.

[27] The notes, undated but perhaps from 1935-1936, are reading notes prepared by Patricia Spence, Russell's third wife (Lintott 2008, 49-50). She may have performed the same service for *A History of Western Philosophy* as well?

The British vilification of German philosophy revived in the 1930s under the auspices of Russell and others (Akehurst 2010, 16). Many people believe, unfortunately, this view of German philosophy to be justified. After the two world wars it is now commonplace. To be sure, in the shadow of World War II, this kind of attack became easier, and seemingly more obvious and morally necessary. According to Akehurst, analytical philosophy came to be regarded as politically safe (*ibid*.; see also Akehurst 2013). But we must think ourselves past that. We must be careful not to replicate the World War I propaganda propagated by intellectual warriors.

The real question is the relation of ideas to history. This is as thorny as the mind-body problem; indeed, it is almost the same as the mind-body problem. Dewey held that there is no separation between ideas and practice, that is, no airy intellectual realm. Russell believed intellectual detachment could improve humanity.

V. RUSSELL'S LEGACY AND PRESENT IMPLICATIONS

Two French figures aligned themselves with Russell's view of globalism in this period. In 1915, Romain Rolland (1866-1944) published *Au-dessus de la mêlée / Above the Battle.* This was the same year in which he won the Nobel Prize in Literature. In 1919 Rolland secured the signatures of many intellectuals, including Russell, to a manifesto, "Declaration of the Independence of the Mind" (Rolland 1920, 209-15). This is a fascinating document for the history of public intellectuals. Rolland takes the same line as Russell. He writes, for example, "Most of the intellectuals placed their science, their art, their reason, at the service of the governments," and "Let us free the mind from these compromises, from these unworthy alliances, from these veiled slaveries! Mind is no one's servitor. It is we who are the servitors of mind. We have no other master." This manifesto ties together themes of several generations. Looking back, Rolland was much impressed by Spinoza, as Russell and Benda were. Looking forward, Rolland was an early champion of Gandhi.

Julian Benda (1867-1956) forms a link between the Dreyfus affair, when he first published essays on the role of intellectuals, and later interwar debates about the role of intellectuals in political life (Benda 1900, 1955).[28] In *The Betrayal of the Intellectuals* (orig. 1927), Benda calls intellectuals

---

[28] On Benda, see Said (1994).

the conscience of mankind. He accuses them of the crime of selling out to politics: "Patriotism to-day is the assertion of one form of mind against other forms of mind." "Our age," he continues, "is indeed the age of the intellectual organization of political hatreds" (Benda 1955, 14, 21). This is the target of his brilliant polemic. I'd like to say one thing about this book here. Like Russell and Rolland, he relies on the idea of eternal, disinterested truths. Like them, his heroes are Spinoza and Socrates. But when he comes to say why it is that intellectuals have degenerated into mere partisan political fighters, he becomes hypocritical. Who started this? The Germans! They are the bad intellectuals: "The nationalist (intellectual) is essentially a German invention;" "the Germans," he continues, "debased philosophy & metaphysics by making it political" (*ibid.*, 174, 59; see also 46, n. 1). Benda cannot rise above partisanship himself. This is a jarring nationalistic note in his high-minded book.

One American who came to prominence in the 1960s takes the story to the present day. Noam Chomsky tirelessly criticizes the self-serving rhetoric and actions of servants of power. Chomsky idolizes Bertrand Russell.[29] Central to the work of Chomsky is the notion that academics just as much as the mass media buy into the status quo with its injustices. "Their job, basically, is to serve as defense counsels for state power....This is a large part of what the academic profession does" (Chomsky 2005, 75, 77; see also 58, 62-3).

All of this has implications for liberal arts education. We aim to develop students as individuals. At the same time, we want them to succeeed. These two aims can conflict, but the ideology of the liberal arts promises that they cohere. Develop yourself, the idea goes, and you'll get a better job. What is the balance between theory and praxis? Are academics relevant?[30] What about professors; do commitments to identity politics limit our perspective, and is a universal human perspective even tenable any more?

---

[29] An honorary member of the Bertrand Russell Society, Chomsky once wrote: "And it's one of the memberships of which I'm most proud. A large picture of Russell is the only one on my office walls" (e-mail to John Lenz, April 26, 2013). At the 4th Annual Conference on Public Intellectuals at Harvard University (2013), Chomsky singled out Russell's enduring of imprisonment for opposition to World War I as one of the most courageous acts of the twentieth century. Chomsky moved into the public sphere in a manner reminiscent of Russell, with his Vietnam-era article "The Responsibility of Intellectuals" (Chomsky 1987).

[30] Senator Ted Kennedy wrote wistfully about 1962 that "academia...still had a voice in public matters in those days" (Kennedy 2009, 181-2).

Whatever justifiable points we can make about political opponents (intellectual ones or others), the most remarkable thing about Russell is that he was just as willing to oppose his own society. "It has been a common belief that the human race is divided into groups, each with its own self-interest and each necessarily hostile to some other group or groups....It is now necessary to proclaim that the interests of all men [human beings] are identical" (Russell 1997, 461; see also 457). The philosopher has a duty different from that of every other human being. For Russell, this duty was to oppose government and majority opinion when necessary and to offer a better vision (459). Sometimes the need for impartiality makes one like a "stranger" to the world, he wrote in 1964 (1997, 461). Edward Said called intellectuals perpetual exiles even within their own societies (Said 1994, xvi, 52-3, and more generally ch. III).

Russell's high-minded view of intellectuals, while it seems remote and perhaps transcendent, did carry great influence. Russell lived long enough to join with Albert Einstein in creating a league of scientists from East and West; this organization, the Pugwash Conferences, was awarded the Nobel Peace Prize for 1995 (Lenz 1996). He also led the group (the Campaign for Nuclear Disarmament, or CND) that created the peace symbol. Rolland, Russell, Einstein, and others proposed a vision of globalism for the twentieth century: globalism before globalization. This combination of intellectual and political harmony, which curiously assumes a duality of mind (intellect) and body (political self-interest), was ultimately more forward-looking than Dewey's seemingly more modern sort of pragmatic action-only politics, although the latter dominates today's academy. One does not have to be all practical to make a difference, and sometimes it gets in the way. Dewey was a professor, but Russell took mind to the streets—around the world, through the decades and into a better future.[31]

Bibliography

Akehurst, Thomas. 2010. *The Cultural Politics of Analytic Philosophy: Britishness and the Spectre of Europe.* London and NY: Continuum.

---

[31] "[N]o man in this century has shown greater moral force than the public Bertrand Russell" (Ruse 1997).

Akehurst, Thomas. 2013. "Bertrand Russell Stalks the Nazis." *Philosophy Now* 97, July/August.

Atkins, Jonathan. 2002. "Academics at War: Bertrand Russell and Cambridge." In *War of Individuals: Bloomsbury Attitudes to the Great War.* Manchester: Manchester University Press, 52-76.

Benda, Julien. 1900. *Dialogues à Byzance.* Paris: Éditions de la Revue blanche.

Benda, Julien. 1955. *The Betrayal of the Intellectuals.* Trans. Richard Aldington. Reprint ed. Boston: Beacon Press. Orig. pub. 1927.

Blackwell, Kenneth. 1985. *The Spinozistic Ethics of Bertrand Russell.* London: Allen & Unwin.

Chomsky, Noam. 1987. "The Responsibility of Intellectuals." In *The Chomsky Reader.* Ed. James Peck. New York: Pantheon. Orig. pub. 1967.

Chomsky, Noam. 2003. *Hegemony or Survival.* New York: Metropolitan Books/Henry Holt.

Chomsky, Noam. 2005. *Imperial Ambitions.* New York: Metropolitan Books/Henry Holt.

Clark, Ronald. 1975. *The Life of Bertrand Russell.* London: Jonathan Cape.

Collini, Stefan. 2007. *Absent Minds: Intellectuals in Britain.* Oxford: Oxford University Press.

Dewey, John. 1915. *German Philosophy and Politics.* New York: Henry Holt.

Dewey, John. 1979. "Reply to William Ernest Hocking's 'Political Philosophy in Germany.'" In *John Dewey: The Middle Works, 1899-1924.* Ed. Jo Ann Boydston. Volume 8. Carbondale, IL: Southern Illinois University Press, 418-420.

Fromm, Erich. 1967. "Prophets and Priests." In *Bertrand Russell: Philosopher of the Century.* Ed. Ralph Schoenman. New York: Little, Brown, 67-79.

Grosby, Steven. 2005. *Nationalism: A Very Short Introduction.* New York: Oxford University Press.

Hardy, G.H. 1970. *Bertrand Russell and Trinity.* New York: Cambridge University Press.

Herman, Edward S. and Chomsky, Noam. 2002. *Manufacturing Consent: The Political Economy of the Mass Media.* New ed. New York: Pantheon.

Kennedy, Edward M. 2009. *True Compass: A Memoir.* New York: Twelve.

Lenz, John R. 1996. "Pugwash and Russell's Legacy." Rev. ed. http://www.users.drew.edu/~jlenz/pugwash.html (November 15, 2014).

Lintott, Brett. 2008. "Russell's Aborted Book on Fascism." *Russell* n.s. 28: 39-64.

Martin, Nicholas. 2003. "'Fighting a Philosophy': The Figure of Nietzsche in British Propaganda of the First World War." *Modern Language Review* 98: 367-380.

Mazower, Mark. 2012. *Governing the World: The History of an Idea.* New York: Penguin.

Menand, Louis. 2001. *The Metaphysical Club: A Story of Ideas in America.* New York: Farrar, Straus and Giroux.

Rolland, Romain. 1920. *The Forerunners.* Trans. Eden Paul and Cedar Paul. London: Allen & Unwin.

Ruse, Michael. 1997. "Introduction" to *Religion and Science*, by Bertrand Russell. New York: Oxford University Press.

Russell, Bertrand. 1912. *The Problems of Philosophy.* New York: Henry Holt.

Russell, Bertrand. 1935. "The Ancestry of Fascism." In *In Praise of Idleness*. London: Allen & Unwin.

Russell, Bertrand. 1939. "The Role of the Intellectual in the Modern World." *American Journal of Sociology* 44: 491-498.

Russell, Bertrand. 1946. *A History of Western Philosophy.* London: Allen & Unwin.

Russell, Bertrand. 1949. *The Scientific Outlook.* 2nd ed. New York: Routledge.

Russell, Bertrand. 1953. *The Good Citizen's Alphabet.* London: Gabberbocchus Press.

Russell, Bertrand. 1968. *The Autobiography of Bertrand Russell.* Volume II. Boston: Little, Brown and Company.

Russell, Bertrand. 1988. *Prophecy and Dissent, 1914-1916.* Ed. Richard A. Rempel. Vol. 13 of *The Collected Papers of Bertrand Russell.* London: Unwin Hyman.

Russell, Bertrand. 1992. *The Selected Letters of Bertrand Russell: The Private Years, 1884-1914.* Ed. Nicholas Griffin. Boston: Houghton Mifflin.

Russell, Bertrand. 1997. "The Duty of a Philosopher in This Age." In *Last Philosophical Testament, 1943-1968*. Ed. John G. Slater. Vol. 11 of *The Collected Papers of Bertrand Russell*. New York: Routledge, 455-463. Written in 1964.

Russell, Bertrand. 2001. *The Selected Letters of Bertrand Russell: The Public Years, 1914-1970*. Ed. Nicholas Griffin. New York: Routledge.

Ryan, Alan. 1988. *Bertrand Russell: A Political Life.* New York: Hill and Wang.

Ryan, Alan. 1995. *John Dewey and the High Tide of American Liberalism*. New York: Norton.

Said, Edward W. 1994. *Representations of the Intellectual*. New York: Vintage Books.

Santayana, George. 1915. "Goethe and German Egotism." *New Republic*, Jan. 2.

Santayana, George. 1916. *Egotism in German Philosophy.* New York: Charles Scribner's Sons.

RUSSELL AND DEWEY ON EDUCATION: SIMILARITIES AND DIFFERENCES

Tim Madigan

JOHN DEWEY AND BERTRAND RUSSELL were two of the premier philosophers of the twentieth century. During their long lives (each lived to be over 90), their paths crossed on several occasions. While cordial enough when in each other's presence, the two men were definitely not on the best of terms. Sidney Hook, who knew and admired them both, once said that there were only two men who Dewey actively disliked—Mortimer Adler and Bertrand Russell. Russell, for his part, never tired of making disparaging remarks about the pragmatists in general and Dewey in particular. This irked Dewey immensely. Still, the two men shared many philosophical traits—an internationalist outlook, a high regard for the scientific method, a concern for social matters, and a suspicion of dogma, especially religious dogma. In this chapter, I will focus upon the educational theories of Russell and Dewey, including the curious fact that each of them (for a short period of time) ran their own elementary schools.

That the Dewey-versus-Russell debate is still going on can be seen in the Winter 1990 issue of *The Wilson Quarterly*, which contains a letter from Alan Ryan (author of books on both Russell and Dewey) commenting upon a previous article which ran in that magazine entitled "John Dewey: Philosopher in the Schoolroom." In comparing Russell and Dewey, Ryan writes that, "The similarities, of course, are many and obvious: both were ardent defenders of an education in which the child learned by doing, both began by doubting the need for any authority in the classroom other than the discipline of the subject matter itself, and both came to think, in Hobbes' memorable words, that children 'are born inapt for society'" (Ryan 1990, 141). But Ryan goes on to say that the differences between them are more striking, and that an absolute barrier divided them—namely, Dewey's pragmatism. To quote again from Ryan:

> For Russell, at any rate, pragmatism was a sort of secular blasphemy. With God gone and most ethics shaky, all mankind had left was a concern for the truth—not a concern for what it would "pay to believe," but a concern for how things really were. By bringing philosophy back into the market-place, Dewey closed the breach that Russell had opened between the concerns of the intellectual and the duties of the plain man... Dewey's passion for closing all gaps and rejecting all dichotomies is ultimately less true to life than Russell's insistence on the tragic dimension of everyday life. A strong sense of the uselessness of truth and its unrelatedness to human affairs still strikes many of us as an indispensable element in the psychology of the serious philosopher. (Ryan 141)

Ryan spells out quite well the bone of contention between the two men: the meaning of truth. But Russell was perhaps not as hesitant to bring philosophy into the marketplace as Ryan suggests. For Russell and Dewey are noteworthy in the annals of educational philosophy for attempting to practice what they preach; each of them, at different times, started their own schools for children. Russell, like Dewey, was (for at least a short while) a philosopher in the schoolroom.

The University Elementary School, popularly known as "The Laboratory School," was set up by the Department of Pedagogy of the University of Chicago and headed by John Dewey from its inception in 1896 to his resignation in 1904. The term "Laboratory School" was no accident, for according to Dewey the school had two aims: "To exhibit, test, verify, and criticize theoretical statements and principles, and to add to the sum of facts and principles in its special line" (Dewey 1972, 437). In this way, Dewey thought that the school would do for pedagogy what similar laboratories did for biology, physics and chemistry: it would provide an opportunity for experimentation. The school eventually grew to 140 students, aged 4 to 15.

Russell opened the Beacon Hill School in 1927, over 20 years after Dewey's experiment in education had ended. It originally had 12 boarders and 5 day students, aged 5 to 12. The school was run by Russell and his second wife, Dora. In 1932 Russell withdrew from any participation with the school after filing for a Deed of Separation from Dora. (They divorced two years later.) Dora continued to run the school until 1943, and was always its staunchest supporter. The Russells' reason for starting a school is described in his autobiography:

> We did not know of any existing school that seemed to us in any way satisfactory. We wanted an unusual combination: on the one hand, we disliked prudery and religious instruction and a great many restraints on freedom which are taken for granted in conventional schools; on the other hand, we could not agree with most "modern" educationists in thinking scholastic instruction unimportant, or in advocating a complete absence of discipline. (Russell 1968, 222-3)

Dewey and Russell each wrote books that detailed the format of their respective schools, and what they hoped to achieve in them: Dewey's *The School and Society* and Russell's *On Education* and *Education and the Social Order* (first published in 1899, 1926, and 1932, respectively). Examining these works, one can see another crucial distinction between the two men—their writing style. Dewey is earnest, dry and straightforward in his presentation, while Russell is not afraid to add playful digressions and pepper his approach with witty asides and colorful anecdotes, such as the following from *On Education*:

> Every author who has had uneducated housemaids knows that it is difficult (the public may wish it were impossible) to restrain their passion for lighting the fire with his manuscripts. A fellow-author, even if he were a jealous enemy, would not think of doing such a thing, because experience has taught him the value of manuscripts. Similarly the boy who has a garden will not trample on other people's flower-beds, and the boy who has pets can be taught to respect animal life. (Russell 1933, 112)

And in his later book, *Education and the Social Order*, Russell writes: "I found one day in school a boy of medium size ill-treating a smaller boy. I expostulated, but he replied: 'The bigs hit me, so I hit the babies; that's fair.' In these words he epitomized the history of the human race" (Russell 1961, 32). One would be hard-pressed to find such anecdotes in Dewey's writings.

While darkly humorous, stories such as these illustrate a concern of both Dewey and Russell—how can the school be used as a means of shaping the student to be a good citizen and a good individual? The two men found much fault with existing school systems, which they felt were too geared towards regimentation, learning by rote, and inculcating an obedience to authority. In addition, they felt that too much educational theory was basically impractical, and was applied to students without first being properly tested. Hence the need for "experimental schools." Neither Dewey nor Russell had any illusions that their schools would become models for universal education, but they did hope to show how theories could be tested and adapted to fit the needs of individual students. As Dewey writes in *The School and Society*:

> I heard once that the adoption of a certain method in use in our school was objected to by a teacher on this ground: "You know that it is an experimental school. They do not work under the same conditions that we are subject to." Now, the purpose of performing an experiment is that other people need not experiment; at least not experiment so much...We do not expect to have other schools literally imitate what we do. A working model is not something to be copied: it is to afford a demonstration of the feasibility of the principle, and of the methods which make it feasible. (Dewey 1980, 56)

This raises an obvious question. To what extent were the Laboratory and Beacon Hill schools successful working models? This is rather difficult to judge, given the short time that both schools were in existence and the precariousness of the support they received, but it seems that their achievements were spotty at best. I will briefly describe what both men hoped to achieve with their schools, and how close they came to reaching this.

Dewey had several key elements in his concept of the well-educated person: a pluralistic world view; acceptance of the fact that one can never fully know objective reality; acceptance of the consequences of one's actions; a concern for social action; and adherence to the scientific method as the best means for achieving knowledge. These elements, especially the last of these, were also in accord with Russell's educational views. "Knowledge will not be viewed as mere knowledge, but as an instrument of progress, the value of which is shown by bringing it into relation with the needs of the world" (Russell 1980, 11). This quotation comes, not from Dewey, as one might expect, but from the prospectus Russell wrote up for the Beacon Hill school. But its view of knowledge is reminiscent of Dewey's instrumentalism.

Both Russell and Dewey stressed the importance of understanding and utilizing the scientific method. Their schools sought to get the students actively involved in the educational process. As Brian Hendley points out in his excellent book *Dewey, Russell, Whitehead: Philosophers as Educators*, both philosophers had a great deal of trouble finding the proper equipment to do this; the desks and chairs available for small children were made for listening, not for working (Hendley 1986, 57). The Laboratory and Beacon Hill schools got the children outdoors as much as possible. Gardening, walks, cooking, and scientific experiments were the order of the day, and each school hated the idea of keeping the young ones constricted and cooped-up in dusty classrooms.

The schools also tried to avoid heavy-handed discipline. This led to the charge against both men that they allowed anarchy to reign supreme. In *The School and Society*, Dewey answered this charge:

> Upon the moral side, that of so-called discipline and order, where the University Elementary School has perhaps suffered most from misunderstanding and misrepresentation, I shall say only that our ideal has been, and continues to be, that of the best form of family life, rather than that of a rigid graded school...If we have permitted to our children more than the usual amount of freedom, it has not been in order to relax or decrease real discipline, but because under our particular conditions larger and less artificial responsibilities could thus be required of the children, and their entire development of body and spirit be more harmonious and complete. (Dewey 1980, 65-6)

Russell's Beacon Hill School followed roughly the same approach to discipline. The teachers at both schools, who were used to the more regimented approach, often had a difficult time putting this into practice. And, as Russell's illustration of the young boy striking the even younger boy shows, knowing when or when not to discipline a child proved a tricky thing. In his *Autobiography*, Russell bemoans the fact that "I found myself, when the children were not at lessons, obliged to supervise them continually to stop cruelty....Young children in a group cannot be happy without a certain amount of order and routine. Left to amuse themselves, they are bored, and turn to bullying or destruction" (Russell 1968, 226). Russell came to feel that the Beacon Hill School had been rather too lenient in regard to discipline.

It should be pointed out that the Laboratory and Beacon Hill schools were very much family affairs for the two philosophers. Dewey and Russell each sent their own children to the schools, and their wives were heavily involved in all aspects of running the schools. In fact, Alice Dewey and Dora Russell, due to their day-to-day work at the schools, had more influence on them than did their husbands, who had less time to devote to them. And it was this husband-and-wife combination that would lead, for different reasons, to the two philosophers abandoning their efforts in regard to the schools.

In 1902, the Laboratory School merged with another prominent Chicago experimental school, the Parker School, which had a much larger budget and staff. Alice Dewey was appointed principal of this combined school in 1903. She did not get on well with the former members of the Parker staff. The President of the University of Chicago, William Harper, who oversaw the school, tried to pacify the warring factions by interpreting Mrs. Dewey's appointment as being for one year only, subject to annual reappointment. She felt differently, and promptly resigned. John Dewey sprang to her defense, and himself resigned as Director of the School of Education, and from his position as professor and head of the University's Department of Philosophy.

Russell's involvement with Beacon Hill also ended at least partly because of his wife, but in his case it was estrangement between the partners that led to the breakup. Both Russell and his wife advocated free love. Once, when Dora returned from a trip, she was informed by her cook that Russell had been sleeping with the children's governess while she was away. Dora reacted by firing the cook! "I had to explain," she wrote in her autobiography, "that, though I loved her for her loyalty, we did not feel quite the same way about these things. I would have to let her go, because she and 'the Masther' [sic] could hardly get on after this. And to the governess, who was a charming girl, I simply said that her job at the school was *not* cancelled" (emphasis in original; Russell 1975, 198). Russell himself was a bit less sanguine when Dora gave birth in 1930 to a child fathered by Griffin Barry, a frequent visitor to the school. When she gave birth to another child by Barry in 1932, Russell had had enough. It was at this point that he washed his hands of Dora and of the school.

While both Dewey and Russell's schools were short-lived, one can still ask if they were successful on their own terms—namely, as working models for making innovations in the American and British school systems. From this perspective, neither school seemed to fulfill this goal. In a way, this is not surprising. The students at each were rather atypical; for the most part, they hailed from upper class or professional households. And at least in the case of Beacon Hill, a good number were "problem children" who had been hopelessly spoiled by doting parents, and whose lack of discipline preceded their introduction to the school. On a brighter note, the parents of the students were exceptionally supportive, and raised a great deal of money to help out each school's perennial financial woes. In addition, individual attention was stressed, something which was often a luxury in most school systems. And certainly the presence of the two remarkable founders was something which very few schools could hope to emulate. Dewey and Russell each complained bitterly about the amount of paperwork their experimental schools generated. Perhaps they had been overly optimistic in their hopes of avoiding this particular hurdle, which is the bane of all administrators. And their hopes of being truly innovative were tempered by their realization that the students would still have to face standardized testing and old-fashioned grading techniques once they entered the realm of higher education.

Perhaps the two main charges levelled against the schools were, first, that they were overly artificial, and second, that they did not live up to the standards of a real laboratory for education. The first charge is one that Dewey in particular took pains to counter. "There is a difference," he wrote, "between working out and testing a new truth, or a new method, and applying it on a wide scale, making it available for the mass of men, making it commercial. But the first thing is to discover the truth, to afford all necessary facilities, for this is the most practical thing in the world in the long run" (Dewey 1980, 56). While granting that his model was highly specialized, Dewey nonetheless hoped to discover new techniques and new approaches to education that could be used under many different conditions.

Russell was perhaps less concerned with the charge that his school was elitist. While Dewey continually stressed the important connection between education and democracy, and the need to provide a school that would offer equal opportunities for all, Russell was ambivalent on the issue of just what his school was aiming to achieve. In *On Education*, he writes that "the ideal system of education must be democratic" (Russell 1933, 16).

And like Dewey, he sought to give the students an international, rather than parochial, education. Indeed, he went so far as to propose the formation of a committee which would oversee all textbooks and train teachers in a manner that would transcend narrow nationalistic feelings. The committee would be composed of individuals from all walks of life, except those who rejected the idea of an international government. This hardly seems a democratic model.

Russell also gave more attention than Dewey did to the special student, the student of superior intellect who feels constrained by the democratic attributes of the school system. In *Education and the Social Order*, Russell observes that "A great deal of needless pain and friction would be saved to clever children if they were not compelled to associate intimately with stupid contemporaries. There is an idea that rubbing up against all and sundry in youth is a good preparation for life. This appears to me to be rubbish. No one, in later life, associates with all and sundry" (Russell 1961, 100).

One need only compare this with Dewey's constant refrain that the American public school system, with its interaction of students from many different creeds, nationalities, and cultures, is an ideal forum for promoting social unity. Russell, unlike Dewey, was torn between the desire to offer equal educational opportunities for all students, and his perception that exceptional students would suffer under such a system. Beacon Hill, with its rather ragtag bunch of rambunctious children, did not reconcile this dichotomy.

The second charge levelled against both schools, that they did not live up to the standards of a good laboratory, is an apt one. Strangely, given the importance both men placed upon the scientific method, neither school underwent a rigorous scientific evaluation. Most of what we know about the schools comes from anecdotal evidence, some of which (such as Dora Russell's writings) is overly partisan. A few studies were done on the schools, but not to the extent that one might expect. While it is, of course, difficult, if not impossible, to scientifically evaluate creativity and attentiveness, certainly there could have been systematic and objective studies done on the methods used in the schools, and the achievements of its students in their later lives. Perhaps the abrupt departure of Dewey and Russell from their respective schools had something to do with the lack of follow-up studies. How sad that these two rare occasions when professional philosophers attempted to practice what they preached should go, for the most part, unstudied. One feels that a golden opportunity was lost because of this.

As educational models, then, the Laboratory and Beacon Hill schools left something to be desired. Their short life, their specialized clientele, their "family affair" quality, and their lack of follow-up studies and precise reports make it next-to-impossible to evaluate their overall effectiveness objectively. Nonetheless, one cannot help but admire the willingness of Dewey and Russell to tackle concrete issues of education, from finding the right sort of equipment for the children to use, to planning lessons, to pleading with parents for financial support. One wonders how many other philosophers would be so willing to get their hands dirty in this way. How nice it would have been, for example, if Rousseau had tried to raise his own children by his educational principles, instead of giving them all up for adoption shortly after their birth.

Returning to what Alan Ryan calls the absolute barrier dividing Dewey from Russell, one gets a sense of this in the afterword Alan Wood wrote for Russell's book *My Philosophical Development*. He quotes from Russell's essay "Reflections on My Eightieth Birthday," in which Russell laments: "I wanted certainty, in the kind of way in which people want religious faith." Wood then adds. "I believe the underlying purpose behind all Russell's work was an almost religious passion for some truth that was more than human, independent of the minds of men, and even of the existence of men" (Wood 260). If this is correct, then it is no wonder that Russell could not abide the pragmatic philosophy of John Dewey, which criticized the "quest for certainty" as being ultimately fruitless, and who judged truths by their practicality. But while this may have been an unbridgeable gulf between them, they still had many remarkable similarities, especially in their wish to unfetter the human mind from hidebound dogmas, ideological prattle and nationalistic fervor. Their work on education ably demonstrates their humanistic concerns.

Bibliography

Dewey, John. 1972. "The University School." In *John Dewey: The Early Works, 1882-1898*. Ed. Jo Ann Boydston. Volume 5. Carbondale, IL: Southern Illinois University Press, 436-441.

Dewey, John. 1980. *The School and Society*. Carbondale, IL: Southern Illinois University Press.

Hendley, Brian. 1986. *Dewey, Russell, Whitehead: Philosophers as Educators*. Carbondale, IL: Southern Illinois University Press.

Russell, Bertrand. 1933. *On Education*. London: George Allen & Unwin Ltd.

Russell, Bertrand. 1961. *Education and the Social Order*. London: George Allen & Unwin Ltd.

Russell, Bertrand. 1968. *The Autobiography of Bertrand Russell*. Volume II. Boston: Little, Brown and Company.

Russell, Dora. 1975. *The Tamarisk Tree*. Volume 1. London: Elek/Pemberton.

Russell, Dora. 1980. *The Tamarisk Tree.* Volume 2. London: Virago Ltd.

Ryan, Alan. 1990. "Dewey and Russell." *The Wilson Quarterly* (Winter): 141.

Wood, Alan. 1959. "Russell's Philosophy." Afterword to *My Philosophical Development*, by Bertrand Russell. London: George Allen & Unwin Ltd.

SOMEWHERE IN ENGLAND:
VOLUNTARY EDUCATION AT BEACON HILL
AND SUMMERHILL

Cara Rice

> Though loneliness and anxiety were my close companions through all those seven years they do not seem to me to be too high a price to have paid for the intellectual excitement, the beauty and the exhilaration of the learning we enjoyed.
>
> —*Katherine Tait (formerly Katherine Russell) describing her experience as a student at Beacon Hill*

1. NEVER QUIET ON THE WESTERN FRONT

The life of Lord Bertrand Russell provides a strong counterargument to charges generally laid against philosophers. Society often claims that those who champion the search for objective truth are privileged and protected. However, events such as the death of Socrates and the execution of Giordano Bruno demonstrate that great thinkers have sacrificed not only their safety but their very lives for the sake of principle. Those who dismiss philosophy frequently say that the subject is irrelevant to the everyday challenges of making money and raising children. Bertrand Russell's life provides a noteworthy rejoinder to this argument. Lord Russell's biography is less bleak than the cases cited above, but he frequently forfeited privilege and freedom in order to stay true to his convictions. For example, Russell protested World War I, served time in prison for his efforts, and protested nuclear arms decades later, facing arrest in the process. Russell also ran for office as a women's suffragist in the face of considerable adversity, including bystanders (many of them female) throwing eggs at him. As the renowned historian Frederick Copleston writes in *A History of Philosophy*,

At the 1948 International Philosophical Congress at Amsterdam a Communist professor from Prague took it upon himself to refer to Russell as an example of an ivory-tower philosopher. But whatever one's estimate may be of Russell's ideas in this or that field of inquiry and reflection, this particular judgment was patently absurd. For Russell has not only written on matters of practical concern but also actively campaigned in favour of his ideas....Thus even at a very advanced age Russell has continued to battle on behalf of the welfare of humanity, as he sees it. And the charge of "ivory-tower philosopher" is obviously singularly inappropriate. (Copleston 1966, 471-2)

Russell's experience in the world of education reflects this ongoing battle on behalf of the welfare of humanity. When Russell became a father, he and his second wife, Dora, knew that no school in England could provide what they believed to be a proper education. Rather than hire tutors, the Russells founded the Beacon Hill School, where lessons were optional and almost all the children voted on rules and policy. Bertrand Russell then went to great lengths to raise funds for the institution. Russell incorporated his philosophy on education into both his family life and his financial matters. Beacon Hill is not only a testimony that children will learn without coercion; the school also shows that Russell did not simply pen a few ideas about education and return to his pipe. His philosophy of education literally became his job, and his philosophy proved workable. This chapter will explore Russell's experience at Beacon Hill, as well as the experience of his fellow radical educator, A.S. Neill, and the school he founded, Summerhill.

2. PILGRIMS' PROGRESS

Lord and Lady Russell based the Beacon Hill school upon the principles of voluntary education, autonomy for students, and the inclusion of almost all the pupils in the majority of the school's decisions. Although Beacon Hill eventually closed, many argue that this was due to circumstances beyond the Russells' control and that the school was based on feasible policies. One of the strongest arguments in Beacon Hill's favor is that Summerhill, the school founded by the Russells' contemporary A.S. Neill and ran in a somewhat similar manner, is still in operation today.

The Russells took no interest in giving their children a conventional education. Both parents opposed the religious instruction and corporal punishment fundamental to British schools at the time. Furthermore, these institutions all encouraged patriotism, a practice with which the pacifistic Russells had little patience. Russell once stated that:

> My own belief is that education must be subversive if it is to be meaningful. By this, I mean that it must challenge all the things we take for granted, examine all accepted assumptions, tamper with every sacred cow, and instill a desire to question and doubt. Without this, the mere instruction to memorize data is empty. The attempt to enforce conventional mediocrity on the young mind is criminal. (quoted in Clark 1976, 423)

Dora and Bertie agreed that education must be voluntary on the students' part and that teachers must approach young people with kindness and respect. The Russells reasoned that if children were allowed to play freely, they would soon discover the positive aspects of democracy. They also believed that very young children should not become overly studious or bookish. The Russells even found the policies of Maria Montessori to be overly academic and inappropriately centered on reading, writing, and mathematics. They both preferred the teaching practices of Margaret McMillan, a reform educator whose main tenet was the necessity that nursery schools give children large spaces in which to play at any safe recreation they chose. Indeed, McMillan helped establish the original need for nursery schools. As Dora Russell writes of McMillan in the *Tamarisk Tree Vol. 2: My School and the Years of War*:

> Margaret and [her younger sister] Rachel's care of children during the war led up to the Education Act of 1918, which first established the principle of the nursery school.... There was nothing [previously] adequate to meet the needs of the critical period up to five years. Significantly, what Margaret sought was not education but nurture. In fact she always refused to distinguish between the two at any age. (Russell 1980, 12)

As the time approached for the Russells' children, Katherine (or Kate, born 1923) and John (born 1921), to attend school, both parents were writing books that addressed the topic of education. Dora Russell's book

The Right to Be Happy argues that a society must nurture human emotion in order for its members to be productive and successful. In his book *Education and the Good Life*[1] Bertrand Russell writes, "The spontaneous wish to learn, which every normal child possesses, as shown in its efforts to walk and talk, should be the driving force in education" (Russell 1926, 28). Russell continues:

> If you insist upon teaching a child, he will conclude that he is being asked to do something disagreeable to please you, and he will have a psychological resistance. If this exists at the start, it will perpetuate itself; at a later age, the desirability of getting through examinations may become evident, and there will be work for that purpose, but none from sheer interest in knowledge. If, on the contrary you can first stimulate the child's desire to know and then, as a favour, give him the knowledge he wants, the whole situation is different. Very much less external discipline is required, and attention is secured without difficulty. (Russell 1926, 156)

Both writers believed that economic or social class should not be a factor in the quality of a child's education. Many people would agree with the Russells' arguments but would make no effort to put them into practice.

Dora and Bertrand, never daunted by convention or unchartered territory, opened Beacon Hill in 1927. For obvious reasons, the school began on a limited scale. Teachers at Beacon Hill made approximately one-third of what most academic instructors earned, a testimony to the staff's support of the school's mission. The founders knew that their small faculty would not be able to educate a large group of children effectively. Of greater importance, the student body would be limited to the children of individuals who would trust a notoriously unorthodox couple to educate their children using untested ideas and providing no religious instruction. Beacon Hill School began its first term with five American and seven English students, including the Russell's children, Kate and John. The students' ages ranged from two to eight years.

At Beacon Hill, no one was to be coerced to attend lessons although all were encouraged to do so. There were few tests or competitions because the Russells did not believe that children were naturally competitive or that

---

[1] Published as *On Education* in England.

such tendencies should be cultivated. Ronald Clark's biography of Russell explains:

> Children below the age of five were given their own playroom where they could do what they liked with a wide range of materials...From five onwards the children were encouraged but not forced to start reading, writing and arithmetic. Elementary French and German were infiltrated into their studies. (Clark, 1976, 424)

The age of five was pivotal at Beacon Hill. This was the age at which children joined Beacon Hill's school council in which they had the same voting power as any of the adults. The council was an essential component of the school as Katherine Tait, the former Katherine Russell, notes in her book:

> We could never be irresponsibly lazy or malicious, and trust to the teachers to control the consequence of our behavior. Whatever we did we had to live with, and our actions were liable to be very critically discussed at school council meetings, which included all the children, and all the teachers, each with one vote. (Tait 1975, 73)

Parents who believed in free inquiry would most likely have found Beacon Hill an encouraging option. Tait recalls her parents' original intentions for the school:

> The children were to have absolute freedom of inquiry: our natural curiosity was to be encouraged in every way and all our questions answered as truthfully as possible. It was hoped that, in this way, we would acquire an interest in learning and a habit of seeking the truth. The teaching was to be based on our appetite for knowledge, rather than on a preconceived program of basic skills and facts to be fed into the living computer of each child's mind. (Tait 1975, 73)

By all indications, the Russells stayed true to this policy. For example, instructors at Beacon Hill did not teach the children about sex, but they were expected to answer all the children's question on the topic honestly. Part of Beacon Hill's prospectus reads:

> we shall aim at stimulating interest by free discussion, and, in later years, by encouraging argument on every arguable question.... We shall aim at producing, not listless intellectuals, but young men and women filled with constructive hopefulness, consciousness that there are great things to be done in the world, and possessed of the skill required for taking their part. (Russell 1980, 11-2)

What the prospectus does not mention is that lessons were optional, that students voted on the rules, and that nudity was permitted. These freedoms, however, rarely brought about complication. When imperatives presented themselves, the staff became creative. For example, Lady Russell knew that the children must participate in a fire drill, but she did not wish to require anyone to do so. Dora simply invited the children to try the new fire escape apparatus, which consisted of an engaging set of slings, and the children voluntarily practiced what they needed to learn.

Beacon Hill was by no means idyllic. Katherine Tait has explained that the absence of conventional rules frequently meant the absence of conventional safeguards:

> We were expected to rule ourselves, under the wise supervision of benevolent adults, and to learn to behave well even when we were not watched, an expectation that made the climate remarkably bracing...Many of the children at Beacon Hill were problems, sent to us as a last resort, and they vented on others the grief and frustrations of their private lives. That their cruelty had been learned at home, and was more their misfortune than their fault, afforded little comfort to their victims. The atmosphere of Beacon Hill probably helped them, but they were not particularly good for us. (Tait 1975, 74-7)

Supervising children privy to so much freedom was difficult for the adults as well. Bertrand Russell was disappointed by how much time he had to spend watching the students play freely to insure everyone's safety. He had not realized that young people could be so rough. Russell discusses bullying in his book *In Praise of Idleness*:

> There is another consideration to which some advocates of freedom attach too little importance. In a community of children which is left without adult interference there is a

> tyranny of the stronger, which is likely to be far more brutal than most adult tyranny…I do not think that educators have yet solved the problem of combining the desirable forms of freedom with the necessary minimum of moral training. (Russell 1935, 156)

Beacon Hill demonstrates that freedom, like everything else we might cherish, comes with a price. All the same, the safeguards of democracy usually prevailed. The teachers and students had equal status in creating and changing the majority of the school's rules,[2] and this helped create a spirit of camaraderie and cooperation. For example, when bullying became a problem at Beacon Hill, the teachers called a meeting and created a resolution that the school did not approve of such behavior. Afterward, the students would approach individuals who were physically harassing others, and they would recite the resolution. According to both Lady Russell and Katherine, this practice was effective, and the potential danger was usually thwarted. Indeed, in a school that did not require deference to the instructors, the children were often cooperative. Katherine Tait would note in her biography of her father:

> The school council made all the rules for the school except in matters of health. Since children outnumbered teachers two to one, we could have outvoted them at any time if we wanted to…we usually accepted the recommendations of their (the teachers') superior wisdom. Except once when we voted to abolish all rules for a trial period, to discover which ones were really important…the consequence was such dreadful anarchy that we were all thankful to return to the rule of law. (Tait 1975, 74)

During Beacon Hill's inception, Bertrand and Dora could not predict the exact nature of the misguided decisions that would take place in a democratically run school, but they knew that Beacon Hill would be an experimental venture and a work in progress.

---

[2] Noted exceptions were the students' bedtimes, meal times, and diet.

3. COMRADE IN ARMS

The practices and policies of Beacon Hill were distinctive but not singular. Alexander Sutherland Neill, a man whom the Russells would always consider a friend, colleague, and comrade-in-arms, also ran a school with optional classwork and a council on which children and adults shared authority. The man known to the scholarly world as A.S. Neill created a school, Summerhill, that most considered to be even more libertarian than Beacon Hill. Both Dora and Katherine would later write that, as progressive as their school might be, no one could say they were as radical as Summerhill. Russell's biography makes a similar comparison when describing the policies of Beacon Hill: "The basic programme, revolutionary half a century ago, was supported by a discipline midway between that of conventional enforcement and the unlimited freedom of Neill's Summerhill" (Clark 1976, 424).

4. YOU, THAT WAY: WE, THIS WAY

Neill founded Summerhill, in 1921, for the same reasons that the Russells began Beacon Hill. He was the son of a teacher, and he had been an academic instructor for over ten years; so he had ample opportunity to observe the shortfalls of a conventional education. Like the Russells, Neill wanted to provide a healthier alternative. However, while Bertrand Russell believed that children should always be carefully encouraged to study, A.S. Neill did not. The latter placed considerably less emphasis on academics. For example, Katherine Tait has explained that most students at Beacon Hill generally began instruction after a short period of freedom because the school grounds, located in a desolate, rural location, provided limited diversion, especially when most of the students were in their classes. Summerhill, on the other hand, was located in a coastal community brimming with activity. If a student wished to go to class or to study, it was truly his or her choice. Summerhill achieved respectable results with this strategy. Albert Lamb, a former student at Summerhill who would go on to edit Neill's work, explains: "The goal was to use childhood and adolescence to create emotional wholeness and personal strength…the key to this growth was to give children freedom to play for as long as they felt the need in an atmosphere of approval and love" (Neill 1992).

The differences between Bertrand Russell and A. S. Neill are noteworthy. After all, the Russells, with no administrative experience, were willing to start their own school rather than send John and Katherine to Summerhill. While Russell believed that young people should never be forced into a classroom, he thought that a school should still give its students every incentive to study and to protect them from distractions:

> There must, at first, be the example of other children at a slightly more advanced stage. There must be no other obviously pleasant occupation open to the child at the moment. There are a number of things the child may do, and he works by himself at whichever he prefers. Almost all children are perfectly happy in this regime and learn to read and write without pressure before they are five years old…
>
> As children grow older, they become responsive to more remote motives, and it is no longer necessary that every detail should be interesting in itself. But I think the broad principle that the impulse to education should come from the pupil can be continued up to any age. The environment should be such as to stimulate the impulse, and to make boredom and isolation the alternative to learning. But any child that preferred this alternative on any occasion should be allowed to choose it.…If a child has been properly trained up to the age of five or six, any good teacher ought to be able to win his interest at later stages. (Russell 1926, 157)

Naturally, Russell thought it ill advised to send children to Summerhill where classwork was optional and numerous forms of recreation were available. Stephen Heathorn notes that when the Russells were still deciding what would be the best choice for their children's education,

> They considered the institutions of temporary pioneers, particularly A.S. Neill's Summerhill School—which perhaps matched closest to their own ideals amongst the experimental schools then operating—but decided that it was not quite right. Russell, in particular, believed in the humanizing potential of knowledge, which needed to be put in balance with the lack of emotional repression and child centered learning that were the hallmark of Sum-

merhill….In a very literal sense, they put their money where their mouths were, for Russell was required to go on several lecture tours (and Dora one) in the USA to generate the money needed to subsidize the project. (Heathorn 2002, 4)

Furthermore, Russell objected to Neill's willingness to emphasize psychology over the intellect. Russell frequently compared his school to that of Neill's, often underscoring the distinctive emphasis on learning and academic study that he felt Summerhill lacked. One time, when he feared that he and Dora might have to close Beacon Hill due to financial problems, he wrote H. G. Wells:

> I believe profoundly in the importance of what we are doing here. If I were to put into one single phrase our educational objectives, I should say that we aim at training initiative without diminishing its strength…You will realize that hardly any other educational reformers lay much stress upon intelligence. A.S. Neill, for example, who is in many ways an admirable man, allows such complete liberty that his children fail to get the necessary training and are always going to the cinema, when they might otherwise be interested in things of more value. Absence of opportunity for exciting pleasures at this place is, I think, an important factor in the development of the children's intellectual interests. (Croall 1983, 159)

The camaraderie remained strong between Neill and the Russells all the same. For example, Neill wrote to Bertrand Russell that *On Education* "is the only book on education that I have read that does not make me swear" (Russell 1998, 420). Neill is more complimentary to the work than the author himself is. Russell writes in his *Autobiography* that *On Education* "seems to me now somewhat unduly optimistic in its psychology" (Russell 1998, 386). The bond between Beacon Hill and Summerhill was such that, during World War II, Neill had a standing invitation from Dora Russell to evacuate his school to the grounds of Beacon Hill.

Bertrand and Dora Russell ran Beacon Hill together until the unofficial end of their marriage. Russell left Beacon Hill in 1932, but Dora continued to run the school until 1943, when the complications that had plagued Beacon Hill from its inception became insurmountable in the face of World War II. At this time the authorities commandeered the quarters for military purposes (Heathorn 2002, 4). Dora, exhausted and severely lacking in funds, had already moved the school once due to financial complications. She chose not to move it again.

As proprietor of Beacon Hill, Dora became increasingly sympathetic to Neill's viewpoint. She always felt that psychology and nurture should perhaps take precedence over intellectual training, and she gradually embraced most of Neill's ideals. Lady Russell's philosophy and methods of education evolved accordingly:

> Over the next few years, when she [Dora] ran the school without Russell [Bertrand], she aimed to let the children express themselves through unorganized play as well as through drama, art, and movement. Though at first she felt unable to go all the way with Neill's libertarian ideas… after a few years she came to the conclusion that his approach was a necessary one, since "the gulf between the old and the new was too wide to bridge by compromise." By the middle of the 1930s, Neill was telling her that he and she were "the only educators." (quoted in Croall 1983, 160)

5. IN FOR A PENNY

As noted above, Beacon Hill remained in operation until World War II, and many would argue that if war ends a business venture that worked for more than 15 years, it does not follow that the blame lies with the prospectus or the proprietor. However, while war was the final factor that closed the school, funding was always an obstacle. Indeed, many fees were never paid. The Russells could have enrolled more students, but they believed that this would reduce the quality of the services they wished to provide. They did not wish to raise the price of tuition because they did not want the offerings of Beacon Hill to become cost-prohibitive. In *Education and the Good Life*, Bertrand defends the importance of the humanities and argues that children from all backgrounds should study them. Russell begins *Education and the Good Life* by explaining that "Whatever I advocate shall be capable of being universal, though the individual should not meantime sacrifice his children to the badness of what is common if he has the intelligence and the opportunity to secure something better" (Russell 1926, 14). Russell follows by examining the debate whether an education should be lofty or practical and whether working class students need to study material that is not demonstrably utilitarian. He continues that, in order for one's education to be truly practical, it must include courses from the humanities because this is how a child becomes a reflective and analytical adult:

> I do not wish to suggest that the humanistic elements in education are less important than the utilitarian elements. To know something of great literature, something of world history, something of world history, something of music and painting and architecture, is essential if the life of imagination is to be fully developed. And it is only through imagination that men become aware of what the world might be; without it, "progress" would become mechanical and trivial. But science can also stimulate the imagination. (*ibid.*, 21)

There was obviously some substance to the Russells' philosophy. Since Summerhill is still in operation, one can argue that Beacon Hill did not close due to idealistic policies. Therefore, while Dora Russell changed part of the school's mission, two of Bertrand Russell's primary tenets, voluntary learning and rules by consent, are demonstrably feasible.

6. IF YOU CAN WAIT, AND NOT BE TIRED OF WAITING

This is not to say that the majority of twenty-first century schools could run on the model of Beacon Hill. Few of them have the conditions that Russell deemed necessary for his approach: a small student body, a rustic environment providing for limited distraction, and, most of all, time. Both the Russells and Neill made clear that children must come to the decision to seek a formal education on their own. In some cases this took a considerable amount of time, and time requires patience. Modern public schools depend on the patience of the tax-payers, a commodity that presents itself in varying amounts.

Beacon Hill and Summerhill still lend encouragement. The challenges listed above are logistical and political and therefore not insurmountable. After all, public education itself was a limited privilege for centuries. Until recently, even the most benevolent individuals from many societies would not advocate universal tax-based education or schools that forbid corporal punishment. These people would have said that such practices might be ideal but not workable. Today, our viewpoints on education continue to evolve.

Currently, many individuals and organizations that wish to reform our schools want what is best for children, but they believe that they must be rigidly practical and disregard idealistic philosophies. Philosophy, however, is one of the most important tools of reform because a philosopher's goal is to separate that which is true from that which we assume to be true. This information is vital to reform. Furthermore, we all must remember that society has, on first hearing, considered almost every idea that has contributed to the Enlightenment to be extraordinary.

In closing, Bertrand and Dora Russell were pioneers in the field of education reform, not over-protected thinkers who spent their lives in a cloistered study. The Russells put their ideas into practice, raised the necessary funding, and created a school that remained operational until World War II. Summerhill, in many ways a sister school, still stands today. Beacon Hill and Summerhill demonstrate that children will, under the right conditions, govern themselves and learn without coercion. As we strategize to improve our school systems today, any experiment that showed some good results merits examination, and this includes the work of Dora and Bertrand Russell.

Bibliography

Clark, Ronald W. 1976. *The Life of Bertrand Russell*. New York: Alfred A. Knopf.

Copleston, Frederick. 1966. *A History of Philosophy*. Vol. 8: Bentham to Russell. Ramsey: London: Burns and Oates.

Croall, Jonathan. 1983. *Neill of Summerhill: The Permanent Rebel*. New York: Pantheon Books.

Heathorn, Stephen. 2002. "Beacon Hill: Research Group." *The Bertrand Russell Research Centre Newsletter*, Autumn.

Neill, A.S. 1992. *The New Summerhill*. Ed. Albert Lamb. New York: Penguin Books.

Russell, Bertrand. 1926. *Education and the Good Life*. New York: Avon Books.

Russell, Bertrand. 1935. *In Praise of Idleness*. London: Unwin Hyman.

Russell, Bertrand. 1998. *The Autobiography of Bertrand Russell*. London: Routledge.

Russell, Dora. 1980. *The Tamarisk Tree.* Volume 2. London: Virago.

Tait, Katherine. 1975. *My Father, Bertrand Russell*. New York: Harcourt Brace Janovich.

RUSSELL IN THE JAZZ AGE

David E. White

MOST OF BERTRAND RUSSELL'S BIOGRAPHERS do not even mention Horace Liveright, yet Liveright was a key player in the development of Russell as a popular philosopher and public intellectual. In particular, it was on commission from Liveright that Russell wrote three of his best-selling books, books that are still in print and that many people have found helpful.

The publishing firm of Boni & Liveright was founded in 1916 to bring modern and controversial literature to American readers. Albert Boni soon left the business and Horace Liveright was forced out in 1930. The company specialized in authors whose material was considered improper, immoral, and indecent. Boni & Liveright are less well remembered today, but the Modern Library series, which evolved out of their publishing program, is universally known. Bertrand Russell became involved with Boni & Liveright through three books, *Education and the Good Life* (1926), *Marriage and Morals* (1929), and *The Conquest of Happiness* (1930), all published in the later years of the firm's history. Our main concern here is Russell's personal and professional dealings with Horace Liveright (1884-1933), and in particular Russell's difficulties with the fast and loose lifestyle of drink, women, and song associated with the firm.

Readers of Russell are often perplexed by his best-selling works of the 1920s. Much earlier, in 1912, he had produced what he called a "shilling shocker" that did well, is still in print and is often assigned even in rigorous introductions to philosophy. *The Problems of Philosophy* was written for the Home University Library, and continues to be admired by professional philosophers. Much later, Russell produced another bestseller, and an especially profitable one, in his *History of Western Philosophy* (1945). Scholars justifiably found fault with Russell for not doing any original research for his history, but the book remains useful as a record of what Russell thought at the time of the Second World War. In the first volume of his autobiography, Russell could not be more blunt: "Most of my work during these years was popular, and was done in order to make money" (Russell 1967, 87). *The A.B.C. of Atoms* (1923) and *The A.B.C. of Relativity* (1925) were further works of popularization, made some money, and were widely admired by public and professional readers. The big money, though, came with the three volumes done for Horace Liveright, all of which are still in print to this day, as well as the lecture tours of America (in 1927, 1929, and 1931) done in part to promote the books. The profits from these books, it should be noted, went primarily to support the education of his own children and other students at the Beacon Hill School, which he and his wife Dora had started in 1927 (editors' note: see Cara Rice's article in this volume for further details).

Bertrand Russell lived a long time, long enough and at a high enough energy level to live quite a few lives. The story of Russell's life as a publicist for liberal causes has not been adequately told, though, and this for various reasons. In the United States the kind of liberalism Russell favored has all but disappeared. The cornerstone of Russell's work in publicity was his reaction to the First World War. Russell reflected on his family background in politics, his own life-long interest in history, his revulsion at public enthusiasm for the war, and the fact that he had already accomplished much of what he set out to do in philosophy and mathematics. The only real question was whether he should continue to run for office or serve in some other capacity.[1] Russell proved his ability to reach a non-technical audience with "The Free Man's Worship" (1903) and he demonstrated his ability to make money by popularizing his own philosophy with *The Problems of Philosophy* (1912). "The Free Man's Worship" was reprinted at least eight times between 1923 and 1930, the period of the American tours discussed here. Russell did not consider himself an educator nor much of a philosopher of education, but within his social philosophy, education held a special place. Of course, Ludwig Wittgenstein did not at all approve of *The Problems of Philosophy*, and there would be much more criticism to come. The difference is that Wittgenstein stands almost alone among professional philosophers in rejecting *The Problems of Philosophy*, but has many allies regarding the worthlessness of, say, *Conquest of Happiness*.

---

[1] At least that is Russell's own account of the non-commercial aspect of the American tours as given in the autobiographical introduction to his *Selected Papers* (Modern Library, 1927).

Bertrand Russell lived many lives, and there are by now many tellings of those many lives. We should abandon the notion there is one essential Russell and look more to the grand design of Russell's life as a sort of pacifist battle plan, and then look at the individual actions under that plan as the encroachments of reality. Russell acknowledged that much of his effort at political propaganda through the American tours of the 1920s was unsuccessful, but he certainly had the ability to inspire others and impressed on them that it is possible to live a good life both in terms of enjoyment and in terms of doing the right thing when called upon. The American tours tended to be inconvenient for Russell, and as Nicholas Griffin points out, he may have been "unduly pessimistic" about his success as a publicist (Russell 239.) Still, he complained constantly, especially to Dora, and at one point told her he saw himself as a male prostitute who would be better off earning a living by writing popular science rather than preaching radical reform (*ibid.*).

The fact of life is that the kind of people who have the leisure time and are willing to pay top dollar (which Russell demanded and got) for a talk on progressive politics are very likely the last people who would have any reason to act in a way urged by such lectures. At least that is the type of audience that so disgusted Russell. In reply to complaints from working people who could not afford to hear him, he said he needed the money to support his family and, later, the Beacon Hill School (Feinberg and Kasrils 1973, 103).

Russell gave complete control of the tours to William B. Feakins, who even while keeping fifty percent for himself produced entirely satisfactory results in terms of the number of people who turned out to hear the "message" and the amount of money Russell brought home. No American publisher succeeded in gaining a similar monopoly on Russell's books. That none succeeded is not to say none tried.

But can we find a single message in these books and explain their continuing appeal to the public, the disdain of professors, and especially the variations in the effect and reception of these works? The Liveright books might be called the *Conquest of Happiness* trilogy since education and marriage, the subjects of the other two Liveright books, are, along with the prevention of war and the rejection of religion, where the principle elements of happiness lie for Russell. Art and the intellect were sources of great pleasure, and to a degree are available to all, but the person who fails at art or science can still be happy. Those whose lives are devastated by war, those who are enslaved to religion, or who never advance in education have greatly diminished chances of lasting happiness.

In 1922, Russell turned 50 and was famous, but it is hard to call him successful. Certainly his political elective career was no success. Few books on the First War even mention his peace efforts (efforts which came to nothing). The logicism of *Principia Mathematica* did not work, and while logical atomism remains a landmark in the history of philosophy, it was not generally adopted (as was Locke's empiricism, Kant's critical philosophy, or Derrida's deconstructionism). His first marriage had failed, painfully. Looking ahead, Russell had a protracted (four-year) legal dispute with Dora ending in their divorce, and neither before nor after Russell's repudiation of Beacon Hill were Russell or Dora or anyone else able to solve the problem of cruelty among children. In 1929 Russell lost to the Church when his invitation to lecture at Columbia was withdrawn, and then in 1940 the Church was able to deprive him of a teaching job at City College of New York, all because of *Marriage and Morals* (editors' note: see Thom Weidlich's discussion of the CCNY case in this volume for more details).

The firm of Boni & Liveright was one of the most important liberal publishing houses in the U.S. during the 1920s. Unlike the Russell biographers who pay no attention to Liveright, both of Liveright's biographers[2] provide useful information on their relationship, although as with accounts of Russell's life the integrity of the social mission keeps getting clouded by mercenary considerations on the one hand and personal indiscretions, or at least complications, on the other.

There are two reasons for looking at Russell's writings in this way. One is the retrospective reason of trying to understand what Russell was attempting and how well he succeeded. The other is the prospective reason of trying to see how we can do our part in supporting Russell's cause, and in bringing into sharper focus what the cause is and what it ought to be.

The publishing firm of Boni & Liveright stems from the chance meeting of Albert Boni and Horace Liveright in 1916 and their plan to pub-

---

[2] *Horace Liveright: Publisher of the Twenties* by Walker Gilmer (David Lewis, 1970) and *Firebrand: the Life of Horace Liveright* by Tom Dardis (Random House, 1995). The Dardis book is rich in documentation and Liveright lore. The large entry on Boni & Liveright by Charles Egleston in the "Dictionary of Literary Biography" makes only passing reference to Russell, and in his *Autobiography* Russell mentions the Liveright books only to point out that he wrote them to make money and that they did. He does say, as he had already written elsewhere (in the Library of Living Philosophers volume, for example) that he stands by the main ideas of the book on education even if he was "unduly harsh" in his methods.

lish a Modern Library of the World's Best Books, a series that would include both good editions of the classics and the best new writing in English or English translation. Russell's contribution to that series did not come until more than a decade later, but the initial contact between Liveright and Russell was in Liveright's letter of 15 December 1919, a two-page document that runs together ideological and mundane concerns.

Boni & Liveright had tried to acquire the rights to the 1918 *Proposed Roads to Freedom* from George Allen & Unwin, its British publisher, but that deal fell through and now Liveright was proposing that Russell contribute to a different venture, called "The New World Series," with books on such topics as the New Society, New Religion, New Morality and, he hoped, The New Psychology by Freud and The New Education by Russell. Liveright could not have been more clear about what he wanted. He desired a book that both said the right things and that would sell well. He wanted a book that people would enjoy reading and that would inspire them to think and act in new ways. Liveright expected Russell would naturally want his work represented in the list of "one of the leading liberal publishers in America." Specifically, Liveright asked Russell for a 50,000 to 60,000 word version of the chapter on education in his 1916 book *Why Men Fight*.[3]

Liveright praises both Russell's writing and his person, and he tells Russell he does not want a technical or theoretical work but one that has "aloofness of viewpoint" and provides "far-seeing inspiration." Clearly what Liveright wanted from Russell was a secular sermon, not an academic treatise. For example, Russell wrote at the end of the chapter on education in *Why Men Fight* that, "Education should not aim at a passive awareness of dead facts, but at an activity directed towards the world that our efforts are to create…. Those who are taught in this spirit will be filled with life and hope and joy, able to bear their part in bringing to mankind a future less somber than the past, with faith in the glory that human effort can create," having said already that there was no point in discussing details until the state of things at the end of the war was known (Russell 1916, 116). In the final chapter of *Why Men Fight*, Russell explicitly compares his task and ours with what St. Augustine did in the *City of God*, that is, the struggle "to create

---

[3] *Why Men Fight* is the title used by the American publisher, Century, in 1916, for the London lectures of 1915 published in the U.K. under the title *Principles of Social Reconstruction*. Russell understood them to be lectures in "Social Psychology and Ethics." *Why Men Fight* was reprinted as a Bonibook (number 32) in 1930, after Liveright had left the firm.

new hope, to build up by our thoughts a better world than the one which is hurling itself into ruin" (Russell 1916, 270).

Liveright's firm was a great success at getting material into print. By 1921 The Modern Library was up to 104 volumes and over the next five years Liveright signed authors such as Pound, Eliot, Cummings, Anderson, Hemingway, Jeffers and Faulkner to join O'Neill and Dreiser on the roster (Gilmer 1970, 27). As part of this very aggressive effort to improve the world, and with the roaring 20s well under way, Liveright tried the direct approach and met with Russell in London in 1923. This time Russell agreed to do an 80,000-100,000 word book on education.

It seems no exaggeration to claim that Liveright holds in the history of American publishing a place roughly comparable to Russell's position in the history of English philosophy, and that with his colorful and flamboyant bohemian lifestyle and his devotion to liberal and radical causes he would be worth a close look in relation to Russell's life even apart from the fact that he commissioned three of Russel's best-selling books.

The letter from Liveright to Russell dated December 12, 1923 is all business and does not continue the conversation on education begun in the face-to-face meeting, but most interestingly it refers to Boni & Liveright's ambition of gaining the American rights to all of Russell's works.

The following February 13, Liveright wrote to Russell apologizing for the delay in carrying on their correspondence and inviting Russell, when he came to America, to stay with Liveright and his wife and enjoy the "beauties of New Rochelle."[4] He also says he hopes Russell will not consider him a "lion-hunter." Liveright is willing to postpone the discussion of education until he can meet with Russell again personally, but he encloses a plan for the publication of all Russell's works in a collected, uniform edition. The list is simply divided into "technical" and "popular," so it is clear that Liveright is entirely serious about reprinting *Principia Mathematica* along with *Principles of Social Reconstruction (Why Men Fight), The Problem of China,* and *Roads to Freedom.* No such set ever appeared, alas, but the reason was not a perceived lack of market for the technical works, but rather that the publishers of the popular works, especially Century and Holt, would

---

[4] By the time Russell did accept the offer of hospitality, Liveright had moved back to Manhattan. One problem with having to commute was that Liveright was so generous with his time and willing to discuss projects with authors so late into the night that he would miss the last train back home.

demand so much in fees that Boni & Liveright could not expect any profit at all from the project.

The two men hit it off famously. Gilmer writes: "With Bertrand Russell . . . Liveright maintained a cordial relationship that became fruitful for both. From the beginning of his association with the publisher in January of 1925 the British writer was amenable to most suggestions Liveright made regarding the text, production, or promotion of Russell's work in America. The author rarely asked to see the proofs of his books after minor corrections had been made, and he generally took Liveright's advice on writing for the American market" (Gilmer 1970, 220).

The best place to begin in evaluating Russell's Liveright books is with Russell's own reflections. In the *Library of Living Philosophers* Russell makes clear that *On Education* (published in America under the title *Education and the Good Life*) is the only work on education he stands by. In the *Autobiography*, Russell writes: "It seems to me now somewhat unduly optimistic in its psychology, but as regards values I find nothing in it to recant, although I think now that the methods I proposed with very young children were unduly harsh" (Russell 1968a, 221).

In *On Education*, Russell claims he is writing as a parent to other parents, offering to share his frustration as a parent who is unhappy with what the established schools have to offer and unwilling, for social reasons, to commit to home-schooling. He quickly discovers that to ensure a good education for one's children one must take the political and philosophical path of social reform (Russell 1926, 8). This line will serve as a good example of how the success of Russell's controversial popular works can be seen as indicative of what Russell and Liveright were trying to do more generally, and how they were perceived by the reading and lecture attending public. Russell proposes to be practical and stay clear of the wider sphere of political and philosophical issues, but he acknowledges we cannot steer entirely clear of them. In particular, there is the great cleavage "between those who regard education as a means of instilling certain definite beliefs and those who think that it should produce the power of independent judgment" (*ibid.*, 9). Russell's concern throughout the 250-page core of the book (entitled "Education of Character") is to deliver non-controversial, psychological knowledge to guide parents through the years of early childhood, and on to nursery school.

After receiving the manuscript *On Education*, Liveright sent Russell two full pages (single-spaced) of substantive suggestions (30 December

1925). Most of these urge Russell to amplify his points, but the longest and most substantive urges him not only to amplify but to be more outspoken on sex education. Liveright eggs Russell on with a series of questions: "Do you or don't you believe in absolute sex freedom? Do you or don't you believe that for some people sexual promiscuity is just as necessary as a change of air, scene or diet?" and so on ending with, "of course you may say that a book on Education shouldn't be a treatise on free love," but it is just such a treatise that parents need to educate their children well. Russell could not have been surprised by Liveright's provocation, since early in 1925 (February 9), before seeing any of the education book, plans were well under way for a book by Russell and Dora with the working title, *Sex Freedom*. Liveright projected sales between 50-100,000 and urges Russell to adopt the "credo" of absolute sex freedom, including the benefits of sex before and outside of marriage. The work eventually appeared (written solely by Russell) under the title *Marriage and Morals* at Russell's insistence. (He thought that *Sex Freedom* sounded "a bit cheap.")

In the summer of 1925, Bennett Cerf acquired The Modern Library for $200,000, a trade that was both Liveright's greatest blunder and Cerf's most important investment, laying a solid foundation for Random House, which continues to issue Modern Library titles under the slogan, "Since 1917 the Modern Library has published the world's best books at the best prices." The Russell volume, *Selected Papers of Bertrand Russell*, appeared as soon as Random House began publishing its own Modern Library titles, in 1927, and included an introduction that Russell had already published as a magazine article in *The Dial*. Although Liveright had nothing to do with this volume directly, both the autobiographical introduction and the selections included are helpful primary evidence in trying to understand Russell's public self-image at the time he was working with Liveright.

Russell's brief exposition of what he takes himself to be doing at this phase of his life places him most clearly in the tradition of the British Moralists of the eighteenth century and the writers associated with the Scottish Enlightenment. We are not, they argued, to allow ourselves to be confined to mere academic study as long as there are so many problems and so much suffering in the world. Russell is careful to avoid anti-intellectualism, saying that he does not claim his move away from mathematics and philosophy is an improvement. It is simply his own response to his present circumstances. He states bluntly that he retains the aristocratic ideals "such as fearlessness, independence of judgment, emancipation from the herd, and leisurely culture," but wants to inspire their cultivation in the new industrial society, and to do so without the aristocratic vices, which he lists as "limitation of sympathy, haughtiness, and cruelty to those outside a charmed circle" (Russell 1968b, 53).

Russell believed, as did the British Moralists and the thinkers of the Scottish Enlightenment, that the key to reform of society along these lines was education, and that what was most important in education was for people to acquire a just conception of what constitutes their own happiness. In a line that sounds as if it were torn from one of Bishop Joseph Butler's eighteenth century sermons, Russell writes, "there is less pleasure to be derived from keeping a beggar hungry than from filling your own stomach" (Russell 1927, 9). A constricted egoism cannot bring individual happiness, but neither can such an egoism be defeated by rational pursuit of self-interest alone. Affection, generosity and pleasure in creation are all needed, and these can be cultivated not as a narrow specialization but only in a philosophy that embraces all life and all science. All that Russell or anyone can do is to raise consciousness and suggest avenues to be pursued.

It is this general attitude that Russell works through and amplifies in his three books commissioned by Liveright and that he argued for to large paying crowds during his lecture tours of the 1920s. Those who do not care for Russell personally, do not share his sense of responsibility for reform and revitalization or simply are offended that one who has already made such magnificent contributions as a narrow specialist should venture out on such a murky and failure-prone venture, are entirely entitled to their opinions and will find nothing in Russell telling them to live their lives otherwise. The mistake these critics make is not in disagreeing with Russell on substantive issues, but rather in dismissing the whole of what he said and did during this time and then pretending not to understand why so many thousands of ordinary people not only were inspired by the Russell of the 1920s and early 30s but continue to purchase, read and benefit from the Liveright books. A decade before John Dewey's famous lectures at Yale, Russell was working himself to the point of exhaustion preaching a "Common Faith," the pacific ideals we must strive for free of any of the superstitions and supernaturalism associated with conventional religion.

Russell stayed with Liveright in New York City during his 1927 and 1929 tours. Shortly before heading over in 1929, Russell wrote, "It will give me great pleasure to see you again when I am in America. I do not see how you could make me more comfortable than you did last time; the visions of sybaritic luxury conjured up by this promise are most enticing" (Dardis 1995, 307-8).

The 1929 visit was particularly memorable. As recounted in Dardis's biography: "After a long welcoming lunch for Bertrand Russell at the Algonquin, to mark the publication of his first book for Horace, *Education and the Good Life*, Horace, accompanied by his guests including the philosopher Horace Kallen...returned to Forty-eighth Street in fine spirits. Horace immediately called up a number of important people to invite them over to meet Russell" (Dardis 1995, 147). Although Prohibition was supposedly the law of the land, liquor was in plentiful supply at the Boni & Liveright office, as was a four-piece orchestra, showgirls, and none other than New York's playboy mayor, Jimmy Walker.

Interestingly enough, while Russell was there to work out the details of his second book, *Marriage and Morals*, he apparently eschewed Liveright's offer to provide him with sexual companionship during his visit. Dardis notes that "Russell also informed his wife that Horace had attempted to obtain bed partners for his stay in New York, but that he had rejected the offer: 'In spite of his efforts, I took up with no ladies'" (quoted in Dardis 1995, 147).

Russell could not endure the permanent partying at Liveright's home in 1929, and after a few days moved to a hotel. The move did not lessen his contact with Liveright, which included not only many parties but an attempt to get *Marriage and Morals* adopted by the Book of the Month Club. The mention of Liveright's courageous campaign for press freedom, which appears in the chapter on "Sex Knowledge" was inserted at Liveright's request, although Russell was happy to comply. Russell did ask Liveright to consider holding back on release of *Marriage and Morals* until after he has toured the American South, since he suspected Southerners of being as strict about the Seventh Commandment (prohibiting adultery) as they were lax regarding the Sixth (against murder).

The final meeting between Liveright and Russell was at Beacon Hill School in 1930. At that meeting Russell and his publisher worked out plans for the third book, *The Conquest of Happiness*, which was published before the end of the year. Their final correspondence concerned changes in *The Conquest of Happiness* and Liveright's departure from the firm. After two best-sellers, the relationship between author and publisher is bound to change with regard to planning the next book. Liveright published some of the best-known and most respected authors of the day, but that fact alone provides no clue regarding the philosophical or literary quality of *Conquest of Happiness*. Knowledge of the publishing background does allow us to see through some of the misleading and contentious accounts that have been presented to the public. Thus Ray Monk makes much of the unhappy circumstances in which Russell found himself in 1930 but says nothing about Liveright's involvement in planning the book. Monk then quips, "It was in these circumstances that Russell decided to write a book telling people how to be happy" (Monk 2000, 114-5). Monk goes on to quote Russell in a way that suggests Russell was claiming to have made an important discovery that he needed to report to the public, and concludes Russell was entirely insincere. In fact, Russell was in unhappy circumstances and badly needed to make money to support his family and the school. Out of this condition Russell did not so much decide to write a book telling people how to be happy as he decided to meet with his publisher and plan a book which, in the first year of the Depression, would have some chance of being as successful as his pre-depression work had been. Winning the approval of philosophers like Ray Monk, not to mention Wittgenstein and his followers, was never a consideration. Russell himself points with satisfaction to the book's success with the public and with the psychiatric profession. In the event, the history of popular and general literature has not been kind to philosophers who scorn *Conquest of Happiness*. The book remains in print almost ninety years after publication, and long after the deaths of everyone involved in its creation it continues to prove useful to those seeking a better life. Admittedly, *Conquest* is popular self-help literature, but it continues to hold its own in an overcrowded field, a field that continues to be neglected and disparaged by professional philosophers.

Russell's own considered opinions on his popular work are more interesting and more tempered than those of his professional critics. Russell admits there are errors of detail and of general tone in the book on education. At the time he wrote, he was determined to apply science to all aspects of life, and he believed someone with a good knowledge of psychology could apply that knowledge to child-rearing. Monk is probably right that Russell's experience with his son John ended up more a counterexample than a supporting example of his educational theories. The shortcomings of this one effort to develop education along scientific lines should not discourage all such efforts. Furthermore, Russell was entirely right on two key points: that the earliest years of life are crucial as regards the child's education, and that there is one great cleavage in all education theories between those who believe the purpose of education is to instill acceptance of certain particular beliefs and those who see the aim of education more in terms of personal development. Russell seems to have a crude and superficial understanding of Rousseau's *Emile*, but in general his ambivalence regarding exactly where one should come down on the great cleavage is helpful for those who want to work through the problem for themselves. Regarding marriage, Russell's second thoughts are quite different. Not only does he admit he got marriage wrong, he also concludes that no general theory of marriage, no application of science to this most important of human institutions, is likely to be generally helpful. Russell does claim to stand by the doctrine of *Conquest of Happiness*, which is somewhat surprising considering how convinced Wittgenstein and company are that it is such a dreadful book. We might have expected Russell to fall back on the excuse that *Conquest* was merely a potboiler. He announces from the start that the book is not for professional philosophers, but his final position seems to be that these professionals are just unable to grasp the value that is apparent to the general public and to the psychiatric profession.

The job of the critic is not just to toss off negative or positive opinions, but to guide the reader who wants to formulate his or her own assessment. Obviously, the philosophical profession has given what guidance it has to give in this matter and that instruction is that if you must read Russell at all, find something more worthy of attention than *The Conquest of Happiness*. Since it is *Conquest* that has met with the harshest criticism, and *Conquest* that Russell never backed off on, it may be *Conquest* that should get the most careful review here. One academic Russell scholar who is more charitable to *Conquest* is Alan Ryan, but his field is politics, not philosophy.

The doctrine of *Conquest*, is, everyone agrees, simple, and it is simply that happiness results from the integration of the person. This integration must be external, between self and society, and internal, between the conscious and the unconscious mind. As Ryan points out, this doctrine is not only simple, it is "very old and absolutely persuasive," associated with classic British moralists such as Bishop Butler and David Hume (Ryan 1993, 165). To a degree Russell recapitulates Butler and Hume in that while their religious differences seem irreconcilable, the moral doctrine of benevolence that has a religious spin in Butler is presented in a secular form by Hume so clearly that we can see that even as Butler uses God-talk, such talk is not essential to his teaching on morals, whatever may have been the case with religion itself. The comparison is a fair one since Butler, Hume, and Russell were all writing for the same sort of audience. Indeed, those who would even consider buying a book about happiness in 1930 would have to be among the more privileged.

Even if Russell's *Conquest* falls short of Butler, Hume and Plato (or even Plato's better commentators), Russell still has some things that Anglo-American philosophy sadly lacked then and still lacks now. Those things include on the one hand vivid images, and on the other practical exercises. Right at the start of chapter 1, Russell presents a party scene filled with drink and petting, then turns autobiographical, and in chapter 2 he elucidates many of the images in *Ecclesiastes*. Then chapter 3 opens with a marvelous, extended sketch of the life of a business man. The various stories and images presented in chapter 4 are obviously intended to show that a discussion of boredom can be highly entertaining.

All three of Russell's books with Boni & Liveright did well in both their initial sales and in their continuing sales; they stand out today as handsome volumes in any Russell collection. At first, *The Conquest of Happiness* did not do as well as the first two, but all book sales suffered from the onset of the Depression.

From every point of view, Russell was one of Liveright's best authors, and Liveright one of Russell's best publishers, but it is overstating the case somewhat to say they had no problems. It is true that Russell never argued the terms offered by Liveright, but he did keep a close watch on his account. On September 28, 1926, for example, Russell noticed a bookkeeping error, and on January 30, 1930, he had to remind Liveright of an overdue royalty check. The relationship with Liveright also involved Russell in conflicts with his U.K. publisher, George Allen & Unwin, and his other American publisher, W. W. Norton. With regard to the lectures, Russell referred all business to Feakins, but he refused to let Unwin represent him with Liveright, and Liveright was furious when Russell let Norton have the very type of book Liveright most wanted, the grand summation of Russell's philosophy written with the American audience in mind (July 11, 1927). Then in 1930 Liveright was outraged when Norton proposed that the rights to Russell's works held by Boni & Liveright be transferred to Norton. Russell (July 14, 1930) claimed to be shocked and could only suggest that the people at Norton had a case of grandiosity or were mildly insane.

Liveright's general admiration for Russell went beyond publishing and promoting his works. In a letter of June 11, 1927 Liveright toys with the idea of starting a school of his own modeled on Russell's and offers to donate whatever Russell wants from the current Boni & Liveright catalog. Liveright had always been a careless spender, to the distress of his colleagues.

IN 1930, LIVERIGHT, WITH HIS HIGH LIVING, high pay and generosity with authors, was forced out of the firm he had founded. Russell was one of the first to be notified of his move to California; Liveright was unready to admit he was leaving the firm for good (July 7, 1930).

Liveright addressed Russell variously as "Russell," "Bertrand Russell" or "Mr. Russell." In the 1950s Russell continued to receive royalty statements from Arthur Pell, an accountant who had been a thorn in Liveright's side for years and who became the model of the modern price-of-everything value-of-nothing kind of publisher after he pushed Liveright out of the firm. Pell always addressed Russell as "Dr. Russell." Russell finally corrected him (October 12, 1959) when he found it necessary to file a change of address.

In closing, Horace Liveright and Bertrand Russell were a potent force, and together helped to create three classic works that remain in print to this day. As Dardis points out, "As far back as 1919 Horace had felt that he had much in common with the great English philosopher, especially in the area of sexual conduct. Considering the difficulty and seriousness of much of Russell's writings, it may seem strange for him to have appeared on Horace's list with three best-selling books, but Russell had, unlike nearly everyone else in his field, an unsurpassed ability to produce very readable prose on the most abstruse subjects" (Dardis, 305-6). Russell's influence as a public intellectual in the 1920s and beyond was due in no small way to the support and encouragement he received from his stalwart publisher, Horace Liveright.

Bibliography

Dardis, Tom. 1995. *Firebrand: the Life of Horace Liveright*. New York: Random House.

Feinberg, Barry and Ronald Kasrils. 1973. *Bertrand Russell's America*. New York: Viking.

Gilmer, Horace. 1970. *Horace Liveright: Publisher of the Twenties*. New York: David Lewis.

Monk, Ray. 2000. *Bertrand Russell: the Ghost of Madness*. London: Jonathan Cape.

Russell, Bertrand. 1916. *Why Men Fight*. New York, the Century Company.

Russell, Bertrand. 1926. *Education and the Good Life*. New York: Boni & Liveright.

Russell, Bertrand. 1929. *Marriage and Morals*. New York: Liveright.

Russell, Bertrand. 1927. *Selected Papers of Bertrand Russell*. New York: The Modern Library.

Russell, Bertrand. 1930a. *The Conquest of Happiness*. New York: Liveright.

Russell, Bertrand. 1930b. *Why Men Fight*. New York: Boni.

Russell, Bertrand. 1967. *The Autobiography of Bertrand Russell*. Volume I. Boston: Little, Brown and Company.

Russell, Bertrand. 1968a. *The Autobiography of Bertrand Russell*. Volume II. Boston: Little, Brown and Company.

Russell, Bertrand. 1968b. *The Wisdom of Bertrand Russell*. New York: Philosophical Library.

Russell, Bertrand. 2001. *The Selected Letters of Bertrand Russell: The Public Years 1914-1970*. Ed. Nicholas Griffin. New York: Routledge.

Ryan, Alan. 1993. *Bertrand Russell: A Political Life*. New York: Oxford University Press.

A CHAIR OF INDECENCY:
THE BERTRAND RUSSELL/CITY COLLEGE CASE

Thom Weidlich

BERTRAND RUSSELL'S ROLE AS A PUBLIC INTELLECTUAL led to one of the most bizarre and upsetting episodes in his life: his denial of a teaching position at the College of the City of New York.[1]

Ironically, when this occurred in 1940, Russell was turning back to technical philosophy, completing his book *Inquiry into Meaning and Truth*, which came out that year. He was moving away from the popular writings that both raised his profile in the United States and at the same time made him a target for more conservative forces that could not abide those writings.

Through his work, especially *Principia Mathematica* (written with his teacher Alfred North Whitehead), Russell had secured himself, until the end of time, a place in the history of philosophy. But he had another, more controversial, side. Russell had publicly opposed World War I and spent time in a British gaol for insulting the United States Army. He wrote popular books promulgating his advanced views on religion, sex, and marriage, which brought him fame and scorn. In the City College case, Russell came under fire for his controversial social writings that sought to replace a religion-based ethos, including religion-based sexual mores. He was also well known to Americans due to the four lucrative lecture tours he took in the states between 1924 and 1931.

Throughout his life, Russell was willing to stick his neck out, as it were, to risk a complacent life by enunciating truths as he saw them, especially the truth that superstitious moral codes such as Christianity must give way to a more rational ethic. Russell railed against a moral code that justified itself through revelation and tradition. His willingness to oppose those

---

[1] For more information on the City College case, including detailed information on all the references made here, see Weidlich (2000), *Appointment Denied: The Inquisition of Bertrand Russell*.

codes—again and again, and very publicly—is ultimately what got him into hot water in New York City in 1940.

When Russell's appointment became public in late February of that year, Bishop William T. Manning, overseer of the city's Episcopal Church, sent a letter of protest to the New York newspapers. "What is to be said," the bishop wrote, "of colleges and universities which hold up before our youth as a reputable teacher of philosophy, and as an example of light and learning, a man who is a recognized propagandist against both religion and morality, and who specifically defends adultery?"

Manning invoked several Russell quotations to prove the philosopher was unworthy of teaching at the publicly funded City College, quotations that other opponents seized on:

> "Outside human desires there is no moral standard."
>
> "God and immortality, the central dogmas of the Christian religion, find no support in science."
>
> "The peculiar importance attached, at the present, to adultery is quite irrational."

Manning was particularly incensed by Russell's 1929 book, *Marriage and Morals*, the philosopher's contribution to the 1920s sexual revolution. Indeed, most of the quotes used against Russell during the City College case came from his writings during the 1920s and early 1930s, when he played the role of the popular moralist.

Bishop Manning's protest spread throughout the city and indeed the country. It was played out in the press for several months. Russell's opponents bristled at his outspoken religious skepticism, at his defense of "companionate marriage" and masturbation, and at his two divorces. They demanded that the Board of Higher Education, which had made the appointment, reverse its decision.

Many, especially the vocal isolationists wary of the ominous events unfolding in Europe, were upset that a foreigner was designated when qualified Americans were available. Russell was labeled "that alien professor." He was also called "an avowed Communist," which, as one of the Left's earliest critics of Soviet Russia, he certainly was not.

The city's Democratic politicians seized upon the selection of such a depraved individual by Fiorello La Guardia's reform Board of Higher

Education to embarrass their nemesis, the mayor. Republican La Guardia's reform movement had been eroding their power. It was generally assumed the mayor supported the choice. But La Guardia declined to speak on it publicly.

Russell's foes were certain he would be unable to refrain from uttering his opinions on sex and marriage in even the most antiseptic of logic classes. The three courses he was to teach at City College concerned the foundations of mathematics; the relation of logic to science, mathematics, and philosophy; and the reciprocal influence of metaphysics and scientific theories. Not exactly the stuff of erotica. "His warped and immoral views necessarily will be reflected in his teachings," wrote the head of the city's Knights of Columbus. Russell's opponents said the issue was not free speech but abhorrent speech that taxpayers objected to paying for.

Those who supported the appointment at first viewed the opposition as the grumblings of a few reactionary malcontents. The noise would soon subside, they thought. But as the protest continued to mount, those of a more liberal view realized that these meddlers posed a real threat. Recalling the persecution of Socrates, another famous philosopher accused of corrupting youth, and the 1925 anti-evolution Scopes trial, they too sprang into action.

The defenders of Russell were academics, freelance intellectuals, and civil libertarians, and they raised the banner of academic freedom. The American Civil Liberties Union, the American Association of University Professors, and the Committee for Cultural Freedom—the last formed by Sidney Hook less than a year before to repel just these sorts of attacks—urged the Board of Higher Education to stand its ground. Chief among Russell's supporters were the City College students themselves, who viewed the attack on the appointment as an affront to their school's good name. Throughout the episode they held rallies in the college's Great Hall.

Russell himself had refused to answer Bishop Manning's charges. "Anyone who decides in youth both to think and speak honestly," he said, "regardless of hostility and misinterpretation, expects such attacks and soon learns to ignore them." But soon even Russell, then teaching in Los Angeles, would be unable to ignore the clamor rising three thousand miles away.

Yet despite the protest, the Board of Higher Education refused, by a vote of 11 to 7, to reconsider its selection (the original vote appointing Russell had been unanimous). The conflict, however, did not end; it moved to a new stage. Mrs. Jean Kay, a Brooklyn housewife, brought a taxpayer's lawsuit to have the court force the Board of Higher Education to rescind the appointment. Mrs. Kay's petition named two grounds: first, that Russell wasn't an American citizen; and, second, that he was of a character unsuitable for a teacher.

Mrs. Kay's lawyer, Joseph Goldstein, charged in an affidavit that Russell had "exhibited practically all his life marked eccentricities and mental quirks, and his conduct throughout his life has been queer and unusual." Not only was Russell "a person entirely bereft of moral fibre," he was also "lecherous, salacious, libidinous, lustful, venerous, erotomaniac, aphrodisiac, atheistic, irreverent, narrow minded, bigoted, and untruthful." Finally, he was not a philosopher at all, but "a sophist."

The case for the board was handled by the city's legal agency, the corporation counsel, which filed a counter-petition to drop the suit. At the hearing on this motion before Justice John E. McGeehan, the assistant corporation counsel, Nicholas Bucci, argued that Mrs. Kay had insufficient cause for her suit. But Bucci only discussed the citizenship issue because he saw it as the only question of law—Russell's character was irrelevant. This omission would prove to be a tactical mistake.

The opposition to Russell found backing on the citizenship question in a New York State law that required all teachers to be American. Bucci argued that this pertained only to primary and secondary teachers, and with the city's public colleges teeming with foreign professors, particularly those fleeing Hitler, he had some evidence.

After Bucci presented his side, there followed what the *Harvard Law Review* was to call the "singular procedure whereby" this matter was decided. Justice McGeehan announced that he was reserving decision on the board's request to drop the suit, and ordered Joseph Goldstein and his co-counsel, former U.S. Congressman William Bennet, to present their evidence, as if for a trial. But the hearing was called to decide on the board's motion to drop the suit. Even Bennet pointed out the irregularity. But Justice McGeehan insisted.

So, Mrs. Kay's attorneys made their case, and in doing so raised a third reason for Russell's ouster that wasn't in the original petition: Bertrand Russell, quite possibly the greatest living philosopher, had not been administered a civil service examination! Bennet and Goldstein argued that teachers in public colleges were civil servants, and that the New York State constitution required civil service positions to be awarded on the basis of exams. Although it seemed an absurd claim, the *New York Times* reported that it jeopardized the jobs of every one of the city's 3,300 public-college teachers—none had been subjected to such exams.

As Justice McGeehan adjourned the court, Bucci reminded him that he still had pending his motion to dismiss Mrs. Kay's suit.

On March 30, three days after the hearing before Justice McGeehan, those who had been awaiting a ruling on the board's counter-petition received quite a surprise. The judge had found against Bucci's request—because he had argued only one of the three points raised by Mrs. Kay—and then gone ahead and ruled on the original petition, without allowing the board an opportunity to answer the other charges. And McGeehan, finding in Mrs. Kay's favor, ordered the Board of Higher Education to revoke Russell's appointment.

In his decision, Justice McGeehan scoffed at the notion that the case was about academic freedom, which he defined as "the freedom to do good and not to teach evil." In selecting Russell, he said, the Board of Higher Education was not bringing a great intellectual to the students, was not boosting the prestige of City College, but merely creating "a chair of indecency."

Ultimately, McGeehan ruled against Russell on a "most compelling" ground: the philosopher's bad character. Still, he admitted he was powerless to act on Russell's views on masturbation, religion, and politics, and on his own life and conduct. He was even powerless, he said, to ban Russell for his defense of adultery, which was only a misdemeanor. But, McGeehan said, there was this: "Dr. Russell's utterances as to the damnable felony of homosexualism" (Russell, it should be noted, did not have a Ph.D. and was not a "doctor").

In the strict "logic" of McGeehan's decision, it was Russell's advocacy of "homosexualism" that forced McGeehan to direct the Board of Higher Education to revoke the philosopher's job offer. The irony is that the quote the judge used to prove Russell "winks at homosexuality" (to use Goldstein's phrase) is actually rather critical of it. "It is possible that homosexual relations with other boys would not be very harmful if they were tolerated," Russell wrote in *Education and the Modern World*, "but even then there is danger lest they should interfere with the growth of normal sexual life later on."

Obviously, McGeehan was searching for any excuse, however absurd, to find in Mrs. Kay's favor. McGeehan was a Roman Catholic and a Bronx Democrat who proudly called himself "an organization judge." It seemed that he was not loath to break procedural regulations to support his judicial activism. Several commentators pointed out the superhuman speed at which his lengthy decision was written—that is, if it was composed in the three-day interval between the hearing and the day it was released. Some suggested it was written before the hearing even began.

The City College students demonstrated their anger at McGeehan's verdict by packing into the Great Hall for yet another rally. Afterward, a five-member contingent traveled downtown to City Hall to protest to the mayor. While there, some newspapermen called the students into the pressroom and told them something that took them completely by surprise: Fiorello La Guardia, that fighter for right and reform, had slashed from his budget the appropriation for Russell's salary.

La Guardia claimed his act was in keeping with his Depression-era policy of eliminating vacant positions. But it was plain that what the mayor was really eliminating was a political headache. 1940 was an election year, and the Little Flower ("Fiorello" in Italian) had national-office aspirations, possibly for vice president. At the very least, he would be running for re-election in 1941. Evidently he felt that the uncertainty swirling around Justice McGeehan's decision left him vulnerable.

It was unclear whether La Guardia's action was legal. His budget needed to be confirmed by the Board of Estimate, and even if it were confirmed, the Board of Higher Education could find money elsewhere to pay Russell's salary. In a month's time, the Board of Estimate would close this loophole by making as part of the conditions of the city's budget that, "[n]o funds herein appropriated shall be used for the employment of Bertrand Russell."

La Guardia's and the Board of Estimate's actions turned out to be unnecessary. Justice McGeehan's decision had done the trick, although officially the fight continued through the appeals process. McGeehan continued to make sure the issues were not given a fair hearing. When the corporation counsel refused to appeal the case, following La Guardia's orders, the Board of Higher Education hired its own lawyers (including future U.S. Supreme Court Justice John Harlan). But Justice McGeehan declared that only the corporation counsel could represent the board. This decision was affirmed by the higher courts.

Russell obtained a lawyer to have him made a party to the proceedings. But Justice McGeehan decided that Russell had no legal status in the case: Mrs. Kay had brought her suit against the Board of Higher Education and could not be forced to face him in court. This decision too was affirmed by the higher courts.

Russell's inability to join the suit was more than just an irritant for him. The City College case happened during one of the worst periods in his life. He was distressed at events in Europe. He was also strapped for funds, and he would have no post come that January. (He had already tendered his resignation to UCLA.) And now no school would risk offering him one. It must have been strange for the world-class philosopher to realize that he had become a victim of the rough-and-tumble world of New York City politics. "Everyone fusses about the public issue; my personal ruin passes unnoticed," he wrote to his American publisher, W.W. Norton. And yet, he refused to cower from the controversy.

That Russell was found to have no say in the matter was ironic in light of Mrs. Kay's professed interest in the case. She had brought the suit, she had explained, for fear that her college-bound daughter might one day come under the evil professor's spell. Yet this was impossible. At that time, liberal arts courses in City College's day session, where Russell was to teach, were open only to men. Decades later Mrs. Kay's son explained that his sister never attended college and that Joseph Goldstein, the lawyer, who was a Democrat, had put his mother up to bringing the suit.

Autumn came and the Board of Higher Education resolved to carry on the fight. Then in October, Albert C. Barnes, the eccentric art collector and friend of philosopher John Dewey, engaged Russell as an instructor at his foundation in Merion, Pennsylvania. The contract was for five years and would commence in 1941, when Russell was to have begun teaching at City College.

And such was the anticlimactic ending of the Bertrand Russell/City College case of 1940. On October 21, eight months after Russell had been appointed, the Board of Higher Education voted in favor of dropping the litigation. On that occasion, one board member wrote to his friend, Mayor La Guardia: "Thus ends, I hope for all time, this melancholy incident. I trust that its end will also serve to wash out the bad feeling that it has brought between so many good people."

In a real sense, what happened to Russell in the City College case transpired because of his role as a public intellectual. Shortly after McGeehan's decision he published an article called "Freedom and the Colleges." In it, he admitted that, given the horrors of the war, academic freedom might not seem such a weighty matter. But, he added, "[l]et it be remembered that what is at stake, in the greatest issues as well as in those that seem smaller, is the freedom of the individual human spirit to express its beliefs and hopes for mankind, whether they be shared by many or by few or by none."

In this role, Russell, like Galileo and Spinoza and so many others, was a rebel. The case highlights that a democratic society does not always know how to deal with its rebels, including those who are public intellectuals. There is no question that Russell's own questioning of society's received wisdom was done with honesty and through the scientific method. The Russell/City College case is, indeed, a cautionary tale.

Russell himself did not quench his bitterness over the incident. On the title page of the British edition of *An Inquiry into Meaning and Truth*, his 1940 return to technical philosophy, he included at the end of his list of attainments: "Judicially pronounced unworthy to be Professor of Philosophy at the College of the City of New York (1940)."

Bibliography

Weidlich, Thom. 2000. *Appointment Denied: The Inquisition of Bertrand Russell.* Amherst, NY: Prometheus Books.

RUSSELL THE POLITICAL ACTIVIST

Peter Stone[*]

BERTRAND RUSSELL SPENT MOST OF HIS CHILDHOOD in the custody of his grandmother. (His parents were both dead by 1876, when Russell was four, and his grandfather died two years later.) On his twelfth birthday, his grandmother gave him a Bible as a gift. A deeply religious woman, she inscribed on the flyleaf of the book some of her favorite Biblical verses. Among these was a verse that would exemplify the political philosophy according to which her grandson would conduct himself—Exodus 23:2: "Thou shalt not follow a multitude to do evil."

Russell abandoned his grandmother's religiosity as a teenager, and never returned to it. But he never rejected the sentiment his grandmother expressed with this quote. In his autobiography, Russell wrote that his grandmother's "fearlessness, her public spirit, her contempt for convention, and her indifference to the opinion of the majority have always seemed good to me and have impressed themselves upon me as worthy of imitation" (Russell 1967, 18). And the spirit of this particular Bible verse governed his actions throughout a long and turbulent life. It was a life filled with political activism. This activism was consistently governed by a radical form of liberal philosophy, a philosophy that evolved over time but that was quite consistent in its essentials. Russell stuck to these principles with a great deal of courage. Then as now, radical liberalism was not always popular, and so he had plenty of chances not to follow a multitude in doing evil. Fortunately, the part of the rebel, the dissident, the political gadfly, was a part Russell was born to play.

Russell came to politics acutely conscious of family tradition. The Russell family's political track record was long and distinguished. The family had risen to prominence at the time of Henry VIII, during which time

---

[*] I would like to thank Stefan Andersson, David Goldman, Fred Johnson, Marvin Kohl, Ben Wade, and Terry Zaccone for helpful comments and suggestions regarding this chapter.

one John Russell became the first Earl of Bedford. (Years later, this earldom was "upgraded" to a dukedom.) Numerous members of the family held high political office over the years. The high point of the Russell family's political fortunes came when another John Russell (Russell's grandfather) served twice as prime minister under Queen Victoria, in 1846-1852 and 1865-1866. A younger son of the sixth Duke of Bedford, John Russell spent most of his life active in parliament. For his long and distinguished career in public service, Queen Victoria named him the First Earl Russell in 1861.

Russell thus took for granted a life surrounded by great men. His grandfather was one such man, and he kept equally impressive company. He had visited Napoleon in exile at Elba; this led radio journalist Studs Terkel to describe Bertrand Russell as "The Man Who Shook the Hand of the Man Who Shook the Hand of Napoleon."[1] Russell's grandfather also knew all the major figures of British political life, including Gladstone, perhaps the most famous British prime minister of the nineteenth century. Some time after the death of Russell's grandfather, Gladstone visited the Russell household. Though only a teenager, Russell was the oldest male family member present, and so as custom dictated, he was left with Gladstone after dinner for drinks and conversation. Russell recounted the story in his *Autobiography*. Apparently, Gladstone spoke to him only once the entire time, when he asked, "This is a very good port they have given me, but why have they given it me in a claret glass?" At that moment, Russell reported, he "wished the earth would swallow me up" (Russell 1967, 73-4). Despite Russell's terror that day, he grew up with as much comfort and confidence around the great statesmen of the day as one could hope for, and so there was plenty of reason to expect that he might take his place among them.

But if the statesman plays a prominent role in the Russell family tradition, then so does the rebel. As Bertrand Russell would proudly recall, William Russell, a younger son of the fifth Earl of Bedford, was executed in 1683 for taking part in the Rye House Plot.[2] Russell's father (also named

---

[1] The journalist Studs Terkel once interviewed Russell, and presumably shook his hand. If you ever had the chance to meet Terkel, then, you can call yourself "The Man Who Shook the Hand of the Man Who Shook the Hand of the Man Who Shook the Hand of the Man Who Shook the Hand of Napoleon."

[2] The Rye House Plot was a plan to assassinate King Charles II and his brother James (later King James II). Both Charles and his brother were known as Catholic sympathizers, and James had even converted in secret to Catholicism. The plot involved many prominent political figures, who feared a restoration of Catholic rule to England which might result in the suppression of hard-won political liberties.

John) had political ambitious much like his father, entering parliament in 1866. These ambitions, however, were rudely dashed when he gave a speech to the London Dialectical Society in which he advocated the discovery of new and better forms of birth control. Amidst a storm of controversy, he left parliament in 1868 and retired from public life, devoting his last years to his voluminous book *An Analysis of Religious Belief*, which he completed in November 1875 just before his death.[3]

Even at its most statesmanlike, however, the Russell family tradition embodied a devotion to liberal reform. The greatest achievement of Russell's grandfather—the achievement for which he is still remembered today—was the passage of the Reform Act of 1832, which greatly expanded the number of men who enjoyed the right to vote, and also corrected other serious problems with the electoral process.[4] He also spearheaded the repeal of the Test and Corporation Acts in 1828, as well as the passage of the Catholic Emancipation Act in 1829. These acts greatly expanded the rights of British Catholics and many non-Anglican Protestants, allowing them to run for political office for the first time in centuries. Russell's grandfather had fought hard for all of these reforms, and had to overcome much strong opposition. His efforts were not forgotten. In 1878, a deputation of Methodists and Wesleyans—people whose religious views would in days past have barred them from political office—gathered outside the window of the dying Lord Russell to cheer and celebrate the fiftieth anniversary of the repeal of the Test and Corporation Acts. The young Russell witnessed this, and later described it as "one of my earliest and most important memories."[5] This legacy of support for enlightened social change—even in the face of bitter resistance—was something Russell never forgot, even if his career did not quite go the way his family expected.

When Russell entered Cambridge in 1890, his grandmother certainly hoped that he would follow in his grandfather's footsteps. Russell's older

---

[3] Russell's father was also a close friend of John Stuart Mill, one of the greatest iconoclastic philosophers of the nineteenth century. Mill even agreed to serve as little Russell's godfather, although he died when Russell was less than a year old. It is interesting to imagine how different Russell's life might have been had he been brought up by so unconventional and intellectually fearless a philosopher as Mill.

[4] In particular, it eliminated many "rotten boroughs." Traditionally British electoral districts were not required to be equal in population. This meant that a small village of pig farmers might have more representatives in parliament than a huge manufacturing city right next door to it. The Reform Act rectified many of these injustices.

[5] He described the incident in a 1940 letter to the *New York Times*. See Perkins (2002, 161).

brother, Frank, had proven to be something of a "problem child." In him, the rebel side of the Russell legacy clearly predominated over the statesman side. As a child, Frank had attempted to run away from home; as a teenager, he left Oxford University under a cloud, and then more or less cut himself off from the rest of the Russell family for many years. Bertrand, by contrast, was hardworking and studious—the perfect figure to carry on the Russell family's statesmanlike legacy. It didn't quite turn out that way.[6] While Russell studied economics and politics quite extensively, he quickly gravitated toward philosophy and mathematics. He took his first tripos (a set of exams) in math, and scored seventh in his class ("seventh wrangler"). He then took his second tripos, and got a First in Moral Philosophy in 1894. The successful completion of the first and second tripos led to Russell receiving a BA from Cambridge that year. He subsequently received an MA from Cambridge in January 1897, and his first major work in philosophy, *An Essay on the Foundations of Geometry*, won him a Prize Fellowship in 1895. (This work was published as a book in 1897.) He therefore seemed destined for a life as an academic philosopher—a distinguished life, but not a political one.

Russell did not, however, abandon all interest in politics. In 1894 he spent three months in Paris working as honorary attaché for the British ambassador to France. His grandmother had secured him the post. Russell had become involved for some time with an American woman named Alys Pearsall Smith. His grandmother strongly disapproved of this choice, and probably still nursed hopes that her grandson might yet become a statesman like his grandfather. By securing him a post abroad—far away from Alys—she hoped both to end the relationship and to steer her grandson toward a promising political career. She failed at both counts. Russell married Alys in December 1894, shortly after his return from Paris, and he detested his work for the ambassador so much that he never felt tempted to make politics his full-time vocation. That said, he continued to take an interest in politics. After a honeymoon in Holland, Russell and his new wife Alys traveled to Berlin in 1895, where he continued his academic work in philosophy. But while visiting the Tiergarten (a large park in Berlin), he had the following epiphany:

---

[6] Ironically, it would be Frank, and not Bertrand, who would ultimately hold political office. Russell's brother served as Under-Secretary for India for the Labour Party's government from 1929 to 1931.

> I remember a cold, bright day in early spring when I walked by myself in the Tiergarten, and made projects of future work. I thought that I would write one series of books on the philosophy of the sciences from pure mathematics to physiology, and another series of books on social questions. I hoped that the two series might ultimately meet in a synthesis at once scientific and practical. (Russell 1967, 184-5)

Thus, even as he rejected a career as a politician, Russell hoped to connect his philosophical pursuits to politics, in ways that were both philosophically satisfying and helpful at addressing real political problems.

Russell did not wait long to try implementing his plan. He and his wife Alys used their time in Berlin to examine the German Social Democratic Party, a primarily Marxist party struggling to liberate Germany from the crushing grip of the Kaiser and his autocratic government. Their studies involved both a detailed investigation into the practices of the party and a careful study of the Marxist philosophy upon which the party's platform was based. When Russell returned to England in 1896, he reported on his investigations in a series of lectures at the newly-formed London School of Economics (LSE).[7] These investigations were published in a book entitled *German Social Democracy* later that year. (While Alys did much of the work, and is acknowledged as a collaborator in print, Russell alone is listed as the book's author.) In this book Russell strongly condemned the Marxist program of revolution even while recognizing the need for drastic change in the politics of autocratic Germany. It was the classic position of a radical liberal, someone who deeply abhorred authoritarian regimes but struggled to find nonviolent paths to achieving social change.

After returning from Germany, Russell settled into academic work in Cambridge. For almost twenty years Russell concentrated his energies upon philosophy, producing classic technical works such as the book *Principles of Mathematics* (1903), the paper "On Denoting" (1905), and the monumental three-volume *Principia Mathematica* (1910, 1912, 1913), the last of which he co-authored with his mentor, Alfred North Whitehead. But

---

[7] The LSE had been founded in 1895 by a number of leading members of the Fabian Society, a group dedicated to the slow and progressive reform of British society. Russell joined the Fabian Society in 1897, and knew most of its leading members, including Sidney and Beatrice Webb and George Bernard Shaw. He also strongly supported the LSE, serving on its advisory committee and providing generous financial donations in its crucial early years.

at the same time, he remained deeply interested in politics, and maintained a level of activism that, given that his primary interests lay elsewhere, was nothing short of remarkable. It was at this time that Russell first became critically concerned with the primary issue that would motivate him politically throughout his long life—the problem of war and peace. Russell himself traced the origins of his passionate antiwar stance to an epiphany he had in 1901. He chronicled this epiphany in the following stirring passage from his *Autobiography*:

> One day, Gilbert Murray came to Newnham to read part of his translation of *The Hippolytus*, then unpublished. Alys and I went to hear him, and I was profoundly stirred by the beauty of the poetry. When we came home, we found Mrs. Whitehead [wife of his mentor] undergoing an unusually severe bout of pain. She seemed cut off from everyone and everything by walls of agony, and the sense of the solitude of each human soul suddenly overwhelmed me. Ever since my marriage, my emotional life had been calm and superficial. I had forgotten all the deeper issues, and had been content with flippant cleverness. Suddenly the ground seemed to give way beneath me, and I found myself in quite another region. Within five minutes I went through some such reflections as the following: the loneliness of the human soul is unendurable; nothing can penetrate it except the highest intensity of the sort of love that religious teachers have preached; whatever does not spring from this motive is harmful, or at best useless; it follows that war is wrong, that a public school education is abominable, that the use of force is to be deprecated, and that in human relations one should penetrate to the core of loneliness in each person and speak to that.

This mystical experience had a clear impact on his politics, particularly with respect to the Boer war, which Britain was currently fighting. "Having been an imperialist, I became during those five minutes a pro-Boer and a pacifist" (Russell 1967, 220-1).

It is worth asking both why Russell had this particular reaction to Evelyn Whitehead's suffering and whether this experience alone led to Russell's political change of heart. With respect to the first question, the answer no doubt lies in Russell's past. Russell led a very lonely childhood; as noted before, his parents were both dead by the time he was four, his grandfather died when he was six, and he was raised by an emotionally cold and distant grandmother. As a child, he had little opportunity to express his pains and fears in a way that brought any comfort; small wonder, then, that he should associate pain and loneliness, and see both together in Whitehead's agonies. With respect to the second question, it is very possible that Russell exaggerated the importance of this mystical experience to his political development. Other factors doubtless influenced him, including his background in radical liberalism.[8] But what is impossible to dispute is that from this time forward, Russell became increasingly preoccupied with finding ways to end war and ensure everlasting world peace.

This new preoccupation had a profound impact on his personal relationships. In 1902, for example, Russell became involved with a club called the Co-Efficients. Its purpose was to discuss world affairs, with the idea that the group's members would be jointly efficient, or "co-efficient," in making a better world. Though the club was founded by Russell's friend Sidney Webb, and involved a number of other friends including George Bernard Shaw, Russell did not long remain a member. To him, the group was more concerned with party politics and advancing British political interests than with creating a more peaceful world.

While Russell quietly came to oppose the Boer War, his opposition did little to move him to act. And yet the quest for a more peaceful world soon led him into political activism. In May 1903, Joseph Chamberlain, the Colonial Secretary in Arthur Balfour's Conservative-Unionist government, initiated a campaign to impose tariffs that would favor products from both Britain and its empire. This proposal would mark a strong move away from Britain's longstanding commitment to free trade, and it greatly angered Russell. Like many other liberals, he saw protectionist measures of this sort as ways by which imperial powers competed against one another. These measures encouraged nationalistic competition, and usually led to war. Above all, they represented a blow against the ideal of an international system that worked for everyone, not just the inhabitants of one country or another; this ideal was both central to liberalism and a critical part of Russell's vision of a more peaceful world. For this reason, Russell undertook a crusade against Chamberlain's tariff proposal, speaking in a variety of meetings and writ-

---

[8] David Blitz has exhaustively analyzed the relative importance of a variety of factors, including Russell's mystical experience, in shaping his views on war and peace. He particularly credits the influence of the logician and pacifist Louis Couturat, with whom Russell had an extensive correspondence at this time. See David Blitz (1999-2000).

ing detailed critiques of the protectionist case for various newspapers.[9] This crusade meant a lot to Russell; indeed, it was one of the few things that he was willing to let distract him from his philosophical work. Free trade, he wrote to a friend at the time, "is to me the last piece of sane internationalism left, and if it went I should feel inclined to cut my throat." Ultimately, the free traders prevailed, and in the 1906 general election the Liberals won a smashing victory.

At the same time, Russell also found time for other political causes, causes unrelated to peace and internationalism but still deeply grounded in his radical liberal politics. Foremost among these was the cause of women's rights. It was a cause that had long animated his family. His mother had been an ardent crusader for women's suffrage. Russell continued the tradition by joining the National Union of Women's Suffrage Societies (NUWSS). In 1907, a seat in parliament in Wimbleton became vacant, and a by-election was to be held. It was a safe Conservative seat, and the Liberal Party declined even to field a candidate. And so the NUWSS asked Russell to run for the seat on a platform committed to women's suffrage. He agreed, but only because he was certain that he would not win. (He was still heavily wrapped up in philosophical work). His opponent was Henry Chaplin, an old-fashioned Conservative warhorse. While Russell lost handily, as expected—3,299 votes to Chaplin's 10,263—he did succeed in raising the visibility of the issue of women's suffrage, which was his only goal.

Russell, however, soon fell out with the NUWSS. On principle, he was committed to universal adult suffrage. Not even every man enjoyed the right to vote in Britain at that time, and Russell was upset at the NUWSS's fear of committing to full adult suffrage. The group was also unwilling to consider compromise positions—say, provisions to extend voting rights for men that did not extend the right to vote to women on equal terms. And so Russell left the NUWSS and joined the People's Suffrage Federation, which advocated universal adult suffrage. To advance this cause, Russell endeavored to run again for parliament, this time in Bedford. This was a very Liberal district, and with the support of the Liberal Party Russell was likely to win. This support, however, was not forthcoming. The party's local leaders had asked him if it was true that he was an agnostic. He said yes. They then asked him if he was willing to attend church occasionally. He said

---

[9] For a detailed discussion of Russell's campaign against the tariff proposal, see Rempel (1979).

no. Russell probably rejected the hypocritical defense of organized religion even more vehemently than he rejected organized religion itself.

During his crusades on behalf of women's suffrage and free trade, Russell displayed a deep-rooted commitment to radical liberal principles. It was devotion to these principles that drove Russell to accomplish so much; it is important to remember that his political activism during this period of his life—activism that included an unsuccessful campaign for parliament—ranked second on his list of concerns, after his philosophical work. This kind of devotion also revealed itself as perseverance in the face of continued opposition—opposition that, in the case of his defense of women's suffrage, could get very unpleasant. This was the sort of devotion to principle that Russell's grandmother had in mind when she bade him not to follow a multitude to do evil. It was a devotion that would serve him well when World War I broke out in 1914.[10]

Russell was shocked when Europe plunged itself into full-scale war in 1914. He himself was no pacifist (although many people to this day fail to realize this, probably because he worked closely with many pacifists). He always recognized that there were wars worth fighting. But he saw no good in the war into which Europe was entering. It represented nothing but endless bloodshed for no good purpose. Even worse, it represented a threat to the ideals of liberal enlightenment that Russell cherished. On the altar of war, Russell feared, Europe would sacrifice everything that made its civilization worth preserving—especially personal freedom and the spirit of human brotherhood. In this war, liberal countries like France and Britain would go to war for the sake of autocratic allies like the Czar of Russia, a symbol for Russell and many liberals of the dark past from which Europe was emerging. *Liberté, egalité, fraternité*—none of these things fared well in times of war. For this reason, Russell made the crusade against war the focus of his life throughout World War I.

Russell's antiwar activism began as part of the short-lived Neutrality Committee, which hoped to prevent Britain's entry into the war. When this failed, Russell became involved with the Union for Democratic Control (UDC), a group that opposed the shadowy and secretive nature of British foreign policy. It was this secrecy that made it possible, Russell and others believed, for allegedly liberal countries like Britain and France to strike deals with the autocratic czarist Russia, for the sake of expanding their re-

---

[10] For a full account of Russell's antiwar activism during World War I, see Vellacott (1981).

spective empires. Such things, it was hoped, would not happen with a more democratic foreign policy. As part of this cause, Russell produced a number of essays on British foreign policy and the ethics of a just war. These essays were collected and published as the book *Justice in War Time* in November 1915. But Russell quickly became frustrated with the timidity of the UDC; it took some time, for example, for the group explicitly to condemn the war, as opposed to the undemocratic manner in which it was entered. He therefore joined the No-Conscription Fellowship (NCF) in March 1916. This group fought to defend the rights of those who refused military conscription, which Britain introduced for the first time in January 1916.

In some ways, Russell was the odd man out in the NCF. Whereas most of its members were pacifists, many of deep religious commitment, Russell was neither a pacifist nor religious. And in order to be a full-fledged member of the NCF, one had to be eligible for the draft; Russell, however, was too old for the draft, and thus could only become an associate member. But in other ways, NCF was a perfect fit for Russell. The fact that a liberal country like Britain was forcing people into uniform against their will, and denying people the right to observe their philosophical and religious principles, was a scandal to Russell. It proved that Russell's worst fear was correct—that whatever the high moral principles proclaimed to justify the war, the course of fighting it would inevitably threaten those very principles. Moreover, Russell greatly admired the conviction of the young men who were refusing to be called up, even if that conviction was religious in nature. It embodied exactly the kind of refusal to follow the multitude into evil that was central to Russell's philosophy of life. It was the kind of spirit that, Russell hoped, might bring people to recognize the madness of war, but even if that were not possible, it was a spirit worth preserving and defending at any cost. Something of value, Russell thought, had to survive the war.

Russell soon became a centrally important figure in the NCF. As the war dragged on, more and more of the NCF's (draft-age) members wound up in prison, leaving associate members like Russell to carry the burden of keeping the group going. And the tireless efforts of Russell and the NCF resulted in some successes in mitigating the lot of those who refused military service. Most famously, Russell helped save the lives of a group of conscientious objectors who had been denied exemption from the draft. In May 1916 the army apparently decided to make an example of these men, and surreptitiously shipped them off to France in the middle of the night. Once the men were sent to the front, they could be ordered to wear the uniform and pick up a gun; refusal could be punished by court-martial and (potentially) execution by firing squad. Word of this episode reached Russell, who with several other draft opponents demanded a meeting with the prime minister. The prime minister, in turn, gave the order that no death sentence was to be issued to any conscientious objector without the express permission of the government. While it is arguable whether any of these men would ever have been shot, the episode captured in a nutshell the kind of brutality that Russell thought war inevitably generated in even the freest and most enlightened society.

Russell was also concerned to combat what he saw as the deeper causes that led to war. From January to March 1916 he gave a series of public lectures on his vision of a better world, a world without wars of this kind. He had originally conceived of it as a joint set of lectures with the novelist D.H. Lawrence, whom he had met in 1915 and for a time greatly admired. But though both he and Lawrence opposed the present war, by 1916 he had come to dislike both Lawrence's volatile personality and his rather wild political views, and had nothing further to do with him. (The feeling was quite mutual, and it was in fact Lawrence who ended their friendship.)[11] In his solo series of talks, Russell discussed the way that human impulses lead them, under the present set of social arrangements, into conflict and war. These impulses, Russell believed, could not be combated or suppressed; doing so would lead them to work their will surreptitiously and unconsciously. Instead, they had to be channeled in more enlightened directions. Human beings had to express themselves creatively, in ways that were fully compatible with similar expression on the part of others (through science and art, for example), and not possessively, in ways that could not be satisfied without the frustration of others (through pursuit of profit, or national pride). Russell went on to suggest how such institutions as property, marriage, education, and religion might be reformed to create the kind of enlightened individual he championed. These lectures, published in 1916 as a book entitled *The Principles of Social Reconstruction*,[12] constitute perhaps the deepest investigation into political theory that Russell ever conducted.

But while Russell enjoyed successes both theoretically and practically in his antiwar work, this work carried a heavy price. In April 1916, shortly after joining the NCF, Russell wrote an anonymous leaflet entitled

---

[11] The friendship between Russell and Lawrence is well-chronicled in Monk (1996).
[12] The title of the American edition of the book—*Why Men Fight*—makes even more plain the link between Russell's project of social reconstruction and the prevention of war.

Two Years Hard Labour for Not Disobeying the Dictates of Conscience. It chronicled the case of a conscientious objector named Ernest Everett who had been denied exemption from military service and court-martialed when he refused to wear a uniform. The government considered the pamphlet an obstacle to recruitment, and so arrested a number of people for distributing the leaflet. When Russell learned of this, he wrote a letter to the London *Times* entitled "Adsum qui Feci," which roughly translates as, "Here I am, I did it."[13] In this letter, he confessed to writing the leaflet and suggested that if anyone should be punished for writing the leaflet, it should be he. While the police were initially reluctant to arrest a prominent and well-connected philosopher, the British Foreign Office ultimately pressured them to do so. Russell wanted to travel to the United States, which was still technically neutral at this point. He even hoped to meet with President Wilson to ask his help in ending the war. The Foreign Office wanted to block any action that might hinder their efforts to drag America into the war, and so wanted an excuse to deny Russell a passport. A criminal prosecution would provide such an excuse. And so Russell was prosecuted in June 1916 under the Defense of the Realm Act (DORA), an act that was passed during the war giving the government wide authority to prosecute the war and suppress obstacles (and opposition to it). Once again, the suppression of personal freedoms exhibited in his case—along with the accompanying political skullduggery that went on behind the scenes—was exactly the reason that Russell so strongly opposed war.

    Russell was ultimately convicted under DORA of hindering recruitment. His punishment was not severe—a fine of £100. Russell refused to pay the fine, and so many of his possessions were confiscated to be sold at auction. Fortunately, Russell's friends successfully bid enough at the auction to pay for his fine and then returned the purchased items to Russell. But worse was in store for him. The Foreign Office did indeed make use of Russell's conviction and denied him a passport. A few months later, it banned him from entering "restricted areas" near the British coast. Again, the reason was cynically political; while the bans of this nature were supposed to be used to prevent spies from contacting enemy vessels, in this case the motive was to prevent Russell from speaking to discontented workers in coastal regions. He had intended to address a gathering of miners in Glasgow in the fall, but the ban prevented him from traveling there. It made no difference;

---

[13] The letter has been published in Perkins (2002, 65-6).

union leader Robert Smillie gave a talk in Russell's place, then announced at the end that the speech he had given was the one Russell had intended to give. (This talk dealt with many of the same themes raised in *Principles of Social Reconstruction*, and was subsequently published in a short book entitled *Political Ideals*.)

But the harshest blow came in July 1916, when the Trinity College Council met and dismissed Russell from his position at Cambridge.[14] Many of the dons at Cambridge, some of whom had been friends of Russell, detested his antiwar activism, and his conviction under DORA provided them with a pretext for getting rid of him. (Russell had his supporters, especially among the younger dons, but unfortunately for him most of the draft-age faculty were away on military service.[15]) Cambridge had been Russell's intellectual home for over twenty years, and he left bitter and disillusioned with how little even his academic compatriots cared about freedom of speech and of conscience.

As the war dragged on, Russell became increasingly convinced that there was little more to be done in opposing the war. He had hoped that the U.S. would mediate among the major powers and achieve a negotiated peace. He even sent an open letter to President Wilson in December 1916, urging him to take on the role of mediator. (The letter had to be smuggled out of England in dramatic fashion, and was ultimately published in many major American newspapers.) Instead, Wilson chose to lead the U.S. into the war. Russell knew that with American involvement, the end of the war could not be far off. And so he began extricating himself from the NCF so as to move on to other things. One of the last actions he performed was to write an editorial for the NCF's newsletter, the *Tribunal*. (Because so many draft-age members of the NCF had been sent to prison, Russell had taken over editing the newsletter.) In this editorial, he lambasted the stupidity of the British government and the thuggish nature of the American government, whose troops were helping Britain and France finally to extract a victory after so much pointless bloodshed. The following passage, in which he predicted how the war would end, attracted particular attention:

---

[14] On Russell's dismissal from Cambridge, see Delany (1986) and Bone (2007).
[15] After the war ended, a number of the younger dons led a movement to reinstate Russell. While they succeeded in getting Russell restored to his former position, Russell never returned to it. He took a leave of absence, then resigned before going back. Russell would not return to Cambridge until 1944, when he was at long last made a full Fellow of Trinity College.

> The American garrison which by that time will be occupying England and France, whether or not they will prove efficient against the Germans, will no doubt be capable of intimidating strikers, an occupation to which the American army is accustomed when at home. I do not say that these thoughts are in the mind of the Government. All the evidence tends to show that there are no thoughts whatever in their mind, and that they live from hand to mouth consoling themselves with ignorance and sentimental twaddle.

For some reason, the British government vindictively decided to use this passage as an excuse to prosecute Russell under DORA once again, this time for disparaging an ally during wartime. Once again he was convicted, and in February 1918 he was sentenced to six months in prison.

Russell was originally sentenced to the second division in prison, which meant hard labor and harsh conditions. But a few of his remaining friends still enjoyed political connections—as did Russell's brother Frank, who had succeeded his grandfather and become the Second Earl Russell—and they persuaded the authorities to assign Russell to the first division. This meant more comfortable conditions, as well as the privilege of practicing his own trade (i.e., philosophy), instead of sewing mailbags all day. He served five months of his sentence before being released. During his time in prison, he managed to read some two hundred books and wrote extensively, though not on politics. (In particular, he completed his book *Introduction to Mathematical Philosophy*, which was based on a set of philosophical lectures he had given the previous fall. This book was published in 1919, and has proven very influential.)

While Russell was ready to move on from crusading against war after his release from prison, he was not ready to abandon politics. In April 1920, the British government assembled, at the request of the Trades Union Congress, a delegation to visit Russia and report on the conditions there. The Bolshevik Revolution had occurred three years earlier, but it was still difficult to obtain accurate information about the changes that had taken place. (This was hardly the fault of the Bolsheviks; the Russian Civil War was still going on, and the British, along with the United States and most of the other major world powers, had intervened in the war on the anti-Bolshevik side.) Russell had grown despondent at the thought of reforming British society, and like many people on the Left was curious if the Russian Communists offered an attractive alternative. For this reason, he asked to join the delegation. The group visited Petrograd and Moscow, then took a trip along the Volga River. While there, Russell had a one-hour personal interview with V.I. Lenin, one of only two delegates granted this privilege. (He also had the chance to hear Leon Trotsky speak, but did not meet with him.) Russell was personally unimpressed by the Bolshevik leader, whom he regarded as doctrinaire and small-minded. He gave Lenin a copy of his *Principles of Social Reconstruction*, and while the book apparently remained on Lenin's bookshelf, there is no evidence that its ideas affected the Bolshevik in any way.

Upon his return, Russell wrote a short book entitled *The Practice and Theory of Bolshevism* (1920). While acknowledging the enormous obstacles facing the Bolsheviks, Russell condemned them for their lack of liberal values and their view of human beings as little more than machines. It was an unpopular position among many of his old friends on the Left, as well as many of his erstwhile allies in the antiwar movement. The need to imagine that some country in the world offered a guide to a better future drove many people who should have known better (such as Sidney and Beatrice Webb and George Bernard Shaw) to overlook what Soviet Russia was becoming. Russell was one of the few figures on the Left not to fall into this form of intellectual dishonesty. (Even Dora Black, who visited Soviet Russia at about this time just shortly before becoming Russell's second wife, was highly optimistic about what she saw. This generated some tension within the new couple.)

Russell was thus a strong anti-Communist from his visit to Russia to the end of his life. But he was no cheerleader for capitalism. In both his earlier anti-Marxist book, *German Social Democracy*, and in *The Practice and Theory of Bolshevism*, Russell recognized how capitalism deprived the majority of people of effective control of their lives, of the ability to make their lives truly meaningful. A few years earlier, Russell had explored a number of alternatives to capitalism in a little book entitled *Roads to Freedom* (1918). Commissioned by the American publisher Henry Holt in 1917, and completed just before Russell's prison term began, this book compared the three leading anti-capitalist visions for a better world—socialism, anarchism, and syndicalism.

Russell recognized that state socialism, in which the government commanded the economy from above, could rectify many injustices, but posed grave threats to human freedom. (Russell is one of the few critics of capitalism to ask hard questions about how, for example, academic freedom, freedom of the press, and artistic freedom will be maintained without private property.) Anarchism, conceived as a rejection of all forms of social organization, could not deal with the real problems that every society must face.[16] Syndicalism, a system whereby all decision-making is organized through democratically-run workplaces that are joined together via federations, is well-suited to meet human needs, but mistakenly assumes that all important decisions revolve around economics. In the end Russell argues for guild socialism, a system that combines the worker-run economic system of syndicalism with a decentralized, democratic government.[17] Such a system would allow people two forums for asserting control over their lives, their workplaces and their communities. Moreover, it would prevent power from being concentrated in the hands of any one group. Like all good liberals, Russell feared that absolute power corrupted absolutely. Unlike many liberals, however, Russell feared private concentrations of power (such as multinational corporations) just as much as he feared state power, and so took it for granted that some alternative to capitalism was required; guild socialism, Russell concluded, was the best option available.

While Russell envisioned guild socialism as the best form of social system available in the modern world, he saw no means for advancing this vision in the years following World War I. He therefore joined the Labour Party, albeit with many reservations. When one of his old friends complained to him about Labour in a letter, Russell responded, "I think you are entirely right in what you say about the Labour Party. I do not like them, but an Englishman has to have a Party just as he has to have trousers, and of the three Parties I find them the least painful." Russell was not content with passive party membership, either. In 1922 and in 1923, he ran for parliament as the Labour Party candidate. (As with his first run for parliament, Russell took care to run in an unwinnable district.) Dora, his second wife, ran for the same seat in 1924. While Russell ascended to the earldom upon the death of his brother in 1931, the Third Earl Russell took little part in the activities of the House of Lords.

---

[16] It is, however, possible that Russell was being unfair to anarchism, as most respectable anarchists (from Peter Kropotkin to Noam Chomsky) reject the idea that anarchism equals rejection of organization. If this is correct, then Russell's position may have been much closer to anarchism then he believed (see chapter 18 of this volume for more on this topic).

[17] Guild socialism was widely discussed in Russell's day among people on the Left, but it has received relatively little attention in recent years. For a detailed discussion of the idea, see Cole (1917).

But throughout the 1920s and 1930s, Russell's interest in politics was primarily indirect. Russell became a father in 1921 and again in 1923. (Long estranged from his first wife, Alys, Russell had divorced and remarried in 1921.) Both Russell and his new wife, Dora, believed that most existing schools had a corrupting influence on children, discouraging independent thought and indoctrinating unsuspecting minds into religious and nationalistic dogmas. To keep their children safe from such dangers, Russell and Dora opened Beacon Hill school in 1927. The school, which remained open until 1943,[18] became one of the most well-known models for progressive education in the world. Beacon Hill is relevant for politics because Russell saw a good educational system as both a central component of any enlightened and free society and one of the most important means of achieving such a society. A society dedicated to Russell's radical liberal principles required citizens who were fearless, thoughtful, ready and willing to challenge authority, skeptical of dogma, respectful of other human beings regardless of nationality or creed—exactly the kind of students Russell hoped would emerge from Beacon Hill. He expressed this view in a number of works, most notably his book *Education and the Social Order* (1932).

As the international situation darkened in the late 1930s, war and peace again became central concerns for Russell. The devastation caused by World War I frightened him, and technological developments since then—especially the development of aerial bombardment, as demonstrated so horribly in Spain and Ethiopia—convinced him that the next war would be even more destructive. This led him to oppose those who urged Britain to rearm and challenge the growing power of Germany. He expressed these views in a book entitled *Which Way to Peace?* (1936). In this book, Russell argued that if a future war broke out, either Britain would win or it would lose. If it lost, Britain would succumb to fascism, and be utterly devastated. If Britain won, it would still be devastated during the war; moreover, whatever government survived the horrors would be an illiberal militaristic autocracy—effectively, a fascist state. (Russell had a lot of firsthand experience with how illiberal nations could become during wartime, and an even more devastating war could be counted upon to render Britain even less liberal.) Thus, war would bring both fascism and destruction to Britain no matter which side won. He therefore concluded that Britain should not

---

[18] Russell and Dora divorced in 1935, but Dora continued to run the school on her own for another eight years.

resist Germany's aggressive reassertion of power in Europe. There was always a chance that such nonresistance would make Germany rethink its actions—it's rather embarrassing to push around countries that are obviously not threatening your own—and even if it did not, Britain might at least succumb to fascism without the horrors of another war. Russell quickly became disenchanted with the argument; he apparently came to recognize that Hitler's Nazi regime was something much worse than the Kaiser's autocratic government during World War I, and that preventing such an evil regime from extending its power was worth risking the devastation Russell thought the war would bring. (It is important to remember that, as horrible as World War II turned out, it was considerably less horrible than Russell envisioned it.) After Britain entered the war, Russell repudiated his earlier opposition to war against Germany in a lengthy letter to the *New York Times* (Perkins 2002, 177-82). Moreover, *Which Way to Peace?* was one of the only books Russell authored that he never allowed to be reprinted during his lifetime.

The end of World War II brought the world into the atomic age. Russell had long believed that peace between highly-advanced, independent, and prideful nations was inherently unstable. Disarmament among such nations was at best a temporary palliative; in the event of a crisis, after all, nations could always quickly rearm. The only long-term solution was the creation of a world government, with an effective monopoly on the use of force, that could effectively outlaw war between nations. (There would still be a role for national governments with regard to purely internal affairs; as noted before, Russell was a big fan of federative arrangements, much as the U.S. government has with its states.) This imperative became all the more important with the creation of the atom bomb. The destruction that wars could generate was now potentially unlimited; this made the goal of a world government paramount if the human race was to survive. It was to this goal, therefore, that Russell was to devote most of the last 25 years of his life.

Russell's crusade against war in the postwar era left him little time to spare for work on other political causes to which he had devoted himself in the past—women's rights, progressive education, guild socialism, etc. But this does not mean that Russell no longer believed in these causes. True, he may have grown more cynical as to the prospects for some of his more utopian ideals; he saw few immediate opportunities, for example, for the reform or abolition of capitalism or of Soviet-style socialism. But the more fundamental reason for Russell's narrowing of focus was a simple reflection of priorities. None of Russell's ideals could be realized if the human race destroyed itself in war. A humane and enlightened social order could come about, if at all, only if humanity survived. And so Russell devoted himself to ensuring this survival, through the only means he thought viable—world government and the abolition of war.

Russell began the postwar era with an intense fear of Soviet Russia. Still an ardent anti-Communist, he thought the USSR represented the primary threat to world peace. It had an expansionist agenda that made a confrontation with the U.S. and other western powers inevitable. As of 1945, the United States was the only nation to possess the power of the atom bomb. For this reason, Russell proposed, on a number of occasions, that the U.S. use the threat of atomic warfare to pressure the Soviet Union into accepting some sort of world government, with a monopoly of control over the bomb. The United States proposed something very similar in the form of the Baruch Plan, which would have created an international agency under the auspices of the newly-created United Nations with full control over atomic weapons. Soviet Russia rejected this plan, perceiving it (not without reason) as a means by which the U.S. might attain world hegemony. The Soviet refusal further convinced Russell that the USSR must be compelled to accept such a plan, on pain of nuclear attack.[19] He was perhaps somewhat naïve about the U.S.'s intentions in proposing the Baruch Plan, but regardless he had decided that a world dominated by the U.S. was superior to a world in which rival powers continued to compete via war, with all the devastation this would entail.

Russell's position changed immediately, however, in August 1949, when the USSR exploded its first atomic bomb. Before this took place, the U.S. might reasonably have expected to force the Soviets to accept its terms; moreover, even if the Soviets refused the U.S. might reasonably have hoped for a swift and sure victory. But with both sides possessing the bomb,

---

[19] Some critics have claimed that Russell advocated a nuclear attack on Soviet Russia. This does not appear to be true. Russell urged the United States to threaten such an attack if the USSR refused to meet its terms. Russell knew this could not be an empty threat—the U.S. had to be ready if the Soviets thought it was all a bluff—but he also thought that the threat would be successful, and so no war would be necessary. Russell also thought that some confrontation with the Soviet Union was inevitable, and so even if there was a chance of nuclear war, it would be better to have it happen when only one power possessed nuclear weapons. This would result in a swift U.S. victory, rather than a prolonged period of mutual annihilation. For more on the evolution of Russell's thought on this question, see Perkins (1994-5) and Blitz (2002).

it would be unreasonable for either side to expect the other to capitulate, and neither side could expect to triumph in a war without being annihilated along the way. For this reason, Russell began to argue that a new course of thinking was required. Both sides had to recognize that the old means by which nations advanced their agendas were outmoded, and that both sides now had a common interest—survival—that outweighed any disagreements they might have. Once both sides realized this, it would be possible to find ways to diminish mutual suspicion and hostility, and put themselves on a path that might lead to the only long-term solution—an abolition of war through a world government. Such a government might permit capitalist and communist countries to continue their respective economic systems, but it would not permit any of them to impose its own ideology on the world. Such imposition, Russell argued, could now not be had without threatening the survival of the species. Russell set forth this argument in a variety of speeches and articles, but the best summary of his position is his book *Common Sense and Nuclear Warfare* (1959).

The late 1940s and the early 1950s were the years in which Russell enjoyed the highest level of social and political respectability he ever attained in his long life. This is none-too-surprising. Russell was as vehemently anti-Communist as could be; any man willing to threaten the Soviets with atomic attack could hardly be considered a "Red." And so for a time Russell enjoyed the favor of many within the political establishment—the same establishment that had put him in jail and fired him from his job during World War I. He finally became a full-fledged fellow of Trinity College, Cambridge in 1944; he won the Order of Merit in 1949; and received the Nobel Prize for Literature in 1950. Moreover, he undertook a number of anti-Communist speaking tours, and wrote a number of anti-Communist essays. Many of these speaking engagements and publications were paid for by the British Foreign Office, eager to showcase what the lifelong antiwar activist and political radical really thought of Soviet Russia.[20]

And yet Russell was far from an uncritical anti-Communist. He went on two speaking tours of the United States at this time, and both times he was highly critical of the shrill and shallow brand of fanaticism that equated any kind of peaceful social reform with Communism. Moreover, he deplored the attacks on civil liberties and the right to due process that were characteristic of the McCarthy era. Such tactics, he thought, only served to

---

[20] For a discussion of Russell's relation with the Foreign Office at this time, see Bone (2005).

make the FBI look like the KGB, and to blur what should be a clear line between authoritarian and free peoples. (He was particularly concerned with the case of Morton Sobell, who was a co-defendant with Julius and Ethel Rosenberg in one of the most famous spy cases in U.S. history.) For expressing these views, he was repeatedly taken to task by many Americans, including some anti-Communist leftists (most notably Sidney Hook). Russell defended himself by denouncing the tendency to act as though everything the U.S. did was right and everything the USSR did was wrong. The following passage, taken from a letter to the *New Leader*, captures the essentials of Russell's attitude:

> The question whether a given person committed a specific crime is logically quite independent of the merits or demerits of Communism. If a murder has been committed and Mr. A is accused, if I think that there is not sufficient evidence against Mr. A I shall not on that account be thought to favor murder. But if a man is accused of the sort of crime that Communists are expected to commit, anybody who thinks that he did not commit it is supposed to be a Communist. (Perkins 2002, 267-8)

Russell recognized this sort of attitude as a serious obstacle to his quest to end war. Given that both the U.S. and the USSR possessed the atomic bomb, the only way to avoid war was for both sides to recognize their common interests. This meant that both Americans and Soviets had to start recognizing that agreement with the other side (about the need to avoid war) did not mean embracing the other side's entire agenda. The typical Cold War mentality that attributed absolute evil to the opposing side therefore had to be resisted.

Russell's quest to get both sides in the Cold War to recognize the obsolescence of war in the atomic age began in earnest at Christmas 1954, when he read a statement on radio entitled "Man's Peril." In it, he challenged his listeners to accept the grave dangers posed by nuclear warfare—dangers hitherto unknown in human history—and to recognize the need to abolish war. The following year, he issued a joint statement with Albert Einstein, known as the Russell-Einstein Manifesto. Russell persuaded a number of Nobel prizewinning scientists from both sides of the Iron Curtain to sign it. It was essential, the statement argued, for people of all political ideologies to recognize their common interest, and see how this common interest dictated changes in the way they approached age-old political problems. "We have to learn," the manifesto declared, "to think in a new way," and it concluded with the following ringing words:

> We appeal as human beings to human beings: Remember your humanity, and forget the rest. If you can do so, the way lies open to a new Paradise; if you cannot, there lies before you the risk of universal death.

The Manifesto called for a conference of scientists (Communist, anti-Communist, and neutral) to assess the dangers of nuclear weapons. A millionaire philanthropist named Cyrus Eaton responded to the call, and offered to house such a conference at his home in Pugwash, Nova Scotia. Russell accepted, and the conference was held in July 1957. The conference led to the creation of an organization which to this day continues to organize other conferences, in which scientists across the political spectrum come together to discuss scientific questions of great public importance. The Pugwash Conferences, as well as their founder, physicist Joseph Rotblat, received the Nobel Peace Prize in 1995.

As he crusaded to end war, Russell stressed the common interest that both sides had in averting Armageddon. No progress would be made, he believed, if his campaign were regarded as a propaganda tool for one side or another—or, even worse, a ploy to allow one side to gain a strategic advantage over the other. He therefore strived to involve parties from both sides of the Iron Curtain, and maintained a polite distance from both Cold War liberals and Communist-aligned peace activists (although he rejected the help of neither when offered).[21] And yet Russell did realize that whatever he did, propagandists from both East and West would attack anything he said that did not fit with their fanatical creeds. He acknowledged this fact in a response to the anticommunist Norman Thomas, which was published in the *New Leader* in February 1957:

> Whoever pursues even-handed justice must expect to incur the hostility of both sides. In Russia, I am regarded as a rabid advocate of American imperialism. For example, *Bolshevik*, in an article devoted to the enumeration of my crimes, says: "Russell now serves the American dollar and tirelessly trumpets the glories and unrivaled virtues of 'the

---

[21] On Russell's relationship with the Communist Left during this period, see Bone (2001).

American way of life,' of American 'democracy.' It costs him nothing to announce that the U.S.A. is the promised land for all nations and to summon nations to submit meekly to the undisputed military and civil power of Wall Street."

"You, on the other hand," Russell said to Thomas, "accuse me of evincing a desire lately, and 'perhaps unconsciously, to use the blackest possible paint in depicting the American scene.' I have no such desire" (Perkins 2002, 267). Russell concluded from attacks by sources such as Thomas and *Bolshevik* that, in the end, his efforts to avoid aligning with either side were proving a success.

Through the late 1950s and early 1960s, Russell continued to press both the U.S. and the USSR to recognize their common interests and start taking steps toward a world international order that could ensure peace. This effort yielded some results, notably an exchange between Russell, Soviet Premier Nikita Khrushchev, and American Secretary of State John Foster Dulles, on the need to end the arms race. (This exchange appeared in the pages of the *New Statesman* in late 1957 and early 1958, and was subsequently published as a book.) But by 1958, Russell had decided to direct much of his attention toward his own country, Britain. Britain had tested its first H-bomb the year before, and Russell thought it added nothing to British security. If anything, it ensured that Britain would be destroyed in any confrontation between the two major superpowers, as the USSR would make sure to strike at a nuclear-armed U.S. ally. Russell argued that Britain should unilaterally disarm, give up the bomb, and declare its neutrality with respect to the two great powers. Such a move would place it in a position to mediate between them, and help them along the road to peace. (Note that Russell did not advocate unilateral disarmament for the United States.)

To this end, Russell became involved with the Campaign for Nuclear Disarmament (CND), a peace group created in 1958 that called for Britain to give up the bomb. (The group's logo is known throughout the world as the "peace symbol.") Russell was elected the organization's first president, with the chairman being Canon Collins, a Christian pacifist and founder of Christian Action. The group organized a number of high-profile events designed to pressure the British government, most notably an annual march from Trafalgar Square in London to the Atomic Weapons Establishment (the facility that designed and built Britain's nuclear warheads) at Aldermaston. While the group's early marches attracted thousands of participants, it ran into strong opposition from within the Labour Party. (It did, however, manage to get the Labour Party's annual conference to commit the party to unilateral disarmament, although the decision was overturned the following year.)

Russell recognized the strong opposition within the British establishment to unilateral disarmament. He quickly began to fear that the CND's annual marches might become yearly *pro forma* exercises, gratifying to those taking part but easy for the powers-that-be to ignore. He was encouraged in this matter by Ralph Schoenman, an American graduate student studying at the London School of Economics under the Marxist Ralph Miliband. Schoenman argued for a campaign of civil disobedience led by prominent public figures, with the aim of both shaming the government and triggering widespread popular resistance. Russell liked the idea, and in 1961 left the CND to found the Committee of 100. The group began by conducting a public sit-down in front of the Ministry of Defence. 5000 people attended the event. The authorities soon decided to crack down on the organization. After a rally on August 6 to mark Hiroshima Day, Russell was arrested for inciting public disobedience of the law (and for ignoring a police ban on the use of microphones at the rally). He was convicted, and sentenced to two months in prison. The court quickly decided, however, to reduce his sentence to seven days; Russell was, after all, 89 years old, an earl, and a Nobel Prize winner, and the authorities were terrified of the public outcry should he die while in prison. Russell served his term in the prison hospital. Ultimately, the campaign of civil disobedience petered out, and Russell resigned from the Committee of 100 in early 1963.

When the Cold War began, Russell thought that peace required above all else the containment of the Soviet Union. He saw that country as expansive in its goals, and this expansionism would inevitably bring it into conflict with the United States. The Soviet acquisition of the atom bomb changed the policies that might be appropriate in dealing with the USSR, but it did not change Russell's mind as to the nature of the threat. The USSR remained the primary threat to world peace in Russell's mind. But as the years went on, Russell came to view both the U.S. and the Soviet Union as equally likely to press for advantages in ways likely to lead to war. By the early 1960s, his thinking had changed to the point that he now saw the U.S. as the country whose aggressive foreign policy was most likely to trigger atomic war and the destruction of the human race. Nowhere is this more evident than in Russell's reaction to the Cuban Missile Crisis. Russell knew that the U.S. government had been trying to overthrow Fidel Castro's government for several years. He therefore saw Cuba's attempt to acquire nuclear weapons from the USSR as a perfectly natural defensive move. It was not, in Russell's eyes, more provocative for the U.S. to have Soviet missiles so close to its border than it was for the Soviets to have U.S. missiles right near its border in Turkey. (The U.S. had stationed missiles there for several years.) He therefore saw Kennedy's blockade of Cuba as an insane overreaction. In effect, Kennedy was announcing that no country had any right to do anything the U.S. disliked, and that the U.S. was willing to risk destroying the world rather than surrender the tiniest measure of power. This attitude, Russell feared, would inevitably lead to World War III.

And so throughout the Cuban Missile Crisis, Russell fired off a stream of telegrams to President Kennedy, to Premier Khrushchev, to Fidel Castro, and to U.N. Secretary-General U Thant. On both sides, he urged restraint lest the world go up in flames. He clearly hoped for some kind of compromise, whereby Cuban missiles might be removed in exchange for a comparable American concession (say, removal of U.S. missiles in Turkey) plus a guarantee that the U.S. would not invade Cuba. But he clearly saw the U.S. as the aggressor state, and throughout his messages to Khrushchev and Castro he constantly reiterated that he recognized the merits of their position, but that unreasonable concessions might be necessary to prevent American recklessness from destroying the world. His view of the situation was well-summarized in a leaflet he released during the height of the crisis. It read as follows:

> YOU ARE TO DIE, not in the course of nature, but within a few weeks.
>
> Why?
>
> Because rich Americans dislike the Government that Cubans prefer, and have used part of their wealth to spread lies about it.
>
> WHAT CAN YOU DO?
>
> You can go out into the street and into the market place, proclaiming: 'Do not yield to ferocious and insane murderers'…
>
> AND REMEMBER:
> CONFORMITY MEANS DEATH. ONLY PROTEST GIVES A HOPE OF LIFE.

After the crisis was over, Russell collected the telegrams he had sent during the crisis (along with whatever responses he had received from the major figures involved) and published them in a book entitled *Unarmed Victory* (1963).

Russell's role in the Cuban Missile Crisis was capped off in an unusual way. On November 10, 1962, a small procession of Russell's neighbors traveled to his home in Wales carrying a banner that read "Thanks to Bert, We're still unhurt." The group wanted to thank Russell for taking such a strong stand for peace. The whole affair was very reminiscent of the delegation that cheered Russell's grandfather to mark the anniversary of one of his greatest parliamentary victories. While it is an open question just how much of a difference Russell's intervention in the Cuban Missile Crisis made, there is no doubt that he appreciated this personal gesture.

Interestingly, while Russell consistently opposed Kennedy's hard-line foreign policy, he also created the Who Killed Kennedy Committee after Kennedy's assassination. This committee was inspired by Russell's correspondence with Mark Lane, an attorney appointed to represent Lee Harvey Oswald before his assassination who would become one of the leading sources of conspiracy theory regarding Kennedy. The committee, which involved a number of leading public intellectuals, did not embrace any particular conspiracy theory, but it did question the seriousness and the thoroughness of the Warren Commission.

Russell's continuous political activity attracted a number of young people to support his efforts. These included Ralph Schoenman, who continued to work with Russell after leaving the Committee of 100 and was now Russell's personal secretary. With so much activity going on, Russell decided that an official organization should be created to carry on the work. And so in 1963, Russell created the Atlantic Peace Foundation and the Bertrand Russell Peace Foundation. The former was created for the study of world peace, while the latter was created to promote world peace. The Russell Peace Foundation persists to this day; it can be found online at http://www.russfound.org/.

Russell's final major political intervention was a campaign against the U.S. war in Vietnam. He was angry that America was brutally suppressing a Third World country for trying to leave the political orbit of the United States; moreover, he thought it inevitable that unless U.S. aggression was stopped, a full-scale military confrontation with the USSR was inevitable. It was the U.S., not the USSR, that in Russell's eyes was now posing the greatest threat to world peace. Russell was also angry with the Labour government in Britain, which supported the American war effort while muttering the occasional meaningless murmur of dissent. His anger led him in 1965 to tear up his Labour Party membership card as a public protest. (While Russell never went without trousers, he apparently decided he could make do without a party.)

In 1966, Russell called for the formation of an International War Crimes Tribunal, to investigate the United States for its conduct in Vietnam. The tribunal, Russell emphasized, would have no legal authority, but it would constitute a way by which people around the world could evaluate the war independently, without regard to the propaganda demands of the major powers. He enlisted a number of prominent intellectuals in the project, most notably the French philosopher Jean-Paul Sartre. To finance the tribunal, Russell sold the rights to his long-anticipated *Autobiography*, and received a handsome sum. (The book appeared in three volumes, in 1967, 1968, and 1969.) He also sold his personal papers to McMaster University, in Ontario, Canada. He would likely have sold them to an American university, which might have fetched him more money, but *Newsweek* magazine claimed that the money from the sale would be sent to fund the National Liberation Front's military activities in South Vietnam. As a result, no American university would touch the papers. (It is possible that the FBI planted this false story in the American media so as to sabotage Russell's efforts; see Griffin 2004.) The papers remain at McMaster to this day, where they form the heart of the Bertrand Russell Archives.

After months of investigation and research, the Tribunal was held in 1967 in Stockholm, Sweden and Roskilde, Denmark. (Russell could not persuade the Labour government to permit it being held in Britain, nor could Sartre persuade President de Gaulle to let France host it.) Russell, who turned 95 in May of that year, was unable to attend in person. The tribunal found the U.S. and its allies guilty on most counts. Since then, it has served as a model for a number of other citizen tribunals, providing a forum for charges to be raised even when governments do not wish to hear them (Klinghoffer and Klinghoffer 2002).

Throughout all of these activities, Ralph Schoenman served as Russell's secretary, confidante, and right-hand man. (The only other person to enjoy such a close working relationship at this time was his fourth and last wife, Edith, who supported him in all his endeavors for peace and even went to prison with him in 1961.) While he doubtless helped Russell accomplish many projects that age would otherwise have thwarted, Schoenman gained a reputation for being both arrogant and attention-seeking. In Russell's absence, he assumed the right to speak for Russell. (This led Jean-Paul Sartre at one session of the International War Crimes Tribunal to tell Schoenman, "Vous, Schoenman, vous n'êtes pas Lord Russell."—"You, Schoenman, you are not Lord Russell.") His close working relationship with Russell led many to accuse him of manipulating Russell. Indeed, the mainstream press, eager to dismiss Russell's crusade for peace, often depicted him as little more than the mouthpiece of his secretary. This dismissive tactic overlooked Russell's long track record as an antiwar activist dating back over fifty years; it also provided a convenient excuse (still practiced by those who dislike Russell's political stances) for ignoring the substance of Russell's arguments.[22] All the evidence of those who knew him best suggests that to the very end he was as alert and intellectually active as a ninetysomething-year-old man could be. Still, by the end of his life Russell came to share many of the criticisms made of Schoenman, and expressed these in a long memorandum he wrote for his political associates. (This memorandum was first published in *Black Dwarf*, a Marxist newspaper, in September 1970.)

On January 31, 1970, Russell drafted his last political statement. Fittingly, it concerned war and peace. In this statement he criticized Israel for maintaining its occupation over territories seized during the 1967 Six-Day War, and for trying to crush resistance to that occupation by force. The statement was read to the International Conference of Parliamentarians in Cairo on February 3—the day after Russell's death at the age of 97.

THIS SHORT ACCOUNT OF THE POLITICAL SIDE of Russell's life is quite incomplete. It omits discussion of several important political events in which Russell became involved—for example, the Sino-Indian border dispute of late 1962, which Russell and his Peace Foundation attempted to mediate. (The story is chronicled in the second half of Russell's book *Unarmed Victory*.) It also omits discussion of many of Russell's books on politics, such as *The Prospects of Industrial Civilization* (1923, co-authored with his second wife, Dora); *Freedom and Organization, 1814-1914* (1934); *Power: A New Social Analysis* (1938); *Authority and the Individual* (1948); *New Hopes for*

---

[22] For an interesting analysis of the way that advanced age can be used to dismiss arguments otherwise meriting attention, see Ross (2001).

a Changing World (1951); *Human Society in Ethics and Politics* (1954); and *Has Man a Future?* (1961). And it does not attempt to address Russell's views on many important social issues closely related to politics, such as his views on sex, marriage, and religion. But enough has hopefully been said to make possible some broad conclusions about Russell's political life.

In considering Russell's political work as a whole, there are two questions worth asking. First, what commitments underlay Russell's politics? And second, what did those commitments lead Russell to do? In particular, what sort of writing did these commitments lead Russell to write?

To begin with the first question, it is fair to describe Russell as a radical liberal. He was a liberal in the sense of being centrally concerned with individual freedom. But his concern with freedom was of a deep nature. He was not content with superficial nostrums such as "Get government off our backs!" but instead tried to get to the root of the idea of freedom. This made him a radical liberal. (The word "radical" comes from the Latin for "root.") For Russell, defending individual freedom meant protecting and nurturing the ability of every individual to flourish, to lead a life of accomplishment and meaning. For Russell, taking this ideal seriously demanded more than liberals had traditionally thought. Many liberals (especially those known as "classical" liberals) acted as though the only threat to freedom came from the government. But while Russell was concerned about preserving people's liberty of thought and action from government interference, he also recognized that there were many other things that could obstruct people's free development. Religion, education, private property—all could shape individuals in ways that stunted their moral, intellectual, and personal growth. Thus, achieving a truly free society required radical changes. This was another sense in which Russell was a radical liberal.

Russell's liberalism was radical in one further sense. Russell's analysis of the conditions necessary for human freedom—indeed, at times even human survival—often placed him in conflict with the political *status quo*. Russell consistently displayed both the intellectual courage to reason through what his principles implied, and the moral courage to act on those principles in the face of fierce opposition. The philosophy behind the verse "Thou shalt not follow a multitude to do evil" truly did animate Russell's politics, whether the issue at hand was the Battle of the Somme or the bombing of Hanoi.

Russell may have displayed principle and courage, but that does not answer the question of how he approached politics as he endeavored to advance his radical brand of liberalism. Russell's political interventions were many and varied, but how should these interventions—in particular, his voluminous body of political writings—be characterized?

One way to do it would be to describe Russell as a political theorist or political philosopher. This would be an obvious strategy for describing a philosopher who wrote books with titles like *The Principles of Social Reconstruction*. And yet it is not a very satisfactory strategy. Russell was indeed a philosopher, who wrote a great deal about the philosophy of mathematics, logic, epistemology (the study of human knowledge), the philosophy of language, and ethics, among other fields. But he never considered himself a political philosopher. He generally thought of his political work as being of a totally different nature than his philosophical work. Russell thus characterized *The Principles of Social Reconstruction* as follows:

> With regard to *Social Reconstruction*, and to some extent with my other popular books, philosophic readers, knowing that I am classified as a "philosopher", are apt to be led astray. I did not write *Social Reconstruction* in my capacity as a "philosopher." I wrote it as a human being who suffered from the state of the world, wished to find some way of improving it, and was anxious to speak in plain terms to others who had similar feelings. If I had never written technical books, this would be obvious to everyone; and if the book is to be understood, my technical activities must be forgotten. (Russell, 1951, 730-1)

Russell was not practicing false modesty; his writings on social and political questions did not display the level of analytic rigor and precision that one might expect from the author of *The Principles of Mathematics* and *Principia Mathematica*, or from the canon of leading political philosophers from Hobbes to Rawls.[23] It was this lack of rigor that led Ludwig Wittgenstein, Russell's most famous student, to remark that Russell's books should be bound in two colors—"those dealing with mathematical logic in red—and all students of philosophy should read them; those dealing with ethics and politics in blue—and no one should be allowed to read them" (quoted in Monk 1990, 471).

---

[23] This is not to say that his works contain no insights that may prove of use to a political theorist. For an argument to this effect, see Hardin (1996).

The level of analytical rigor in Russell's political writings can be gauged fairly effectively by looking at three of his most important political books—*The Principles of Social Reconstruction* (1916), *Power: A New Social Analysis* (1938), and *Human Society in Ethics and Politics* (1954). In *Principles*, Russell argues for the essential role of impulses, as opposed to rational satisfaction of desires, as central to human nature. And yet he never offers a rigorous account of what impulses are, how many types of impulses we have, how one type of impulse gets transmuted into another, or the relationship between desire and impulse. At the start of *Power*, Russell declares his intention of proving "that the fundamental concept in social science is Power, in the same sense in which Energy is the fundamental concept in physics" (Russell 1938, 10). And yet while the book offers many interesting reflections upon the concept of power, it certainly does not offer a truly systematic account of the concept (and certainly nothing comparable to the treatment that the concept of energy would receive in a physics textbook.) Finally, Russell devotes the first half of *Human Society* to developing a theory of ethics, in a fairly sophisticated manner. He promises to devote the second half to applying this theory to politics, but in fact he does nothing of the kind. Again, while he makes many interesting observations about politics in the modern era, these observations never come together in any kind of systematic theory.

If Russell does not write about politics as a philosopher, then how *does* he write about politics? Russell himself, as noted above, described himself as writing about politics merely as a concerned human being, but this may indeed be too modest a characterization after all. In an essay entitled "Russell: The Last Great Radical?" the political theorist Alan Ryan describes Russell as a political polemicist, a pamphleteer in the tradition of Thomas Paine (Ryan 1996). This is probably the fairest characterization of Russell's interventions in politics. They are not the interventions of an ordinary Joe, but neither are they the work of a professional philosopher. Rather, they are the actions of a deeply principled public intellectual—an intelligent and highly-educated person who finds the political conditions of his time wanting and feels a heartfelt calling to do something about it.

Some may characterize Russell's interventions in politics as a waste of his great mind. As noted before, this was Wittgenstein's view. It also seemed to have been the view of Russell's brother-in-law, who once said that using Russell's mind in ordinary political debates was like "using a razor to chop wood" (quoted in Moorehead 1992, 134). Russell himself felt routinely drawn away from politics by the lure of the philosophical work he loved so much. He also felt the lure of personal commitments, especially toward the various women he loved throughout his life. Yet he also felt that the stakes in politics were high enough to demand his attention. Russell expresses this idea in the memorable prologue to his *Autobiography* as follows:

> Love and knowledge, so far as they were possible, led upward toward the heavens. But always pity brought me back to earth. Echoes of cries of pain reverberate in my heart. Children in famine, victims tortured by oppressors, helpless old people a hated burden to their sons, and the whole world of loneliness, poverty, and pain make a mockery of what human life should be. I long to alleviate the evil, but I cannot, and I too suffer. (Russell 1967, 4)

Russell may not have been able to eliminate evil from the world, and yet clearly he thought there were things he could do to alleviate it. This led him back again and again to the realm of practical politics as a public intellectual.

This discussion of Russell's political life began by noting the two traditions embodied in Russell's heritage, the tradition of the statesman and the tradition of the rebel. Russell the political activist was a public intellectual of the first order. In that role he certainly benefited from his family's tradition of statesmanship; it provided him with qualities like political courage that served him well. And yet in the end, the public intellectual is more of a rebel—a rabble-rouser, if you will—than anything else. For the role of the public intellectual is to identify the ways in which a society falls short, and to suggest ways that it might do better. There is no way to perform this task without embracing the spirit of the rebel. It was a spirit that Russell embraced in passages like the following:

> An individual may perceive a way of life, or a method of social organisation, by which more of the desires of mankind could be satisfied than under the existing method. If he perceives truly, and can persuade men to adopt his reform, he is justified. Without rebellion, mankind would stagnate, and injustice would be irremediable. The man who refuses to obey authority has, therefore, in certain circumstances, a legitimate function, provided his disobedience has motives which are social rather than personal. (Russell 1938, 172)

If Russell's life is any indicator, the world could use a few more rabble-rousers.

One final note before leaving Russell's politics. It is important to note that Russell's legacy as a public intellectual is carried on to this day. One example will have to suffice. As noted earlier, Russell wrote an anonymous pamphlet during World War I; when those who distributed the pamphlet were arrested, Russell publicly announced his authorship of the pamphlet and challenged the authorities to stop him. A similar episode occurred in Turkey just a few years ago. In September 2001, a Turkish publishing house published a collection of essays by renowned linguist and political analyst Noam Chomsky. The collection contained criticisms by Chomsky of the Turkish government's brutal campaign to suppress the Kurdish independence movement. By November, the Turkish government had charged the publishing house's owner with publishing "Propaganda against the indivisible unity of the country, nation, and State of the Republic of Turkey." When the publisher appeared in court the following February for his trial, he was accompanied by—Noam Chomsky. Chomsky had flown to Turkey to be present at the trial. He argued before the court that he had written the remarks that generated the criminal charges, and so if the publisher of those remarks was facing trial, then so should he. The prosecution declined to press charges against Chomsky, and was embarrassed into dropping the charges against the publisher. Anyone wishing to see Russell's legacy as a public intellectual being carried on today would be well to examine the life and work of Noam Chomsky (see chapter 18 of this volume for a more extensive comparison of Russell and Chomsky).[24]

Bibliography

Blitz, David. 1999-2000. "Russell and the Boer War: From Imperialist to Anti-Imperialist." *Russell* n.s. 19 (2): 117-42.

Blitz, David. 2002. "Did Russell Advocate Preventive Atomic War against the USSR?" *Russell* n.s. 22 (1): 5-45.

Bone, Andrew G. 2001. "Russell and the Communist-Aligned Peace Movement in the Mid-1950s." *Russell* n.s. 21 (1): 31-57.

Bone, Andrew. 2005. "Bertrand Russell as Cold War Propagandist." *Bertrand Rus-*

---

[24] Not coincidentally, Chomsky has long admired Russell. He has a large poster of Russell in his office at MIT, and he holds an honorary membership in the Bertrand Russell Society.

sell Society Quarterly 125-126 (February-May): 9-33.

Bone, Andrew G. 2007. "Bertrand Russell's Wartime Dismissal from Trinity College, Cambridge." In *Free Speech in Fearful Times: After 9/11 in Canada, the U.S., Australia, & Europe.* Eds. James L. Turk and Allan Manson. Toronto: James Lorimer, 19-41.

Cole, G.D.H. 1917. *Self-Government in Industry*. London: G. Bell and Sons.

Delany, Paul. 1986. "Russell's Dismissal from Trinity: A Study in High Table Politics." *Russell* n.s. 6 (1): 39-61.

Griffin, Nicholas. 2004. "How the Russell Papers Came to McMaster." *Bertrand Russell Society Quarterly* 123 (August): 21-7.

Hardin, Russell. 1996. "Russell's Power." *Philosophy of the Social Sciences* 26 (3): 322-47.

Klinghoffer, Arthur Jay and Klinghoffer, Judith Apter. 2002. *International Citizens' Tribunals: Mobilizing Public Opinion to Advance Human Rights.* New York: Palgrave Macmillan.

Moorehead, Caroline. 1992. *Bertrand Russell: A Life*. New York: Viking.

Monk, Ray. 1990. *Ludwig Wittgenstein: The Duty of Genius.* New York: Penguin.

Monk, Ray. 1996. "The Tiger and the Machine: D.H. Lawrence and Bertrand Russell." *Philosophy of the Social Sciences* 26 (2): 205-46.

Perkins, Ray. 1994-5. "Bertrand Russell and Preventive War." *Russell* n.s. 14 (2): 135-53.

Perkins, Ray, ed. 2002. *Yours Faithfully, Bertrand Russell: A Lifelong Fight for Peace, Justice and Truth in Letters to the Editor.* Chicago: Open Court.

Rempel, Richard. 1979. "From Imperialism to Free Trade: Couturat, Halevy and Russell's First Crusade." *Journal of the History of Ideas* 40 (July-September): 423-43.

Ross, William T. 2001. "Bertrand Russell in His Nineties: Aging and the Problem of Biography." *Journal of Aging and Identity* 6 (2): 67-76.

Russell, Bertrand. 1938. *Power: A New Social Analysis.* London: Allen & Unwin.

Russell, Bertrand. 1951. "Reply to Criticisms." In *The Philosophy of Bertrand Russell.* Ed. Paul Arthur Schilpp. 3rd ed. New York: Tudor, 679-741.

Russell, Bertrand. 1967. *The Autobiography of Bertrand Russell, 1872-1914.* Boston: Little, Brown and Company.

Ryan, Alan. 1996. "Russell: The Last Great Radical?" *Philosophy of the Social Sciences* 26 (June): 247-66.

Stone, Peter. 2006-7. "Chomsky and Russell Revisited." *Bertrand Russell Society Quarterly* 132-135 (November-August): 13-22.

Vellacott, Jo. 1981. *Bertrand Russell and the Pacifists in the First World War.* New York: St. Martin's Press.

A PUBLIC INTELLECTUAL ON WAR AND PEACE: RUSSELL'S "LITTLE BOOKS" DURING THE GREAT WAR AND THE COLD WAR

David Blitz

BERTRAND RUSSELL WAS, like few others before him, and even fewer after him, a public intellectual, concerned with bringing intellectual acumen to bear on policy issues.[1] Traditionally, most intellectuals concern themselves solely with their academic specialty, unlike Russell, who roamed much more broadly. While Russell wrote and intervened on issues including social justice, human happiness, and world government, this paper will focus on Russell's contributions to the public understanding of an issue that preoccupied him from the late 1890s through to the 1960s: war and peace.

RUSSELL'S "BIG" AND "LITTLE" BOOKS: TWO STRANDS TO BE UNIFIED

Russell is best known for what can be termed his "big books": the blue cover Cambridge volumes *Principles of Mathematics* (1903) and *Principia Mathematica* (1910-1913).[2] In these works, along with his most famous article, "On Denoting" (1905), Russell established the program of logicism—reducing mathematics to its logical foundation—and analysis— eliminating complex entities in favor of their (re)construction from simpler and more basic components (sense data and later, events). These works were highlights of what has now been termed analytic philosophy, and which in its "early" phase—from the mid 1890s to the mid 1910s—has been the object of considerable academic research.[3]

---

[1] A contemporary comparison would be Noam Chomsky, who made a significant academic contribution—his theories of syntax—and has played a major role as a radical critic of the powers that be, especially as concerns the military-industrial-academic complex and war.

[2] Co-authored with Alfred North Whitehead; second edition 1925-1927, with the assistance of Frank Plumpton Ramsey for revisions in volume 1.

[3] See the series *History of Analytic Philosophy*, edited by Michel Beaney, which has published over 20 volumes, most of which deal with this time period.

But Russell also produced a number of volumes which can be termed, in comparison with to his major writings, "little books," to designate the many shorter volumes Russell wrote on public policy issues related to war and peace, especially during two significant periods of conflict in world history: the Great War of 1914-1918, and the nuclear arms race at its height from 1958-1967. To the contrary of those, such as Ray Monk,[4] who argue that Russell ceased to be a valued intellectual after *Principia*, the thesis of this chapter is that Russell's little books are just as important, in terms of Russell's life and perhaps our own, as his big books.

Russell, in his *Autobiography*, recognized the dual aspect of his life and work, in terms of both theoretical and practical philosophy:

> The serious part of my life ever since boyhood has been devoted to two different objects, which for a long time remained separate and have only in recent years united into a single whole. I wanted, on the one hand, to find out whether anything could be known; and, on the other hand, to do whatever might be possible toward creating a happier world. (Russell 1967, 326)

And he continued:

> Nearly three-quarters of a century ago, walking alone in the Tiergarten through melting snow under the coldly glittering March sun, I determined to write two series of books: one abstract, growing gradually more concrete; the other concrete, growing gradually more abstract. They were to be crowned by a synthesis, combining pure theory with a practical social philosophy. Except for the final synthesis, which still eludes me, I have written these books. (*ibid.*, 329)[5]

In a sense, the "big books" of the first decade and a third of the twentieth century were the abstract component, supplemented by a number

---

[4] The title of the second volume of Monk's otherwise well researched biography of Russell betrays the bias: *Bertrand Russell: The Ghost of Madness* (2000), while that of the first volume implies an individual cut off from the population at large, even though it covers the period of Russell's activism during World War I: *Bertrand Russell: The Spirit of Solitude* (1996).

[5] For an analysis of this project in terms of residual Hegelianism in Russell's thought at the time he formulated the project, see Nicholas Griffin (1991), ch. 3. Ken Blackwell argues for the importance of Spinoza in Russell's thinking about the link between the theoretical and the practical.

of later volumes,[6] while the "little books" which form the subject matter of this chapter were the concrete component. How to combine or reconcile them was no simple matter, and Russell himself indicated that he had not fully done so. The abstract series represents the highest aspirations of the human mind—the contemplation of theoretical knowledge, especially in logic, mathematics and science. The concrete series includes Russell's efforts to promote human happiness through improved forms of social, political, and economic organization, and to prevent the death and destruction, and given nuclear weapons, the possible annihilation of humanity due to war.[7] A pair of somewhat neglected, but very interesting books by Russell indicate the way in which the two strands of theoretical and practical philosophy could be combined: *Power: A New Social Analysis* (1938), in which Russell argues that power plays the unifying role in social science that energy plays in natural science; and *Human Society in Ethics and Politics* (1954), where Russell introduces the notion of "compossibility" of wills and interests as the key to a morally just society.

RUSSELL'S FIRST, UNSUCCESSFUL VENTURE INTO PUBLIC LIFE

Russell's first venture into the public arena was to stand for election in 1907 in Wimbledon division as a supporter of women's suffrage. The effort, against a well-established incumbent, was unsuccessful (as expected), and mired by incidents such as the following, as described by the *New York Times*: As Russell was being introduced at a meeting in Wimbledon, ruffians brought into disrupt the meeting responded with "guffaws, shouts, shrieks, catcalls, and toots on motor car horns."[8] When Russell rose to speak, a man who had been hurling insults through a megaphone shouted "Let 'em loose." The *Times* article continued: "That was the signal for the rats to make their debut in British politics. An instant latter forty whopping big fellows were scampering over the floor, terrorizing the audience, and especially the women. To say that the meeting adjourned in great disorder is an extremely

---

[6] These include *Analysis of Mind* (1921), *Analysis of Matter* (1927), *Inquiry into Truth and Meaning* (1940), and *Human Knowledge: Its Scope and Limits* (1948), all of which are summed up in his intellectual autobiography: *My Philosophical Development* (1959).
[7] The other component of what Russell terms the concrete component is his social philosophy, in particular his critique of both capitalism and communism as systems, and his defence of individual liberty and moderate socialism—topics which go beyond the scope of this paper.
[8] "Rats as Political Agents: Used Successfully to Break up Woman Suffrage Meeting," (*New York Times,* May 12, 1907).

conservative statement" (*ibid.*). Russell, in his *Autobiography*, reproduces a contemporary English newspaper report, which limits the number of rats to two (Russell 1967, 232).

But rats, whether two or twenty times that number, were small fare in comparison to the reception given Russell when he presented at a meeting called to celebrate the first (Menshevik) revolution in Russia in 1917. Russell describes his encounter with thugs (he calls "veragos") armed with wooden boards studded with rusty nails and led by army officers out of uniform. As the "veragos" disrupted the meeting, the attendees fled the hall, and Russell found himself pursued by two of the "veragos," while London police stood by and did not intervene.

> While I was wondering how one defended oneself against this type of attack, one of the ladies among us went up to the police and suggested that they should defend me. The police, however, merely shrugged their shoulders. "But he is an eminent philosopher", said the lady, and the police still shrugged. "But he is famous all over the world as a man of learning", she continued. The police remained unmoved. "But he is the brother of an earl", she finally cried. At this, the police rushed to my assistance. (Russell 1968, 27)

Russell continues that he was ultimately saved by a young woman who interposed herself between him and the thugs, and herself escaped without further injury. So much for Russell's first real forays into public life. He was again a candidate for public office in 1922 and once more in 1923, when he was an unsuccessful socialist candidate in the district of Chelsea.

RUSSELL AND THE GREAT WAR

But it was in matters concerning war and peace that Russell was to be most active, bringing to bear his philosophical abilities to analyze complex situations. Russell had become a pacifist as the result of a debate during the Boer War (1899-1902) with the French logician Louis Couturat (Blitz 2000). This aspect of his thinking was re-activated by the outbreak of war in August 1914. Russell's activities during the period 1914-1918 exposed him to more than veragos with nail-infested boards. When war broke out, Russell, along with other anti-war intellectuals, called for British neutrality. As Great Britain joined the war, Russell became a founding member of the

Union for Democratic Control (UDC) and then the No-Conscription Fellowship (NCF) after conscription was introduced in 1915. For his efforts Russell endured a series of sanctions by his university and the state. In June 1916, Russell was tried in the Mansion House, with Sir Charles Wakefield (the Lord Mayor of the City of London) as president, for a pamphlet he had written in April published by the NCF. The pamphlet supported Ernest Everett, a teacher who, as an absolute conscientious objector, had refused alternative service. Russell was charged with "impeding recruiting and discipline" in the armed forces, was found guilty and fined 100 pounds or 61 days in prison. Russell refused to pay, and his personal belongings, including over 1500 books, were seized. Friends put up 150 pounds to buy the books and his other belongings at auction.[9]

Subsequent to this conviction, the British government refused Russell a passport to lecture at Harvard, and the following month, on July 11, the Council of Trinity College dismissed him from his lectureship he held. In September of that year, Scotland Yard officers served Russell with an order forbidding him to enter prohibited areas where soldiers were quartered or munitions were produced, including a prohibition from going to the sea coast as well. This whole period of repression culminated in May of 1918, when Russell was tried for having written an article "The German Peace Offer," in which he suggested that US troops stationed in Europe might be used as strike breakers in the post-war period. Russell was accused of making statements "likely to prejudice his Majesty's relations with the United States of America," convicted, and sentenced to six months in jail in the second division (for common criminals); he ultimately served four and half months at Brixton Jail, in the first division (with improved living conditions; Clark 1975, 338-53).

Throughout all this, Russell persisted in his efforts to sensitize the public to the evil of war. As early as 1914, his "War: The Offspring of Fear" was published as a pamphlet, No. 3 in a series of anti-war publications by the UDC.[10] During 1914-1915, he published a series of articles in journals

---

[9] Russell's detailed defence, along with the prosecutor's charge by A. H. Bodkin, was published as *Rex v Bertrand Russell: Report of the Proceedings before the Lord Mayor at the Mansion House Justice Room 5 June 1916*, by the No-Conscription Fellowship. See also Clark (1975, 282-9).

[10] Other pamphlets published by the UDC included: *The Morrow of the War* (No. 1), a statement of the UDC policy against the war; Norman Angell's *Shall This War End German Militarism* (No. 2); and H. N. Brailsford's *The Origins of the Great War* (No. 4). It was a series of 10 pamphlets in all, each sold for the price of one penny.

and magazines, subsequently issue as the book *Justice in War Time* (1915). To enlarge his audience, he also delivered several series of lectures to the general public. One of these was held at Caxton Hall, London, delivered over the course of 8 Tuesday evenings from January to March of 1916, and subsequently published as *Principles of Social Reconstruction*. A second series of lectures was given in South Wales in June 1916, the first of which was attended by thousands of miners, and the second of which attracted an equally large number of steel workers.[11] In October 1916, he was to undertake a further series entitled "The World as It Can be Made," also directed at the general public, but was inhibited by the travel ban; these proposed lectures formed the basis for *Political Ideals*.[12] These were Russell's principal writings presented for and available to the general public,[13] about which the following may be noted.

War: The Offspring of Fear (1914)

Russell's first pamphlet about the Great War was issued in 1914 by The Union of Democratic Control. It likely appeared just a month after the war began, in September, as the latest reference in the text is to a *Times* article of Aug. 27; Britain had declared war on Germany on Aug. 4. The pamphlet is divided into sections presenting in turn the views of the "average citizen" in each country involved in the conflict, including Austrian, Russian, German, and Western (England, France, Belgium) viewpoints. (Turkey which entered the war on Oct. 28, is not included, so the pamphlet was surely published before that date.) Russell first presents the war as a conflict between Germans and Russians: "a great race conflict, a conflict of Teuton and Slav, in which certain other nations, England, France, and Belgium, have been led into co-operation with the Slav" (4-5). But this first

---

[11] Clark (1975, 294-7). Russell wrote *Introduction to Mathematical Philosophy* (1919) while in prison.

[22] Russell also gave a more theoretical course of lectures on his metaphysical system, "Philosophy of Logical Atomism," begun before his 1918 trial, which he completed after his conviction, but before he entered prison. The lectures were published in the academic journal *Monist*, and, much later, as a book.

[13] Russell wrote the first chapter, "General Statement of the Problem" of a volume entitled *I Appeal Unto Caesar*, subtitled "The Case of the Conscientious Objector," and credited as to authorship to Mrs. Henry Hobhouse, the wife of a prominent war resistor. Russell's co-authorship, including probable organization of the rest of the text, was kept secret. The book had four printings and some 18,000 copies were distributed. See Blackwell and Ruja (1994, II.342).

analysis is supplemented by two more: war as a failure of alliances, and, as the title of the pamphlet suggest, war as "the offspring of fear." Alliances entangle partners and draw them into conflicts stoked by the mutual fear of the antagonists. "If civilization is to continue, Europe must find a cure for this universal reign of fear with its consequence of mutual butchery" (11).

Russell proposed the creation of a League of Peace, which would promote mediation to resolve conflicts, and failing this, use force to restrain the party that refuses mediation, or the aggressor in the case where both refuse. Appropriately generalized, this could spell the end of war: "If a sufficient number of nations entered into such a League, they could make aggressive war obviously doomed to failure, and could thereby secure the cessation of war" (12). Failing such a post-war League, Russell recommended for Great Britain a policy of non-intervention in future European conflicts.

Justice in War-Time (1915)

Justice in War-Time first appeared as a paperbound pamphlet issued by the National Labour Press in England, with a preface by Russell dated Sept. 1915. Russell included six journal and magazine articles he had published during the first year of the war, including "An Appeal to the Intellectuals of Europe" to unite against the war, and "The Ethics of War." The latter essay defined four kinds of war—wars of colonization, wars of principle, wars of self-defence, and wars of prestige. Interestingly for a pacifist—in a sense only to be clarified by an article written during the following world war on "non-absolute pacifism"—Russell thought only one of these four was never justified: wars of prestige, under which he classified the Great War of 1914. Key to his analysis of the remaining three was his notion of "civilization," an issue which will recur in his analysis of the dangers during the World War II and the post-World War II environment. On Russell's view, wars of colonization were justified (in the past) if a "superior" civilization displaced an inferior one as a result. This notion of "higher" and "lower" was inherited from the Euro-centric anthropology of Russell's day, and would today be rejected by scholars of world cultures. Russell noted two instances of the second category, wars of principle, which he believed were also justified: the American Revolution for self-government and independence, and the Civil War, considered as a war against slavery. Russell felt that wars of self-defence could, in most cases, be better dealt with by passive resistance—refusal to cooperate with the invader. He recommended this policy to the British if Germany were to invade; although he felt that wars of self-defence could be justified, using the "higher" and "lower" criteria, if an inferior civilization invaded a superior one.

A second, expanded edition appeared in 1916 in the United States, with two added chapters: "The Danger to Civilization," of which Russell considered the current war to be an example, and a detailed analysis of "The Entente Policy, 1904-1915" in response to a criticism of Russell by his friend, Gilbert Murray. Two brief appendices, on Britain's relations with Belgium and France, were also added. The second US printing, dated 1917, included a "Publisher's Preface to the Second Edition," which featured "A Personal Statement" by Russell, detailing his reaction to the military order, dated Sept. 1, 1916, forbidding him from visiting prohibited areas near the sea coast, and in land locations where military production was centered, in addition to the previous refusal by the government to allow Russell to go to visit Harvard for a series of lectures, and his dismissal as a lecturer at Trinity College, Cambridge.

"The Philosophy of Pacifism" (1915)

Russell was one of the featured speakers at a Conference on the "Pacifist Philosophy of Life," held at Caxton Hall, London on July 8-9, 1915. Russell's talk was reprinted twice: in the edited volume of papers presented at the conference, and as the first pamphlet in a series of "Peace and Freedom Pamphlets," published by the League of Peace and Freedom, which organized the conference.[84] Russell repeated his arguments that war is the evil to be opposed, but added an important qualification to his argument that passive rather than armed resistance could overcome aggression. He noted that the success of passive resistance presupposed a degree of consciousness and organization then lacking in European populations, and he proposed an alternative means of preventing war: a world government empowered with a monopoly of the use of armed force:

> Nevertheless, it is hardly to be expected that progress will come in this way, because the imaginative effort required is too great. It is much more likely that it will come, as the reign of law within the State has come, by the establishment of a central government of the world, able and willing to secure obedience by force, because the great majority of men

will recognize that obedience is better than the present international anarchy. A central government of this kind will command assent, not as a partisan, but as the representative of the interests of the whole. Very soon resistance to it would seem to be hopeless, and wars would cease. Force directed by a central authority is not open to the same abuse, or likely to cause the same long-drawn conflicts, as force exercised by quarrelling nations, each of which is the judge in its own cause. Although I firmly believe that the adoption of passive instead of active resistance would be good if a nation could be convinced of its goodness, yet it is rather to the ultimate creation of a strong central authority that I should look for the ending of war. But war will only end after a great labour has been performed in altering men's moral ideals, directing them to the good of all mankind and not only of the separate nations into which men happen to have been born. (Russell 1915b)

While this conclusion appears in the edited volume, it was not included in the pamphlet. As there is no evidence that Russell changed his mind on world government—a point to which he returns throughout his life—the only conclusion is that this was done by the editors who presumably disagreed with him. Russell's pacifism was non-traditional in two ways: it allowed, exceptionally, for justified wars, such as Russell's subsequent support of the Allies in World War II, and it allowed for the use of force by a central, or world government, in contrast with traditional pacifist refusal to use force in any circumstances.

Political Ideals (1916)

"Political Ideals" was first issued as a 12-page pamphlet by the National Council for Civil Liberties in 1916, and was to be the first in a series of lectures entitled "The World as It Can be Made." Due to the prohibition on his movements having been extended to Glasgow, where the talk which formed the content of the pamphlet was to be delivered, it was read by Robert Smillie, President of the Miners' Federation." Russell revealed this interesting detail in the Foreward to the first British edition of the book as a whole—which appeared only in 1963! Russell expressed his protest against the restrictions imposed on him in the Foreword to the pamphlet:

> My profession hitherto has been that of a lecturer on mathematical logic. The government has forbidden me to fulfill an engagement to practice this profession at Harvard, and the Council of Trinity College have forbidden me to practice it in Cambridge. In these circumstances it became necessary for me to lecture on some more popular subject, and I prepared a course on the Philosophical Principles of Politics. Then came an order from the War Office which, using its power to deal with enemy aliens and potential spies, forbid me to enter any "prohibited area." As three of the towns in which my lectures were arranged are in prohibited areas, I cannot fulfill my engagements there. This is the first lecture of the proposed course. (Russell 1916b)

The American edition of the five lectures appeared as a hard bound book in September, 1917, with "Political Ideals" as the first chapter, and subsequent chapters on "Capitalism and the Wage System," "Pitfalls in Socialism," "Individual Liberty and Public Control," and "National Independence and Internationalism." It is of note that there is no chapter on war as such; nonetheless the government did its best to prevent its author from speaking to the public.

Principles of Social Reconstruction (1916)

The chapters of *Principles of Social Reconstruction* were written in 1915 and delivered as a series of eight lectures, in Caxton Hall, London, on consecutive Tuesdays from January 18–March 7, 1916 (and so actually preceded the lectures that made up *Political Ideals*, though this volume was published after it). *Principles of Social Reconstruction* deals explicitly with war in just one chapter, "War as an Institution." But by the time it was published (1917), Russell was well known in the United States as an anti-war campaigner, who had previously written a public letter to President Wilson in the hope that he would not only keep the US out of the war, but help to end it;[14] and so the American publisher retitled it *Why Men Fight: Proposed*

---

[14] As reported by the *New York Times* on page 1, the delivery of the note was dramatic: "Mysterious Girl Brings Russell's Peace Plea Here: Famous English Philosopher and Mathematician Asks Wilson to Stop War Ere Europe Perishes: Says Soldiers of All Armies Are Eager to Quit Fighting—Wilson's Duty Like Lincoln's" (*New York Times*, Dec. 23, 1916, 1). The article led the third column of page 1, in stark contrast to the main headline spread over columns 5-8: "Germany Likely to Submit Terms Asking Wilson to Act as Mediator: Must Push War, Says King George."

Measures to End the International Duel. In it Russell develops a model of human nature that he hopes will explain both why war occurs and how it can be prevented, and in that sense the American title highlights its essential content.

Russell's model of human nature was based on two factors: desire and impulse. Though in theoretical matters Russell privileged reason, in practical matters he considered reason to be secondary to the passions, of which he identified two components: desire and impulse. Desire is closer to reason in that it sets out a conscious goal; impulse is the spontaneous tendency to act in a certain, often stereotyped way, independently of any objective. It is closer to compulsion than to reason. Of the two passions, impulse usually trumps desire—that is to say, the spontaneous tendency (impulse) overshadows and even countermands the more thoughtful tendency (desire). Finally, within impulse, Russell identified two further components: the creative tendency responsible for knowledge and all that is good in life, and a possessive one, which in its destructive phase leads to war. It was the analysis of these tendencies underlying human nature which was to be the basis of Russell's philosophy of politics, essential to that part of his Tiergarten program which started from the concrete (in this case, world affairs) and rose to the abstract (a philosophy of politics):

> My aim is to suggest a philosophy of politics based upon the belief that impulse has more effect than conscious purpose in moulding men's lives. Most impulses may be divided into two groups, the possessive and the creative, according as they aim at acquiring or retaining something that cannot be shared, or at bringing into the world some valuable thing, such as knowledge or art or goodwill, in which there is no private property. (Russell 1916d)

Russell then proposed, basing himself in large part on William James' "The Moral Equivalent of War," that the destructive impulses be replaced by constructive ones, and that non-violent challenges be developed to replace the excitement of war.[15] This is a theme to which he returned in 1950 in his Nobel Prize speech, when, in the midst of the Korean War, he proposed that a constructive outlet for the excitement otherwise provided by war be found:

---

[15] Russell had favorably reviewed James' "Moral Equivalent of War;" the review is reprinted in *Collected Papers*, 6: 291.

In Australia, where people are few and rabbits are many, I watched a whole populace satisfying the primitive impulse in the primitive manner by the skillful slaughter of many thousands of rabbits. But in London or New York some other means must be found to gratify primitive impulse. I think every big town should contain artificial waterfalls that people could descend in very fragile canoes, and they should contain bathing pools full of mechanical sharks. Any person found advocating a preventive war should be condemned to two hours a day with these ingenious monsters. More seriously, pains should be taken to provide constructive outlets for the love of excitement. Nothing in the world is more exciting than a moment of sudden discovery or invention, and many more people are capable of experiencing such moments than is sometimes thought. (Russell 2010, 168)

Precisely how these "moral equivalents" of war could be developed on a scale large enough to end international armed conflict remains unresolved, but Russell's project is thereby still a live one: to find challenging alternatives that involve facing danger and exercising heroism, but that do not involve killing and maiming one's fellow humans.

FROM ABSOLUTE TO RELATIVE PACIFISM

During the 1920s, Russell largely devoted himself to the school he and his then-wife Dora Black ran, and to public speaking tours in the US to help finance the school, although at the same time he produced a large number of books, including sum-ups of his trips to Russia and China, volumes analyzing matter and mind, volumes on general philosophy, books popularizing the latest developments in physics, a volume on educational policy, and more.[16] During this decade, war was not on the immediate horizon,

---

[16] See *The Practice and Theory of Bolshevism* (1920) and *The Problem of China* (1922). Among other volumes published in this period Russell produced the two "Analysis" volumes applying neutral monism—*Analysis of Mind* (1921) and *Analysis of Matter* (1927)—as well as two "ABC" books popularizing science—*ABC of Atoms* (1923) and *ABC of Relativity* (1925). In philosophy he published *An Outline of Philosophy* (1927) and *Sceptical Essays* (1928), as well as a second edition of *Our Knowledge of the External World* (1929). He also published two books on social issues—*On Education Especially in Early Childhood* (1926), based in large part on the work at the school he and Dora Russell had run, and *Marriage and Morals* (1929), the volume that would be cited by those who refused him permission to teach at City College of New York in the early 1940s.

but the Great Depression at its end ushered in a new period of international conflict, and in the 1930s, Russell foresaw and dreaded the outbreak of another world war. He advocated, for the first and only time, in *Which Way to Peace?* (1936) that individuals refuse to participate in any European war, a position he was to soon modify. A major motivating factor was Russell's belief that aerial warfare had developed to the point that bombardment of cities would be fatal to civilization—something to be avoided at all costs. The book concluded with the following appeal (in all-capitals) to individual, absolute pacifism, with the only proviso that the policy was intended to be applied to wars among "civilized states," an important qualification for Russell's subsequent change of position during World War II:

> TO ABSTAIN FROM FIGHTING, AND FROM ALL VOLUNTARY PARTICIPATION IN WAR BETWEEN CIVILIZED STATES; TO USE EVERY EFFORT TO PERSUADE OTHERS TO DO LIKEWISE; TO BRING ALL POSSIBLE INFLUENCE TO BEAR TO PREVENT PARTICIPATION OF HIS COUNTRY IN WAR; AND, WITHIN THE LIMITS OF HIS CAPACITY, TO AIM AT SIMILAR RESULTS IN OTHER COUNTRIES ALSO. (Russell 1936b, 223)

In order to achieve wider circulation for the book, the publisher, Michael Joseph, issued the concluding chapter 12 as a separate pamphlet, in which the above quote again featured prominently, as the next-to-last paragraph of the book. The publisher's note introducing the pamphlet stated "In order that *Which Way to Peace?* may be assured the widest possible circulation, we have taken the unusual course of arranging this special printing of one of its important chapters for free distribution" (Russell 1936b). The table of contents and an order form preceded the reproduction in full of the concluding chapter.

Russell modified this position once World War II broke out to what he termed "relative, political pacifism": allowing for war against an enemy that is a threat to civilization itself (a position he shared with Albert Einstein, who also broke with his pacifism at this time). This was, in a sense, a return to Russell's position in *Justice in War-Time*: some wars are justified, though Russell was now more restrictive in the sort of wars falling under that category—only defensive wars against an enemy so ferocious that it aimed not merely at territorial gain or occupation, but the extinction of one's civilization (or in Einstein version of the doctrine, destruction of one's people—genocide).[17] As a result Russell did not allow *Which Way to Peace?* to be reprinted. Russell now saw Nazi Germany as a threat to civilization, and also recognized that aerial bombardment could be survived, as instanced by the resistance of the British RAF and the London population to the Luftwaffe attack. In a letter to the editor to the *New York Times* in 1941,[18] and in a more theoretical article in 1943. Russell returned to the position akin to that he held in *Justice in War-Time* during World War I: war is an evil to be avoided, but some wars are justified—in particular, self-defence against an attack by an enemy of civilization (in this case, the Nazis).

> I think myself that the most useful kind of pacifism, and also the one most likely to become influential, is *relative political pacifism*. According to this view, there are causes, but only a very few, for which it is worth while to fight; but whatever the cause, and however justifiable the war, war brings about such great evils that it is of immense importance to find ways short of war in which the things worth fighting for can be secured. I think it is worth while to prevent England or America being conquered by the Nazis, but it would be far better if this end could be secured without war (Russell 1943-44, 8-9; italics added).

After World War II, Russell, with the defeat of Nazi Germany followed by the rise of the Soviet empire over Eastern Europe, took a decidedly anti-Soviet position, believing that Stalin had replaced Hitler as the main threat to civilization. He expressed this privately in letters to his friends immediately after the conclusion of the war in Europe, and he made a speech at the Westminster School in 1948 during which he considered, though I argue elsewhere, did not advocate, a preventive war against the Soviet Union (Blitz 2002). But the mere mention as a possibility was enough for many to consider that he did propose the atom-bombing of the Soviet Union before it achieved a nuclear weapon of its own, a controversy which probably denied him a Nobel Peace Prize for his subsequent work.

---

[17] See Blitz, David (2000) "Russell, Einstein and the Philosophy of Non-Absolute Pacifism," *Russell: the Journal of Bertrand Russell Studies*: Vol. 20: 2, Article 3.
[18] "Long-Time Advocate of Peace Approves Present War," *New York Times*, 16 Feb., 1941, sec. 4, 8. The title was provided by the *Times*, which subtitled the nearly page-long letter, "Professor Bertrand Russell States Reasons for Changing Position."

Nonetheless, this controversy indicates just how far, at least as a possibility, Russell's non-absolute pacifism could go. Just as in his "Ethics of War," Russell had countenanced past colonial wars so long as they represented a victory for European civilization, Russell now countenanced the possibility of a war against the Soviet Union if it continued its aggressive behavior. But to the general public, Russell's qualifications, always preceded by the logician's "if," were stripped of this conditional, and appeared as a direct call and advocacy war with the USSR, including the use of atom bombs. This controversy dogged Russell throughout the 1950s.

THE DANGER OF NUCLEAR WAR

Russell's next (and last) phase as a public intellectual on war and peace was prompted by the development of the H-bomb. Russell had not openly objected to the use of the A-bomb at Hiroshima and Nagasaki at the time, but in an address to the House of Lords in 1945, to which he had been named after the death of his brother in 1931, he had foreseen the development of an even more deadly weapon—the H bomb.[19] Whereas the A-bomb could destroy a city, an H-bomb war could devastate whole countries, and through residual radiation, all of humanity. After the death of a Japanese fisherman due to the secondary effects of radiation poisoning in 1954, Russell addressed the British public and the world in his famous BBC broadcast of December 23: "Man's Peril," in which he formulated his slogan for the survival of the human race: "Remember your humanity and forget the rest."[20]

Following on this address, Russell was instrumental in organizing the Russell-Einstein Manifesto against War, and was a co-founder of both the Campaign for Nuclear Disarmament (CND) and subsequently, the direct action Committee of One Hundred. The CND inaugurated regular marches to Aldermaston, where the US stocked nuclear weapons in Britain. When this form of protest became routinized and ineffective, Russell, along with

---

[19] Russell, "The International Situation," Hansard, House of Lords, v. 138 (28 November 1945).
[20] The talk, delivered on Dec. 23, 1954, was widely distributed as a 4-page pamphlet, by the Friends Peace Committee; in the US it also appeared as the cover article in the April 2, 1955 issue of *Saturday Review*, entitled "Man's Duel with the Hydrogen Bomb," along with a photo of a pensive Russell holding his pipe. See Russell (2003, 82-89).

much younger associates, created the Committee of One Hundred. The campaign of civil disobedience that ensued, including Russell's use of a microphone to address a rally in Hyde Park, led in September 1961 to Russell (along with dozens of others in the Committee) being charged with inciting a public disturbance. Both Russell and his wife Edith were sentenced to two months in prison, reduced to one week after an appeal was lodged concerning his and his wife's medical conditions. But whether in jail or out, Russell, as he did during the First World War, produced a series of books on the problems of war and peace, all directed to the general public.

The first of these was a collection of letters between Russell, Khruschev and Dulles on the issue of nuclear disarmament that first appeared in the *New Statesman* and was reproduced as the *Vital Letters of Russell, Khruschev, Dulles* (1958). The others, save one, are entirely texts by Russell, for which we have his handwritten manuscripts. The exception is the last, *War Crimes in Vietnam* (1967), for which only a typescript in large font exists, and was most likely approved, but not exclusively written, by Russell. Three of the books were issued as special publications: *Common Sense and Nuclear Warfare* (1959) was given expedited publication by Allen and Unwin, and *Has Man a Future?* (1961) and *Unarmed Victory* (1963) appeared first as Penguin Specials. A sixth volume: *Bertrand Russell Speaks his Mind* (1960) was the transcript of a series of 13 films Russell made in 1959. Included during this period is Russell's shortest publication: a single sentence constituting the whole of a very brief *History of the World in Epitome* (1962)—a facetious text on a serious topic: nuclear Armageddon. All were directed to the general public and each expresses another component of Russell's philosophy of politics.

Vital Letters of Russell, Khruschev, Dulles (1958)

In late October of 1957 (following the founding of the CND) one of its leaders, the author J. B. "Jack" Priestley, wrote an article entitled "Britain and the H-Bomb," which the *New Statesman* immediately published. Kingsley Martin, the editor of the *New Statesman,* sent Russell a note to this effect on October 24, asking whether he "would like to follow it up in any way, by article or letter."[21] Russell immediately contributed a short letter supporting

---

[21] All letter citations are from material in the Bertrand Russell Archives at McMaster University.

Priestley, adding a few points in support of the policy calling for Britain to reconsider its policy of producing nuclear bombs, as part of a more general correspondence with other respondents. Martin reported to Russell on November 7 that these would be published as a pamphlet.

This got Russell thinking of a more significant statement that he could make to provide further momentum to the issue. On November 18, 1957 he sent Martin a letter with an enclosure: "I enclose what purports to be an open letter to Khruschev and Eisenhower and I shall be very glad if you are willing to print it. I should not wish to be paid for it, but should wish to retain the right to let anybody in any country re-print it…" This was unusual, the more so that it was gratis, and Martin reacted appropriately, noting in his response to Russell, "I was delighted to get your article; it arrived on Wednesday morning in time for us very cheerfully to pull the paper to pieces so that your open letter could be given proper prominence" (Martin to Russell, 21 Nov. 1957). He added, as only a publisher might, "I am taking you at your word about not wishing payment," and granted him the right to reprint it as desired.

Thus began an interesting exchange. Russell's open letter generated a reply from Khruschev, which forced Eisenhower to have his Secretary of State, John Foster Dulles, respond to both Russell and Khruschev. This prompted a second reply from Mr. K, never a man to be short on words, and a final sum-up by Russell—five letters in all. The letters were printed soon after in book form as *Vital Letters of Russell, Khruschev, Dulles* by the London publisher McGibbon and Kee, with an introduction by Kinglsey Martin and a cartoon by Vicky.

Russell began his letter to Khruschev and Dulles "Most Potent Sirs," more in reference to their possession of nuclear bombs than to any intellectual prowess, and called for the two to "meet in a frank discussion of the conditions of co-existence, endeavoring no longer to secure this or that more or less surreptitious advantage for your side, but seeking rather for such agreements and such adjustments in the world as will diminish future occasions of strife" (Russell 1958, 19). This would be the leitmotif of Russell's subsequent campaign. And he concluded, "I believe that if you were to do this the world would acclaim your action, and the forces of sanity, released from their long bondage, would ensure for the years to come a life of vigour and achievement and joy surpassing anything known in even the happiest eras of the past" (*ibid.*).

Khruschev and Dulles maintained their respective government's position, largely of critique of the other side, but the key thing was that they responded. For Russell, this was a first step in engaging a process of reduction in world tensions leading to nuclear disarmament, and the ultimate goal of the abolition of war.

Martin was quite pleased when Khruschev did in fact reply—more free copy, and from the head of one of the two superpowers! In his letter of December 13, 1957 to Russell he was more sanguine about prospects of a response from the other superpower leader: "I may add that I am not hopeful of receiving a reply from Eisenhower!" In a letter of March 12, he indicated that he had "put out feelers to Tito and Truman as possible participants in the correspondence"; this did not occur. However, as noted above, Dulles did respond on Eisenhower's behalf.

Following Khruschev's second response, Russell in his second letter concluded that "Mr. Khruschev and Mr. Dulles appear as rival fanatics, each blinded to obvious facts by mental blinkers" (Russell 1958, 73), though he went on to say "Although the letters of Mr. Dulles and Mr. Khruschev are not such as we might hope from men conscious of holding the future of mankind in their hands, they do, nevertheless afford some substantial grounds for hope," which Russell found in each side's contention that it would not be the first to launch an unprovoked nuclear attack against the other, though of course, each suspected that the other side might (*ibid.*). In the end, Russell appealed to ordinary Americans and Russians, as well as citizens of the rest of the world, to deal with the nuclear peril in a rational way by forgoing military solutions to the East-West divide.

In private, Russell was more to the point. In his letter to Martin accompanying his sum-up of the debate with Khruschev and Dulles, Russell noted, "It is awful that the continued existence of the human race should be dependent upon the whims of a pair of nincompoops" (Russell to Martin, March 24, 1958).

Common Sense and Nuclear Warfare (1959)

Russell spent the early part of 1958, among other things, preparing his intellectual autobiography, *My Philosophical Development,* for publication. In April he sent in a blurb, as requested by the publisher. By July the work was in press, but Russell then brought up the matter of including as a preface material written by Alan Wood for an intellectual biography of Russell, which remained unpublished at the time of Wood's death. For technical reasons the posthumous publication was included as an appendix, but what is of interest is that in the midst of negotiating this addition, on November 6, 1958 Russell wrote to his publisher George Unwin to announce an additional piece of news: he had just completed another book, unannounced, that he wished Unwin to publish as soon as possible, without royalties in exchange for a lower price that would make the book widely available. Moreover, the typescript was enclosed!

> I have written a very short book (some 21,000 words) which I am calling *Common Sense and Nuclear Warfare*, though I am open to suggestions for a more attractive title, and the typescript of which I am enclosing with this. The book is topical and propagandist and is intended to appeal equally to the East and the West. I have endeavored to avoid anything showing a bias either way and I hope that its arguments may not fail to make an appeal in Communist countries as well as in the West. I should like to see the book published, not only in England and Ameridca, but also in various Western European countries and, if possible, in Russia. As my object is to persuade as many people as possible, I should like the book to come out quickly and cheaply. I am quite willing to forgo all royalties if that will lower the price. (Russell to Unwin, November 6, 1958)

Just as Kingsley Martin of the *New Statesman* could not turn down a free Russell paper, Unwin, Russell's longtime British publisher, made every effort to accommodate a royalty-free book; he did suggest, though, that the paperback be published at an "un-economic" price, but that the hardback, intended for libraries, carry a minimal royalty. Unwin also agreed to send the book to press immediately, without waiting for a specimen page or cost estimate. Russell was pleased, and on November 11, five days after announcing the existence of the book, he sent a blurb for its back cover to Unwin: "The purpose of this book is to suggest that the danger of nuclear war is not one which is due to hostility of the West towards the East or of the East towards the West, but is a common peril of both sides, and indeed, of all mankind. A common peril calls for a common defense." And Russell went on to propose a series of tension-reducing measures which amount to a philosophy of a sort, namely, a philosophy of conflict resolution.

The book can be traced back in Russell's notes to a rough draft entitled "The Nuclear Peril," dated July 26, 1958, which was subsequently renamed to *Common Sense and Nuclear Warfare*. From manuscripts in Edith's handwriting, it can be seen that Russell dictated the work beginning August 29, and completed it on November 3, producing a total of 21,275 words exclusive of the table of contents and book list of suggested readings at the end.

A number of aspects of this work are noteworthy, which make it the centerpiece of the little book series for several reasons.

The most important reason is what can be termed the philosophy of conflict resolution that Russell proposes. After setting out the disastrous consequences of brinkmanship and the nuclear war to which it leads, Russell devoted the central chapters to "Methods of Settling Disputes in the Nuclear Age," "Program of Steps Towards Peace," "New Outlook Needed before Negotiations," and "Steps Towards Conciliation." True to conflict resolution principles and his stated goal, Russell adhered to a strictly neutral position as between the contending powers. He proposed psychological measures, such as abandoning mutual fear and suspicion of bad faith; political measures, such as a committee of reconciliation made up of neutral powers such as India to act as intermediaries and a world authority to ultimately assure compliance; military measures, such as the abolition of nuclear tests, mutual inspection and step by step disarmament.

Russell was up-to-date in his readings and references. The 13 volumes referenced in the "Books Recommended" section were all published in 1958, including Russell's own *Vital Letters*, the Resolutions of the Third Pugwash Conference, a book by Seymour Melman on nuclear inspection, Linus Pauling's *No More War*, and Antoinette Pirie's book on fallout. Russell carefully read each book, as is evidenced by the marginal lines he drew in each at interesting passages, and the list of such highlightings on the back cover of each volume that he added so that he could return to these passages later, as he wrote his own work.[22]

Russell included two Appendices, dealing with misconstruals of his positions. The first was on "Unilateral Disarmament," where he pointed out that he argued for unilateral disarmament for Great Britain alone, not either

---

[22] These volumes can all be found in Russell's library at the McMaster University Archives, and I recommend a pleasant afternoon or two for any visitor there recreating Russell's intellectual readings for that year.

the US and the USSR alone. In particular, he quite correctly denied having called for US unilateral disarmament. Nuclear arms for Great Britain made no sense, as they could not be used to defend the country and only made it a target for the USSR in the event of war with the US. However, it was only as a result of mutual disarmament and a negotiated process that Russell hoped for the bilateral disarmament of the two superpowers.

The claim that Russell preferred to be "red than dead," while his US critics preferred the reverse, is incorrect. Russell did state that if one or the other superpower were intent on war and could not be stopped, that it was rational for the other to concede and prefer temporary conquest to immediate bilateral destruction. But this had two caveats. First, it applied to the USSR relative to the US as well, so that the Russians should prefer "better yanks than dead"; Second, Russell hoped that the rational strategy of conflict resolution he proposed would prevent this situation arising.

The second Appendix dealt with the charge of "Inconsistency"—that Russell had previously, in the 1945-1953 period, advocated attacking the USSR (the opposite of the claim he was now charged with having in the first Appendix). Russell stated, referring to the period of the Baruch proposal for nuclear disarmament, which he considered both "wise and generous," that "I thought, at that time, that it would be worth while to bring pressure to bear upon Russia, and even, if necessary, to go so far as to threaten war on the sole issue of the internationalizing of atomic weapons. My aim, then as now, was to prevent a war in which both sides possessed the power of producing world-wide disaster" (Russell 1959, 89-90).

But Russell pointed out that times had changed and that a new and very different strategy was needed. Two key events stood out: Stalin, an intransigent dictator, had died; and the H-bomb, far more powerful than the A-bomb, had been developed. Russell's policy changed with the times, which he considered both rational and insane. "To achieve a single purpose, sane men adapt their policies to the circumstances. Those do who not are insane" (Russell 1959, 91).

Russell launched a mini-campaign to distribute his book as widely as possible among influential politicians in the West and the East. A preliminary list was prepared for Unwin by Ritchie Calder, to which Russell added names, including all the authors mentioned in his suggested readings, Khruschev, Tito and Gomulka, as well as Nehru, Sukarno, Dulles, Gaitskell and Bevan in the Labor Party, and Lord Samuel, his close friend in the House of Lords.

Manchester Talk for CND (1959)

Russell did not limit his efforts to inform and mobilize the public to the written word. He delivered public speeches, and used the film and TV media to reach them, besides BBC radio, a medium he had used since the 1930s.[23] This and the following section illustrate Russell in public and on film. By this time, Russell was active in the Campaign for Nuclear Disarmament, and addressed one of the first rallies of the group, in Manchester for May Day (May 1) 1959.[24] He read his text, but responded as follows when he was interrupted by a heckler just over 14 minutes into the talk (notes in square brackets are added to indicate surrounding sounds):

> BR: "...It's a terrible thing about governments, that they will not believe the things that are necessary to believe if you are going to take sane measures to prevent this appalling holocaust with which we are threatened. We..."
>
> *[Interruption by heckler]*
>
> Heckler: "You support atheistic communism. Bertrand Russell, you are a traitor." *[Commotion in the hall. BR asks for the comment to be repeated by a member of the hosting committee.]*
>
> BR: "Oh yes, a traitor. Quite so."
>
> *[Laughter, applause from the audience.]*
>
> BR *[raising his voice]*: "Who do you think is the greater traitor: the man who wishes to see some people left alive in this country, or the man who pursues a policy that means that they must all die?" *[applause]* "No, if there are any traitors, it is the people who want us to go on with this suicidal policy, not the people who want it stopped" (14:39 to 15:41).

Russell returned to the issue raised by the heckler later in his talk:

> Some people say, and I daresay the gentleman who accused me of being a traitor might be one of them; some people say it's a cowardly thing to want to survive; heroes face

---

[23] See Blitz (2004).
[24] "Speech at Manchester," Bertrand Russell Archives, RA3: 0919.

death with equanimity; they don't mind dying for cause. Well now, I am prepared to die for a cause if it's going to do any good, but I don't quite see—I don't quite see—the nobility of saying everybody else is to die too. *[applause over unidentifiable comment by heckler]* (16:31 to 17:09)

Bertrand Russell Speaks His Mind (1960)

This volume, published in 1960, is the transcript of a series of 13 films, each 15 minutes long, made in 1959. The number 13 was chosen as this would fit into the three month scheduling typical of TV networks at the time (a quarter of a year). In December of that year, Nick Caris Carter, an independent film producer, proposed to Russell a series of programs on his "personality and philosophy." Carter, referring to Russell's *Common Sense and Nuclear Warfare*, proposed that TV would allow Russell to reach a "wider public at home and abroad" (Carter to Russell, 1 Dec. 1958). Russell responded that he was interested, especially as it would afford him the opportunity to speak about the danger of nuclear warfare even though he agreed to discuss other matters, which he considered as secondary. In short order, Russell and Carter agreed to a series of films, to be made over the incredibly brief period of two weeks with Woodrow Wyatt, then a Labour MP, as the interviewer.

The result was a series of 13 films, each, each 15 minutes long, all of them filmed over the period of a week, one each morning and one each afternoon, in April 1959. Of these, four were immediately shown on the BBC, although the bulk were made available to the reading public in *Bertrand Russell Speaks His Mind*. Of the 13 films, two dealt with war-related topics, "War and Pacifism" (3) and the "H-Bomb" (12), though Russell was able to set out his views on topics including "Philosophy" (1), "Religion" (2), "Communism and Capitalism" (4), "Taboo Morality" (5), "Power" (6), "Happiness" (7), "Nationalism" (8), "Great Britain" (9), "The Role of the Individual" (10), "Fanaticism and Tolerance" (11), and (13) "The Possible Future of Mankind." Russell broke no new ground in the series, but it was his most intensive use of the medium of film.

Nor was this Russell's first venture on television. He had been interviewed by John Freeman on BBC in December 1958, during which he addressed the supposed inconsistency of his views on war and peace; but this would be the first series of interviews on topics agreed upon in advance.

A series of letters between Russell and Wyatt in February of 1959 discussed both the topics to be discussed, and the payment to Russell for his effort. The Wyatt interviews constituted one of two series of interviews Russell filmed; the other was a set of three interviews with the socialist theorist Ralph Miliband in 1965, when Russell was 93 years old. The interviews were entitled "War and Peace," "Wealth and Poverty," and "Man and the Twentieth Century."

Has Man a Future? (1961)

Russell's campaign against nuclear war continued through the CND and then the Committee of 100, whose sit-down demonstrations had begun in February 1961. This was in the immediate background to a March 7, 1961, letter from A. Godwin, Chief Editor of Penguin Books: "I should like to interest you in writing for us a brief Penguin Special, the starting point of which would, of course, be your present campaign for non-violent resistance in the cause of nuclear disarmament." Russell was interested, and Godwin arranged a meeting with Dieter Pevsner, editor for the Penguin Specials—topical, mass-produced, cheap books of just the sort Russell was interested. Russell and Pevsner met on March 27, and Russell agreed to a volume entitled *Has Man a Future?*, the first of two Penguin specials by Russell in the little book series. The book was to be 35,000 words, about 120 pages, to be sold at 2s6d, with a £300 fixed sum royalty on the first printing, and 7.5 percent on any subsequent printing.

Has Man a Future? is more expository, and somewhat longer as a result than *Common Sense and Nuclear Warfare.* It explains the background to the A-bomb and the H-bomb and lays out steps towards eliminating their danger, as well as further steps towards solving territorial disputes. It also argues in favor of world government, with a hopeful chapter on what a stable, post-nuclear world might look like:

> Man can look forward to a future immeasurably longer than his past, inspired by a new breath of vision, a perpetual hope fed by a continuing achievement. Man has made a beginning creditable for an infant—for, in a biological sense, Man, the latest of species, is still an infant. No limit can be set to what he may achieve in the future. I see in my mind's eye, a world of glory and joy, a world where minds expand, where hope remains undimmed, and what is noble is no

longer condemned as treachery to this or that paltry aim. All this can happen if we will let it happen. It rests with our generation to decide between this vision and an end decreed by folly (127).

History of the World in Epitome (1962)

In 1962, the shortest separate publication by Russell appeared, on the theme of the folly of nuclear war, entitled *History of the World in Epitome* and subtitled *For Use in Martian Infant Schools*. Printed on gold colored paper as a small, stapled pamphlet, it was illustrated by two line drawings by Franiszka Themerson and an image of a the cloud rising from a nuclear bomb. The text consisted of the single sentence, "Since Adam and Eve ate the apple, man has never refrained from any folly of which he was capable," followed by the ominous "The End."

Besides its brevity (and in fact because of it) this anti-nuclear pamphlet, issued on the occasion of Russell's 90th birthday, holds two further distinctions. First, the complete text was first published some two years earlier in the *Hartford Courant* newspaper in Connecticut, when Mrs. Stephanie May, an anti-war activist (identified by the *Courant* as a "Bloomfield housewife") returned from a visit to England, having met Russell. The *Courant* stated, "She brought with her a copy of an unpublished manuscript of a history of the world by one of the world's most influential philosophers and educators, Lord Bertrand Russell,"[25] followed by a reproduction of the complete text, making this the first publication of the pamphlet. Secondly, the full sentence appeared as part of the cover of Norman Cousins' *In Place of Folly* (1961), where it occupies the top third of the cover page of the paperbound edition.

Unarmed Victory (1963)

Russell's second Penguin special appeared in 1963, this time at Russell's request. A lot had happened since the appearance of the first book. In September 1961 Russell and Lady Russell had been sentenced to two months in jail, commuted for medical reasons to one week, for a sit-down and march in August commemorating the A-bombing of Japan. But more

---

[25] Barbara Carolson, "Bloomfield Mays Home from Anti-Nuclear Trip," *Hartford Courant*, May 13, 1960, pg. 8A.

importantly, in October 1962 the Cuban Missile Crisis occurred. Less noticed but also ominous was the China-India Border dispute in the following month. Russell wanted to sum up the experience of the two latter disputes, in which he had played a role through telegrams to world leaders at the time. A meeting with Dieter Pevsner in early December 1962 led to an agreement for a 40,000-word volume, to be called *Unarmed Victory*, in which Russell would set out the lessons of the Cuban crisis, along with those of the Chinese/Indian dispute. Proofs were sent by March 6, 1963 and the book came out in paperback from Penguin and hardcover from Unwin at the end of that month.

The manuscript for *Unarmed Victory* in the Russell archive consists of three component parts: 1) original typescript material with handwritten corrections, 2) reproductions of telegrams sent to and from Russell, especially to Khruschev and Kennedy, and from the former (but not the latter), during the Cuban Crisis; and 3) telegrams from Russell to Nehru and Chou En-Lai during the Border Dispute; along with handwritten material (in Edith Russell's hand), especially for the conclusion. The book was in part a collection of statements, with historical details added, as well as a general conclusion along the lines of previous volumes about steps to take to avoid nuclear war.

The most interesting principle of note was Russell's view that the "winner" in these disputes, or rather the more praiseworthy protagonist, is the side that backs down first. Russell did not wish to conclude who was "just" in first acting or responding, as the case may be; he was not concerned with the niceties of just cause. Rather, he assumed conflicts would from time to time arise, with various degrees of blame and injury on each side. What counted was the side that first opted for conflict resolution. In that sense, Russell praised Khrushev for backing down and withdrawing the missiles from Cuba, and he praised China for unilaterally withdrawing from Indian territory. This was, like his previous pronouncements on the Soviet Union in the immediate post-world war period, and his views on unilateral disarmament post 1955, immediately misunderstood by many commentators, especially in the West, who now were convinced that Russell sided with the Reds, having supported Khruschev and Castro in their most recent adventures. This, given the underlying principle of conflict resolution, is quite wrong as an understanding of what motivated Russell.

War Crimes in Vietnam (1967)

The last of the little books is the most controversial, namely the 1967 *War Crimes in Vietnam*. Unlike previous volumes, there is only a typescript in the Russell archives for this one, with no handwritten sections; the typescript is in large type, different from the normal type of previous ones as well; and the final typescript was submitted to the publisher by Christopher Farley, one of Russell's assistants, not Russell directly. The question arises as to how much of the book was Russell's and how much was due to his assistants, including Ralph Schoenman, who wrote the Appendix on North Vietnam. Some have suggested that Russell had been entirely manipulated by his young associates, who were responsible for his supposed one-sided support of the North Vietnamese and National Liberation Front, and his sharp critiques of the Labour Party under Wilson for collaboration with the US war of President Johnson. This is not the case.

It can be surmised from the typescript and the detailed content of many of the chapters, that the book was largely written for Russell, who presumably approved it, reading it in the large-font type. But the sentiments are those of Russell, and however authorship of one page or another may ultimately be attributed, the design was his. Here is Russell, in a speech on "Vietnam Victory" from this same time period:

> And yet despite all this, despite the fact that the US is the most powerful military force the world has ever known, despite the fact that her air force is not equaled and her sea power is not hampered; despite the fact that the automatic weapons in the hands of her soldiers fire several hundred rounds of bullets per minute; despite the fact that the Vietnamese are an agrarian people, with very little industry, these people, like the Greeks at Marathon, have defeated a great and cruel colossus. When I think back to 1940 during the blitz and recall the mood of Englishmen at that time, I know clearly and without hesitation what our responsibility to the Vietnamese is. Do you remember our feelings when the Nazis were bombing our cities? Do you recall the determination which swept Britain never to surrender and never to accept a Nazi occupation of our country? Did we suffer gas and chemicals at that time? Was our country cut in half? Were our people in concentration camps? Was our countryside raised with gas, chemicals

and jelly gasoline and fragmentary/fragmented bombs? No, none of this occurred. And yet Churchill spoke for all of us when he declared that we would fight on the beaches, that we would never surrender. I should like this conference to declare its fervent hope for the victory of the people of Vietnam, total, unequivocal and swift.[26]

These are the sentiments expressed in *War Crimes in Vietnam*, but here in what is incontrovertibly Russell's own words, diction, and framework. Russell, in the last of his little books, had come back to yet another of his principles, that of the non-absolute nature of pacifism, in favoring the military victory of the Vietnamese over an aggressor which had not only assaulted their territory, but also destroyed their homes and indiscriminately killed their population. In justifying this appeal Russell went back to Churchill, World War II, and the all-out fight, which Russell supported, against a similar aggressor at that time.

CONCLUSION

In conclusion, Russell's activities as a public intellectual on the issue of war and peace passed through a number of phases:

1. *Opposition to World War I:* For his opposition to the war, Russell was dismissed from his university position, prohibited from travelling freely in his own country, refused a passport to travel abroad, fined and then sentenced to jail. During this time he produced books and pamphlets directed at the public on the causes of war, freedom during time of war, political ideals, human nature and its relation to war, and a vision for social reconstruction after the war.

2. *Interwar Period and World War II:* As World War II approached, Russell adopted a position of personal, absolute pacifism; but with the outbreak of World War II, he modified this significantly to allow, exceptionally, for justified wars against an enemy aiming at the destruction of civilization. Following the war, he transferred his determination to fight the Nazis to an opposition to the Soviet Union under Stalin that was so fierce that he appeared to advocate a preventive nuclear attack on Russia.

3. *Cold War and the Nuclear Threat:* Russell slowly increased his opposition to the United States, which reached a crescendo over the war in

---

[26] "Vietnam Victory," Bertrand Russell Archives (RA 3496, from 4:17 to 6:20).

Vietnam. After the explosion of the H-bomb Russell began to advocate for the elimination of nuclear weapons and in order to achieve this, of war itself. His actions included the Russell-Einstein Manifesto, the Campaign for Nuclear Disarmament and the Committee of 100. During this period Russell produced no fewer than half a dozen "little" books on current dangers and proposals for disarmament and conflict resolution.

In all these phases, through various modifications of his position, Russell remained, at great personal cost, a public intellectual on issues of war and peace. His words bear careful examination even today, as the world goes through a new cycle of war, that if improperly resolved can only lead to more death and destruction, but if resolved properly, can lead to more permanent peace, the essential condition for social justice and human happiness as Russell envisaged them.

Bibliography

Blackwell, Kenneth. 1985. *The Spinozistic Ethics of Bertrand Russell*. London: George Allen and Unwin.

Blackwell, Kenneth and Ruja, Harry. 1994. *A Bibliography of Bertrand Russell.* 3 volumes. New York: Routledge.

Blitz, David. 2000. "Russell and the Boer War: From Imperialist to Anti-Imperialist." *Russell* n.s. 19 (2): 117-42.

Blitz, David. 2002. "Did Russell Advocate Preventive Atomic War against the USSR?" *Russell* n.s. 22 (1): 5-45.

Blitz, David. 2004. "Seeing and Hearing Russell." *Bertrand Russell Research Centre Newsletter* 3 (Autumn): 4.

Clark, Ronald W. 1975. *The Life of Bertrand Russell.* New York: Alfred A. Knopf.

Griffin, Nicholas. 1991. *Russell's Idealistic Apprenticeship.* New York: Oxford University Press.

Monk, Ray. 1996. *Bertrand Russell: The Spirit of Solitude 1872-1921.* New York: The Free Press.

Monk, Ray. 2000. *Bertrand Russell: The Ghost of Madness 1921-1970*. London: Jonathan Cape.

Russell, Bertrand. 1914. *War: The Offspring of Fear.* London: The Union of Democratic Control.

Russell, Bertrand. 1915. *Justice in War-Time.* Manchester and London: The National Labour Press.

Russell, Bertrand. 1916a. *Justice in War-Time.* 2nd ed. Chicago: The Open Court Publishing Company.

Russell, Bertrand. 1916b. *The Philosophy of Pacifism.* London: League of Peace and Freedom.

Russell, Bertrand. 1916c. *Political Ideals.* Salisbury: The National Council for Civil Liberties.

Russell, Bertrand. 1916d. *Principles of Social Reconstruction.* London: George Allen and Unwin.

Russell, Bertrand. 1917. *Why Men Fight: A Method of Abolishing the International Duel.* New York: The Century Co.

Russell, Bertrand. 1936a. "A Reprint of Chapter 12 from *Which Way to Peace?* by Bertrand Russell." London: Michael Joseph Ltd.

Russell, Bertrand. 1936b. *Why Way to Peace?* London: Michael Joseph Ltd.

Russell, Bertrand. 1943-44. "The Future of Pacifism." *American Scholar* 13 (Winter): 7-13.

Russell, Bertrand. 1958. *The Vital Letters of Russell, Khruschev, Dulles.* London: MacGibbon andKee.

Russell, Bertrand. 1959. *Common Sense and Nuclear Warfare.* London: George Allen and Unwin.

Russell, Bertrand. 1960. *Bertrand Russell Speaks His Mind.* London: The World Publishing Company.

Russell, Bertrand. 1961. *Has Man a Future?* London: George Allen and Unwin.

Russell, Bertrand. 1962. *A History of the World in Epitome (for Use in Martian Infant Schools).* Gaberbocchus.

Russell, Bertrand. 1963. *Unarmed Victory.* London: George Allen and Unwin.

Russell, Bertrand. 1967. *War Crimes in Vietnam.* London: George Allen and Unwin.

Russell, Bertrand. 1967. *The Autobiography of Bertrand Russell, 1872-1914*, Volume I. Boston: Little, Brown and Company.

Russell, Bertrand. 1968. *The Autobiography of Bertrand Russell, 1914-1941*, Volume II. Boston: Little, Brown and Company.

Russell, Bertrand. 1992. *Logical and Philosophical Papers, 1909-13.* Ed. John G. Slater. Vol. 6 of *The Collected Papers of Bertrand Russell.* New York: Routledge.

Russell, Bertrand. 2003. *Man's Peril*, 1954-55. Ed. Andrew G. Bone. Vol. 28 of *The Collected Papers of Bertrand Russell.* New York: Routledge.

Russell, Bertrand. 2010. *Human Society in Ethics and Politics.* New York: Routledge.

RUSSELL IN POPULAR CULTURE

Tim Madigan

IN DIRECTOR/SCREENWRITER JOHN MICHAEL MCDONAGH'S 2011 Quentin Tarantino-like comic film *The Guard*, there is a bizarre scene where three hit men, for no apparent reason, while driving down an Irish road get into a heated debate over who the world's greatest philosopher might be.

> *Hit Man #1*: Bertrand Russell.
>
> *Hit Man #2*: The fuckin' English. Everything has to be fuckin' English. Name your favorite philosopher, and lo and behold, he's English.
>
> *Hit Man #3*: He's Welsh.
>
> *Hit Man #2*: Uh?
>
> *Hit Man #3*: Bertrand Russell was Welsh.
>
> *Hit Man #2*: Bertrand Russell was Welsh?
>
> *Hit Man #3*: Yep.
>
> *Hit Man #2, after a pause*: You know I never knew that. Didn't think anybody interesting was Welsh.
>
> *Hit Man #3*: Dylan Thomas?
>
> *Hit Man #2*: Like I said.

It is amusing that the chauvinistic characters are willing to reconsider Russell's greatness once they can stop thinking of him as an Englishman, but no doubt Lord Russell himself, given his cosmopolitan leanings as well as his oft-professed love for his Englishness, might have been doubly offended by their banter, not to say their subsequent actions of gunning down a police officer in cold blood. Still, it's yet another example of Russell's ubiquitiousness. His name and image often pop up in the most unexpected places.

In addition to being an important public intellectual, for much of his long life Russell was also a noted public figure. Indeed, thanks to the many interviews he did over the years, from newspaper articles to radio debates and all the way up to appearances on television, he was a well-known figure to most people, and became something of a symbol for philosophy itself. So it's not perhaps surprising that references to him—often quite remarkable ones—appear in many areas of popular culture. In yet another celebrated violent film, for example, the pacifistic philosopher makes an unlikely "appearance." In the 1976 classic film *Taxi Driver*, the troubled character Travis Bickle, played by Robert De Niro, tries to tell his fellow cabbie "The Wizard" (played by Peter Boyle) about the demons that are haunting him. The Wizard launches into the following soliloquy:

> Look at it this way. A man takes a job, you know? And that job—I mean, like that—That becomes what he is. You know, like—You do a thing and that's what you are. Like I've been a cabbie for thirteen years. Ten years at night. I still don't own my own cab. You know why? Because I don't want to. That must be what I want. To be on the night shift drivin' somebody else's cab. You understand? I mean, you become—You get a job, you become the job. One guy lives in Brooklyn. One guy lives in Sutton Place. You got a lawyer. Another guy's a doctor. Another guy dies. Another guy gets well. People are born, y'know? I envy you, your youth. Go on, get laid, get drunk. Do anything. You got no choice, anyway. I mean, we're all fucked. More or less, ya know.

Bickle, unable to follow the logic of this, says "I don't know. That's the dumbest thing I've ever heard," to which the Wizard gives the following reply: "It's not Bertrand Russell. But what do you want? I'm a cabbie" (imdb). Who can argue with *that* logic?

But it's not only in the movies that references to Russell may be found. While reading a biography of the cartoonist Al Capp, of "Li'l Abner" fame, I was shocked to find the following unexpected Russell reference. Capp, noted for his drawings of rather voluptuous women and sly sexual references in what was ostensibly a family strip, created a character named "Adam Lazonga" who was renowned as the world's greatest lover, and who became a mentor to the naïve Abner, teaching him how to woo the ladies

"Dogpatch style." "Capp," the authors relate, "modeled Lazonga's physical appearance after George Bernard Shaw, the playwright and novelist, whose play *Pygmalion* was built on a similar teacher/student theme, but Lazonga's eccentric views and behavior were based on English philosopher and mathematician Bertrand Russell, recently in Boston's local news because he had accepted a position as a lecturer at Harvard after having been dismissed from the City College of New York. In interviews, Capp refused to connect Russell to his comic strip character, saying only that Shaw had been the model for the way Adam Lazonga looked. In the end, it didn't matter. Lazonga had become a vehicle for another lighthearted romp" (Schumacher and Kitchen 2013, 100-101). Actually, it *does* matter. Since all good Russellians know that after losing the City College job Russell most certainly did *not* go to teach at Harvard, or any other U.S. University (see Thom Weidlich's chapter in this volume for details), one has to wonder about the veracity of this claim, especially since Capp himself denied the connection. Still, the thought of Lord Russell cavorting with Daisy Mae, Moonbeam McSwine, and Stupefyin' Jones in Dogpatch, USA is an image one can't easily remove from one's mind. "Dogpatch Style," indeed.

    Another cartoonist who made use of Russell's image is the counterculture hero Robert Crumb (in many ways the anti-Capp, given the latter's rightwing ideology and the former's anarchistic attitudes). In 1970, the year of Russell's death, Crumb drew a short comic called "Meatball," in which various dignitaries, including Lord Russell, are mysteriously hit in the head by a flying meatball. Crumb, an iconoclastic figure who seems to have an affinity for Russell's excoriating wit, also made use of him in another of his sketches, as recounted by Laura Cumming, reviewing an exhibition of his work at Whitechapel Gallery in London: "His cartoons often come to proleptic halts—Mr. Sketchum, aka Crumb, thinks he'll send his cartoons to Mr CND [Campaign for Nuclear Disarmament], aka Bertrand Russell; an H-bomb drops; it's all over" (Cumming 2005). And, as Peter Stone relates in this volume, Russell is the major figure in the recent graphic novel *Logicomix*, where, thankfully, neither Mr. Sketchum nor a meatball trouble his equipoise.

    Not only was Russell a figure referred to by those, like the Wizard or Robert Crumb, with no connection to himself. Many of his close associates used him as a character in their fiction. This is perhaps not surprising, given that he was on intimate terms with some of the major writers of the twentieth century, including Joseph Conrad, Virginia Woolf, D. H. Lawrence, T.S. Eliot, and Aldous Huxley, and had an influence on all of them (thanks, in no small part, to his sometime-lover and longtime confidante Lady Ottoline Morrell, who introduced him to many of them and who also often appears, usually unfavorably, in their works).

Of all the above-mentioned writers, Russell seemed fondest of Conrad. He identified strongly with the blistering critique of colonialism found in the latter's classic *Heart of Darkness*, and he named both of his sons—John Conrad and Conrad—after him.

Conrad was deeply moved to learn in 1921 that Russell had bestowed his name upon his firstborn son, and wrote the following to him: "Of all the incredible things that come to pass—that there should be one day a Russell bearing my name for one of his names is surely the most marvelous…I am profoundly touched—more than I can express—that I should have been present to your mind in that way and at such a time" (Conrad 1983, 374). Unlike his relations with some of the other noted authors he knew, Russell and Conrad remained good friends their entire life, perhaps because they seldom met face-to-face—theirs was mostly an epistolary relationship. There is no record that Russell was ever a character in any of Conrad's writings, however, but he most certainly was so in other of the Bloomsbury Group's works.

Virginia Woolf often came across Russell at various Bloomsbury events, often in tow with his fellow Cambridge colleague G.E. Moore, who was an inspirational figure to the movement. In a diary entry written in 1924, Woolf notes of Russell that "He has not much body of character—this luminous vigorous mind seems to be attached to a flimsy little car, like that on a large glinting balloon…he has no chin, and he is dapper nevertheless. I should like the run of his headpiece" (Woolf 1978, 295). Woolf attended his lectures on Social Reconstruction and shared many of his progressive views on Women's Liberation, sexual liberalism and education. Some critics see elements of Russell in the character Mr. Ramsey in Woolf's *To the Lighthouse* (1927) but he seems mainly based upon her father, Leslie Stephen, an earnest freethinker himself. She does, however, make mention of Russell's book *The Scientific Outlook* in her novel *Three Guineas*.

Russell had a more tempestuous relationship with D. H. Lawrence, and directly influenced the character Sir Joshua Malleson in Lawrence's 1917 novel *Women in Love*. Sir Joshua is a comic and repulsive figure, described as having an eighteenth century appearance, with a propensity for showing up at the most awkward moments in order to pontificate on matters that bore everyone silly. He is described as follows: "A learned, dry baronet of 50, who was always making witticisms and laughing at them heartily in a harsh, horse laugh," talking in his "rather mincing voice, endlessly, endlessly, always with a strong mentality working, always interesting, and yet always known, everything he said known beforehand" (Lawrence 1920/1960, 50). In one scene, looking ludicrous in an old-fashioned bathing suit, Malleson splashes about the lead characters, one of whom refers to him in the following manner:

> Gerald had dived in, after Sir Joshua, and had swum to the end of the pond. There he climbed out and sat on the wall. There was a dive, and the little Countess was swimming like a rat, to join him. They both sat in the sun, laughing and crossing their arms on their breasts. Sir Joshua swam up to them, and stood near them, up to his arm-pits in the water. Then Hermione and Miss Bradley swam over, and they sat in a row on the embankment. "Aren't they terrifying? Aren't they really terrifying?" said Gudrun. "Don't they look saurian? They are just like great lizards. Did you ever see anything like Sir Joshua? But really, Ursula, he belongs to the primeval world, when great lizards crawled about" (*ibid.*, 93).

This is, to put it mildly, a harsh representation, and Sir Joshua is a desiccated figure throughout the novel—rather sinister, constantly talking and annoying all the other characters. Lawrence and Russell had once been close allies, but had had a bitter falling out by the time that Lawrence wrote the novel. It should be noted that Russell gave as good as he got, referring to Lawrence's views as fascistic and Lawrence himself as a hater of mankind.

Other Bloomsbury writers were a mite less cruel but still saw Russell as a figure of fun—earnest, loquacious, somewhat ridiculous but above all satyr-like in his approach to women. In T.S. Eliot's poem 1918 "Mr. Appolinax," for instance, we read:

> When Mr. Apollinax visited the United States
> His laughter tinkled among the teacups.
> I thought of Fragilion, that shy figure among the birch-trees,
> And of Priapus in the shrubbery
> Gaping at the lady in the swing (Eliot 1963/1991, 24).

This was written, it should be noted, before Russell began a long affair with Eliot's wife, Vivienne—Priapus indeed. Yet Eliot and Russell (unlike Lawrence and Russell) seemed to have remained on good terms, and both would eventually receive the Nobel Prize for Literature.

Perhaps the most amusing of all the literary versions of Russell may be found in Aldous Huxley's 1921 book *Crome Yellow*, where he appears as the character Mr. Scogan. Set during a weekend frolic among people very like the Bloomsbury set, the novel introduces the character thusly:

> Next to Mary a small gaunt man was sitting, rigid and erect in his chair. In appearance Mr. Scogan was like one of those extinct bird-lizards of the Tertiary. His nose was beaked, his dark eye had the shining quickness of a robin's. But there was nothing soft or gracious or feathery about him. The skin of his wrinkled brown face had a dry and scaly look; his hands were the hands of a crocodile. His movements were marked by the lizard's disconcertingly abrupt clockwork speed; his speech was thin, fluty, and dry. Henry Wimbush's school-fellow and exact contemporary, Mr. Scogan looked far older and, at the same time, far more youthfully alive than did that gentle aristocrat with the face like a grey bowler. Mr. Scogan might look like an extinct saurian (Huxley 1921/2001, 10).

Like Sir Joshua, there is yet another comparison to a lizard (one wonders how many of Russell's other contemporaries thought of him in this way). And, like Mr. Apollinax, Mr. Scogan is also a priapic figure, as he tries to seduce the innocent (or so she seems) young Mary:

> "It has become customary for serious young women, like Mary, to discuss, with philosophic calm, matters of which the merest hint would have sufficed to throw the youth of the sixties into a delirium of amorous excitement. It is all very estimable, no doubt. But still"—Mr. Scogan sighed.—"I for one should like to see, mingled with this scientific ardour, a little more of the jovial spirit of Rabelais and Chaucer."
>
> "I entirely disagree with you," said Mary. "Sex isn't a laughing matter; it's serious."
>
> "Perhaps," answered Mr. Scogan, "perhaps I'm an obscene

old man. For I must confess that I cannot always regard it as wholly serious."

"But I tell you..." began Mary furiously. Her face had flushed with excitement. Her cheeks were the cheeks of a great ripe peach.

"Indeed," Mr. Scogan continued, "it seems to me one of few permanently and everlastingly amusing subjects that exist. Amour is the one human activity of any importance in which laughter and pleasure preponderate, if ever so slightly, over misery and pain" (*ibid.*, 72).

While in many ways just as off-putting as Sir Joshua or Mr. Appolinax, Mr. Scogan is a more good-natured caricature who is genuinely amusing, and the reader looks forward to his various intrusions into the text. Scogan provides a great deal of fun whenever he appears. For instance, at the end of the novel, in order to debunk the craze of spiritualism that has swept over the party-goers, Scogan dresses up as a gypsy woman and manages to fool everyone with sly prognostications about the future.

As with Eliot, Russell stayed on good terms with Huxley, although the two did seem to enjoy needling each other. (Russell once remarked that one could predict Huxley's subject of conversation by knowing which volume of the Encyclopedia Britannia he'd been reading.)

One final rather unexpected Russellian connection with popular culture that has had rather more long-lasting relevance than the above examples is with the peace symbol. As was mentioned in the allusion to Robert Crumb earlier, Russell was an active participant in the Campaign for Nuclear Disarmament (CND), as detailed so ably by David Blitz in this volume. The logo for the CND was designed in 1958 by Gerald Holtom (1914-1985), a well-known British artist. Using the semaphore symbols for N and D ("Nuclear Disarmament"), the logo soon became the international symbol for peace itself. Russell was an admirer of Holtom's work and a strong supporter of the use of his symbol, so while he didn't create it (as some have incorrectly stated) he certainly played an important role in popularizing it. In 1961, for instance, Russell broke with the CND after finding it too non-confrontational. Some members "proposed a Gandhian method of protest—nonviolent civil disobedience. Bertrand Russell agreed, resigned from the CND, and became president of the newly formed Committee of 100 against Nuclear War" (Kolsbun 2008, 46). A group of 100 prominent peace activists, including Russell and his wife Edith, along with the actress Vanessa Redgrave, staged a sit-down at London's Ministry of Defence on February 18, 1961. They were photographed under a giant banner stating "Committee of 100 Action for Life" which was proudly festooned with four giant peace symbols. The photo—as we would put it today—went viral, and the rest is history. How interesting that Bertrand Russell, himself a symbolic figure of rationality, should also have been instrumental in popularizing one of the world's most famous symbols. All he was saying was give peace a chance.

Bibliography

Conrad, Joseph. 1983. *The Collected Letters of Joseph Conrad*. New York: Cambridge University Press.

Cumming, Laura. 2005. "The Artist Who Ain't Bruegil", *The Guardian*, April 2. Found at http://www.theguardian.com/artanddesign/2005/apr/03/art.robertcrumb

Eliot, T.S. 1963/1991. *Collected Poems: 1909-1962*. New York: Harcourt, Bracey & Company.

Huxley, Aldous. 1921/2001. *Crome Yellow*. Chicago: Dalkey Archive Press.

imbd, *Taxi Driver* quotes. Found at http://www.imdb.com/title/tt0075314/quotes

Kolsbun, Ken with Michael S. Sweeney. 2008. *Peace: The Biography of a Symbol*. New York: National Geographic Society.

Lawrence, D. H. 1920/1960. *Women in Love*. New York: The Viking Press.

Ryan, Alan. 1993. *Bertrand Russell: A Political Life*. New York: Oxford University Press.

Schumacher, Michael and Denis Kitchen. 2013. *Al Capp: A Life to the Contrary*. New York: Bloomsbury USA.

Woolf, Virginia. 1978. *The Diary of Virginia Woolf, Vol. 2, 1920-1934*. London: The Hogarth Press.

For further examples please see Rick Stapleton's "100 Years of Bertrand Russell in Literature and Film" in the *Hamilton Arts and Letters* 10th Anniversary Issue, Issue 11, No. 1, www.HALmagazine.com, 2018.

THE WORLD AS I FOUND IT:
TWENTIETH CENTURY BRITISH PHILOSOPHY THROUGH A LITERARY PRISM

Robert Heineman

THE WORLD AS I FOUND IT WAS ORIGINALLY PUBLISHED by Ticknor & Fields in 1987 and republished by *New York Review of Books* in 2010. (1) Although he is not a major novelist, Bruce Duffy encapsulated the world of twentieth-century British philosophy in his historical novel, called by Joyce Carol Oates one of the "five great non-fiction novels written" in the twentieth century. (2) The covers of both editions utilize works from the era of Vienna's greatness. The first uses a stark painting from 1912 by Egon Schiele; the second a surrealist effort by Gustav Klimt, circa 1902-1903.

The 2010 reprinting includes a brief introduction by David Leavitt. Leavitt teaches literature at the University of Florida and has published several novels and a biography of Alan Turing. He has also been co-editor of *The Penguin Book of Gay Short Stories*. (3) I mention this because Duffy, who is married with two children, deals openly with Ludwig Wittgenstein's secret gay life, and sexual proclivities and relationships are featured prominently in Duffy's depiction of British philosophy emanating from Cambridge. Leavitt's introduction to *The World as I Found It*, however, focuses on the literary qualities of the book, in particular, Duffy's ability to construct dialogue and to offer detailed descriptions. Here we shall argue that by employing imaginative construction of individual relationships, Duffy's approach offers useful insights into how important components of British philosophy developed in the twentieth century.

Duffy selectively examines the chronology of the lives of three major twentieth century British thinkers and links these in what must often be characterized as a disturbing fashion. Duffy has made careful use of his literary license so that the book is essentially factually correct. But the literary form has allowed him to probe far more deeply than simple history or biography could allow. Thus, he is able to focus on what for him are salient events in the lives of the major thinkers and the development of philosophy itself and to construct dialogue and interactions that provide insightful portrayals of the thoughts and characters of the protagonists. This juxtaposition of behavior and philosophical endeavor can be jarring in its revelation of contradictions and inconsistencies.

I am suggesting that Duffy has used literary form to provide a framework for insights into twentieth-century British philosophy that might otherwise remain uncovered. Wittgenstein's anguished life and his life experiences offer ample opportunity for deeper analysis. Bertrand Russell, then, serves both in lifestyle, temperament, social background, and philosophical bent as the photographic negative against which Wittgenstein emerges. Duffy balances this duo of philosophers with G.E. Moore, who serves as literary and philosophical ballast for the unfolding drama. Affable, completely candid, and happily monogamous, Moore is simply there as a respected philosopher and contented academic.

Duffy makes frequent use of flashbacks and vignettes so that a simple sequential description of the unfolding of the narrative does not do justice to the nuances of behavior and thought that he is seeking to portray. But in terms of an overall view he begins with a discussion of Wittgenstein's family in Vienna and Wittgenstein's loss of interest in his original studies in aeronautics in England. After a visit with Friedrich Gottlob Frege, he receives the support of that logician in a letter to Russell. Frege warns Russell that Wittgenstein is argumentative and aggressive.

Meanwhile the text shifts to Russell enjoying a respite with Lady Ottoline Morrell at her beach abode. After having sex up against one of the trees in the area, Russell spends some time trying to explain through sketches in the sand his efforts to provide a symbolic basis for language and logic. Later Wittgenstein, in abrupt fashion, without the courtesy of introducing himself (much to Russell's irritation) enrolls in Russell's lecture course. Once they meet and Russell remonstrates with Wittgenstein for what he deems his lack of professional courtesy, Wittgenstein becomes a persistent late-night visitor to Russell's rooms, haranguing him for hours on end.

At this point Duffy introduces the third major figure, or protagonist—although that may be too strong of a word in this case: G. E. Moore. Moore's *Principia Ethica* (1903) had become a major force in philosophy by this time and would continue to have influence throughout the first half of the twentieth century. Moore and Russell are described in some detail at high table—Moore being a fellow who thoroughly enjoys his meals. Russell cannot hide his envy of Moore—although they are united in their opposition to John McTaggart's philosophy of idealism, and Duffy notes that they have effectively destroyed its claims to philosophical legitimacy. Moore, unlike Russell, is a model of innocence and candor, and when Russell asks him directly, "Do you like me?" Moore responds "No," however much he might respect him. (4) Meanwhile Moore falls in love with Dorothy Ely, marries her, and unlike the other two philosophers becomes a happy domestic and continues contentedly teaching at Cambridge.

Meanwhile, after a brief stay in Vienna, Wittgenstein returns to Cambridge with a two-page destruction of Russell's theory of logical forms. Duffy depicts Russell as recognizing the merit of Wittgenstein's criticisms and argues that from that point on the two men function as collaborators rather than as master and student. Wittgenstein also begins attending Moore's lectures and, again much to Russell's irritation, Moore invites him to join the Apostles, a prestigious group of leading Cambridge intellectuals—which Wittgenstein does for a short period only.

After having seriously undermined Russell's efforts at a grand synthesis in philosophy, Wittgenstein leaves for a remote cabin in Norway, not to return to England until after World War I. While away, Wittgenstein is called home to Vienna, where his father, Karl, is dying. Wittgenstein has been a tremendous disappointment to Karl, who has been a highly successful industrialist, and who does not understand his son's approach to philosophy and, as a consequence, sees no use whatsoever in it. Yet, of all the family, Wittgenstein stays at his father's side until the very end.

With the outbreak of World War I, the paths of Russell and Wittgenstein diverge even more dramatically. Wittgenstein volunteers and serves through heavy combat in the Austrian army against the Russians, although his sister, Gretl, is continually trying to convince him to obtain an exemption from service. He is captured by the Italians and serves the last two years of the war as an Italian prisoner of war. It is during this period that he writes the *Tractatus Logico-Philosophicus,* drawing on inspiration that he received from an army safety manual. Meanwhile, Russell, with the imposition of universal conscription in England, comes out strongly against the war and is eventually sentenced to prison. As a result of having been convicted of a crime, his tenure at Cambridge is put in jeopardy. And through the efforts of his critics, led by McTaggart, but defended by Moore (even though by this time he and Moore were estranged), he is dismissed from Trinity College.

Section Three of the book focuses on the year 1931 at Beacon Hill, the progressive school founded by Russell and his wife Dora. Wittgenstein has communicated to Moore and Cambridge that he would like to return and become a professor. To do this he needs his doctorate, which requires a Viva—a defense of his work. Cambridge and Moore ask Russell to join Moore in the interrogation, and Russell, with a sense of quiet vindication, agrees as long as the event occurs at Beacon Hill. Duffy's rendition of the event places it two years later than it actually occurred and moves it from its location at Cambridge. His change of date and location allow him to bring into play a fuller range of relationships than if he had remained historically accurate.

IN THE INTERVENING YEARS WITTGENSTEIN has served for several years teaching at a rural school in Trattenbach, Austria—a very unpleasant time for him. He leaves Trattenbach, denounces philosophy as currently propounded, returns to Vienna, builds a modernistic house for Gretl, and renounces his entire fortune. He and his close companion Max, whom he met at Trattenbach, meet Moore and Dorothy at the train station and proceed in cramped fashion by auto to Beacon Hill.

Duffy presents the Beacon Hill educational effort by Russell and his wife Dora as an exercise in controlled chaos. At that time the children were being terrorized by a new student, Rabe, who had serious psychological problems and whom Russell could not get rid of because he could not locate the woman who left him there. Russell is also making the most of his sexual opportunities with the staff, in particular one Miss Marmor, a lady of substantial athletic bent. Wittgenstein arrives with Moore, and old envies and rivalries reemerge. These are submerged, barely, for the purposes of completing the Viva, and Duffy gives brief coverage to Moore's discussion of Wittgenstein's abandoning the kind of philosophy that he had espoused in the *Tractatus*. (It might also be noted here that Wittgenstein had tried to prevent publication of the *Tractatus*, having abandoned its underlying assumptions, but Russell had encouraged its publication and written an introduction for it.) There is never any question that the Viva will be completed successfully by Wittgenstein.

Taking a broader perspective on the event, Duffy has fashioned it to bring together the social, personal, and philosophical dynamics of the era and the book's major players. To accomplish this, he locates the event at Russell's school, where the unpleasant dynamics of Russell's open marriage, the temper of Wittgenstein, and the placid security of Moore all come into play.

For many degree candidates, the doctoral defense can be a nerve-wracking experience, with a successful defense not by any means assured. Wittgenstein's Viva offers a sharp contrast to most doctoral defenses. Although his standing as a major thinker was by this time unquestioned, neither Moore nor Russell was prepared to award the Viva simply by acclamation, i.e., by simply applauding Wittgenstein upon his entrance into the room. It appears instead that Wittgenstein left his examiners in something of an intellectual fog. After a halting beginning and some perfunctory dialogue initiated primarily by Moore, Wittgenstein apparently concluded the session by grasping his two interlocutors each on the shoulder and declaring that they probably would never really understand his thought. (5) Moore's letter of approval to the Cambridge authorities seems fundamentally to agree with Wittgenstein's assessment in that Moore acknowledges his lack of thorough comprehension of Wittgenstein's thought, while at the same time declaring its importance. (6)

The remainder of the book moves quickly from the Anschluss through World War II to Wittgenstein's death. Max, who left Wittgenstein in anger at the Beacon Hill event, reappears in Vienna as an SS officer and assists Gretl, her sister, and Gretl's son out of Austria. Wittgenstein accepts a teaching position at Cambridge, and he and Russell become permanently at odds—with Russell arguing that Wittgenstein has simply lost his way and Wittgenstein seeing nothing useful in Russell's later work. Russell and many of the Cambridge dons in philosophy are continually sniping at the band of disciples who follow and worship Wittgenstein's personal style and philosophy. Wittgenstein dies of prostate cancer in the home of Dr. Bevan, his personal physician, and his wife, who take him in and care for him during the last months of his life.

There is much to be derived from this work. Aspects that I wish to treat in some depth are, first, the impact of the relationships between life and intellectual work for the three protagonists—especially Russell and Wittgenstein. And, second, how these dynamics can be seen as contributing significantly to what were to become major philosophical currents in British philosophy during the twentieth century.

Wittgenstein, in criticism of Russell, asserted that he alone was a "practicing philosopher." Russell could legitimately have disagreed on this point. It is true that in his early work he placed tremendous reliance on logic and the bases therefore. He, of course, never abandoned his faith in reason and logic, but throughout much of his life he engaged in political and other activities through which he tried to promote the importance of rationalism. Unfortunately, as Duffy's discussion often illustrates, many times Russell's calm application and promulgation of reason were belied by the chaos and passion actually occurring. Duffy continually points to the complications from Russell's amorous adventures and to the envy of other academics that Russell had difficulty concealing. And later in life some of Russell's positions became far removed from what rational statesmen would, or could, undertake. (7) Important components of Russell's *Weltanschauung* are perhaps best summarized by Duffy in his description of Russell's responses to the press while in a hospital bed recovering from a plane crash into the sea in which 19 passengers died. What, one interrogator inquires, was the secret to Russell's long life? Russell, now in his late seventies, replies heredity and lack of worry.

Lack of worry was in stark contrast to Wittgenstein's outlook on life, for he was a forever driven man. His philosophical positions were deeply rooted in his psyche, which was indelibly troubled. Riven by guilt stemming from his family's demands and questions, his sexual orientation, his horrible wartime experiences, and his family's concealed Jewish heritage, Wittgenstein was never to find peace, and he certainly did not find succor in philosophy. A genius whose conceptual capacity was extraordinary, Wittgenstein soon saw that Russell's search for certainty could never be successful. Individuals experienced life through language, but one could never be clear or certain about language itself. Thus, at the very foundations of his belief system—if that is the appropriate term—Wittgenstein remained religious and mystical throughout his life. Unlike Russell and Moore, he believed that there had to be more beyond either formally constructed logic or the tangible.

Duffy situates Moore, personally and philosophically, between the lives and the ideas of Russell and Wittgenstein. A philosopher of prominence and influence since his publication of *Philosophica Ethica* in 1903, Moore remained throughout his life a contented academic. He was totally monogamous and his marriage to Dorothy was happy and dull. He broke with Russell early in the twentieth century, but he never did so with Wittgenstein. And Wittgenstein, despite Moore's rather pedestrian approach to philosophy and life, clearly respected and valued Moore and his ideas. Once he had joined the faculty at Cambridge, Wittgenstein would regularly visit with Moore and his family on Tuesday evenings, and he and Moore would discuss a wide range of topics. Duffy's presentation of these visits strongly suggests that they provided an essential respite for Wittgenstein in what for him was an otherwise disturbing world.

Duffy depicts sexual activities as one of the most important influences on his thinkers' world views. Although there may still be some debate over the issue, Duffy clearly accepts that Wittgenstein was homosexual and in imaginative fashion provides several graphic descriptions of Wittgenstein's engagement in such activity. In particular, Duffy's first unnerving description of Wittgenstein's subjection to a night of sodomy in the trenches by Grundhardt, a surly and obstructionist infantryman in Wittgenstein's platoon, combines Wittgenstein's physical sensations with his philosophical epiphanies to the point that the event becomes surreal. Later, however, Duffy makes clear that Wittgenstein's prowling the Prater for evenings of oral sodomy left him feeling guilt-ridden. Paraphrasing Wittgenstein's feelings Duffy has him believing that "he had sunk to the very bottom...Sin reeked from his pores." (8)

Paralleling Wittgenstein's sexual drives is Russell's continual heterosexual philandering, which is covered in much more detail, probably because factually Duffy is on stronger ground on this point. Russell is forthright about his desires with women to whom he is attracted, and engages in affairs in serial fashion. What is clear from Duffy's presentation is that Russell feels no guilt whatsoever in his sexual approaches and his consummation of these various proposals, although many of these lead to complications that a more focused heterosexual could have avoided.

Moore's sexual activity also receives some treatment and remains securely within the confines of marital bliss. The vignette that really stands out in this respect occurs during Wittgenstein's Viva. Through the window in the library at Beacon Hill, Russell can see that Max is in the process of seducing Lily, whom he has just hired and who has rebuffed his forthright advances, by taking her behind the barn. Wittgenstein, who warned Max not to play any games with Lily, also sees what is happening. Moore, as usual, is oblivious to the barnyard goings on, but later that evening Dorothy confides to him that while out strolling in the meadow she had seen Max having his way with Lily. Moore is intrigued, Wittgenstein is furious, and Russell is deeply jealous. Here Duffy represents the fairly intense philosophical dialogue of the doctoral defense as simply the epiphenomena of underlying passions, passions rooted in sexual proclivities.

Several other life experiences for Russell and Wittgenstein that exemplify their differences and that are treated in detail by Duffy deserve some comment here. One is their wartime experiences. Wittgenstein volunteers for service in the Austrian army and Duffy spends considerable space narrating his combat experience, his efforts to lead men, and his mixed feelings towards the ignorance, superstition, and perseverance of his comrades in arms. Duffy admits in his addition to the 1995 reprint that much of this is imaginative reconstruction on his part, but his point—which he makes very effectively—is that life in the trenches was unpleasant and often horrifying. Russell, on the other hand, spends much of the war as a public opponent, but his opposition reaches fever pitch with the imposition of universal conscription. At this point, the government finally prosecutes Russell and he serves six months in prison. Although his prison conditions were reasonably comfortable and he publicly displayed an upbeat attitude toward spending a few months in study and writing, Duffy portrays him as really quite unhappy with having to serve in confinement. In characterizing their reactions to the war we could argue that both thinkers were engaging in their beliefs, perhaps Russell more so than Wittgenstein. There is no question, however, that, in contrast to Russell's experience, Wittgenstein's war must have had moments of real terror and suffering.

Another area deserving more extended treatment is the effects of their worldview on their attempts at education. Russell's experiment at Beacon Hill, however modest the results, implemented his attachment to the power of rational approaches to problems and projects, although to be fair he and Dora both devoted a lot of personal, warm attention to the children. Each child, for example, is personally tucked in every evening by either Russell or his wife, who by this time was pregnant with another man's child.

Wittgenstein, on the other hand, after the war studied for and received his teaching credentials and journeyed to the small rural community of Trattenbach, where he taught for a number of years. Those years did not go particularly well. Wittgenstein was a strong disciplinarian and did not suffer dolts easily. On numerous occasions he administered corporal punishment and finally was forced to leave when one of the pupils claimed that he had been seriously injured—falsely as he later admitted. Earlier Wittgenstein had lied to cover up his mistreatment of a female student, whom he had struck—something that bothered him ever after. Wittgenstein, who prided himself on his scathing attacks on other philosophers for intellectual obfuscation and dishonesty, found unsettling the fact that he himself had stooped to duplicity to save his own skin, so to speak. So for Duffy the effects of Russell's educational effort illustrated the limits of rationality, and the educational arena reinforced in turn the frustration and guilt that accompanied Wittgenstein throughout his life. Again at his Viva, for example, Wittgenstein focuses on the ambiguity of the term "pain," as he does in other venues. Moore, whose *Principia Ethica* had urged the bedrock nature of the good irrespective of a logic framework, questioned why the term "pleasure" might not work just as well.

Finally, on a comparative note I believe it worthwhile to examine briefly the mutual attachment between Wittgenstein and the young followers who bonded with him throughout his life. Duffy gives no indication that there were any physical aspects to these relationships, but they occurred with regularity, and in the post-WW II years he accumulated a dedicated retinue of disciples who repeated his attacks on traditional philosophy and adopted his mannerisms and dress. Several of these became well-known philosophers in their own right, but others moved in other directions. Francis Skinner, for example, became very close to Wittgenstein, even though his mother had hoped that he would move into the study of law or medicine. Wittgenstein, however, convinced him to become something useful—an auto mechanic.

Wittgenstein's genius is without question. His grasp of music, architecture, logic, and math were extraordinary, and his belief in the mystical and religious were vital to him. Although obviously intellectually powerful in the areas of logic and math, Russell had none of the breadth of Wittgenstein and appears not to have been able to engender the kind of individual attachments that grew up around Wittgenstein. And the latter's belief in the mystical and religious was completely foreign to Russell, as was Wittgenstein's disparagement of the philosophical efforts of those who strove for a universal truth, or simply truth.

We might also note Wittgenstein's acuity in music. Duffy relates an incident in which Wittgenstein invites Russell to accompany him to a recital by the Cambridge University Musical Society. At the conclusion Wittgenstein goes up to the musicians and points out possible improvements, with the result that he was asked to practice with them, an invitation that he readily accepted. Moore had some facility at the piano with simple melodies—

Duffy recounts his verbal rendering of "Foggy, Foggy Dew" at his wedding reception—but nowhere is it suggested that Russell was musically capable or even inclined.

As a conclusion, it may be useful to draw on two incidents, factually based, that both enhance and support the value of Duffy's effort to contextualize Cambridge's contribution to twentieth century philosophy.

Duffy's portrayal of Wittgenstein as aggressive, raw, guilt-driven, and brilliant as a scholar and academic is consistent throughout the book and is compatible with the depictions of others. Wittgenstein brooked nothing in the way of what he regarded as trivial or frivolous. Russell, on the other hand, while conceding the power of Wittgenstein's logic, could never break with his aristocratic upbringing, his sociability, or his belief in the power of reason.

In an especially poignant incident, Bryan Magee in his autobiography *Confessions of a Philosopher* relates his embarrassment, indeed his irritation, when he visited Russell for lunch, and Russell, who by then was in his late eighties, insisted on cutting the meat and dishing up the meal, while Magee, a much younger man at age twenty-nine, sat rather haplessly by as Russell apportioned the meat and vegetables on the right, walked behind Magee's chair to serve each from his left. Magee tried at least to pour the wine, but Russell insisted that the host must always serve—that's the way it had to be done. Magee is suggesting that Russell was incapable of discerning what the average luncheon guest, at least, would have seen as the practical absurdity of his behavior. But for Russell it was a rational issue. As he put it in response to Magee's discomfort: "A difference in age can have quite an irrational effect." (9)

Russell simply could not extricate himself from the social expectations within which he was raised. Again, in one of the book's opening liaisons, Duffy notes, for example, that Russell and Lady Ottoline were to be alone at the beach, which, of course, included two maids, a cook, a chauffeur, and "one or two odd guests." (10) In contrast, we see again and again Wittgenstein retreating to the isolation of his cabin in Norway and, while at Cambridge, utilizing for his teaching and his residence rooms that were spartan in the extreme.

Duffy has provided no revisionist or new interpretations of philosophy or of the thinkers featured by him. This work creates a social, historical, and personalized context for completing an understanding of Russell and Wittgenstein. Duffy has offered not only a running, roughly chronological, tableau of the important life phases of these thinkers, he has also created dialogue which for the most part is entirely plausible. Thus, the reader can sense how ideas and personalities interact. What Duffy's rendition says about twentieth-century British philosophy remains really for each reader to puzzle out for himself or herself.

This reader must conclude that with the advent of Wittgenstein the twentieth century search for truth suffered heavy, perhaps fatal, blows, and probably was misguided from its inception. Duffy makes it easier to understand how and why Russell, unable to move outside his aristocratic social standards and cultural assumptions, could have believed that some form of universal truth was possible. Enter stage right Wittgenstein, who rejected almost *in toto* the upper class milieu in which he was raised. In this process, his perspective on philosophy as then articulated became thoroughly corrosive, and in many respects his arguments brought Russell to his knees philosophically. But Russell was certainly not alone in this regard. Impressed by the *Tractatus*, Wittgenstein's supporters among the logical positivists of the Vienna Circle also were to be sorely disappointed and intellectually stymied. By the time of his visits with these thinkers the power of the mystical had become so important to Wittgenstein that he famously spent important time with them reciting the poetry of Rabindranath Tagore. (11)

Duffy's work leaves the reader wondering whether western thinkers will ever be able to recoup some kind of basis for universals. Has the disappearance of the Russellian context, as ably presented by Duffy, left philosophers flailing about desperately for substitute forms of support? Or have the observations of a psychically driven, guilt-ridden, socially bereft man kicked away entirely any ladder upon which they once could have so confidently ascended?

Endnotes

1. *The World As I Found It* was first published in 1987. (Duffy, Bruce. 1987. *The World As I Found It*. New York: Ticknor & Fields.) The book was reissued in 1995 with a short address given in 1991 in the American Literature Today series at Stichting John Adams Institute in Amsterdam. This issue was published by the Mariner Books imprint of Houghton-Mifflin, New York. The most recent issue of the book was published by *New York Review of Books* in 2010. This reprint contains an eight-page introduction by David Leavitt. The

1995 reissue has a cover designed specifically for that work, whereas both the 1987 and 2010 issues use copies of early twentieth-century Viennese artists for covers. Page references in this chapter will be to the 1987 edition unless otherwise specifically noted.

2. Quoted in front material of the 2010 edition.

3. Leavitt, David and Mitchell, Mark (eds.). 1994. *The Penguin Book of Gay Short Stories*. New York: Penguin Books.

4. Duffy, op. cit., 98.

5. See Monk, Ray. 1990. *Ludwig Wittgenstein*. New York: The Free Press. 271-2. Duffy offers his version of the Viva on pages 264-71.

6. Monk, op. cit., 272.

7. Russell, himself, appeared to have been embarrassed by his book *Which Way to Peace?* in which he took a thoroughly pacifist position toward the Nazi threat. Although there were at least two additional impressions in 1937, the book was never republished. (Russell, Bertrand. 1936. *Which Way to Peace?* London: Michael Joseph Ltd.). Ray Monk in the second volume of his biography of Russell remarks that those who would take the time to read Russell's writings on "political, social and moral questions" during the second half of his life "would, I think, be shocked at how sloppy and ill-considered much of it is." (Monk, Ray. 2001. *Bertrand Russell: The Ghost of Madness 1921-1970*. New York: Free Press. xii.)

8. Duffy, op. cit., 398.

9. Bryan Magee, *Confessions of a Philosopher*. New York: The Modern Library, 1999, 206.

10. Duffy, op. cit., 36.

11. Monk, Wittgenstein, 243, see also 408-10. Duffy deals with this at op. cit., 473.

WOULD BERTRAND RUSSELL HAVE USED E-MAIL? A CONTINUING PERPLEXITY

Chad Trainer

1. INTRODUCTION

Available in the 1970s as an aid to U.S. military and academic research the internet was "almost unknown to the general public" as recently as 1990. By the end of 1995, however, millions of civilians were using the internet on a daily basis. As 1996 drew to a close, the "Net" and the "Web" were part of the ordinary person's parlance.

At the time the general public began its involvement with the internet, many of its advocates touted the new technology because it facilitated the formation of "virtual communities" free from the fetters of geographic boundaries and afforded an avenue of expression that at the time was free from restraints of corporately owned newspapers and broadcasters. By 2007, about 1.25 billion people were connected to the internet (19% of the global population). At their 2011 Summit, the G8 nations' leaders saw fit to summarize their position on the internet:

> For citizens, the Internet is a unique information and education tool, and thus helps to promote freedom, democracy and human rights. The Internet facilitates new forms of business and promotes efficiency, competitiveness, and economic growth. Governments, the private sector, users, and other stakeholders all have a role to play in creating an environment in which the Internet can flourish in a balanced manner. (G8 2011, 2)

The Pew Research Center reported in 2011 that half of a recent survey's participants said they used social-networking sites such as Facebook and LinkedIn. According to Facebook, as of 2012 the network had over 800 million active monthly users world-wide.

Inferences regarding the positions Bertrand Russell would have taken on the use of e-mail and the internet in general are bound to be conjectural. However, he left us enough reflections that we can reasonably draw conclusions about the attitudes he would have adopted toward the high-tech devices of our day. Moreover, a spate of current books about cyber culture seems to capture many of what I think would have been Russell's sentiments.

Several questions come to mind: Would Russell have thought his own life more likely to benefit or suffer from using the internet? Would Russell consider the daily lives of most people to be better or worse as a result of the internet? Finally, has the advent of the internet marked an improvement or setback in the progress of geopolitics?

I contend Russell would hold that the quality of human life has suffered as a result of the internet. This paper considers the answers that Russell might have given to these three questions. Russell would have held that the high-tech age, for all its advantages, poses obstacles to such cherished ideals as wisdom and leisure. I defend this conclusion notwithstanding the fact that Russell's own work in mathematical logic arguably helped lay the groundwork for cyberspace.

2. CYBERSPACE IN RUSSELL'S PERSONAL LIFE

Defensibly or not, Russell shared the Greek philosophers' opinion that practical activities are illiberal and slavish. For example, his understanding of modern physics was beyond question, but he lacked a comparable command of his own physical environment. His biographer Ronald W. Clark writes,

> In strong contrast to his philosopher-friend Wittgenstein, engineer, architect and dab-hand at most jobs, Russell could be stretched by having to make a cup of tea. He had, moreover, a certain disinclination for the menial task; in theory the most democratic of men, Russell could not shake off the legacy of [his aristocratic family home] Pembroke Lodge; and the instinctive Russell outlook which divided life into below-stairs and above-stairs. (Clark 1976, 427)

Russell's friend Rupert Crawshay-Williams reports that Russell was guilty of a "total ignorance of the mechanics of machines" (Crawshay-

Williams 1970, 137). "[T]he idea that he should actually know what to do in a domestic/mechanical emergency was laughable" (*ibid.*, 33). And, according to Russell's own daughter, he was "hopeless" at handiwork and domestic matters generally (Tait 1975, 94, 117).

In a similar vein, we can readily envision Russell mastering the more abstruse aspects of cyber technology, while at the same time lacking any savvy at or even interest in the most rudimentary interactions the modern computer keyboard involves. All this corresponds tidily to Russell's exaltation of science as knowledge over science as technique.

Russell cherished routine and the seclusion of a study "to which none was allowed without invitation" (Clark 1976, 428; see also 491).[1] His prolonged trances of speculation have been fodder for his biographers. As biographer Ray Monk reports, "On one walk he became so immersed in a discussion of the rather arcane subject of 'egocentric particulars' that he forgot which way he was going and added eight miles to their route home" (Monk 1996, 502). A thinker given to concentration of such intensity that, by his own report, he "forgot to breathe and emerged panting as from a trance" can hardly be thought to have welcomed the sort of on-the-go slapdash skimming and correspondence involved with our twenty-first century's devices and gadgets (Russell 1956, 211).

In his adult years at least, there was certainly no dearth of social opportunities for Russell. This is substantiated by the reports of his endeavors to literally hide from the adoring admirers who all too frequently attempted to visit him. Architect Peter Blake recounts that, during the time he was sharing a residence with Russell, the latter was not always as gregariously inclined as one might have expected:

> On Sundays, at Little Datchet, young couples—philosophy professors or students from CCNY—would arrive from Manhattan to express their solidarity with Diddy [i.e., Russell[2]]. On one such occasion, as a young, adoring couple bade him farewell at the door of Little Datchet, we overheard the wife saying, "Lord Russell, it was so wonderful to bask in your light." Ever after, we would remind Diddy, come Sunday, that some people were expected for

---

[1] For more on Russell's love of routine, see Wood (1957, 49-60), Clark (1976, 572), and Tait (1975, 130). See also "Appendix on Christopher Farley's View of Russell and E-mail."
[2] "Diddy" was what Russell's son Conrad called him. Evidently, it was the name that gained currency among the inner circle at Russell's Pennsylvania home.

> lunch "to bask in your light," a prospect that did not amuse him quite as hugely as one might think. (One Sunday, when the usual visitors arrived, Diddy could not be found, and Peter sent me off to look for him; I found him sitting in a tree, quite far up, fully and properly dressed, puffing away at his pipe and looking out at the Pennsylvania Dutch landscape. "Diddy, come down! They've come to bask in your light!" He said "Damn them," and that he didn't quite know how to get down from his perch. I lent him a hand, while he grumbled. (Blake 1993, 41-2)

In light of this, there can be little doubt that Russell would not be favorably impressed with the increased volume of communications that e-mail renders feasible.[3]

I believe the spirit of Russell is discernible in the words of Donald Knuth, a computer science professor at Stanford University, who has washed his hands altogether of e-mail: "E-mail is a wonderful thing for people whose role in life is to be on top of things. But not for me; my role is to be on the bottom of things. What I do takes long hours of studying and uninterruptible concentration" (quoted in Freeman 2009, 213). Since the activities in which Russell engaged also entailed long hours of studying and uninterruptible concentration, he would agree with Knuth's views.

Long before e-mail, Russell bemoaned the changing traditions of correspondence. In 1969, he remarked:

> Undoubtedly the art of letter writing has been lost in the twentieth century through the development of the telephone and, to a lesser extent, the greater ease of travel. In my youth it was imperative to master the art of letter writing if one was to make one's way in the world....It was a world remote from the age of the tape recorder, the telex machine and the "hot line", *and I cannot say that its passing necessarily denotes progress.* Today favours are still sought in clubs and over lunch, but the growth of bureaucracies has produced a new form of letter which is archaic, deliberately

---

[3] Ken Blackwell has suggested to me that Russell could well have valued e-mail as a more efficient means of communication with his wives and mistresses. Russell wrote especially frequently to Lady Ottoline Morrell—sometimes two or even three times a day. Even so, "The resulting hoard of letters is an enormous treasure. It could not have been replaced by dashing off e-mails, texts, and (God forbid) tweets" (Blackwell-Trainer Correspondence, July 26, 2013).

uninformative and completely lacking in subtlety. The Civil Service rule books on letter writing must form part of the obituary notice of the twentieth century. (emphasis added; Russell 1969, ix-x; see also Powers 2010, 53)

I think we can glean from these comments what Russell would make of e-mail. He also once protested "It is impossible to read in America, except in the train, because of the telephone" (Wood 1957, 145). The mind reels at what he would make of portable phones, text messaging, and the like.

3. THE INTERNET IN DAILY LIFE

There are reasonable grounds for concluding that Russell would object to e-mail and the internet at least in their present forms and mores, especially with respect to (i) the cult of busyness, (ii) privacy, (iii) the role of deliberate thought in our lives, and (iv) literacy.

(i) The Cult of Busyness

Many people feel an imperative to participate in online life because of how busy they consider themselves to be. The irony here is that the high-tech devices apparently intended to facilitate our work have had the opposite effect. E-mail and the net not only *permit* us to do our work almost anywhere and anytime but they also allow our bosses and ourselves to *expect* us to do our work at almost any place or time (Freeman 2009, 164-6, 195, 208-10). Regardless of what one may think of legislation limiting the number of hours employers can expect employees to work, it is noteworthy that high-tech instruments have made it more difficult for those entrusted with protecting workers (e.g. the U.S. Department of Labor) to monitor and regulate the the number of hours worked off of the work site. However, such technology has made it easier for employers more concerned with the "bottom line" to monitor hours worked with reckless disregard for how invasive its monitoring measures may be.

In his 2009 book, *The Tyranny of E-mail*, John Freeman discusses how "The technology that was supposed to set us free to work from anywhere, to check in and clock out on our own time, has now become the longest employee leash ever invented because we can't seem to log off" (Freeman 2009, 135; see also Johnson 2001, 44; Honoré 2004, 187ff; and

Powers 2010, 157ff). "Sixty-five percent of North Americans," Freeman says, "spend more time with their computer than their spouse" (Freeman 2009, 95). According to Freeman, "people who earned between $30,000 and $60,000 were three times as likely as people making less than $30,000 to bring work home. It's almost considered chic to be a workaholic" (*ibid.*, 164). As e-mail use grows, the stresses of working at this frantic pace will only compound, becoming an ever-stronger feedback loop (*ibid.*, 163; see also Powers 2010, 51f).

As early as 1935, Russell was decrying how *"there is far too much work done in the world, [and]…immense harm is caused by the belief that work is virtuous"* (emphasis in original; Russell 1935, 9; see also 12). No good purpose, he argued, is served by labor-saving devices if the expectations and demands for labor increase at least as much as the amount of labor the device in question is supposedly saving (cf. Freeman 2009, 161). These concerns remain legitimate today. Carl Honoré, a twenty-first century Canadian journalist based in London, observes how "technology is a false friend. Even when it does save time, it often spoils the effect by generating a whole new set of duties and desires" (Honoré 2004, 218; see also Mozorov 2011, 285).[4]

As Russell would have it, "The morality of work is the morality of slaves, and the modern world has no need of slavery" (Russell 1935, 14). He would hardly celebrate the proliferation of tasks this high-tech age facilitates.

(ii) Privacy

In 1928, Russell observed that as economic and political organization increase, so does our need to respect one another's privacy (Russell 1928, 97-8). Far from *respecting* one another's privacy, the high-tech gadgets we employ these days regularly *disrupt* it.[5] It is easy to imagine

---

[4] As Freeman would have it, "Technology that appears to transcend the limits of the physical world merely shifts the costs of its use elsewhere" (Freeman 2009, 194). See also Powers (2010, 48, 185).

[5] An altogether different and, in a sense, even opposite problem with the Internet is its facilitation of *excessive* privacy. Thus, critics have warned that "far from creating a true global village," electronic networks will make it possible that "Users may turn away from their television sets only to withdraw into narrow communion with other residents of their exclusive 'cyburbia'" (Everett-Green 1996, 159)—what Cullen Murphy calls a "Möbius strip of the likeminded" (Murphy 2012, 79). Noam Chomsky remarks that "A teenager in the U.S. talking on the Internet to somebody in Tibet…is an instance of isolated individuals, and it probably has pathological elements. In my view, it will probably be personally harmful to society" (Chomsky 2010, 59).

Russell taking umbrage at the business world's disregard for our privacy. Lori Andrews' *I Know Who You Are and I Saw What You Did* is a provocative account of how "laws protect us against outsiders tapping our phones and reading our private mail. Even prisoners can send mail to their lawyers without having those letters read by prison officials. But everything we post on social networks is fair game for the engineers behind Facebook and any other data miner" (Andrews 2011, 12; see also 44-5). A *Wall Street Journal* 2010 investigation found that, in spite of its professed privacy policy, many of Facebook's most popular applications provided marketing and internet tracking companies with its users' "identifying information" (*ibid.*, 25).[6] Vastly greater sums of money and talent are expended on developing data aggregation technologies than thwarting or preventing them (*ibid.*, 41; see also 45-6). Moreover, "Your private data is being used not just to sell you products but to deny you certain opportunities" (*ibid.*, 35; see also 55f and chapter 10 generally).[7] Rebecca MacKinnon, in her book *Consent of the Networked*, explains the "increasingly opaque and unaccountable ways" in which "power over citizens' digital lives is being exercised" at the "digital intersection of governmental and corporate power" (MacKinnon 2012, 243; see also 64).[8] And a book with something of a Russellian ring throughout is

---

[6] For a timeline regarding the erosion of Facebook's privacy policy, see Andrews (2011, 126-8) and MacKinnon (2012, 144ff).

[7] Andrews also explains:

> Data aggregation about identifiable people can quickly turn into a means to target them. Even information originally collected for benign purposes can turn deadly. In *Delete: The Virtue of Forgetting in the Digital Age*, Viktor Mayer-Schönberger describes how the Dutch government in the 1930s created a registration system to keep better track of its citizens. The population registry listed each citizen's "name, birth date, address, religion, and other personal information" for the purpose of better facilitating government administration and welfare planning. However when the Nazis invaded the Netherlands during World War II, they seized possession of the registry and used it to go after the Dutch citizens who were Jewish or gypsy (Andrews 2011, 72-3).

[8] Cf. Andrews (2011, 70). As Andrews sees things,

> Rather than Big Brother watching, it is Big Business that is monitoring, recording, analyzing, and even selling your private information (Andrews 2011, 39).

Andrews adds,

> There are several federal laws related to computer hacking and the regulation of electronic communications that could be applied to the unauthorized collection of information about people from social networks and other parts of the Web. The Computer Fraud and Abuse Act, the Stored Communications Act, and the Wiretap Act could have been interpreted to protect people. Courts, however, generally have refused to use these laws to protect against the collection of personal information through cookies or the interception of transmissions from a person's computer (*ibid.* 43).

In 2010, Visa, MasterCard, and PayPal announced their plans to start refusing transactions for parties interested in making donations to WikiLeaks (Assange 2012, 16). "In a halting

Evgeny Morozov's *The Net Delusion: The Dark Side of Internet Freedom*.[9] Morozov points out that

> The West excels at building and supporting effective tools to pierce through the firewalls of authoritarian governments, but it is also skilled at letting many of its corporations disregard the privacy of their users, often with disastrous implications for those who live in oppressive societies. Very little about the currently fashionable imperative to promote Internet freedom suggests that Western policymakers are committed to resolving the problems that they themselves have helped to create. (Morozov 2011, 101)

Morozov continues:

> It's not a given that IBM should be selling SMS-filtering technology to authoritarian states; that services like Google Buzz should be launched with minimum respect for the privacy of its users; that researchers at public universities like the University of California should be accepting funding from the Chinese government to work on better video surveillance technology; or that Facebook should be abdicating their responsibility to thoroughly screen developers of its third-party applications. (Morozov 2011, 178)[10]

---

statement at the Frontline Club in London in October 2011, Assange explained that Visa, MasterCard, PayPal, and Bank of America had successfully starved WikiLeaks of the cash it needed to survive. The financial embargo on the group had reduced the group's funding from donations of more than three hundred thousand dollars in the twenty-four hours before the embargo to a trickle of less than ten thousand dollars a month" (Greenberg 2012, 320). MacKinnon observes, "The response to WikiLeaks' release of classified cables is a troubling example of private companies' unaccountable power over citizens' political speech, and of how government can manipulate that power in informal and thus unaccountable ways" (MacKinnon 2012, 86; See also 93, 128, and 148 and Assange 2012, 92-3.). Russell would probably have been able to relate to the darkness of Morozov's view that "It is becoming more and more difficult to convince the world that Google and Twitter are not just the digital-age equivalents of Halliburton and Exxon Mobile" (Morozov 2011, 239).

[9] Morozov also has a later book about how "Internet-centrism has become something of a religion" and there is a consequent need for applying a "secularization of communication...to contexts as different as politics and crime prevention" (Morozov 2013, 62).

[10] Or as Morozov says in his second book, "Last time I checked, much of this proverbial 'Internet' was built by for-profit companies with the explicit objective of making money, not defending human rights. Why should we be reengineering our political institutions with this model in mind?" (Morozov 2013, 125). According to MacKinnon, "much of the censorship in North Africa and the Middle East is being carried out largely with North American software" (MacKinnon 2012, 191; see also 58ff, 138, and 182 and Andrews 2011, 63).

Of special concern to Russell in this arena would be the potential excesses of *police power* (Russell 1938, 192-3). He would have been in full sympathy with the Electronic Frontier Foundation's warnings in the mid-90s about the dangers computer technology poses to civil rights and privacy.[11] Andrews reports: "Social networks have become a cop's best friend…A survey by the International Association of Chiefs of Police of 728 law enforcement agencies from 48 states and the District of Columbia found that 62% of the agencies used social networks in criminal investigations… The U.S. constitution['s]…protections against improper government action are routinely being ignored as social networks are used to uncover possible criminal behavior, to prosecute the offender, and to enhance the penalty" (Andrews 2011, 162-3).[12]

As of this writing, the world is aghast at the revelations of Edward J. Snowden, a former intelligence analyst employed by one of the consulting firms[13] with which the U.S. National Security Agency (NSA) works. The scandal concerns the consulting firm's use of computer surveillance programs, such as XKeyscore. XKeyscore "allows analysts to search with no prior authorization through vast databases containing e-mails, online chats and the browsing histories of millions of individuals…[T]raining materials

---

[11] Everett-Green (1996, 159), See also Assange (2012, 33-40). "[I]n contrast to the protection of offline speech, people have been penalized for exercising their rights of expression on Facebook or other social networks" (Andrews 2011, 76). "The FBI had lobbied hard for a system under which the police would have a software key to unlock all encrypted communications in order to uncover criminal activity" (Alexander 1998, 180).

[12] A problem to which MacKinnon points are the priorities of private intermediaries, such as Google, Facebook, and Twitter for whom "the operational costs of defying government orders often appear to outweigh the risks of upsetting some customers—certainly in the short and medium term" (MacKinnon 2012, 89-90; see also 199.) As Julian Assange points out,

> these companies have some serious ethical liability that stems from the fact that they're building these systems and they've made the economic choice to basically sell their users out. And this isn't even a technical thing. This isn't about technology at all, it's about economics. They have decided that it is more important to collaborate with the state and to sell out their users and to violate their privacy and to be part of the system of control—to be paid back for being a part of the surveillance culture, to be part of the culture of control—than to be resistant to it, and so they become part of it. They're complicit and liable. (Assange 2012, 58; See also Morozov 2013, 181-9)

This is where Eric Schmidt and Jared Cohen seem to miss the point when blithely depicting technology companies as enjoying "all the values of a democratic society with none of the baggage of being a government" (Schmidt and Cohen 2013, 180-1).

[13] The increase in the number of private contractors the NSA uses is noteworthy. In the early 2000s, the NSA used ten primary contractors; nowadays it uses over 1,000. "So there is a smearing out of the border between what is government and what is the private sector" (Assange 2012, 53).

for XKeyscore detail how analysts can use it and other systems to mine enormous agency databases by filling in a simple on-screen form giving only a broad justification for the search. The request is not reviewed by a court or any NSA personnel before it is processed."[14]

The inventor of the World Wide Web, Tim Berners-Lee, is now maintaining it is high time to upgrade the protections in the Magna Carta so as to duly allow for the Internet age.[15]

(iii) The Role of Deliberate Thought in Our Lives

Russell perceived the conflict between a speedy life and one of sufficient deliberation. A prime example of his views is his reaction to the new possibilities of travel in his day. In 1958, Russell reflected,

> There is no reason whatever to suppose that the new possibilities of travel will do anything to promote wisdom. On the contrary they will, as air travel has already done, cause people to spend more time in locomotion and, therefore, less in thought. Already, the foreign ministers of the Great Powers spend so much time in visiting each other's countries, and also those smaller countries which they hope to influence, that they have become unable to acquire even those elements of knowledge which are of most importance if their policies are to have even a modicum of good sense.

---

[14] Glenn Greenwald, "XKeyscore: NSA Tool Collects 'Nearly Everything a User Does on the Internet,'" Guardian, July 31, 2013. Greenwald continues:

> Under US law, the NSA is required to obtain an individualized FISA warrant only if the target of their surveillance is a "US person," though no such warrant is required for intercepting the communications of Americans with foreign targets. But XKeyscore provides the technological capability, if not the legal authority, to target even US persons for extensive electronic surveillance without a warrant provided that some identifying information, such as their e-mail or IP address, is known to the analyst…A 2010 *Washington Post* article reported that "every day, collection systems at the [NSA] intercept and store 1.7bn e-mails, phone calls and other type of communications."…In 2012, there were at least 41 billion total records collected and stored in XKeyscore for a single 30-day period. (*ibid.*)

Even such digital age mavens as Schmidt and Cohen counsel, "We need to fight for our privacy or we will lose it, particularly in moments of national crisis, when security hawks will insist that with each terrible crime, governments are entitled to access more private, of formerly private, information" (Schmidt and Cohen 2013, 256). A good overview of the history of the NSA's warrantless domestic surveillance practices since 9/11 is available at Assange (2012, 167-9).

[15] MacKinnon (2012, 111).

> Bustling activity will more and more take the place of reasonable consideration. (Russell 1958)[16]

This tension between the speed with which an activity can be performed and the likelihood that it will be undertaken with due deliberation is noteworthy and relevant to understanding how Russell would view the online world. I think he would be underwhelmed by people's fetish for *multitasking*. Evidence is accumulating that we are not as adept at it as we may fancy.[17] Typing and publishing have certainly become more convenient. However, thanks to electronic communication, sustained reading is more challenging than ever (Freeman 2009, 98), along with the "focused, linear attention" it develops (*ibid.*, 179). In 2006, Jakob Nielsen, a veteran consultant on Web page design, conducted an "eye-tracking study of Web users" which found that "hardly any of the participants read online text in a methodical, line-by-line way, as they'd typically read a page of text in a book" (Carr 2010, 134ff).[18] Nicholas Carr's *The Shallows* addresses this subject. Carr

---

[16] Robert Everett-Green, Senior Features Writer for the *Globe and Mail*, credits Fedor Dostoyevsky with one of the "earliest and most prescient warnings about electronic media" in the novel *The Brothers Karamazov* (1879-1880):

> We are assured that the world is becoming more and more united, is being formed into brotherly communion, by the shortening of distances, by the transmitting of thoughts through the air," he wrote. In the novelist's view, however, the devices responsible for these transmissions would only stimulate "meaningless and foolish desires." Dostoyevsky's novel was published only about four years after Alexander Graham Bell secured his patent on the telephone, which may be regarded as the first instrument of cyberspace. (Everett-Green 1996, 159)

[17] Freeman cogently argues that "a work climate that revolves around multitasking and constant interruptions has narrowed our cognitive windows down to a core basic facility: rote, mechanical tasks" (Freeman 2009, 140-1). Rather, "the ability to think clearly and critically and develop an argument comes from reading in a focused manner" (*ibid.*, 179).

[18] According to Carr, "the Net diminishes…the ability to know, in depth, a subject for ourselves, to construct within our own minds the rich and idiosyncratic set of connections that give rise to a singular intelligence" (Carr 2010, 143). In contrast to readers of online text, Chomsky speaks of how

> There's no point in reading a book if you let it pass before your eyes and then forget about it ten minutes later. Reading a book is an intellectual exercise, which stimulates thought, questions, imagination.
>
> I suspect that will disappear…I can see from correspondence that people are constantly asking questions about something they saw on YouTube but not about an article or a book…Take, say, electronic books…[W]hen I read a book I care about, I want to make comments in the margins, I want to underline things. I want to make notes on the flyleaf. Otherwise I don't even know what to go back to. You can't do that the same way with an electronic book. Words just pass into your eyes. Maybe they don't even stay in your brain. (Chomsky 2013c, 104)

As Carr puts it, "when we start using the Web as a substitute for personal memory, bypassing

despairs, "In the choices we have made, consciously or not, about how we use our computers, we have rejected the intellectual tradition of solitary, single-minded concentration, the ethic that the book bestowed on us. We have cast our lot with the juggler" (*ibid.*, 114).[19]

In 1951, Russell expressed regret that, "The radio and cinema between them take up a great deal of time that would formerly have been spent in reading….[I]t is difficult to compete with broadcasting. If you broadcast, you may reach five million people. If you write a book, even a very successful one, you are not likely to reach more than a hundred thousand" (Russell 1994, 1). With broadcasted material becoming more convenient and prevalent than ever, Russell would find it *gloomy* that people are reading even less than in his day. I think he would have appreciated Leo Marx's description of technology as a *hazardous concept* prone to *stifle and obfuscate analytic thinking* (Morozov 2011, 294).[20]

William Powers, in his *Hamlet's Blackberry*, criticizes our current society's "unexamined faith in nonstop connectedness" (Powers 2010, 28). His musings on the subject include the following:

> Skillful life management yields wisdom and happiness. It's a terrific ideal, but the busier our days become and the more others control the reins, the harder it is to imagine achieving it (*ibid.*, 92).

> We don't ask these questions because they're philosophical and, unlike technology, which is concrete and quantifiable, philosophy seems abstract and squishy. So we avoid them, focusing instead on the tools themselves, breathlessly trying to keep up with the hot new devices and the latest trends. This is shortsighted since, in the end, it's the philosophical questions that really matter (*ibid.*, 34-5).

> If…there are no gaps in your connectedness, you never get to that place where the most valuable benefits are. We're

---

the inner processes of consolidation, we risk emptying our minds of their riches" (Carr 2010, 192).

[19] There is a critical difference between "information—random fact and disaggregated data—and knowledge, facts and data arranged in a way to tell a story, to explain a mystery, to solve a puzzle. The Web supplies information, while reading printed texts results in knowledge" (Herring 2007, 139). "Web-based 'reading' contributes to an even more cursory reading comprehension, along with a decline in literacy" (Herring 2007, 132).

[20] Morozov also mentions that "in the era of the Internet…the perpetual revolution it has unleashed has shortened the time and space left for analytical thinking" (Morozov 2011, 313).

> eliminating the gaps, when we should be creating them. (*ibid.*, 31)

Freeman discusses the manner in which *true agency* entails a level of deliberation incompatible with the "bite-sized moments of attention" all too characteristic of computer and e-mail activity (Freeman 2009, 158, 160).[21] He cites Herb Simon's point that "a wealth of information creates a poverty of attention, and a need to allocate that attention efficiently among the overabundance of information sources that might consume it" (*ibid.*, 139-40). Noam Chomsky points out that "Access to the Internet is a great thing. A huge amount of material is available. On the other hand,…[t]here's no point in having a lot of data available unless you can make some sense out of it. And that takes thought, reflection, inquiry. I think these capacities are being degraded to an extent" (Chomsky 2013c, 104-5; see also Morozov 2013, 9).

Can we really believe such developments would be welcomed by a man who, in 1916, lamented, "Men fear thought as they fear nothing else on earth more than ruin, more even than death" (Russell 1916, 115)?

(iv) Literacy

Russell believed that society has an excessively utilitarian conception of education (Russell 1934, 138). Were he alive today, he would have criticized the establishment's celebration of computer literacy over traditional literacy.[22] Chris Shute, author of *Bertrand Russell: Education as the Power of Independent Thought*, observes that society tends to put less value today on knowing material well enough that it can be recited from memory. Although much is made of knowing how to *access* data through comput-

---

[21] As Robert Reich says,
> There's something insistent about home faxes, voice mails, e-mails, beepers, cell phones, and car phones. They must be responded to. Or you have to use them to contact someone else if you gain some piece of knowledge that the other person is likely to value and expects you to share at once. After all, the sole purpose of these gadgets is to locate us when we're doing something else. They put us, literally, on call. They break into our lives like burglars. They lay claim even to those small units of time and space that used to be entirely private, like when we're behind the wheel of a car, in an airplane, or walking from place to place. (Reich 2001, 117)

[22] With the popularity of text messaging, for example, there are mounting concerns that "standards of English would drop as text abbreviations entered the mainstream" (Stewart 2006, 165).

ers,[23] "to lose entirely the mechanisms by which we furnish our minds with permanent resources in the form of memorable ideas and beautiful words would be a sad loss of intellectual independence" (Shute 2002, 35-6). John Seely Brown, a researcher of learning, argues that the traditionally organized approaches to learning are *passé* in the twenty-first century and that competence at *navigating* the high-tech age's array of resources is this century's version of *literacy* (cited in Selingo 2013, 174). Russell would be utterly unable to see any good coming from the prevailing consensus that literacy is now "nothing but a quaint notion" (Carr 2010, 111; see also 112).[24]

The internet's lack of quality control results in the spread of much nonsense.[25] Concerns have also arisen about the ability of blogs to amass the power of the press without incurring the press' responsibility for "accuracy and fairness" (Alexander 2006, 164). Chomsky worries that people coming to the internet without sufficient discriminatory powers run the risk of being "drawn into completely crazed cocoons of wild interpretations….Built into the Internet is a system for creating cults" (Chomsky 2007, 151-2; see also Chomsky 2013b, 53).

4. GEOPOLITICS AND THE INTERNET

A staple of Russell's 1931 *Scientific Outlook* was his express distinction between science as knowledge and science as technique. Russell certainly included science as knowledge among the components of the good life. However, he believed the world's progress in science as technique has unfortunately outpaced the world's moral progress (Russell 1923, 70). It follows then, for him, that science as *technique* was increasingly perilous until and unless we make comparable progress in properly appreciating life's ultimate purposes.

From Russell's perspective,

---

[23] Indeed, "today's librarians have become more technicians than scholars" (Herring 2007, 13).
[24] As Jeffrey J. Selingo explains in his book, *College Unbound*, "the rush to embrace technology as a solution to every problem has created tension on campuses over whether the critical role higher education plays in preparing the whole person to be a productive citizen in a democratic society is at risk. Indeed, in an increasingly complex world, the foundation of learning—a liberal-arts education—is more important than ever" (Selingo 2013, xvii).
[25] "[T]he Web in general [has]…simply become too commercial and much too often overcrowded with junk….Even information once found on the Web may not be found when searched for again at a later date" (Herring 2007, 50).

Man hitherto has been prevented from realizing his hopes by ignorance as to means. As this ignorance disappears he becomes increasingly able to mould his physical environment, his social milieu and himself into the forms which he deems best. In so far as he is wise this new power is beneficent; in so far as he is foolish it is quite the reverse. If, therefore, a scientific civilization is to be a good civilization it is necessary that increase in knowledge should be accompanied by increase in wisdom. I mean by wisdom a right conception of the ends of life. This is something which science in itself does not provide. (Russell 1931, ix-x; see also Russell 1957, 159, 204; and Russell 1952, 110)

Computer science would be no exception to these rules concerning science as *technique*. That is, computer science as *technique* would most likely have impressed Russell as having grim prospects as long as the world lacks appropriate conceptions of life's final aims.

Since the mid-2000s, the internet, along with mobile phones, have become sufficiently common that they have begun to have geopolitical repercussions, such as a means to announcing political demonstrations and influencing and/or reacting to election results. To give the high-tech age its due, in contrast with old-fashioned newspapers, the rapidity with which people can use Facebook and Twitter to communicate makes it more difficult for would-be censors to obstruct the dissemination of data (Andrews 2011, 67). Some have credited WikiLeaks with catalyzing the so-called Arab Spring (Assange 2012, 157-8; Greenberg 2012, 3; MacKinnon 2012, 24; Sanger 2012, 283-6; but see Chomsky 2013c, 112). In any case, when the Tunisian street vendor Mohamed Bouazizi set himself on fire on December 17, 2010, not just satellite television news but mobile phones[26] and social networking websites rendered this local suicide *viral*, thereby precipitating a Jasmine Revolution in that country the repercussions of which are still playing themselves out to this day (Almond 2012, 172). Digital activism of this sort has prompted many to tout high-tech devices as a force for the spread of democracy (e.g., Brown 2012, 106).[27]

---

[26] Mobile phones have enjoyed politically significant roles in China, Ukraine, Kuwait (Stewart 2006, 165), Kenya (Albarado 2008, 181), and Iran (Ray 2010, 223).

[27] As the social thinker Jeremy Rifkin depicts such developments, "The Internet generation, which began by challenging the centralized media conglomerates in the West with peer sharing of music and information, is now beginning to flex its peer power in the Middle East by challenging the centralized political rule of autocratic governments" (Rifkin 2011, 18).

As early as 1924, though, Russell noted that his long experience with statesmen and governments had made him skeptical: "I am compelled to fear that science will be used to promote the power of dominant groups, rather than to make men happy. Icarus, having been taught to fly by his father Daedalus, was destroyed by his rashness. I fear that the same fate may overtake the populations whom modern men of science have taught to fly" (Russell 1924, 5).[28]

I think Russell would have been similarly skeptical of the internet with regard to the motives and practices of governments.[29] He was a self-described Cassandra doomed to prophecy evil and not be believed (Russell

---

[28] As Assange sees it, "underpinning the high-tech communications revolution—and the liberty that we have extracted from that—is the whole neoliberal, transnational, globalized modern market economy. It is in fact the peak of that….[I]t really is the top of the pyramid of the whole neoliberal system" (Assange 2012, 27). Assange continues:

> [S]ome people that seem to be in the authority about war start talking technology as if they understand it. Such people are often talking about cyber war and not one of them, not a single one, is talking about cyber peace-building, or anything related to peace-building. They are always talking about war because that's their business and they are trying to control technological and legal processes as a means for promoting their own interests. So when we have no control over our technology such people wish to use it for their ends, for war specifically. That's a recipe for some pretty scary stuff. (*ibid.*, 32)

Assange understands the "most probable scenario for the future" generally to be "an extremely confining, homogenized, postmodern transnational totalitarian structure with incredible complexity, absurdities and debasements, and within that incredible complexity a space where only the smart rats can go" (*ibid.*, 159).

[29] Speaking of the motives and practices of governments, one can only believe that an advantage to the high-tech age that Russell would have applauded would be the ease with which whistleblowers and dissidents can safely disclose governments' misconduct. He regretted that, in America, "in addition to the official Government of that country, there is another entrenched in the Pentagon and CIA capable…of giving orders to the official Government" (Perkins 2002, 353-4). One can easily imagine him singing the praises of WikiLeaks. The best evidence for this is at the very end of his pamphlet *War: the Offspring of Fear* where he says:

> Secret diplomacy must cease. Of all the features in our present methods which tend to defeat the will for peace, and which might be altered without waiting for the consent of other nations, the chief is secret diplomacy. Where a settled policy rather than a sudden crisis is in question, no obligation or debt of honour ought to be created without the full previous knowledge of the House of Commons and the country. So long as this principle is not observed, democratic government is a farce and a pretence. No national or human interest is served by secrecy: the only interest served is that of the official clique who are thus enabled to pursue unchecked a policy entailing terrible liabilities, and to keep the support of men who would execrate their policy if they knew what it was. (Russell 1915, 11-2).

Considering the escalation in the volumes of material the U.S. government is routinely classifying (Greenberg 2012, 5; Morozov 2013, 95), I think Russell would have shared Noam Chomsky's sentiments that "Many of the classified documents have little to do with genuine

1931, 259). For all his reverence for science, he had misgivings about even space exploration as the product of governments' "baser motives" (Russell 1959, 18; see also Trainer 2003). It is not much of a stretch to contend that Russell would think computer technology would be employed more to promote the power of dominant groups than to make men happy.

Russell once quipped "the bulk of the public expenditure of most civilized Governments consists in payment for past wars or preparation for future wars" (Russell 1935, 10-1). One can readily picture Russell claiming that the nature and ultimate fate of cyberspace is discernible by considering its origins in the military-industrial complex. He would say the net gain or loss regarding cyberspace technology for human welfare depends, ultimately, on the fate of the *military* applications of the technology.

Morozov acknowledges that "under the conditions of Western liberal democracies…the Internet has been weakening the state and decentralizing power." However, he argues, since these are the only circumstances with which western observers are acquainted, the consequence is a *Western failure to grasp the importance of the Internet to authoritarian regimes* (Morozov 2011, 289).[30] "One of the temptations that Western observers should avoid," Morozov adds, "is to interpret the fact that authoritarian governments are adjusting their operating methods as a sign of democratization" (*ibid.*, 90).[31] Rather, authoritarian governments have proven to be singularly

---

security but a lot to do with preventing the population from knowing what the government is up to" (Chomsky 2013c, 110). "Bradley Manning," Chomsky writes, "is charged with doing something which, in my opinion, is not a crime but a service to the country….I think Manning should be applauded and the government should be harshly condemned for throwing out the basic principles of law and human rights" (*ibid.*, 113).

Russell would also probably agree with Morozov that "one can't be calling for imposing more restrictions on sites like WikiLeaks, as many American policymakers did in the summer of 2010, and be disparaging China and Iran for similar impulses" (Morozov 2011, 241).

What is less clear, however, is how Russell would have reacted to corporations' efforts to globally enforce intellectual property rights on the internet—efforts Assange and his ilk denounce as "heavy-handed and wide-reaching internet censorship" (Assange 2012, 174). Since Russell earned a living as a writer, would he disagree with Assange or would he have settled for Chomsky's view that the likes of creative artists ought to be publicly funded so as to eliminate the whole piracy issue (Chomsky 2013c, 106-8)?

[30] Morozov also discusses Western governments' selective advocacy of Internet freedom (Morozov 2011, 224).
[31] Morozov also issues the following warnings:

> Denying that greater information flows, combined with advanced technologies like face or voice recognition, can result in the overall strengthening of authoritarian regimes is a dangerous path to take, if only because it numbs us to potential regulatory interventions and the need to rein in our own Western corporate excesses. (Morozov 2011, 178)

adept at rapidly mastering the latest innovations in controlling the internet (Morozov 2011, 139-40).[32]

We need look no further than China's Golden Shield Project (a.k.a. the "Great Firewall") for an example of how a government can monitor internet use, block access to sites, and tamper with search systems. "These are capabilities that the Master of the Sacred Palace could scarcely have imagined, and might devoutly have wished for" (Murphy 2012, 126). It is true that Twitter and Facebook's coverage of the June 2009 Iranian election were important in filling the void resulting from the traditional media's ban on covering that country's opposition rallies. However, the Iranian authorities had only to employ Twitter and Facebook in order to "collect names and trace relationships" (Murphy 2012, 240).[33] The 2009 and 2010 developments in Iran and Belarus flaunt how supposedly people-empowering, democratizing technologies, such as mobile phones and text messaging, have played into oppressive governments' hands by providing them with a

---

> Where the pundits and the policymakers have failed is in understanding the sophistication and flexibility of the censorship apparatus built on top of the Internet. (*ibid.*, 96)

> In virtually all authoritarian states, governments maintain control over communication networks and can turn them off at the first sign of protests. (*ibid.*, 53-4)

One can readily envision Julian Assange marveling at the naïveté exhibited when contrasting "authoritarian regimes" with those of the West:

> My experience in the West is that it is just so much more sophisticated in the number of layers of indirection and obfuscation about what is actually happening. These layers are there to give deniability to the censorship that is occurring….Western societies specialize in laundering censorship and structuring the affairs of the powerful such that any remaining public speech that gets through has a hard time affecting the true power relationships of a highly fiscalized society, because such relationships are hidden in layers of complexity and secrecy." (Assange 2012, 123; see also 130)

[32] MacKinnon also reports Internet scholar Manuel Castells' warning that "digitally empowered citizens may have won important victories, but these victories are not necessarily permanent 'because the powerholders in the network society' will do everything possible to 'enclose free communication in commercialized and policed networks'" (MacKinnon 2012, 13). "The more strategic and forward-thinking a government is," according to MacKinnon, "in managing and controlling the companies that operate a country's information networks—both in terms of their technical structure and their legal governance—the more likely it is that dissent can be kept within manageable boundaries" (MacKinnon 2012, 53-4). Examples of tyrannical governments sabotaging or being empowered by the high-tech age are available at MacKinnon (2012, 58).

[33] When the Mubarak government was caught off-guard by a 2008 Facebook-organized protest in support of suppressed strikers, the government had only to use Facebook to track down the protesters (Assange 2012, 23). This April 6 Youth Movement went on to "play a role" in the 2011 Egyptian revolution (*ibid.*, 164).

means to conducting "antidissident surveillance" (MacKinnon 2012, 56).[34] A couple of days after Egypt's first Tahrir Square protest, President Hosni Mubarak had only to react to the social network devices by pulling the plug on that country's internet (Andrews 2011, 61; see also Murphy 2012, 239-40; Assange 2012, 24). And on June 3 of that year, in an attempt to quell antigovernment protests in Syria, that country's government shut down Internet access (Almond 2012, 28).[35] Morozov cogently argues:

> Unbridled cyber-utopianism is an expensive ideology to maintain because authoritarian governments don't stand still and there are absolutely no guarantees they won't find a way to turn the Internet into a powerful tool of oppression. If, on closer examination, it turns out that the Internet has also empowered the secret police, the censors, and the propaganda offices of a modern authoritarian regime, it's quite likely that the process of democratization will become harder, not easier. Similarly, if the Internet has dampened the level of antigovernment sentiment—because people have acquired access to cheap and almost infinite digital entertainment or because they feel they need the government to protect them from the lawlessness of cyberspace—it certainly gives the regime yet another source of legitimacy. If the Internet is reshaping the very nature and culture of antigovernment resistance and dissent, shifting it away from real-world practices and toward anonymous virtual spaces, it will also have significant consequences for the scale and tempo of the protest movement, not all of them positive.
>
> That's an insight that has been lost on most observers of the political power of the Internet. Refusing to acknowledge that the Web can actually strengthen rather than undermine authoritarian regimes is extremely irresponsible and ultimately results in bad policy, if only because

---

[34] "[I]f we're talking about everybody in the Third World being spied on, realistically what does that mean? It means their telephone systems, which are their link to the rest of the world, are spy devices when someone chooses to use the data collected in that way" (Jacob Appelbaum, in Assange 2012, 49; see also 45). "Ten years ago this was seen to be a fantasy, this was seen to be something only paranoid people believed in..." (Assange 2012, 40).

[35] Rebecca MacKinnon's diagnosis of this problem is that "In our dependence, we have a problem: we understand how power works in the physical world, but we do not yet have a clear understanding of how power works in the digital realm" (MacKinnon 2012, 13).

it gives policymakers false confidence that the only things they need to be doing are proactive—rather than reactive—in nature. But if, on careful examination, it turns out that certain types of authoritarian regimes can benefit from the Internet in disproportionally more ways than their opponents, the focus of Western democracy promotion work should shift from empowering the activists to topple their regimes to countering the governments' own exploitation of the Web lest they become even more authoritarian. There is no point in making a revolution more effective, quick, and anonymous if the odds of the revolution's success are worsening in the meantime. (Morozov 2011, 27-8)

It is easy to imagine Russell concurring with Morozov's assessment that "*If the hidden costs of digital activism include the loss of coherence, morality, or even sustainability of the opposition movement, it may not be a solution worth pursuing*" (emphasis added; *ibid.*, 304).

5. CONCLUSION

I maintain that Russell would take minimal interest in belonging to the *digerati*. He would argue instead that the Information Age is fraught with more costs than gains. He would deplore the way the world of high-tech devices has increased an already overworked people's workload. The utterly inelegant expressions that are the standard fare in e-mail and text messaging would have impressed him as vulgar. He would also have abhorred the manifold distractions so typical of our modern daily routines and would denounce our high-tech age as posing yet even more serious obstacles to sustained thinking.

Last but hardly least, Russell believed that the human race has survived up to now thanks only to dominant groups' ignorance of the ways to implement their destructive designs. Now, with the technological wonder that is cyberspace, Russell would argue that the politically empowered groups have one more tool to distract and oppress the rest of us.[36]

---

[36] An earlier version of this paper was presented June 2, 2012 at the 39th annual meeting of the Bertrand Russell Society at Plymouth State University in Plymouth, New Hampshire.

Appendix on Christopher Farley's View of Russell and E-mail

Christopher Farley served as secretary for Bertrand Russell and a director of the Bertrand Russell Peace Foundation. On Feb. 29, 2012, Ken Blackwell of the Russell Archives asked Christopher Farley about Bertrand Russell and the use of e-mail. Farley replied as follows:

> I realize that I have failed to answer your suggestion that I speculate about how BR might have responded to the arrival of e-mail. It has been useful for me to have delayed responding, and am surprised to feel considerable confidence in my conclusions.
>
> I contend that BR would not have wished to have any direct involvement in it (unless perhaps if it had arrived in his own childhood). There are various reasons for this conclusion:
>
> 1. BR was a creature of habit. He insisted on an ordered day. Breakfast—brought to his bedroom—was invariably at the same hour of day. Likewise his first appearance, fully dressed, his first cup of China tea, his first visitor (if any), lunch, etc.
>
> 2. BR was very comfortable with a pen. He liked to write longhand, and could "hear" what he would have spoken. His handwriting was legible, fast, and unadorned by corrections.
>
> 3. BR retained some of the values long passed. He would have continued to recognize that all manner of incoming correspondence deserved whenever possible a personal reply as a matter of courtesy.
>
> 4. BR's use of an earlier means of communication, the telephone, is not a reliable guide to his response to e-mail. He liked occasionally to hear the voices of relatives and friends.
>
> 5. BR would have recognized the advantages offered by e-mail, and would have welcomed a secretary using it to speed events and to seek information for him.

Bibliography

Albarado, Lawrence. 2009. "Citizen Journalism: A News [R]evolution." In Encyclopaedia Britannica, Inc. *Britannica Book of the Year*. Chicago: Encyclopaedia Britannica, Inc.

Alexander, Steve. 2010. "Computers and Information Systems." In Encyclopaedia Britannica, Inc. *Britannica Book of the Year*. Chicago: Encyclopaedia Britannica, Inc.

Almond, Mark. 2012. "The Arab Spring: The End of the Beginning." In Encyclopaedia Britannica, Inc. *Britannica Book of the Year*. Chicago: Encyclopaedia Britannica, Inc.

Andrews, Lori. 2011. *I Know Who You Are and I Saw What You Did: Social Networks and the Death of Privacy*. New York: Free Press.

Assange, Julian. 2012. *Cypherpunks: Freedom and the Future of the Internet*. New York: O/R Books.

Bergen, Peter L. 2011. *The Longest War: The Enduring Conflict between America and Al-Qaeda*. New York: Free Press.

Blake, Peter. 1993. *No Place like Utopia*. New York: Alfred A. Knopf.

Brown, Michael Barratt. 2012. "A New Revolution." *Spokesman* 116.

Carr, Nicholas. 2010. *The Shallows: What the Internet Is Doing to Our Brains*. New York: Norton.

Chomsky, Noam. 2007. *What We Say Goes*. New York: Metropolitan Books.

Chomsky, Noam. 2010. *Indigenous Resistance*. San Francisco: City Lights.

Chomsky, Noam. 2013a. *Nuclear War and Environmental Catastrophe*. New York: Seven Stories Press.

Chomsky, Noam. 2013b. *On Western Terrorism: From Hiroshima to Drone Warfare*. London: Pluto Press.

Chomsky, Noam. 2013c. *Power Systems: Global Democratic Uprisings and the New Challenges to U.S. Empire*. New York: Metropolitan Books.

Clark, Ronald. 1976. *The Life of Bertrand Russell*. New York: Alfred A. Knopf.

Crawshay-Williams, Rupert. 1970. *Russell Remembered*. New York: Oxford University Press.

Everett-Green, Robert. 1996. "Cyberspace." In Encyclopaedia Britannica, Inc. *Britannica Book of the Year*. Chicago: Encyclopaedia Britannica, Inc.

Freeman, John. 2009. *The Tyranny of E-Mail: The Four-Thousand-Year Journey to Your Inbox*. New York: Scribner.

G8. 2011. "Renewed Commitment for Freedom and Democracy." G8 Summit, Deauville, France. http://ec.europa.eu/commission_2010-2014/president/news/speeches-statements/pdf/deauville-g8-declaration_en.pdf (September 28, 2014).

Greenberg, Andy. 2012. *This Machine Kills Secrets: How WikiLeakers, Cypherpunks, and Hacktivists Aim to Free the World's Information*. New York: Dutton.

Greenwald, Glenn. 2013. "XKeyscore: NSA Tool Collects 'Nearly Everything a User Does on the Internet,'" *Guardian*, July 31.

Herring, Mark Y. 2007. *Fool's Gold: Why the Internet Is No Substitute for a Library*. Jefferson, NC: McFarlans & Company.

Honoré, Carl. 2004. *In Praise of Slowness: How a Worldwide Movement is Challenging the Cult of Speed*. New York: HarperCollins.

Johnson, Haynes. 2001. *The Best of Times: America in the Clinton Years*. New York: Harcourt.

MacKinnon, Rebecca. 2012. *Consent of the Networked: The Worldwide Struggle for Internet Freedom*. New York: Basic Books.

Monk, Ray. 1996. *Bertrand Russell: The Spirit of Solitude*. New York: Free Press.

Morozov, Evgeny. 2011. *The Net Delusion: The Dark Side of Internet Freedom*. New York: Public Press.

Morozov, Evgeny. 2013. *To Save Everything, Click Here: The Folly of Technological Solutionism*. New York: Public Affairs.

Murphy, Cullen. 2012. *God's Jury: The Inquisition and the Making of the Modern World*. New York: Houghton Mifflin Harcourt.

Perkins Jr., Ray. 2002. *Yours Faithfully, Bertrand Russell: A Lifelong Fight for Peace, Justice, and Truth in Letters to the Editor*. Chicago & La Salle: Open Court.

Powers, William. 2010. *Hamlet's Blackberry: A Practical Philosophy for Building a Good Life in the Digital Age*. New York: HarperCollins.

Ray, Michael. 2008. "Social Networking: Making Connections on the Web." In Encyclopaedia Britannica, Inc. *Britannica Book of the Year*. Chicago: Encyclopaedia Britannica, Inc.

Ray, Michael. 2010. "Twitter Takes on the World: 140 Characters at a Time." In Encyclopaedia Britannica, Inc. *Britannica Book of the Year*. Chicago: Encyclopaedia Britannica, Inc.

Reich, Robert. 2001. *The Future of Success*. New York: Alfred A. Knopf.

Rifkin, Jeremy. 2011. *The Third Industrial Revolution: How Lateral Power Is Transforming Energy, the Economy, and the World*. New York: Palgrave MacMillan.

Russell, Bertrand. 1915. *War: The Offspring of Fear*. London: Union of Democratic Control.

Russell, Bertrand. 1916. *The Principles of Social Reconstruction*. New York: The Century.

Russell, Bertrand. 1923. *The Prospects of Industrial Civilization*. New York: Routledge.

Russell, Bertrand. 1924. *Icarus*. New York: E.P. Dutton.

Russell, Bertrand 1928. *Skeptical Essays*. New York: Routledge.

Russell, Bertrand. 1931. *The Scientific Outlook*. New York: Norton.

Russell, Bertrand. 1935. *In Praise of Idleness*. London: Allen & Unwin.

Russell, Bertrand. 1938. *Power*. New York: Routledge.

Russell, Bertrand. 1952. *The Impact of Science on Society*. Simon & Schuster.

Russell, Bertrand. 1956. *Portraits from Memory*. New York: Simon & Schuster.

Russell, Bertrand. 1957. *Why I Am Not a Christian*. New York: Simon & Schuster.

Russell, Bertrand. 1958. "Let's Stay off the Moon." *Maclean's Magazine*, August 30.

Russell, Bertrand. 1959. *Common Sense and Nuclear Warfare*. New York: Simon & Schuster.

Russell, Bertrand. 1969. *Dear Bertrand Russell: A Selection of His Correspondence with the General Public 1950-1968*. Introduced and edited by Barry Feinberg and Ronald Kasrils. Boston: Houghton Mifflin.

Russell, Bertrand. 1994. "The Use of Books." In Kenneth Blackwell and Harry Ruja, eds. *A Bibliography of Bertrand Russell*. Volume I. New York: Routledge.

Russell, Bertrand. 1998. "On Curious Learning." In Harry Ruja, ed. *Mortals and Others*. Volume 2. New York: Routledge.

Sanger, David E. 2012. *Confront and Conceal: Obama's Secret Wars and Surprising Use of American Power.* New York: Crown Publishers.

Schmidt, Eric and Cohen, Jared. 2013. *The New Digital Age: Reshaping the Future of People, Nations, and Business*. New York: Alfred A. Knopf.

Selingo, Jeffrey J. 2013. *College (Un)bound: The Future of Higher Education and What It Means for Students*. New York: Houghton Mifflin.

Sheldon, John B. 2011. "Cyberwarfare: The Invisible Threat." In Encyclopaedia Britannica, Inc. *Britannica Book of the Year*. Chicago: Encyclopaedia Britannica, Inc.

Shute, Chris. 2002. *Bertrand Russell: Education as the Power of Independent Thought.* Nottingham: Educational Heretics Press.

Stewart, Alan. 2006. "Text Messaging: WAN2TLK." In Encyclopaedia Britannica, Inc. *Britannica Book of the Year*. Chicago: Encyclopaedia Britannica, Inc.

Tait, Katherine. 1975. *My Father Bertrand Russell*. New York: Harcourt Brace Jovanovich.

Trainer, Chad. 2003. "Earth to Russell: The Limits to Russell's Views on Space Exploration." *Philosophy Now*, March/April, 20-2.

Wood, Alan. 1957. *Bertrand Russell: The Passionate Skeptic*. New York: Allen & Unwin.

THE LOGIC OF STORYTELLING
AND THE STORYTELLING OF LOGIC[*]

Peter Stone

THE GRAPHIC NOVEL *LOGICOMIX*, by Apostolos Doxiadis and Christos Papadimitriou, tells the history of modern logic through the life story of the philosopher Bertrand Russell. As one of the founders of analytic philosophy, Russell tried—and failed—to derive the entirety of mathematics from logic, and thereby set mathematics upon absolutely certain foundations. His life therefore provides an excellent thread upon which to hang a story about modern logic. Doxiadis and Papadimitriou, however, prioritize storytelling over historical accuracy; they therefore omit or alter a number of facts regarding Russell and logic in the interest of telling a "good yarn." There is nothing inherently wrong with prizing entertainment or aesthetic value over attention to the historical record. Unfortunately, the unifying theme developed in *Logicomix* is both extremely old, extremely popular (i.e., large numbers of people respond to it), and extremely pernicious. This theme holds that those who engage in intellectual work are abnormal, useless, even dangerous. *Logicomix* develops this theme using Russell by characterizing his study of the foundations as a complete failure; by implying that this study posed the risk of insanity; and by depicting Russell as inept and incapable of relating to real human concerns, both political and personal. While Doxiadis and Papadimitriou are to be commended for trying to introduce Russell and modern logic to a wider readership, the theme they use to unify

---

[*] Earlier versions of this paper were presented at meetings of the Bertrand Russell Society (BRS); the Bay Area Russell Set (BARS), a local chapter of the BRS; and the Pacific Division of the American Philosophical Association (APA). I would like to thank participants at these events for their helpful comments and observations. This paper was originally published in Seyed Javad Miri (ed.), *Social Theory, Religion and Critical Discourses: Critical Theory in the Postmodern Globe* (Saarbrücken: LAP Lambert Academic Publishing, 2011) and in *Islamic Perspective* 5 (2011), http://iranianstudies.org/journals/islamic-perspective-journal-number -5-2011/. I would like to thank Seyed Javad Miri for permission to reprint the paper here.

this introduction reinforces dangerous popular prejudices—prejudices that Russell himself worked tirelessly to help others overcome.

1. INTRODUCTION

> "*Logicomix* was inspired by the story of the quest for the foundations of mathematics...Yet, despite the fact that its characters are mostly real persons, our book is definitely not—nor does it want to be—a work of history. It is—and wants to be—a graphic novel." —*Logicomix*, 315

In 2008, Apostolos Doxiadis (hereafter AD) and Christos H. Papadimitriou (hereafter CP) published *Logicomix: An Epic Search for Truth* (Doxiadis and Papadimitriou 2009). The book purports to tell, in graphic novel format, the story of the early formative years of modern logic. It tells the story through the eyes of Bertrand Russell, who was importantly responsible for the field's development through such groundbreaking works as *The Principles of Mathematics* (1903) and *Principia Mathematica* (1910, 1912, 1913), the latter of which was coauthored with Russell's mentor, Alfred North Whitehead. The graphic novel depicts Russell in his seventies, at the start of World War II, reflecting upon his life and work and drawing lessons from them for a large audience.[1]

Logicomix was certainly not the first effort to bring philosophy to a mass audience via graphic nonfiction. Previous attempts include the "For Beginners" series (http://www.forbeginnersbooks.com/); the "Introducing" series published by Icon/Totem Books (http://www.introducingbooks.com/); and the "Action Philosophers" comic books written by Fred van Lente and illustrated by Ryan Dunlavey (http://www.eviltwincomics.com/ap.html).[2] But while *Logicomix* may not be the first, it may well prove the most successful of these attempts. *Logicomix* was first published in Greece, where it proved a runaway bestseller. An English translation followed the following year, and it proved similarly successful. It was on the *New York Times* bestseller list, and named one of *Time* magazine's top 10 nonfiction books of 2009. A Dutch edition has already appeared, and translations are

---

[1] Many of the members of his audience are pacifists and isolationists anxious to hear Russell argue for keeping the U.S. out of the war in Europe. They will be disappointed by the end of the novel, though not more than their opponents in the audience.
[2] Russell puts in an appearance in one of these series (Robinson and Groves 1998).

scheduled to appear in Brazil, China, Denmark, Finland, France, Germany, Israel, Italy, Norway, South Korea, Taiwan, and Turkey. The book has also received numerous awards, including the 2010 Annual Book Award of the Bertrand Russell Society.³

AD and CP have thus won both critical praise and extensive sales for their book. In doing so, they have no doubt increased public awareness of both the development of modern logic and the pivotal role played in that development by Russell. Both logicians and Russellians therefore clearly owe AD and CP an enormous debt of gratitude. But that gratitude should not lead them to admire *Logicomix* uncritically. While many people will be introduced to Russell's life and thought through *Logicomix*, that introduction will be marred by the way the book treats Russell's life and thought. For *Logicomix* does both Russell and logic a serious injustice.⁴

The injustice done to Russell by *Logicomix* is not strictly a matter of factual inaccuracy. *Logicomix* does take some liberties with the details of Russell's life, as its authors freely acknowledge. To mention just two such liberties, the book eliminates Russell's brother Frank entirely, and assigns Frank's pivotal role in introducing Russell to mathematics to a fictional tutor (55-56; 77). It also depicts Russell meeting with the logicians Gottlob Frege and Georg Cantor, although no such meetings ever took place. "Historically keen readers," the authors cheerfully add, "can have fun locating many more such deviations from fact" (315). These deviations were necessary, they claim, in order to tell an interesting story about Russell's life. But at the same time, the authors do not want simply to tell a good story whose main character happens to be named "Bertrand Russell." If historical accuracy did not matter to them at all, they could simply have depicted Russell fighting space invaders on Mars. Rather, AD and CP use Russell's life to tell a good story. This requires tidying up the story a bit, pruning small inconvenient facts that might distract from the larger narrative. But this poses no problems, the authors claim, so long as the story told is still the story of Russell's life, in every respect that matters. AD and CP make the point as follows:

> [A]part from the simplification that was necessary to accommodate it into a narrative work of this kind, we have

---

³ All of this information about *Logicomix*, as well as many more facts, can be found at the book's website—http://www.logicomix.com.
⁴ I shall focus in this essay on the way *Logicomix* treats Russell. How the book treats the history of logic is beyond the scope of my concern here.

> not taken any liberties with the content of the great adventure of ideas which forms our main plot, neither with its central vision, its concepts, nor—even more importantly—with the philosophical, existential and emotional struggles which are inextricably bound with it (316).

AD and CP have changed facts in the interest of storytelling, they recognize, but the story they tell is still Russell's story.

Or so they claim. In fact, however, the authors used Russell to tell a very different story. It is a story that has been told many times before. It is a story with a great deal of popular resonance, and it is therefore no surprise that the authors would make use of it, or that audiences around the world should take to it. It is a story about the dangers inherent in being too intelligent, or too logical, or using reason too much, or pursuing truth too vigorously. It is a story that depicts intelligent people, people who use reason in an effort to solve difficult problems, as different, abnormal, foolish, amoral, possibly even insane. Such people are "not like us," not like ordinary people, and therefore properly the subject of ridicule and contempt. *Logicomix* depicts Russell's life as one long story of this kind.

After briefly discussing the authorship of *Logicomix*, I shall discuss how the authors frame Russell's life in the book. This framing, I shall argue, draws upon recognized themes in Russell scholarship, but distorts them in the interest of delivering an anti-intellectual message. I shall then document a number of ways in which the events of Russell's life are changed to conform to the demands of this story. This shaping often yields an interpretation of Russell's life which could not possibly be sustained if the actual facts were considered. In particular, I shall catalog how AP and CP 1) play up the extent to which Russell's intellectual efforts proved a failure; 2) suggest a link between logic and madness; and 3) exaggerate to the point of distortion Russell's disconnection from both personal relationships and political affairs.

I shall conclude by discussing the implications of what AD and CP have done to Russell's life. The central message of *Logicomix* is pernicious for two reasons. First, it is undesirable for people to entertain such suspicions of deep intellectual activity. Second, it is particularly unfair for such suspicions to be aroused and reinforced by a study of Russell's life. Russell's life does not support such suspicions, and Russell himself would have been saddened and depressed by the thought that it might. In short, *Logicomix* may tell an entertaining story, but it also tells a potentially *harmful* story—harmful in the sense of reinforcing prejudices that desperately need debunking. And above all, it does not tell *Russell's* story.

2. THE PROBLEM OF AUTHORSHIP

Logicomix is the joint effort of two men, AD and CP, with the assistance of Alecos Papadatos and Annie Di Donna. All four individuals play prominent roles in the book itself, which cuts periodically from the story of Russell to the story of how the book was written. This latter story reveals that at least two distinct perspectives went into the crafting of *Logicomix*,[5] and these perspectives were frequently in conflict.[6]

On one side is AD, whose perspective is largely shared by Papadatos and Di Donna. It is AD who initiates the book project. On the other side is CP, who is recruited by AD to serve as the book's expert on logic (12). The priorities of the two sides are not the same, and sometimes clash. CP, not surprisingly, repeatedly intervenes during the story to insist upon the inclusion of some basic logic, so that the reader will be able to follow the events being described (e.g., 97-98). It is the extraordinary work Russell carried out on the foundations of mathematics—work that ultimately led to Gödel's Incompleteness Theorem, the Turing Machine, and the computer—that excites CP. AD, in contrast, set out in *Logicomix*, not to introduce people to logic, but to tell an "honest-to-God, real yarn. Simply, a...*story*" (13). The ideas are distinctly secondary for AD, Papadatos, and Di Donna. "[W]e focus on the *people!* Their *ideas* interest us only to the extent that they spring from their *passions*" (23). AD scoffs at the idea of producing a "logic for dummies" graphic novel, whereas CP seems sympathetic to the idea (12).

AD and CP's differing perspectives lead them to evaluate Russell's work differently. CP, mindful of the role modern logic played in the development of the computer, regards Russell's work as very fruitful, even though it failed to accomplish everything Russell set out to achieve. AD, however, emphasizes the failure of Russell to achieve the aim he set for himself—to achieve absolutely certain knowledge in the world of mathematics—and misses no opportunity to mention this fact, much to the consternation of CP

---

[5] The story's accuracy is of course an open question, as is how seriously the authors intend it to be taken. I see no reason for deception on the authors' part here, however, and so I shall take the story essentially at face value.

[6] The conflict between the authors over the nature of the story is very prominent, and has been noted by several reviewers (Monk 2009; Stone 2009).

(272, 283). In doing this, AD claims to rely upon Russell's own assessment of his project as a failure, but this claim is disingenuous without substantial qualification. Russell lived for over half a century after completing his major work in logic, and his own assessment of the work changed with both new developments in the field and with his own emotional state. The 1930s, for example, witnessed the end of Russell's second marriage in a nasty divorce and custody battle; the beginning of his extremely rocky third marriage; the death of his older brother; and the promulgation of Gödel's Incompleteness Theorem, which may have dealt the final blow to his hopes that unshakable foundations for mathematics might yet be found. At that time, not surprisingly, he often spoke of his life as a failure (Andersson 1994, 13). In later years, he usually took a more sanguine perspective regarding his life and work. AD clearly relies upon Russell's self-assessment during the 1930s; it is not surprising that he ends Russell's story just as World War II begins.

AD must therefore have reasons for dwelling upon Russell's self-assessments as a failure, given that it would not have been hard to find more positive assessments (even by Russell himself). One could, of course, speculate about personal motivations. For example, AD is apparently a frustrated mathematician himself. Unfortunately, "his overarching ambition to join the pantheon of mathematicians from Euclid to Hilbert ended in ruins, and he dropped out of Columbia [where he had been admitted at only fifteen] after six years."[7] (Psaropoulos 2010). One might, I think, reasonably detect a few sour grapes in his efforts to paint one of the most important figures in the history of logic and mathematics as a complete failure. But whatever his personal motivations might have been, his interests as a storyteller are clear. AD, as noted before, wanted to make a compelling and readable story out of Russell's life. And the story he decided to tell about Russell emphasizes the failure of Russell's ambition. It is clearly a compelling story; the immense popularity of the graphic novel is proof of this. AD believed that telling the story of Russell's life in this way would enable him to "tell a good yarn," and his belief was undeniably correct.[8]

AD's decision to depict Russell's life story as a failure was thus part of a broader strategy to craft an entertaining story out of Russell's life. The story he ultimately told was, in many ways, a tragic one. But is it an accurate

---

[7] John Psaropoulos, "Beauty is Truth, Truth Beauty," *Athens News*, January 18, 2010.
[8] This is not to suggest that Russell's life could not be used to tell an entertaining story using a different approach. It is merely to point out that the approach that AD did employ clearly did produce an entertaining story.

story? In the next section, I shall consider both *Logicomix*'s elements of tragedy and the veracity of these elements. Ultimately, as I shall show, these elements are part and parcel of the book's strongly anti-intellectual theme, and the legitimacy of those elements thus stand or fall with the legitimacy of that theme. After cataloging those elements in the next section, and showing how they collectively use Russell's life to deliver an anti-intellectual message, I shall conclude by considering that message in more detail.

3. RUSSELL'S LIFE AS TRAGEDY

> *Ils sont fous ces logiciens!* ("Zey are crazy zese logicians")
> —*Logicomix*, 281

Logicomix sets out to tell a (suitably dramatized) story about Russell and modern logic. AP and his collaborators repeatedly describe this story as a tragedy. The story, AP notes, "is going the way of *all* stories, *passions* leading the way…a *tragedy*, with *logicians as heroes*" (98). But despite the authors' protestations that they are simply relating Russell's tale, it takes work to make Russell's life fit into the narrative structure of a tragedy. CP notes this lack of fit near the end of the book. "I have two problems with your *version*" of Russell's work in logic, he says, "*One*, it *didn't* fail… and *two*, it *wasn't* a *tragedy*!" (303).[9] But AP certainly attempts to make Russell's tale into a tragedy. Understanding how he does this is important, because it demonstrates how the authors, out of a desire to tell a compelling story, use Russell's life to deliver a deeply anti-intellectual message.

Logicomix depicts Russell's life as tragic. While fundamentally not a bad man, he suffers a terrible fall. That fall does not destroy him, but it does leave him suitably chastened and scarred from the experience. At the root of that fall lay Russell's strong intellectual ambition, which led him to search for the foundations of mathematics. That ambition drove him to produce his most important works in philosophy, notably *The Principles of Mathematics* and (with Whitehead) *Principia Mathematica*. One might think that the production of so much important work in philosophy would make for a good life. But *Logicomix* strives to deliver the opposite message. For it was this deep and profound intellectual work that led directly to Russell's fall.

---

[9] To which Annie Di Donna responds, "It isn't exactly a comedy, eh?" (303). The glib nature of her response reflects a complete lack of concern with what makes a tragedy a tragedy.

But what was the nature of this fall? Just how did Russell suffer? What horrible fate befell him? *Logicomix* offers three answers. First, Russell's work was a failure; it never produced the result he most deeply sought—certain and unshakable foundations for the entirety of mathematics. Second, his work took a great toll on him, and put him at risk of insanity. Third, his work distracted him from the ordinary affairs of life, leaving him completely unequipped to deal with those affairs whenever he deigned to notice them. I have already discussed the first answer—that Russell's work was a failure. In the rest of this section, I shall discuss the second and third answers, and show how together, the three answers make Russell's life into a cautionary tale about the dangers of rigorous intellectual work.

First, *Logicomix* suggests that by seeking the foundations of mathematics in the world of logic, Russell was courting madness, a fate that had befallen others who had worked in the same field. The graphic novel does this by developing two themes in Russell's life. Both of the themes are widely accepted as accurately reflected in Russell's life; *Logicomix*, however, connects the two themes together in questionable ways. The first theme, developed most extensively by Stefan Andersson (1994), holds that the "quest for certainty" was critically important to Russell.[10] Philosophical certainty offered Russell the prospect of obtaining what a religious creed offered to its believers. Russell did not hold any religious creed to be intellectually defensible; the treasure it offered its believers was fool's gold. But philosophy and mathematics could legitimately offer certainty, and the psychological comforts it provides, where religion could not. While he ultimately came to reject this goal as unobtainable, it clearly motivated much of the work resulting in *Principia Mathematica*.

It is easy to find Russell making this point. Russell's essay "The Study of Mathematics," first published in 1929, makes religious truth and mathematical truth sound very similar. There he describes mathematics as possessing "not only truth, but supreme beauty—a beauty cold and austere, like that of a sculpture, without appeal to any part of our weaker nature, without the gorgeous trappings of painting or music, yet sublimely pure, and capable of a stern perfection such as only the greatest art can show" (Russell 1929, 60). Later, in his *Autobiography*, he reaffirmed this view as follows: "I wanted certainty in the kind of way in which people want religious faith.

---

[10] On the quest for certainty, and the problems it has generated for philosophy, see Dewey (1960).

I thought that certainty is more likely to be found in mathematics than elsewhere" (Russell 1969, 326). With passages like this in mind, Russell biographer Alan Wood once wrote, "I believe the underlying purpose behind all Russell's work was an almost religious passion for some truth that was more than human, independent of the minds of men, and even of the existence of men" (Wood 1959, 260).

Moreover, there have been many other intellectuals who have sought certainty in some branch of philosophy or science as a substitute for the comforts of religion. Russell's own era produced a number of examples. G.E. Moore was motivated in his pursuit of ethical knowledge by a desire for some sort of substitute for God (Regan 1986). The British neo-Hegelian philosophers—who influenced both Moore and Russell before the latter took philosophy in a radically different direction—also saw in philosophy a solution to a crisis of religious faith (Andersson 1994, 106). Indeed, in the words of Charles Pigden, "in the late nineteenth century Absolute Idealism functioned as a sort of methodone program for high-minded Victorian intellectuals, providing them with moral uplift as they struggled to get off the hard stuff of official Christianity" (Pigden 2008). Clearly, Russell was breaking little new ground here.

AD and CP are thus on firm ground in depicting the young Russell as partaking of a "quest for certainty" very analogous to a religious quest. They are equally on firm ground with regard to their second theme, according to which Russell is depicted as haunted by the "ghost of madness." Russell's uncle William, his eldest son, John, and most likely his granddaughter Lucy suffered from schizophrenia. And Russell himself was terrified of the prospect of losing his sanity. (It was a fear deliberately cultivated by his grandmother, who used the family insanity as a weapon in an unsuccessful attempt to prevent Russell's first marriage.) This theme receives its most sophisticated treatment in Ray Monk's two-volume biography of Russell (1996, 2000). AD and CP rely extensively upon both Monk and Andersson in constructing their story.

AD and CP thus do no violence to Russell's life by portraying his "quest for certainty" as well as the "ghost of madness" that haunted him. They do commit violence, however, by linking the two together. AD and CP suggest that Russell's quest for certainty was somehow connected to the specter of madness. Russell himself never drew this connection. While he recognized his quest for mathematical certainty as somewhat religious in nature, and while he recognized his deep-seated fear of madness, he never claimed that the quest placed him in danger of madness, or that he saw it as a possible escape route from madness. The connection between Russell's work on his logic and the prospect of madness is entirely the invention of AD and CP.[11]

Logicomix's authors go to some lengths to establish this connection between logic/mathematics and madness—a connection which, admittedly, they are not the first to propose. They rely particularly upon an essay by Gian-Carlo Rota (1997) which notes that many logicians "found shelter in asylums at some time in their lives" (Rota 1997, 4).[12] Rota mentions this claim, however, only in passing, without making any effort to document it other than to remark about the many eccentricities of the logicians around Princeton University during the time he spent there. It falls to AD and CP, therefore, to make the connection seem plausible. They make some effort to do so, but this effort requires them to make several highly questionable moves. They play up the madness of the few demonstrably insane logicians in the story (Cantor, Gödel). They also draw attention to the logicians who were sane but who had insane family members (Russell himself, Hilbert). They also count as suspect the sanity of those who had extremist political views (Frege)[13] and those who were functional but eccentric and socially maladjusted (Wittgenstein, arguably Turing). And they fail to note the figures in the book with no remotely plausible connection with madness (Whitehead, Von Neumann). Clearly, the authors are casting their net rather widely. I suspect that using their approach I could establish a connection

---

[11] Russell comes closest to drawing such a connection in a short essay entitled "Insight and Insanity" (Russell 2009). In this essay, Russell reflects upon the way in which brilliant thinkers often have an attachment to their ideas that is initially indefensible. This attachment, however, pushes them to develop the ideas in ways that are ultimately borne out. This sort of irrational attachment can, Russell notes, generate insane behavior. However, while Russell does note Georg Cantor as an example of genius coupled with madness, he nowhere suggests a specific connection between *logic* and madness. Moreover, this essay should properly be regarded as an example of Russell's thinking at an unusually pessimistic time of his life. I would like to thank Ken Blackwell for information regarding this essay.

[12] Not surprisingly, it is AD who brings this source to CP's attention (24). Interestingly, AD has also written a novel about mathematicians, entitled *Uncle Petros and Goldbach's Conjecture*, in which madness is again connected with mathematics (Doxiadis 2001).

[13] The case of Frege is instructive. The authors depict him as an obvious lunatic, complete with a mustache reminiscent of Nietzsche in his declining years. As a result of this treatment, numerous reviewers describe Frege as mad (e.g., "Bertrand Russell: The Thinking Person's Superhero" 2009; Addiego 2009; Holt 2009; Harvey 2010; Smith 2010). And yet there is no evidence of insanity on Frege's part except for the repulsive (anti-Semitic, pro-Nazi) political views he held late in his life. But that makes him a wicked man, not a madman. On the importance of distinguishing between wickedness and madness, see Szasz (1979).

between madness and cosmetology, or madness and ichthyology—or perhaps even between madness and graphic novel authorship. (Robert Crumb, anyone?)[14]

And yet the authors of *Logicomix* confidently insist that the connection between logic and madness is clear and self-evident in the lives of Russell and his contemporaries. When CP observes to the authors that "I can see how you are building towards your *'logic and madness'* theme," Annie Di Donna responds, "It's *life* zat is building zat!" (77). But even if "life" really were building the logic and madness theme—if the story of Russell et al. really did unambiguously connect logic and madness—it would presumably do so in a particular way. The authors of *Logicomix*, however, remain coy about the connection throughout their book. They claim to remain agnostic as to the causal relationship—whether the pursuit of logical truth leads to madness, or whether people prone to madness are liable to pursue logical truth, or whether some other relationship obtains. To the extent that they assert a causal relation at all, it is usually from madness to logic, although they find it difficult to reach any kind of consensus (230). But despite the authors's protestations, it is difficult to read *Logicomix* without perceiving causal arrows running from logic to madness. Certainly this is the way that reviewers of the book perceived the story, judging by the following:

> The interplay of logic and madness is a recurring theme of *Logicomix*, as Russell struggles to stave off madness himself (with only partial success, as readers will learn). (Cowan 2009)

> One of the messages of this tale appears to be that the search for absolute certainty makes you just as prone to mental instability as religious extremism.[15]

> [W]hat we see emerging in the course of the novel is… how an obsessive straining for the dizzy heights of logic can unbalance the mind and blind one to the needs of others. (Smith 2010)

---

[14] In an interview about the book, CP goes so far as to claim that he and AD "were both very interested in the very curious fact that the majority of the protagonists of this great intellectual adventure ended up going insane." CP declines to elaborate upon this claim, and I simply cannot see any way he can sustain this claim about "the majority" of *Logicomix*'s characters. The interview is online at http://www.youtube.com/watch?v=Gbx9M-n7nCU&feature=PlayList&p=7A69553A9BEF7C20&playnext_from=PL&index=24.

[15] Tom Paulson, "Super-Geeks' 'Epic Search for Truth,'" *Seattle Post-Intelligencer*, 9 October, 2009.

To the extent that *Logicomix* suggests anything in particular about logic and madness, it is the possibility that the pursuit of logical truth can endanger the mental well-being of the pursuer.

Nowhere does *Logicomix* suggest this more clearly than in its depiction of Russell's encounter with Cantor (an entirely fictional encounter—the real Russell and Cantor never met). It is true, as the graphic novel suggests, that Cantor struggled with mental illness much of his life, and wasted much of his time concocting crazy theories—that Jesus Christ was really the son of Joseph of Arimathea, for example (135). But there is no evidence that Cantor's mental problems were *caused* by his groundbreaking work in mathematics. And yet what other lesson could possibly be drawn from *Logicomix*'s treatment of Russell and Cantor? Russell travels to meet Cantor, explaining to his wife along the way that he will be meeting "a true mythical hero," a man "who ate of the tree of knowledge of the infinite." Cantor did this, Russell informs the reader, in defiance of the words of "the great Gauss," who "warned mathematicians, 'Don't deal directly with infinity…Never look at it face to face!'" (126). (Could this possibly be foreshadowing?) After a (short but informative) discussion of Cantor's ideas regarding infinity, Russell leaves his wife and goes to Cantor's university. He is directed to a nearby building which turns out to be an asylum. There Russell is shocked by Cantor's insane behavior, realizes that he is mad, and flees (132-136). That night, Russell dreams that he is summoned by the "guardians of infinity." The spirit of Gauss appears, and denounces Russell as a "traitor" for messing with infinity, and wrecking the foundations of knowledge, causing the entire edifice to collapse (137-140).[16] And the lesson Russell draws from this? "My encounter with Georg Cantor should have—if nothing else—made me aware of the possibility that the journey I had embarked on was fraught with dangers" (141).

But Cantor's story does not end there. Later in the book, Russell discovered the infamous paradox that will forever bear his name. When Cantor learns of the paradox, he exclaims:

---

[16] Earlier in *Logicomix*, Russell the student has an exchange with one of his mathematics professors. Russell declares that "the rotten foundations [of mathematics] will give way. The edifice of mathematics will collapse" in the face of the new rigorous approach he will bring to it. The professor responds by asking, "Aren't you concerned that its fall will crush you too?" Russell answers, "No! You see, I don't plan to be inside it" (90). Once again, the foreshadowing is not very subtle.

> Glory be to *almighty God!!!* I'm a *free* man at last! Don't you understand??? The *Englishman* proved the *'set of all sets'* is an *impossibility!* My *monster,* the usurper of *God's absolute greatness* thus no longer exists!!! I'm saved…" (168-9)

The Cantor depicted in *Logicomix* should be recognizable to anyone familiar with the mad scientists that populate B-movies from the 1950s. Cantor went wrong when he tampered in God's domain. And ironically enough, his own creation took its revenge on him, like Frankenstein's monster. The mad scientist is only saved in the end when his creation is destroyed.[17] That creation is a mathematical theory in *Logicomix*, and not a 50-foot-long Gila monster created by atomic radiation, but the principle remains the same. The lesson for future generations concerning the dangers of messing about in logic is quite clear.

If *Logicomix* is to be believed, there is a correlation between undertaking serious intellectual work (of the sort carried out by Russell and Whitehead in writing *Principia Mathematica*) and going mad. *Logicomix* posits a similar relationship between serious intellectual work and disconnection from everyday life. Once again, one could conceivably draw the causal arrows either way. Perhaps working on the foundations of logic renders one incapable of normal functioning outside the intellectual world. Or perhaps only an individual who lacks the ability to function normally regarding non-intellectual matters would spend so much time living the life of the mind. But just as *Logicomix* suggests that serious intellectual work leads to madness, so the graphic novel also suggests that such work leads to social and personal dysfunction. Write a *Principia Mathematica*, and abandon all hope of dealing sensibly with ordinary worldly affairs, at least until *Principia Mathematica* is well behind you.

Logicomix establishes this connection by consistently depicting Russell as obsessed with his work. This causes him to treat as distractions everything else in the world. Thus, while working on his mathematical philosophy, he is shown ignoring a newspaper headline regarding the Boer War. He does this because thanks to his work on the *Principles of Mathematics*, he "drifted father and farther away from humanity's concerns, small

---

[17] In reality, Russell's paradox did nothing of the kind. "When Cantor heard of Russell's paradox, he did not react like a madman, the way *Logicomix* caricatures him. He calmly observed that it did not apply to his own theory of sets, which evolved into the present-day foundation of mathematics" (Holt 2009).

or large" (158). He is also shown ignoring his first wife, Alys, noting later that "the treasures of Logic came at a price" (157). Here and elsewhere in the book, his obsession with logic is depicted as the primary cause of his disintegration of his marriage (182-3).[18] Reviewers have noted that the book chronicles both "the roots of Russell's need for certainty" and "the collateral damage it caused in his and his loved ones' lives" (Hawcock 2009), not to mention his "inconsiderate prioritization of work over family" (Cowan 2009; cf. Lott 2009).

These incidents are not simply false but grotesquely misleading regarding Russell. Russell's marriage to Alys effectively ended with Russell's confession that he no longer loved her, although Alys' refusal to grant a divorce kept the couple married for almost two decades after this. Russell made this confession in 1902—the year before the publication of *The Principles of Mathematics*, and long before *Principia Mathematica* was even conceived (Russell 1967, 222). Many factors contributed to the breakup of the marriage, the most obvious of which being Russell's extreme inexperience with relationships. This inexperience led him into marriage with the first woman in his adult life who would have him. This inexperience, in turn, can be blamed on both his social isolation as a child and his days at overwhelmingly-male Cambridge. But the quest for certainty via logic was responsible for little if any of the trouble.

Nor is it true that Russell neglected the world outside of mathematics while developing his work. This point is worth developing at some length. Russell was groomed for a political career from his earliest years; his grandmother had high hopes that he would become a statesman—perhaps

---

[18] A secondary cause, albeit one closely related to the first, was Russell's growing love of Evelyn Whitehead, wife of his mentor and collaborator, Alfred North Whitehead. Or so *Logicomix* would have you believe. In reality, while there is evidence that Russell had a crush on Evelyn, there is no evidence whatsoever that he engaged in anything more than timid flirtation. Russell was certainly never ready to throw away his marriage to Alys, nor did he ever urge her to leave her husband, as the book depicts (192-6). Moreover, Evelyn clearly knew about the crush, and took advantage of it in her own ways; in particular, she was able to get Russell to loan her and her husband substantial amounts of money—without Alfred's knowledge (Monk 1996; 140-1). And yet *Logicomix* not only invents an obsession on Russell's part with Evelyn; it portrays Evelyn both as an innocent victim of his obsession and as solely responsible for deflecting that obsession. "At least one of zem," Di Donna sniffs, "was remembering she was married to his closest friend" (229). What Di Donna is doing here is the equivalent of drawing a morbidly obese picture of Russell (a man who was extremely thin his entire life), and then chiding him for not taking better care of himself.

even prime minister like his grandfather.[19] While a student at Cambridge, he studied economics extensively, and even considered making it, and not logic and mathematics, the focus of his studies (King 2005). After completing his studies, he spent several months in Berlin, where he had the following famous epiphany:

> I remember a cold, bright day in early spring when I walked by myself in the Tiergarten, and made projects of future work. I thought that I would write one series of books on the philosophy of the sciences from pure mathematics to physiology, and another series of books on social questions. I hoped that the two series might ultimately meet in a synthesis at once scientific and practical. (Russell 1967, 184-5)

Soon thereafter, he returned to Germany after marrying Alys. Together they closely studied Marxism, both by reading Marx's books and by observing the German socialist movement of the day. The result was Russell's first book, *German Social Democracy*, published in 1896—a year before his first book on mathematics, *An Essay on the Foundations of Geometry*. Russell retained an interest in socialism his entire life, and supported democratic socialist alternatives to Marxism (notably guild socialism; see Harrison 1986).

And all of this happened before Russell even began work on *The Principles of Mathematics*! Between the start of that book, and the completion of *Principia Mathematica*, Russell found time for many other political adventures. He campaigned on behalf of free trade in 1903, giving many speeches and writing a number of articles (Rempel 1979). In 1907 he ran for parliament as a candidate pledged to support women's suffrage, garnering a respectable vote in a safely conservative district (Harrison 1984). In 1910, he sought the Liberal Party's nomination for another parliamentary race, but was denied it on account of his agnosticism. In short, while writing *Principia Mathematica*, Russell found time to be more politically active than most people ever become. This is what AD and CP call "drifting away from humanity's concerns."

AD and CP are guilty of more than omission regarding Russell's political activism. When they allow Russell's social conscience to intrude upon

---

[19] Lord John Russell served as prime minister in 1846-1852 and in 1865-1866. During his long political career, he shepherded through parliament a number of reforms, most notably the expansion of the franchise via the Reform Act of 1832. For his lifetime of political service, he was made the First Earl Russell by Queen Victoria.

Logicomix, they do so in ways that reinforce the picture of a dangerously obsessed logician.[20] Consider their depiction of Russell's famous moment of "mystical illumination," during which Russell encountered Evelyn Whitehead in the throes of an apparent heart attack. Russell credits the event with igniting his social conscience, and inducing him to take a greater interest in humanity. *Logicomix* accepts that the incident led Russell to "new concern with the welfare of my fellow human beings" (235). But it also situates the incident after the completion of *Principia Mathematica*. In other words, it suggests that Russell the maniacally-obsessed logician experienced a moment of personal illumination—something clearly incompatible with his obsessive work on logic—after his work on logic was substantially (and unsuccessfully) concluded. But the incident really took place in 1901—before even the *Principles of Mathematics* had been completed (Russell 1967, 220). During the early 1900s, Russell *both* slaved away at his work on logic *and* strove for a deeper connection with his fellow human beings. For the story *Logicomix* wishes to tell about Russell, this fact is most inconvenient, and so accuracy is sacrificed so that Russell can be depicted as socially and emotionally useless throughout his days of logic.[21]

But AD and CP do not permit Russell anything like a sensible engagement with the world outside of logic even after his moment of "mystical illumination." They claim that at this point, and only at this point, "*the real world* begins to *barge* into Russell's cloistered life" (221). This intrusion takes the form of World War I, during which Russell was extremely active as an antiwar crusader. Anyone who has ever heard of Russell has heard of this activism, which earned Russell a fine, a prison term, and dismissal from Cambridge University. And so AD and CP cannot ignore this episode

---

[20] AD claims in an interview that he used Russell as the protagonist for *Logicomix*, rather than some other logician, because "he was the only one of these characters who was not a meganerd." Indeed, he there acknowledges Russell to be "a political activist, a womaniser, traveler, adventurer, great talker, a wit and a dandy" (AFP 2009). Too bad that the Russell depicted in *Logicomix* is none of those things. Instead, he is socially inept and disconnected from the real world—in other words, nerdy, all too nerdy.

[21] AD and CP rub further salt into the wound they inflict on Russell by depicting him as specifically oblivious to the Boer War. During his moment of mystic illumination, Russell writes, he "became during those five minutes a pro-Boer and a pacifist" (Russell 1967, 220-1). But even before the incident, Russell had been keenly aware of the war. After the war broke out in late 1899, according to Russell, "I used most afternoons to walk the four miles to the station in order to get an evening paper" so as to obtain news about the war (*ibid.*, 201). This is the man AD and CP would have you believe would not so much as read a newspaper headline about the war. For more on Russell's evolving views on the Boer War, see Blitz (1999-2000).

of Russell's life, or pretend it didn't happen. But even here, Russell cannot simply be a man of deep moral concern, trying to inject a note of sanity into an insane world. Instead, he is a man who "started giving lectures...trying to apply the Higher Logic to human affairs" (235). In other words, if *Principia Mathematica* was the theory for Russell, then his antiwar activism was supposed to be the practice. This is an utterly daft idea, as Russell surely would have realized. And so the real Russell never claimed that he was bringing his "Higher Logic" to bear in opposing the war. But the Russell of *Logicomix* does not realize this, and so goes merrily along attempting the ridiculous application of modern logic to politics—and, not surprisingly, having no discernible effect.[22] Even the politically concerned Russell is an inept fool at practical matters, or indeed at anything other than mathematical logic.

After the war, Russell "returned to pure thought" (254)—or so *Logicomix* would have you believe. No mention of his decision not to return to academia, but to become a full-time public intellectual and crusader for progressive ideas. No mention of his visit to the newly-formed Soviet Union in 1920, during which time he had a personal audience with Lenin. No mention of his time spent in China, where he became very popular with modern-minded college students. No mention of the books on Russia and China that resulted from these trips—or indeed, of any of the popular books Russell produced during the 1920s and 1930s. No mention of his campaigns for parliament in 1922 and 1923. No mention of his popular speaking tours of the United States. If one relied solely upon *Logicomix*, one would surely regard Russell's antiwar activism as an odd aberration in a life devoted wholly to logic—the exact opposite of reality.

After World War I, only two parts of Russell's life outside of logic receive any attention in *Logicomix*. Both are told in such a way as to make Russell seem as inept and impractical as possible. First, there is his second marriage, to Dora Black.[23] This marriage was an open one by mutual

---

[22] The real Russell does claim to have seen large crowds celebrating the start of the war, and that this sight led him to reconsider the strength of the irrational in human affairs (Russell 1968, 4). The veracity of Russell's memory is debatable on this point; others have questioned the existence of any such enthusiastic crowds. But *Logicomix* goes one step further, and turns the crowds into an antiwar march that magically becomes a *prowar* march the second the war is declared (239). If AD and CP believe this story to be plausible, one must question whether they have ever met an antiwar protester before.
[23] Russell's third marriage had begun by the dawn of World War II, when *Logicomix* ends, but it receives no attention in the book. His fourth, and most successful, marriage took place after this date.

consent, and both Bertie and Dora took numerous lovers. (Only Dora is depicted with a lover in the book.) But the marriage ultimately fell apart. There are numerous reasons for this failure, not the least of which was Dora's decision to have two children with another man. Russell firmly believed that children should only be born and raised within monogamous relationships, a view which Dora ignored and which Bertie shelved for the sake of (temporary) marital peace (Monk 2000). But none of this complexity makes it into *Logicomix*. Instead, the reason for the marriage's failure was simple—in his "attempt to remold human nature," Russell "had been blinded by theory, and not for the first time in [his] life" (292). Indeed, according to *Logicomix*, Russell was *always* blinded by theory in everything he did, both within the world of logic (a world in which, according to AD, Russell completely failed) and without.[24]

Second, there is Russell's creation, with Dora, of the progressive school Beacon Hill. Here again Russell makes catastrophic and obvious mistakes solely because, as a man who lives in the world of ideas, he is incapable of doing anything remotely practical. Beacon Hill is caricatured in a manner that the worst enemies of progressive education could not top. Russell and Dora created the school because existing schools indoctrinated students with religious bigotry and patriotic chauvinism. But according to *Logicomix*, they did it because "*Russell*, the inveterate *modernizer*, could not accept an *old* educational system" (278). His "new-fangled" educational system is obviously daft. Present at its opening is a gullible American couple, the sort that would clearly buy into any new fad foisted off on them (279). Beacon Hill supposedly has no rules of any kind, and yet Russell attempts to lecture on geometry to young children under normal classroom conditions, completely oblivious to how badly this plan will work (280). In the end, the authors equate Russell's educational experiment with that of Wittgenstein, who as a teacher had no particular pedagogical theory and simply lashed out physically at students who annoyed him. "Zey both want," Di Donna concludes, "to fix everything with *ze brain!*" (281).[25] One would never know

---

[24] One reviewer noted that Russell "depends solely on logic to master courtship, marriage and child-rearing." As a result, *Logicomix* becomes the story of one "nerdy fumble" on Russell's part after another (Cowan 2009).

[25] CP's response—"What *else* is there?"—is both absolutely correct and yet utterly incomprehensible to Di Donna, AP, and the rest of the *Logicomix* team. The resulting stunned silence leads CP quickly to add, "Just kidding." It is made quite clear here that, whatever CP's value as a technical consultant on modern logic, it is the worldview held by AD and Di Donna that largely dictates the content of *Logicomix*.

from *Logicomix* that Beacon Hill lasted for sixteen years, from 1927 to 1943 (although Dora ran the school alone after her divorce from Bertie). The ill-conceived, foolish experiment depicted in the book would not have lasted sixteen days. Again, Russell certainly made his fair share of mistakes as both a parent and an educator.[26] But for the authors of *Logicomix*, Russell's life was nothing but one long mistake in these areas—a mistake made due to Russell's ineptitude with practical matters.

The picture of Russell that emerges from *Logicomix* is clear and consistent. Russell is a brilliant man, but that brilliance extends only to theoretical matters. When confronted with reality, Russell is, quite simply, a complete screw-up. He is incapable of relating to real people or real problems without utterly making a mess of things. And even in the realm of ideas, his position is nothing to be envied. For the results he sought he never obtained—and it's good that he never obtained them, for the mere pursuit of these ideas can drive people mad. And at the very least, the pursuit of these ideas renders a person singularly unsuited for real human society.

Little wonder, then, that the authors of *Logicomix* describe Russell's story as a tragedy. A tragedy, according to Aristotle, depends upon the "tragic flaw" of its protagonist to set the action in motion. It is hard to identify the tragic flaw of *Logicomix*'s Russell as anything other than a dedication to deep and critical thought. It is this "flaw" that leads him to the brink of madness—a precipice over which many logicians (notably Cantor) are supposed to have stumbled—in a search that ultimately proves completely fruitless. And it is this "flaw" that makes Russell into a neglectful spouse, a terrible father, and an inept public figure. Russell concludes the preface to his autobiography by writing, "This has been my life. I have found it worth living, and would gladly live it again if the chance were offered me" (Russell 1967, 4). These are hardly the words of a man whose life has been one long tragedy; one cannot imagine Hamlet or Oedipus penning them. But then again, the man who wrote those words—the real Russell—is simply not the man depicted in *Logicomix*.

---

[26] The biggest mistake Russell made, on most accounts, was to think he could be a schoolmaster and a parent at the same time. Russell recognized that favoritism towards his own children at Beacon Hill would cause problems for both them and the other students. But as a result, Russell often failed to fulfill the specifically parental duties he owed his children. The authors of *Logicomix* recognize this fact, but once again twist it to serve their agenda. Thus, Russell is depicted lecturing his son that "It's your *duty* to put yourself in the place of the children to whom I'm *not 'Daddy'*" (291). Once again, if Russell does something wrong in the book, it's because he foolishly ignores common sense in pursuit of some abstract theoretical principle.

4. CONCLUSION

> "Sorry, *readers*. Myths can be a bit *ugly!*"
> —*Logicomix*, 301.

Logicomix is no doubt being read both by longtime fans of Russell and/or modern logic and by newcomers to these topics. The former know the facts, by and large, but most of the latter are learning all they will ever learn about these topics from this book. I would much rather these readers learn of Russell's life and work through *Logicomix* than fail to learn of him at all. The worst form of publicity is no publicity at all, and so the authors of *Logicomix* deserve credit for raising awareness of both Russell and the history of modern logic. But while the world may be better off with *Logicomix* than not, it is still worth asking whether the result is as good as it could have been. *Logicomix* has made many people aware of Russell; if only it could have made them aware of the real Russell as well.

Newcomers to Russell will take away from *Logicomix*, not the details it provides regarding Russell or modern logic,[27] but the broader theme of the book—its overall "message," if you will. But just what is this message? Clearly, it concerns the place of logic and reason in life. As noted before, in *Logicomix* Russell tells the story of his life in flashback on the eve of World War II. His occasion for doing so is a (fictional) lecture entitled "The Role of Logic in Human Affairs" (31). The lecture's title is not a coincidence. But just what does *Logicomix* want to say about this role? Just what is logic's role?

Logicomix's apparent answer is, not too large. But getting more precise than this is difficult. The book does not have Russell foreswear logic or intellectual work altogether. From start to finish, Russell believes that "*rational* tools should be employed" (33). And at the end of the book, Rus-

---

[27] Indeed, even book reviewers have trouble keeping facts straight. One *Logicomix* reviewer describes it as follows:

> Covering a span of 60 years, it tells the story of Russell's life, taking in his childhood, brought up by his grandparents after he was orphaned aged four, his four marriages, the writing of his great work *Principia Mathematica*, his rivalry with Ludwig Wittgenstein, and his quest for nuclear disarmament in the last decades of his life (Flood 2009).

Logicomix never mentions Russell's work for nuclear disarmament, nor does it mention his last two marriages. It would have been surprising if these topics had come up, given that "a span of 60 years" could not possibly cover all of Russell's 97-year-long life.

sell still describes himself as a "rationalist" (296). But one must not allow reason to overstep its boundaries. It is this mistake, the Russell of *Logicomix* claims, which he made during his quest for the foundations of mathematics. But just what sort of mistake is this? Just how might reason wind up overstepping its bounds? There are many ways to answer this question, not all of which are compatible with one another. And yet the reviewers of *Logicomix* quite enthusiastically identified *many* different candidates for Russell's intellectual mistake. Some of these candidates have clear textual support in the graphic novel; others appear to be the inventions of the reviewers. But regardless, the real Russell simply cannot be accused of quite so many different forms of stupidity as the reviewers of *Logicomix* identify. Whatever Russell's failings regarding the limits of reason, he simply did not make all of them at once.

Consider the following ways in which reason can overstep its boundaries, each of which was identified by at least one *Logicomix* reviewer as the book's "message:"

1. One could take one's beliefs to be more certain than the evidence warrants. A chastened Russell expresses this view at the end of the book, when he announces a desire to attack "your conviction that you are *absolutely right* in your views" (296). This is indeed a serious intellectual error, but it is not clear that anyone in *Logicomix* makes it. Surely there was no way for Russell to know in advance that his quest to set mathematics upon absolutely certain foundations was doomed. Nor was Hilbert (another major part of the "quest for certainty" in *Logicomix*) irrational to believe that all mathematical claims might be either provable or disprovable, before Gödel proved otherwise. To believe that one must not believe beyond what the evidence authorizes—an admittedly very Russellian point—is not the same as believing that one can never believe absolutely, unless one has good reason to believe that one will never obtain evidence authorizing absolute certainty. It took Russell et al. decades to establish this fact in the realm of mathematics. Moreover, there is no evidence presented in *Logicomix* that Russell ever mistakenly thought he had completed his quest for certainty. Russell's dream might have been hopeless, but his pursuit of it was not obviously irrational.

2. One could accept the Aristotelian idea that one should not seek further precision than a given subject allows. This possibility is frequently conflated with possibility #1. For example, one review of *Logicomix* claims that the "book's main theme…is the tension between reason's

clean drive for *precision and certainty*, and the humane but messy world of the passions" (my emphasis; Smith 2010). This review clearly runs together the quest for precision and the quest for certainty. Moreover, accepting this point does not make Russell irrational either. Contra Aristotle, there may be no way of knowing in advance what the maximum level of precision is, or whether that level grows over time. And the authors provide no reason for thinking that Russell was irrationally optimistic regarding the precision of his results.

3. One could take valid beliefs to authorize other beliefs in an indefensible manner. I take this to be Russell's point when he declares at the end of *Logicomix*, "when Logic congeals into all-encompassing and perfect-seeming theories, then it can actually become a very evil con trick" (296). This statement runs together "all-encompassing" and "perfect-seeming" theories, conflating this possibility with possibility #1. Nevertheless, the avoidance of "all-encompassing" theories—theories that make proclamations about areas over which they have nothing defensible to say—is a valid, if rather trivial goal. The Russell of *Logicomix* clearly fails to achieve this goal, insofar as he uses his work in mathematical logic to authorize his antiwar activism or provide him with pedagogical principles. The real Russell, however, did nothing so ridiculous. At the end of *Logicomix*, Russell urges his audience to "try another old triad: Responsibility, Justice…even a sense of Good vs. Evil, i.e. all the concepts my Viennese friends considered 'beneath the dignity of serious minds'" (297). Again, it is perfectly valid to claim that one needs more than logic to resolve questions of justice. But again, the real Russell never pretended otherwise.[28]

4. A closely related mistake would be to neglect one's *conscience* out of a belief that principle will somehow dictate correct behavior. The Russell of *Logicomix* finds himself confronted by antiwar activists who demand that he oppose U.S. entry into World War II, just as he opposed British entry into World War I. Russell responds by entreating his audience, "think twice—*at least twice!*—before deciding whether to take arms against the sea of Europe's troubles…or not" (297)! Russell in effect

---

[28] It is also strange to depict Russell as attacking the logical positivists of the Vienna School for regarding good and evil as "beneath the dignity of serious minds." For one thing, Russell *shared* the Vienna School's noncognitivism, according to which words like "good" and "evil" literally had no meaning. For another, neither Russell nor the Vienna School took noncognitivism to render good and evil unworthy of attention. For noncognitivists, statements about good and evil might be meaningless, but this need not be a reason to stop making them (Pigden 2008).

recognizes "a clash between a belief in intuited truth and a strict reliance on methodical deduction," and concludes that "truth can only be found in the conscience of each individual" (Miller 2009). But the point is surely not generally valid. Some people were told by their "consciences" to support World War II; others were told to oppose it. Should both perspectives be deemed equally valid?[29] (And it is important not to forget that there were Germans in that same war who obeyed their "consciences," to horrible effect.) There are times when putting the "voice of conscience" ahead of principle can lead one badly astray, just as following principles blindly can.

5. Finally, one could simply like one's behavior to make sense. This is obviously not a mistake of any kind, and yet at times *Logicomix* suggests that it is. "Logicians hate contradictions," notes CP, "But what is life…if not a bundle of contradictions" (216)? In *Standpoint* magazine, reviewer Hannah Stone picks up on this point, suggesting that the authors of *Logicomix* "realise that reason and unreason can and must coexist."[30] If AD et al. simply mean that one will never be able to eliminate all contradictions and/or irrationalities from one's belief system, they are surely correct. And this is sad and unfortunate. But this point is far different from suggesting that one should *cease attempting* to eliminate contradictions and/or irrationalities.

Sadly, this last idea appears to be the lesson drawn by some readers of Logicomix. One reviewer summarizes the point of the book with the simple equation, "Life > logic" (Holt 2009). According to another, the graphic novel shows that "the devotees of logic and mathematics discovered they were perhaps being just as fundamentalist [as religious fanatics] in trying to rid their world of uncertainty and mystery."[31] (Paulson 2009). Apparently, it's a good thing that there are still areas of the world that we don't understand (and never will), and don't you forget it. With messages like these in

---

[29] Several reviewers believe that the Russell of *Logicomix* is attempting to "question the antiwar protesters' certainty that the USA should not help Europe fight the Nazis" (Smith 2010; see also Lukes 2010). But Russell's point—don't be too certain, but follow one's conscience—works just as well against a supporter of the war.

[30] Of course, Stone also describes the Russell of *Logicomix* as "a lone ranger, battling against impossible odds to reach his goal of absolute truth, often despairing but never giving up." But by the end of *Logicomix*, Russell *had* clearly given up the goal of absolute truth, and embraced the position (whatever it may be) of the authors. For Stone, apparently, Russell must not only be doomed and foolish, but he must remain blind to the bitter end.

[31] Paulson, "Super-Geeks' 'Epic Search for Truth.'"

the public sphere, it is little wonder that so few children pursue careers in science.[32]

Logicomix thus concludes with a vague and unspecified attack upon reason attempting to do too much in some sense. The precise sense, however, is difficult to discern. It is therefore hard to resist concluding that the book's message amounts to, "Don't think too hard." It is easy to see how a reader of *Logicomix* could receive this message from the book. After all, it devotes most of its space to depicting Russell and other logicians as very smart people who were at best socially maladjusted failures and at worst clinically insane. Moreover their maladjustment and/or insanity are continually linked to their deep intellectual work. Brainy people are not "like the rest of us," and their being "different" is a direct result of their use of their brains. This message is an unfortunate one to deliver at a time when so many pressing social problems require serious intellectual effort if solutions are to be found. It is doubly unfortunate because Russell himself would have wholeheartedly rejected the message. Far from urging caution lest intellectual activity be permitted to overstep its bounds, Russell tirelessly promoted the embrace of reason and the rejection of irrationalism his entire life. He once quipped that "most people would rather die than think. And in fact, they do." But *Logicomix* would have the reader believe that it is thinking, not the lack thereof, that is truly dangerous.

Russell lived for almost three decades after the story told by *Logicomix* ends. He has now been dead for forty years. To the extent that his reputation survives, it is for being a fearless thinker, with an unshakable faith in the importance of human reason in all areas of life. Defenders of human reason should therefore be happy to see a graphic novel that helps keep the memory of Russell alive. But they should be saddened that the authors of this novel feel the need to deprecate Russell's devotion to intelligence, and to discourage others to follow it.

---

[32] It is worth adding that even an anti-intellectual book can make intellectual work sound attractive to some. Those science fiction B-movies from the 1950s depicted scientists as amusingly eccentric at best and dangerously insane at worst. And yet some children nevertheless saw those movies and were inspired by them to become scientists. As I indicated before, it is definitely better that there be some graphic novel about logic out there than none at all.

Bibliography

"Bertrand Russell: The Thinking Person's Superhero." *The Independent*, September 2, 2009.

AFP. 2009. "Greek 'Maths' Comic Is Surprise International Bestseller." *Independent*, October 12.

Addiego, Walter. 2009. "Graphic Novel Explores Mathematics." *San Francisco Chronicle*, October 31, E1.

Andersson, Stefan. 1994. *In Quest of Certainty: Bertrand Russell's Search for Certainty in Religion and Mathematics up to* The Principles of Mathematics (1903). Stockholm: Almqvist & Wiksell.

Blitz, David. "Russell and the Boer War: From Imperialist to Anti-Imperialist." *Russell* n.s. 19 (Winter 1999-2000): 117-142.

Cowan, David. "*Logicomix*: An Epic Search for Truth (with a Connection in Frankfurt)." *eSkeptic*, September 9, 2009. http://www.skeptic.com/eskeptic/09-09-09/. Accessed March 16, 2010.

Dewey, John. 1960. *The Quest for Certainty*. New York: Capricorn Books.

Doxiadis, Apostolos. 2001. *Uncle Petros and Goldbach's Conjecture*. New York: Bloomsbury.

Doxiadis, Apostolos and Papadimitriou, Christos H. 2009. *Logicomix: An Epic Search for Truth*. New York: Bloomsbury.

Flood, Alison. 2009. "Bertrand Russell's Mathematical Quest Adds up to Unlikely Graphic Novel Hit." *Guardian*, April 27.

Harrison, Brian. 1984. "Bertrand Russell: The False Consciousness of a Feminist." *Russell* n.s. 4, no. 1 (Summer): 157-205.

Harrison, Royden. 1986. "Bertrand Russell: From Liberalism to Socialism?" *Russell* n.s. 6, no. 1 (Summer): 5-37.

Harvey, R.C. "Logicomix, A Tour de Force." http://www.tcj.com/history/logicomix-a-tour-de-force. Posted January 21, 2010. Accessed March 16, 2010.

Hawcock, Neville. 2009. Review of *Logicomix* by Apostolos Doxiadis and Christos Papadimitriou. *Financial Times*, September 5.

Holt, Jim. 2009. "Algorithm and Blues." *New York Times*, September 27.

King, J. E. 2005. "Bertrand Russell on Economics, 1889-1918." *Russell* n.s. 25 (Summer): 5-38.

Lott, Rod. Review of *Logicomix* by Apostolos Doxiadis and Christos Papadimitriou. http://www.bookgasm.com/reviews/comics/logicomix/. Posted October 23, 2009. Accessed March 16, 2010.

Lukes, Steven. 2010. "Let's Get Logical: *Logicomix* Reviewed." *Print Magazine* 64, no. 1, February.

Miller, Laura. 2009. "Logic Made Fun: A New Comic Romps through One of the Philosophy's Greatest Debates." *Salon.com*, December 14.

Monk, Ray. 1996. *Bertrand Russell: The Spirit of Solitude 1872-1921*. New York: The Free Press.

Monk, Ray. 2000. *Bertrand Russell: The Ghost of Madness 1921-1970*. London: Jonathan Cape.

Monk, Ray. 2009. "A Graphic Novel about Logic? The Idea Is Not as Far-Fetched, or as Innovative, as One Might Think." *Spectator*, September 30.

Pigden, Charles, "Russell's Moral Philosophy," *The Stanford Encyclopedia of Philosophy* (Fall 2008 Edition), Edward N. Zalta (ed.), URL = <http://plato.stanford.edu/archives/fall2008/entries/russell-moral/>.

Regan, Tom. 1986. *Bloomsbury's Prophet: G.E. Moore and the Development of His Moral Philosophy*. Philadelphia: Temple University Press.

Rempel, Richard. 1979. "From Imperialism to Free Trade: Couturat, Halevy and Russell's First Crusade." *Journal of the History of Ideas* 40 (July-September): 423-43.

Robinson, Dave and Groves, Judy. 1998. *Introducing Bertrand Russell*. New York: Totem.

Rota, Gian-Carlo. 1997. "Fine Hall in Its Golden Age: Princeton in the Early Fifties." In *Indiscrete Thoughts*. Boston: Birkhäuser.

Russell, Bertrand. 1929. "The Study of Mathematics." In *Mysticism and Logic*. New York: W.W. Norton.

Russell, Bertrand. 1967. *The Autobiography of Bertrand Russell*. Volume I. Boston: Little, Brown and Company.

Russell, Bertrand. 1968. *The Autobiography of Bertrand Russell*. Volume II. Boston: Little, Brown and Company.

Russell, Bertrand. 1969. *The Autobiography of Bertrand Russell.* Volume III. Boston: Little, Brown and Company.

Russell, Bertrand. 2009. "Insanity and Insight." In *Mortals and Others: American Essays 1931-1935*, ed. Harry Ruja. New York: Routledge Classics.

Smith, Barry C. 2010. "Drawing Distinctions." *The Philosophers' Magazine* 49: 101-3.

Stone, Hannah. 2009. "A Good Look at Logic." *Standpoint Magazine*, November. http://standpointmag.co.uk/node/2306/full (August 28, 2014).

Szasz, Thomas. 1979. "The Freedom Abusers." *Inquiry*, February 5, 4-6.

Wood, Alan. 1959. "Russell's Philosophy: A Study of Its Development." In *My Philosophical Development*, by Bertrand Russell. London: George Allen & Unwin, Ltd., 255-77.

BERTRAND RUSSELL AND *THE CONQUEST OF HAPPINESS*

Tim Madigan

BERTRAND RUSSELL WAS ONE OF THE MOST IMPORTANT PHILOSOPHERS of the Twentieth Century. He came to prominence during the early years of that century primarily through his technical work on the relationship between mathematics and logic, as expressed in such seminal writings as the article "On Denoting" (1905) and the monumental three-volume work *Principia Mathematica* (1910-1913) he co-wrote with Alfred North Whitehead, his friend and colleague at Trinity College, Cambridge. These and later works would have been enough to guarantee his importance to the world of philosophical thought. But in addition to his concern for logical reasoning and critical thinking, Russell was also an important public intellectual. His natural ability to write clearly and his willingness to tackle a myriad of social problems throughout his life helped to make him one of the best-known figures of his time. He was awarded the Nobel Prize in Literature in 1950 primarily for his non-technical writings on the history of philosophy and for his works which attempted to demonstrate how logical thinking can play a vital role in promoting happiness and a good life.

It is therefore not surprising that many of Russell's more popular writings, especially those dealing with cultural, economic, and political issues, addressed strategies for ways in which people could attempt to maximize their happiness. In the words of political scientist Alan Ryan: "In his innumerable essays on 'how to be happy'…Russell's recipe always involves imagination, individuality, independence of other people's good and bad opinion; happiness is less a matter of pleasure than of experiencing one's vitality, a doctrine which is defended in *The Conquest of Happiness* in an extended hymn to 'zest'" (Ryan 1988, 16). I will explore Russell's concept of "zest" later in the chapter, but first I will briefly examine how he came to write this particular book, and then look at why he chose to devote the first half of it to the concept of "conquering unhappiness."

As David White relates in the chapter "Russell in the Jazz Age," the philosopher was commissioned to write *The Conquest of Happiness* by the flamboyant New York publisher Horace Liveright. He had previously published Russell's books *Education and the Good Life* in 1926 and *Marriage and Morals* in 1929, both of which were bestsellers for the American publishing house, as well as for Russell's British publishing house Allen & Unwin. Wishing to capitalize on the success of these works, Liveright proposed to Russell that he write a popular book specifically on the topic of how to be happy. *The Conquest of Happiness* was published in 1930. It is important to note that this book predates the contemporary fascination with self-help publications by several decades.

Unfortunately, unlike the first two Liveright publications, *The Conquest of Happiness* did not sell nearly as well, primarily due to the collapse of the world economy shortly before its appearance—a cause of extreme unhappiness for millions. "The diminished sales figures for this volume," writes Liveright's biographer Tom Dardis, "demonstrate what had happened to the U.S. book trade within only a year into the depression. *Conquest* sold just 13,000 copies, as compared with 25,000 for his first two books" (Dardis 1995, 309). Due to the collapse in sales of all of his books, Liveright was pushed out of the publishing house he founded that same year, 1930, and died in poverty three years later.

While initially not as successful as many of his earlier books, Russell's *Conquest of Happiness* continued to sell steadily over the years and has never been out of print. It remains one of the most read and commented upon of all his works, and continues to be consulted by those wondering how they might become happier people. Liveright and Russell remained on cordial terms right up until the former's death, in part because they had a remarkably good working relationship (something that was not the case with many of Liveright's other celebrity authors, such as Russell's fellow Nobel Laureates in Literature T. S. Eliot, William Faulkner, Ernest Hemingway, and Eugene O'Neill). According to Walker Gilmer, "Russell never questioned the terms of his contracts with Liveright, never demanded additional advances or royalties, and never looked for special treatment" (Gilmer 1970, 220). Moreover, Liveright recognized the timeless nature of Russell's exploration of happiness as well as appreciated Russell's examination of the causes of unhappiness, several of which he could relate to personally, as he confesses in his final letter to the philosopher: "Let me reiterate that reading your book not only gave me one of the greatest intellectual pleasures that I have had in a long time, but I know it is going to give me a great deal to think about for a long time to come. It seems that I have all of the vices that make for unhappiness; envy, sense of sin, fear of public opinion, and what not" (Gilmer 1970, 222).

Bertrand Russell's use of the word "conquest" in the title of *The Conquest of Happiness* reinforces his primary contention that happiness, except in rare cases, is not something that simply presents itself to people but rather is something that must be achieved (conquered). Russell's advice centers on the premise that happiness has as much to do with eliminating the causes of unhappiness as it does with engaging in activities that bring us happiness. Like Aristotle and his idea of intrinsic and extrinsic values (as expressed in *The Nichomachean Ethics*) Russell in *The Conquest of Happiness* explains that happiness depends partly upon external circumstances and partly upon oneself. In *The Conquest of Happiness*, he proposed that in order to be happy one must first conquer unhappiness.

According to Russell, happiness in itself is natural for each person and depends on engaging in activities to achieve real (affordable, accessible) things. But because of erroneous views or habits, the irrational can take over in humans and become a cause of unhappiness. So, Russell distinguishes between several types of unhappiness. All of them are a reflection of negative emotions, personal experiences, and a reaction to something external. The conquest of happiness means overcoming erroneous and irrational views, and returning to healthy and reasonable ideas. Russell believed that it is important to understand your needs and desires and to correlate them with real opportunities. Another, no less important way to happiness, lies in refusing to pay close attention to oneself and one's own experiences, and in paying attention to the surrounding world instead. A sincere interest in the world around us and in other people positively shapes the activity/action through which each person should be developing. Thus, happiness is associated with a clear mind, proper activity, and self-realization.

The world is filled with avoidable and unavoidable misfortunes, psychological entanglements, a struggle to attain financial security, and a number of other variables that contribute to unhappiness. In *Conquest*, Russell spends as much time discussing the causes of unhappiness as he does the causes of happiness. Russell's advice centers on the premise that happiness has as much to do with eliminating the causes of unhappiness as it does with engaging in activities that bring us happiness. Such a perspective seems quite simplistic and yet it is relatively profound, in that many people seem oblivious to the idea that happiness can be attained if one removes the causes of unhappiness. In other words, one can be happy only if one is not unhappy.

Russell acknowledges that there are many causes of unhappiness, some of which have roots in the social system and others are the result of one's individual psychology. The social system, according to Russell, creates war, economic exploitation, unequal access to a quality education among all members of society, and tactics of fear designed to make people feel uneasy about their place in society. Elaborating on war, for example, Russell states that the social system cannot avoid war when "men are so unhappy that mutual extermination seems to them less dreadful than continued endurance of the light of day" (p.15).

The relevance of Russell's view on "what makes people unhappy" is evident in abundance in contemporary society as social systems, including democracies, create inequality in all the same forms described by Russell; that is to say, war appears to be a constant, as do economic inequality and education inequality, and a wide variety of scare tactics are used by most social institutions (e.g., politics, government, insurance companies) in an attempt to keep people in support of the status quo. Individuals who are particularly upset with the existing social system and who seek change seem to be particularly unhappy with nearly every social institution and are generally very unpleasant to be around. Such individuals are filled with anxiety; become excessively preoccupied by things beyond their control; have a lack of interest in anything but their self-imposed struggle; are generally incapable of enjoying simple things in life, like play and leisure and pride in their sense of workmanship; and seem to lack a sense of well-roundedness. But in addition to these outside causes of unhappiness, Russell also explores internal ways of thinking that can contribute to an unhappy existence.

In chapter 2 of *Conquest*, Russell describes what he calls "Byronic unhappiness." The origin of the concept of "Byronic" dates back to the characteristics of English Romantic poet Lord Byron (1788-1824), or more specifically to his poetic themes, especially romanticism, melancholy, and melodramatic energy. Essentially, the Byronic individual has a self-absorbed, brooding personality. The Byronic personality may also include descriptions that include a proud, moody, cynical, defiant, and lonely person. Russell, it should be noted, was an admirer of Byron's poetry, and identified with his anti-establishment views and his willingness to shock the public in order to get across unconventional views on politics, religion, and human sexuality. But for this very reason he was aware that such deviant views can cut one off from one's fellow beings, and thus be the source of extreme dissatisfaction and isolation.

Russell (1930) depicted Byronic individuals as being truly unhappy and yet also "proud of their unhappiness, which they attribute to the nature of the universe and consider to be the only rational attitude for an enlightened man" (p.25). Russell counters that there is no superior rationality in being unhappy and that the wise person should allow himself to be as happy as circumstances permit. Unless you are a Byronic person, chances are you will try to avoid being around those who are "happy with being unhappy" as their negative attitudes may rub off on you.

Russell further argues that it is *competition* that most interferes with one's pursuit of enjoyment. Competition (which Aristotle would call *agon*) leads to what Russell calls the "struggle for life" and this struggle is enough to lead many members of the masses to believe that "life is too grim, too tenacious" and too tough to bear (1930, 55). In the contemporary era we can see that competition is all-prevalent. We are in competition with others over minor things like finding a parking spot or securing a seat on a subway or picking which line will go faster at the grocery store. We are in competition for major things too, such as acquiring wealth, finding a spouse, and securing a job promotion. Major institutions have elements that are in constant competition, too. And because competition results in more losers than winners, those who are not best fit to adapt to the environment risk dissolution. Competition is indeed a source of unhappiness for many.

In chapter 4 of *The Conquest of Happiness*, Russell discusses *boredom* as a source of unhappiness. Russell suggests that boredom is exclusively a human emotion. Animals may become listless, pace up and down, and yawn, but in a state of nature what they experience is not analogous to boredom. According to Russell, the opposite of boredom is excitement. Thus, if we are not excited by our environment or circumstances, we are bored by it. Russell states, "The desire for excitement is very deep-seated in human beings, especially in males. I suppose that in the hunting stage it was more easily gratified than it has been since" (1930, 57). He recognized that we all have a tendency to fall into patterns of behavior that can lead to being in a rut, and such listlessness can become self-perpetuating.

Fatigue was the next cause of unhappiness described by Russell (chapter 5). As is the general case throughout *The Conquest of Happiness*, Russell does not provide a definition of the concepts he uses and this includes the term "fatigue." This may be due in part to the philosophical nature of his writing and/or a belief that the parameters of certain concepts are, more or less, understood by professionals and laypersons alike. The contemporary definition of fatigue includes such descriptions as physical and/or mental exhaustion that can be triggered by stress, medication, overwork, or mental and physical illness or disease and a condition characterized by a lessened capacity for work and reduce efficiency of accomplishment, usually accompanied by a feeling of weariness and tiredness. Based on these definitions, it is easy to comprehend how fatigue can lead to negative consequences.

Russell himself said that fatigue can become a "grave evil" and, of course, a cause of unhappiness (1930, 68). Laborers and peasant women, Russell found, were old by the time they reached thirty years of age. As with contemporary views of fatigue, Russell also linked stress and anxiety due to fatigue. As a bit of sound advice, Russell proclaimed that a great many worries could be diminished by realizing the unimportance of the matter which is causing the anxiety. Russell describes how he once had a considerable amount of anxiety due to public speaking. In fact, he often dreaded giving a talk in front of others to the point where he became exhausted from the nervous strain. However, he gradually taught himself "to feel that it did not matter whether he [I] spoke well or ill, the universe would remain much the same in either case" (1930, 73). Once Russell learned to downplay the importance of giving public talks, the nervous strain he experienced diminished almost to the vanishing point. And, in fact, a considerable part of his income throughout his life came from giving public lectures. He used these venues to try out the ideas that he would later put into writing in such books as *The Conquest of Happiness*.

The next cause of unhappiness discussed by Russell is envy. He states, "Next to worry probably one of the most potent causes of unhappiness is envy. Envy is, I should say, one of the most universal and deep-seated of human passions" (1930, 82). Envy combines traits of jealousy and competition. To be envious of another is to want what others have, or to despise them because of what they have.

Envy, along with anger, gluttony, greed, lust, pride, and sloth, is one of the traditional "Seven Deadly Sins." So, it is not surprising that, in chapter 7 of *Conquest*, Russell discusses the idea of "the sense of sin."

Earlier in his book (chapter 1), Russell had described a "sinner" as someone who commits an act that leads to disapproval, especially one's own self-disapproval. Further, if the person is religious, a sinful act is interpreted as the disapproval of God.

Interestingly, Russell described narcissism (admiring oneself and wishing to be admired) as a habitual sense of sin. He acknowledged that, up to a point, it is normal to want to be admired and to admire one's own accomplishments, but when such self-directed admiration becomes excessive, it becomes a grave evil. Russell describes "the sense of sin" as one of the most important underlying psychological causes of unhappiness as there exists a corresponding feeling of unease and discomfort. A person who offends his or her rational code of conduct experiences unhappiness because there were alternative behaviors that could have been employed. Upon reflection on an act that violates one's own code of conduct, remorse is likely to take residence within one's consciousness via self-reflection. This remorse, beyond making a person unhappy, is likely to make the individual feel inferior. Worse yet, the unhappy person is likely to act out in a number of harmful ways, including setting unrealistic and excessive expectations on others' behaviors and by holding grudges against those who now seem superior. Russell states, "Nothing so much diminishes not only happiness but efficiency as a personality divided against itself" (1930, 107).

The final cause of unhappiness discussed by Russell is the fear of public opinion. He states, "Very few people can be happy unless on the whole their way of life and their outlook on the world is approved by those with whom they have social relations, and more especially by those with whom they live" (1930, 126). Hoping to gain the approval of the general public, and especially those closest to us, is still important to many people today. Russell believes that the fear of public opinion, like every other form of fear, is oppressive and stunts growth. Furthermore, it is difficult to achieve any kind of greatness while a fear of this kind remains strong and it is impossible to achieve happiness if we must constantly concern ourselves with the tastes and desires of our neighbors or close relations. He offers this summation: "I think that in general, apart from expert opinion, there is too much respect paid to the opinions of others, both in great matters and in small ones" (1930, 136). Still, it would be advisable for employees to heed the directions of their employers; for people to abide by the laws of a particular society; and for spouses to heed their partner's concerns.

After laying out in Part One of *The Conquest of Happiness* the chief causes for what makes us unhappy, Russell then tackles what he considers to be the causes of happiness in Part Two. The key to Russell's view of happiness resides in the realization that happiness is not, except in very rare cases, something that simply happens; rather, it is something that must be achieved (conquered) through effort.

After asking the question "Is Happiness Still Possible?" at the beginning of Part Two, Russell gives a vigorous affirmative. He addresses such causes of happiness as affection, family relations, health, work, impersonal interests, and effort. He lays particular emphasis on what he calls "zest." By this, he means a hearty pleasure or appreciation for life. In chapter 11 of *Conquest*, Russell equates zest to a thirst for happiness. "Genuine zest," he asserts, "is part of the natural make-up of human beings except in so far as it has been destroyed by unfortunate circumstances" (1930, 100). He goes on to say that "Loss of zest in civilized society is very largely due to the restrictions upon liberty which are essential to our way of life" (p.100). Society necessarily places limits upon our actions, and we must understand the reasons for these limitations if we are to truly be happy. Paradoxically, achieving happiness necessitates a certain amount of resignation. "To teach an attitude of inactivity and withdrawal towards life," he notes, "is clearly to teach something very inimical to zest" (p.101).

Resignation, therefore, also has its part to play in the conquest of happiness, and it is a part no less essential than that played by effort. Russell discusses this in detail in Chapter 16 of *Conquest*. He argues that a wise person will learn to resign from the pursuit of certain desired but unattainable forms of happiness so as not to interfere with actual attainable forms of happiness. In other words, sometimes we have to resign ourselves to the reality that not everything we desire in life will happen (or as the Rolling Stones would put it—you can't always get what you want).

And here Russell, somewhat begrudgingly, admits that he has come to appreciate Aristotle's concept of "The golden mean"—the middle ground between two extremes. "The golden mean," he writes, "in an uninteresting doctrine, and I can remember when I was young rejecting it with scorn and indignation, since in those days it was heroic extremes that I admired" (1930, 132). This was in Russell's more Byronic stage of life, when he sought joy by rejecting conventional thinking, including Aristotle's teachings. "Truth, however," he adds, "is not always interesting, and many things are believed because they are interesting although, in fact, there is little other evidence in their favor" (p.132). Sometimes, in order to be happy, we must resign ourselves to the fact that there are goals we cannot achieve. But this is all the more reason why we need to focus our attention on goals that are in fact achievable.

So, good things do not come to those who wait; instead, they come to people who actively seek happiness and conquer the obstacles that come between one's pursuit of happiness and happiness itself. One can see the similarity here with Aristotle's idea that happiness (which he calls *eudaimonia* or "good spirit") involved genuine effort. Happiness will also come when one learns to stop pursuing the unattainable. Again, like Aristotle, Russell is stating here that we must use our rational minds to determine what are realistic goals for ourselves. "Happiness is not, except in very rare cases, something that drops into the mouth, like a ripe fruit, by the mere operation of fortunate circumstances," he writes. "That is why I have called this book *The Conquest of Happiness*. For in a world so full of avoidable and unavoidable misfortunes, of illness and psychological tangles, of struggles and poverty and ill-will, the man or woman who is to be happy must find ways of coping with the multitudinous causes of unhappiness by which each individual is assailed" (1930, 133).

In the final chapter of *The Conquest of Happiness* (Chapter 17), Russell explains that happiness depends partly upon external circumstances and partly upon oneself. Some people are born with certain advantages and yet we all, potentially, have the opportunity to pursue happiness. The happy person is one who has affections, wide interests, pursues happiness with a zest, is free from suffering, is a citizen of the universe, and not giving a damn about what others think of you or what others think is important.

After reading Russell's *The Conquest of Happiness* and reflecting upon its meaning and relevance to contemporary society, we can conclude that happiness is not, except in very rare cases, just a matter of good fortune. For in a world so full of avoidable and unavoidable misfortunes, of illness and psychological tangles, of struggle and poverty and ill will, the man or woman who is to be happy must find ways of coping with the multitude of causes of unhappiness by which each individual is assailed. Individuals must then pursue activities that will bring them happiness while also resigning to the fact that not everything one wants in life is achievable.

Russell, in his role as a public intellectual, exemplified these traits. One must remember that for much of the second half of his life Russell made his living as a writer. He did not have the luxury, for most of this time, of drawing upon an academic salary to pay for his and his family's upkeep. His wonderful ability to write memorable copy on a deadline is not something one should easily dismiss. Through his social activism, frequent media appearances and nonstop issuance of manifestoes, he made philosophy exciting and relevant to a new generation. Russell became the stereotypical image of a philosopher in the minds of many non-academics, much as Einstein became the stereotypical image of a scientist. Both showed that one could be a deep thinker and still be passionately involved in life's struggles (and even have an active sex life, too). It's not surprising that this Jazz Age book still has much to offer. Russell truly knew what "zest" really means.

Bibliography

Dardis, Tom. 1995. *Firebrand: The Life of Horace Liveright.* New York: Random House.

Delaney, Tim and Tim Madigan. 2017. *Friendship and Happiness: And the Connection Between the Two.* Jefferson, NC: McFarland.

Gilmer, Walker. 1970. *Horace Liveright: Publisher of the Twenties.* New York: David Lewis.

Monk, Ray. 2000. *Bertrand Russell: The Ghost of Madness, 1921-1970.* New York: The Free Press.

Russell, Bertrand. 1930. *The Conquest of Happiness.* London: Allen & Unwin.

Ryan, Alan. 1988. *Bertrand Russell: A Political Life.* New York: Hill and Wang.

RUSSELL ON THE ETHICAL VALUE OF LOGIC

Landon D.C. Elkind

Logic or Ethics, with an Inclusive "OR"

IT IS WELL TO START AN ESSAY ON LOGIC with the notion of *inclusive* "OR". We often use "or" in the exclusive sense to mean that one or another claim is true, but not both. For example, in the 1939 film *Mr. Smith Goes to Washington*, when Senator Jefferson Smith exclaims, "Either I'm dead right, or I'm crazy!" we do not understand him to be entertaining the possibility that he is both dead right and crazy. But this is of course logically possible, and so logicians often allow that the default use of "OR" is inclusive, so that it means that one claim, or another, or both, are true.

When it comes to Bertrand Russell's contributions to logic and ethics, Russell is an unhappy victim of scholars' predisposition to prefer the exclusive "OR" to the inclusive one. Russell was preeminent in both fields. In ethics, his writings made a deep and lasting mark on society, beginning in 1896 with his first book, *German Social Democracy*, through his social commentaries during and after World War I, especially his 1929 *Marriage and Morals*, and continuing into his righteous opposition to nuclear Armageddon in radio addresses like his 1950 "Man's Peril" carried on the *BBC*. This lasting society-wide impact in ethics earned Russell the 1950 Nobel Prize in Literature "in recognition of his varied and significant writings in which he champions humanitarian ideals and freedom of thought" (The Nobel Prize, 2020).

Russell's logical contributions were no less impressive. He invented type theory, which has seen a rich variety of applications throughout computer science and mathematics after being unhappily eclipsed from philosophers' attention by set theory. With Alfred North Whitehead, Russell co-authored in 1910 the groundbreaking three-volume *Principia Mathematica* on the heels of his 1903 *The Principles of Mathematics*, a rich and robust defense of the philosophy of mathematics known as logicism, according to which all mathematical truths are logical truths. Russell produced ample and insightful illustrations of how these logical innovations could guide and invigorate new research in philosophy in his 1914 *Our Knowledge of the External World: As a Field for Scientific Method in Philosophy*, his 1921 *The Analysis of Mind*, and his 1927 *The Analysis of Matter*. His writings on both scientific philosophy and practical affairs were widely read and published globally. Again, he was preeminent by the measure of his writings in either logic or (inclusive) ethics.

Yet scholars have, unfortunately, tended to praise his work on logic and bury his ethical writings, or vice-versa: they typically praise one or the other, but not both. They see these sides of Russell's contributions to thought as independent of one another but that happen to be stuck to the same person, much like two sides of a coin can look totally different but still be stuck together.

This has made it possible to evaluate Russell's contributions in ethics and logic apart from one another. The orthodox view among scholars is accurately reflected by Ray Monk's two-volume biography of Russell, where we find, for instance, the following:

> As a philosopher of mathematics, Russell had achieved rare greatness; as a journalist and political commentator, he was to produce a staggering amount of second-rate writing. The problem as many of his friends identified, was partly that he approached politics with a logician's desire for absolute clarity, and thus, impatient with the messy realities of political life, was inclined to oversimplify every issue…His best philosophical writing is subtle, nuanced and unafraid of complexity. He supports his views with rigorous and sophisticated arguments, and deals with objections carefully and respectfully. In most of the journalism and political writing that he produced in the second half of his life, however, these qualities are absent, replaced with empty rhetoric, blind dogmatism and a cavalier refusal to take the views of his opponents seriously. (Monk 2001)

I here aim to refute this opinion. Russell applied his logical prowess no less in *Principia* than in *Proposed Roads to Freedom*. As we will see, in ethical works Russell argues more methodically than has been widely acknowledged. In his ethical writings, as in his scientific ones, he argues from data that are taken as true, reasons from first principles, and suspends endorsement of a conclusion where none is reachable. In fact, many of the same methodological moves occur in his ethical and scientific works alike. His whole mode of argumentation belies opinions like the one above, even though logical allowance must be made for unwieldy ethical subject-matters.

It is also mistaken to set up, as if they were in opposition, the logical, technical mode of writing and the ethical subject-matter. The ethical subject-matter is not necessarily outside the scope of "technical philosophy"—indeed, I should think that Russell's insights in ethics are to *logically* develop various detailed and comprehensive policy recommendations from clear initial principles about human psychology and his account(s) of human desires, with a refusal to give a conclusion where none is warranted. And that seems a very fruitful model for research in ethics.

We will see that Russell's philosophical method in logic is equally applied to ethical subjects. But more importantly, we will also discuss Russell's belief that there is a quite close connection between logic and ethics. Russell thought the discipline of logic had ethical worth. And even though Russell's view as to the place of ethics among the sciences was complicated and changing, Russell nonetheless held that logicians could boast of ethical insights. So the received opinion, besides being historically inaccurate, also misses something vitally important in Russell's philosophy about the mutual interrelations between ethics and logic.

The Logical Methodology in Russell's Ethical Works

RUSSELL EXPLICITLY ENDORSES WHAT HE CALLS *the regressive method* in ethics, too. A thorough critical discussion of this method is beyond the scope of our topic here, but the idea is simple enough. Roughly, the regressive method involves starting with some *data*, i.e., claims in whose truth we have strong confidence, and tracing them backwards to principles that are logically adequate to recover this data, and to withstand some potentially dramatic revisions required to clarify it.[1]

---

[1] Notably, Russell does not insist that the premises discovered by this method are, or even should, be epistemically certain. A robust argument for this claim occurs in Irvine (1989).

Russell describes the regressive method in his 1907 "The Regressive Method of Discovering the Premises of Mathematics:"

> In every science, we start with a body of propositions of which we feel fairly sure. These are our empirical premises, commonly called the facts, which are generally got by observation. We may then ask either: What follows from these facts? or, what do these facts follow from? The general laws of science are propositions logically simpler than the empirical premises of the science, but such that the empirical premises, or some of them, can be deduced from these laws. The laws only become as certain as the empirical premises if we can show that no other hypotheses would lead to the empirical premises, or if (what may happen in mathematics) the laws, once obtained, are found to be themselves obvious, and thus to be capable of themselves becoming empirical premises. (Russell 2014, 572)

The regressive method in sciences, if successful, results in logically simpler premises sufficient, and sometimes also necessary, to deduce some of the facts of observation, whether sensory observation or intellectual. This method applies equally in ethics according to Russell, at least during the period when he considered ethics to be a science (we will return to his changing view on the status of ethics in the final section). In his 1909 "The Elements of Ethics," Russell says:

> It is the business of the philosopher to ask for reasons as long as reasons can legitimately be demanded, and to register the propositions which give the most ultimate reasons that are attainable…Thus in the case of ethics, we must ask why such and such actions ought to be performed, and continue our backward inquiry for reasons until we reach the kind of proposition of which proof is impossible, because it is so simple or so obvious that nothing more fundamental can be found from which to deduce it. (Russell 1992, 218)

Russell, at least in 1909, thought ethics embraces the regressive method. An ethicist works backwards from the data that some actions are good, and others bad, to the principles that suffice to deduce the ethical data.

The orthodoxy as to Russell's ethical prowess, or alleged lack thereof, fits poorly with Russell's stated view about ethics as a discipline.² It demands, firstly, that Russell's ethical writings drastically failed his explicit standards in ethical philosophy.

This alone does not supply textual evidence against the orthodox view. But Russell's ethical writings do. Not only did Russell claim in 1909 that ethical theorizing possesses a logical structure, proceeding from ultimate premises discovered by the regressive method to the data and other consequences of ultimate premises: in notable ethical works, Russell argued to basic ethical principles, and then from those basic principles to everyday applications and consequences.

As one example of this pattern, consider his 1916 *Principles of Social Reconstruction*. There Russell begins his book on political philosophy by outlining beginning logical principles:

> My aim is to suggest a philosophy of politics based upon the belief that impulse has more effect than conscious purpose in moulding men's lives. Most impulses may be divided into two groups, the possessive and the creative, according as they aim at acquiring or retaining something that cannot be shared, or at bringing into the world some valuable thing, such as knowledge or art or goodwill, in which there is no private property. (Russell 1916, 5)

The first chapter of his 1916 book is an extended defense and explanation of this basic claim of human psychology. He argues that reason alone cannot control human action and, further, that will and desire play more minor roles in guiding our actions than impulse (Russell 1916, 16). Having defended and elaborated on this foundational principle in the first chapter, the rest of Russell's book repeatedly applies his foundational principle of human psychology to politics and society. That is, his principle is a premise, and is heavily used in developing his arguments. This is unexpected if we think that Russell argued without methodological rigor in his ethical works.

For instance, in discussing the abolition of war, Russell ties the difficulty directly to our impulses: "The fundamental problem for the pacifist

---

² Russell's views about the nature of ethics changed significantly after the publication of this piece (Russell 1992, 213). I discuss how Russell's changing view of the discipline of ethics bears on my thesis in the concluding section.

is to prevent the impulse towards war which seizes whole communities from time to time." (Russell 1916, 92-3) This is complicated by such impulses being ineliminable for human well-being: "A great many of the impulses which now lead nations to go to war are in themselves essential to any vigorous or progressive life." (Russell 1916, 93) So Russell's proposed solution is to provide outlets for the human impulse to conflict that do not lead to war. Just as private duels, which arise from the same impulses to conflict, were abolished by the substitution of intrastate political contests, so war can be abolished by introducing a world state and allowing intra world-state political competition (Russell 1916, 107-8). Crucially, Russell thinks that this can be done, as it must, "without any fundamental change in human nature" (Russell 1916, 108).

Our takeaway from this portion of Russell's 1916 book chapter on war is that the argument is methodical. It has an apparent logical structure. We might reconstruct it as follows:

1. Human action is predominantly caused by impulses. [Premise, basic principle]

2. The human impulses that cause wars cannot be extinguished consistent with human well-being. [Premise]

3. If (1) and (2), then the human impulses that cause wars must be rechanneled to contests besides warfare, e.g., political contests.

4. Therefore, the human impulses that cause wars must be rechanneled into contests besides warfare, e.g., political contests. [by (1), (2), and (3)]

This is a rigorous and sophisticated argument that springs chiefly from premise (1), which itself was an insight produced by applying the regressive method in ethics. Here is a fine example of Russell reasoning carefully from first principles in ethics just as he does elsewhere.

This is not an isolated incident in Russell's *Principles of Social Reconstruction*. For example, in a chapter on property, Russell argues against his age's capitalist system. He held that it stifled our creative impulses: "The chief defect of the present capitalistic system is that work done for wages seldom affords any outlet for the creative impulse" (Russell 1916, 136). So it violates his "chief test" for economic systems: "whether it leaves men's instinctive growth unimpeded" (Russell 1916, 135). This argument of Russell's can also be readily reconstructed in a patently valid argument form.

This methodical argumentation is not confined to one book: it pervades Russell's other works in ethics. In his 1919 *Proposed Roads to Freedom*, he argues against a government bureaucracy being given total discretion over which artists and writers receive funding. This policy, he says, is contrary to the very impulses that move us to make creative works:

> Art springs from a wild and anarchic side of human nature…It is impossible for art, or any of the higher creative activities, to flourish under any system which requires that the artist shall prove his competence to some body of authorities before he is allowed to follow his impulse. (Russell 1919, 175-6)

Russell prefers an option that allows persons to follow their creative impulses without needing to persuade a bureaucrat. We see here again how Russell's argument carefully ties his case against a proposed policy to his basic claim, that the source of artistic activity is our creative impulse. This is the organizing principle of his discussion of art in the ideal society: people must have "liberty to follow the creative impulse" (Russell 1919, 172).

This fundamental claim about the springs of human action, that they are largely due to either our creative or possessive impulses, equally animates his discussion throughout *Proposed Roads*. The book's closing chapter identifies a life guided by creative impulses as possessing "a certain fundamental happiness, of which it cannot be wholly robbed by adverse circumstances" (Russell 1919, 187). This is why the "main method" for fighting character vices is "a free outlet for all impulses that do not involve domination" (Russell 1919, 189). The creative impulse is indeed the centerpiece of Russell's program for an ideal political society:

> The world that we must seek is a world in which the creative spirit is alive, in which life is an adventure full of joy and hope, based rather on the impulse to construct than on the desire to retain what we possess or to seize what is possessed by others. (Russell 1919, 212)

This is just what we would expect from Russell's methodical argumentation in his ethical works: he has a basic principle about human psychology and leverages it, time and again, to develop a case for or against some proposed policy of achieving a desired social outcome, like ending war.

Russell's Changing View on the Place of Ethics in Philosophy

PART OF WHY THE RECEIVED OPINION HAS TAKEN ROOT among scholars is that Russell's views as to the place of ethics in philosophy changed over his ninety-seven years. In his 1910 "The Elements of Ethics," he explicitly endorses many of the views held by his college friend and Cambridge colleague, G. E. Moore, as Moore developed them in *Principia Ethica*.[3] Among these views is that ethics is a science in its own right:

> ...the object of ethics, by its own account, is to discover true propositions about virtuous and vicious conduct...these are just as much a part of truth as true propositions about oxygen or the multiplication table...Thus the study of ethics is not one something outside science and coordinate with it: it is merely one among the sciences. (Russell 1992, 217)

In the previous section, I cited Russell's works from the 1910s, which largely bear out this view of ethics. But his view of the place of ethics changed shortly after World War I, as he says in a footnote to the 1952 reprinting of "The Elements of Ethics" (Russell 1992, 213).

The clearest repudiation of his 1910 conception of ethics occurs in his 1927 *An Outline of Philosophy*.[4] In the chapter on ethics, Russell writes:

> There is a view, advocated, e.g., by Dr. G. E. Moore, that 'good' is an indefinable notion, and that we know *a priori* certain general propositions about the kinds of things that are good on their own account...I formerly held this view myself, but I was led to abandon it...I now think that good and bad are derivative from desire. (Russell 1927, 238)

---

[3] "What follows is largely based on Mr. G. E. Moore's *Principia Ethica*, to which the reader is referred for fuller discussions" (Russell 1992, 218).
[4] See also (Russell 1935, 235-7) and (Russell 1925, 37-41).

Russell even goes so far as to divorce ethics and philosophy, and presumably rejects the view that the inquiry regarding fundamental ethical principles is a science:

> Ethics is traditionally a department of philosophy…I hardly think myself that it ought to be included in the domain of philosophy… (Russell 1927, 233)

Nonetheless, Russell retains a scientific method in ethics: he still holds that ethics involves the discovery of basic and general principles from which one can derive rules to guide our conduct:

> As a provisional definition, we may take ethics to consist of general principles which help to determine rules of conduct…It is not the business of ethics to arrive at actual rules of conduct, such as: "Thou shalt not steal"…Ethics is expect to provide a basis from which such rules can be deduced. (Russell 1927, 233-4)

It may be a reach to say that this is the regressive method that we saw practiced in the 1910s, but it is similar in respect of seeking basic ethical principles from which to derive normative rules. In other words: it is a significant departure from his view in the 1910s that Russell denies that true or false claims are the end result of this method in ethics, but even though the results of applying the method in ethical investigations are rules and not claims, Russell nonetheless uses a method.

This fact is borne out in Russell's writings. In his 1929 *Marriage and Morals,* Russell says, "The general principle upon which the newer morality differs from the traditional morality of puritanism is this: we believe that instinct should be trained rather than thwarted" (Russell 1929, 311). This is, firstly, quite consonant with his 1910s ethical principles as to human impulses. This applies especially to his definition of the good life: *"The good life is one inspired by love and guided by knowledge"* (Russell 1925, 28). Note: love and knowledge are not possessive.

Second, the general principle given in *Marriage and Morals* is clearly an overarching claim that imbues the arguments of this 1929 book. Indeed, Russell says that any sexual ethic "has to be derived from certain general principles" (Russell 1929, 315). And Russell walks his talk; he consistently ties his critiques and support of policies, like no-fault divorce and widespread birth control, to his basic principles.[5] Russell also affirms a need for fundamental principles from which ethical rules can be derived in his other works; furthermore, he holds that, although the fundamental principle itself lies outside the scope of scientific inquiry, the derivation of ethical rules from such fundamental principles is part of science (Russell 1935, 228-30).[6]

Thus, even though Russell's views as to the fundamental principles of ethics changed, this did not prevent Russell from arguing methodically in ethics, as he did in other areas of inquiry.[7] As such, we have seen that Russell thought that the deployment of rigorous methodology in ethics was essential, and he practiced this conviction. We might restate this point as follows: Russell held that logical methods were quite applicable in ethics. In the rest of this paper, we will see, conversely, that Russell believed there was ethical value to the study of logic.

Russell's Belief in the Ethical Value of Logic

RUSSELL HELD THAT LOGIC HAS ETHICAL VALUE IN TWO WAYS. It has aesthetic value as something that we can enjoy and appreciate. It also has social value in its improvement of our rational faculties.

Let us take aesthetic value first. Russell held that logic was beautiful. Indeed, in his 1907 "The Study of Mathematics," republished in the 1917 *Mysticism and Logic, and Other Essays*, he says of mathematics, which is a branch of logic according to Russell, the following:

> Mathematics, rightly viewed, possesses not only truth, but supreme beauty—a beauty cold and austere, like that of sculpture, without appeal to any part of our weaker nature, without the gorgeous trappings of painting or music, yet sublimely pure, and capable of a stern perfection such as only the greatest art can show. The true spirit of delight, the exaltation, the sense of being more than man, which is the touchstone of the

---

[5] See, for instance, Russell 1929, 126-7, 278, 293, and especially Russell 1925, 28-30.
[6] See also Russell 1925, 37.
[7] See especially his 1955 book, *Human Society in Ethics and Politics*. As he states in the preface, the whole agenda of that book is, first, to develop an ethic, and second, to apply it to modern political issues (Russell 1954, 7).

> highest excellence, is to be found in mathematics as surely as in poetry. (Russell 1917, 60)

The particularly appealing aspects of logic and mathematics are "the purity and strictness of its reasoning" and in mathematical texts imbued with this logical character, "in the greatest works, unity and inevitability are felt as in the unfolding of a drama..." (Russell 1917, 65-6). And the view that mathematics is part of logic itself has an aesthetic element: "The discovery that all mathematics follows inevitably from a small collection of fundamental laws is one which immeasurably enhances the intellectual beauty of the whole..." (Russell 1917, 67).

Beauty in logic and mathematics, Russell says, partly stems from their systematic nature and the interconnections of systematic mathematics (Russell 1917, 66). The beauty in logic and math also comes from the independence of their content from us: "It is only when we thoroughly understand the entire independence of ourselves, which belongs to this world that reason finds, that we can adequately realize the profound importance of its beauty" (Russell 1917, 69).

Russell held that logic and mathematics also had ethical value for society in a practical way. Part of this is derivative: theoretical inquiries can change habitual patterns of thought, often for the better; for example, the development of steam and electric power was made possible through mathematical inquiry (Russell 1917, 72). And the aesthetic appreciation of logic and math, in Russell's view, instils a valuable sense of wonder and appreciation in us, one that can inspire us to learn for the sake of learning, that is, to give us "the love of truth" (Russell 1917, 73).

Even more important is the impact philosophy can have on liberating the mind from mental prisons. Philosophy, in Russell's view, can help us escape the contingent and sometimes harmful social and cultural norms of our time, and to envision a society liberated from them. In his 1912 popular book, *The Problems of Philosophy*, Russell gives his clearest expression of this view:

> The value of philosophy is, in fact, to be sought largely in its uncertainty. The man who has no tincture of philosophy goes through life imprisoned by the prejudices derived from common sense, from the habitual beliefs of his age or his nation, and from convictions which have grown up in his mind without the co-operation or consent of his deliber-

ate reason. To such a man the world tends to become definite, finite, obvious; common objects rouse no questions, and unfamiliar possibilities are contemptuously rejected. As soon as we begin to philosophize, on the contrary, we find…that even the most everyday things lead to problems to which only very incomplete answers can be given. Philosophy, though unable to tell us with certainty what is the true answer to the doubts which it raises, is able to suggest many possibilities which enlarge our thoughts and free them from the tyranny of custom. Thus, while diminishing our feeling of certainty as to what things are, it greatly increases our knowledge as to what they may be; it removes somewhat the arrogant dogmatism of those who have never travelled into the region of liberating doubt, and it keeps alive our sense of wonder by showing familiar things in an unfamiliar aspect. (Russell 1912, 242-4)

This brings us to a further point: why did Russell write a *popular* philosophy book? The answer is of course that he thought that philosophy was good for us: it embiggens our sphere of interests and concerns beyond ourselves and our affairs; philosophical contemplation thereby achieves "freedom and impartiality" that we often do not enjoy in everyday life (Russell 1912, 248).

Moreover, philosophy deflates our dogmatic airs. It brings us to see how the world might be different, and how some apparent necessities are in fact accidents. The social and political value of all this is immense: it leads us to sympathize beyond personal features, like nation, politics, sex, race, gender, and so on, and to reject our social group's dogmatic inheritances. This benefit of philosophy is helpfully captured by Russell's impartiality test in "Philosophy for Laymen":

> I recommend the following exercise: When, in a sentence expressing a political opinion, there are words that arouse powerful but different emotions in different readers, try replacing them by symbols, A, B, C, and so on, and forgetting the particular significance of the symbol. Suppose A is England, B is Germany, and C is Russia. So long as you remember what the letters mean, most of the things you will believe will depend upon whether you are English, German, or Russian…In thinking about political problems this kind

> of emotional bias is bound to be present, and only care and practice can enable you to think as objectively as you do in the algebraic problem. (Russell 1921, 47)

So not only does philosophy help us to scrutinize beliefs and customs of our community, but also to set aside our feelings in considering political questions by encouraging generalization. This led Russell to claim that if both of these benefits of philosophy "became common, the gain in diminishing the acerbity of disputes would be incalculable" (Russell 1921, 47).

Russell evidently held that logic was crucial to philosophy playing this social role. After all, Russell believed that philosophy and logic are "indistinguishable," and logic consists of course of completely general claims (Russell 1986, 65). Partly because of its general nature, Russell says that studying logic, which is "the essence of philosophy," liberates thought itself:

> Modern logic, as I hope is now evident, has the effect of enlarging our abstract imagination, and providing an infinite number of possible hypotheses to be applied in the analysis of any complex fact. In this respect it is the exact opposite of the logic practised by the classical tradition. In that logic, hypothesis which seem *prima facie* possible are professedly proved impossible, and it is decreed in advance that reality must have a certain character. In modern logic, on the contrary, while the *prima facie* hypotheses as a rule remain admissible, others, which only logic would have suggested, are added to our stock, and are very often found indispensable if a right analysis of the facts is to be obtained. The old logic put thought in fetters, while the new logic gives it wings. (Russell 1914, 58-9)

So logic has this ethical benefit on its practitioners, and one that would be society-wide if it was sufficiently common. Contrast this ethical value of modern logic with the noxious effects of the older, traditional, Aristotelian logic. As is well-known, Russell abhorred the practice of teaching Aristotelian logic that was common in his day. In a 1968 essay, he writes:

> If you wish to become a logician, there is one piece of advice which I cannot urge too strongly, and that is: Do NOT learn the traditional formal logic. In Aristotle's day, it was a creditable effort, but so was Ptolemaic astronomy.

To teach either in the present day is a ridiculous piece of antiquarianism. (Russell 1968, 38)

Why is that? As Russell explains in his 1948 *History of Western Philosophy*, Aristotelian logic has the pernicious ambition of certifying as necessary beliefs that seem obvious.

Take, say, "all humans are mortal." This claim strikes as true, and perhaps obviously so. But it is not certifiable by logic alone because, logically speaking, it could be false:

> …there is nothing self-contradictory about an immortal man. We believe the proposition ['All men are mortal'] on the basis of induction, because there is no well-authenticated case of a man living more than (say) one hundred and fifty years; but this only makes the proposition probable, not certain. It cannot be certain so long as living men exist. (Russell 1946, 220-1)

However, Aristotle held that there was a human species whose essence could certify this claim, at least in Russell's telling of Aristotle. And some philosophers have held, and continue to hold, that philosophy aims at establishing necessary truths. It is often a happy accident that these necessary truths conform to our beliefs before we engage in philosophy.

These are the vices of the traditional, Aristotelian logic, and of the traditional mode of doing philosophy. They are antithetical not just to Russell's conception of logic, and so of philosophy, but to his view as to why logic and philosophy are valuable. For Russell, certifying the obvious, even the apparently innocent claim that all humans are mortal, is not logic's task. Logic shows us new possibilities that may be, not old possibilities that must be. It should not dogmatize about the 'obvious' because this risks mistaking the obvious for the true, thereby poisoning the results of our scientific inquiry: "The logic which thus arises is not quite disinterested or candid… Such an attitude naturally does not tend to the best results" (Russell 1914, 46).

So to ourselves and society, the ethical value of logic, and so the value of philosophy, consists in strengthening our critical capacities. It forces us to bracket our feelings as misleading guides to the truth. By showing the genuine logical connections between claims, it undercuts the haze of obviousness that often clouds our ethical judgments. And it opens the way to improving society, unhindered by our present ills. As Russell writes, "Thus, while it [logic] liberates imagination as to what the world *may* be, it refuses to legislate as to what the world *is*" (emphasis in original; Russell 1914, 8).

This perk to society of studying logic makes for a powerful combination with its aesthetic value. We saw that Russell believed logic could enlarge our interests and concerns. At the same time, it can minimize the muddying effects of bias and emotion in our thinking. This clears the way to clear-eyed appraisal of our politics and society, and to advocacy of the interests of those beyond our immediate and severely limited sphere of interaction. Such was the way that Russell managed to advocate for lofty ambitions, like a world without warfare and freed from the threat of nuclear annihilation, a universal basic income, women's suffrage, liberty in our sexual relations, an end to retributive criminal punishment, free higher education for those that desire it, a student-centered educational model, and more. Perhaps someday, immortal humans, say, will join the ranks of such ideas, if enough of us mind our logic studies.

We have seen that Russell argued methodically, with logical rigor, in his ethical writings, and even explicitly affirmed the importance of this. But we also saw that Russell believed that logic itself was ethically valuable, and not just for aesthetic reasons: logic is also vital to our moral development and social improvement. Without logic, we will not know for sure if, as a society, we can abandon our antiquated ideas and customary habits for a bold new vision of what our society could be. With logic, we can see that there is nothing contradictory about a world without war, without sickness, without poverty, without want, and without fear. As Russell saw, it is through the study of logic—"the science of the possible" (Russell 1986, 65)—that such possibilities become open to us. By moral reflection using logical tools, we are startled into action because logic, by its general nature and the impersonal and beautiful character its content, encourages us to develop what Kenneth Blackwell calls "the ethic of impersonal self-enlargement," an ethic that transcends our selfish desires and personal circumstances (Blackwell 1985, 17). Logic has this ethical value both because of its aesthetic quality, which turns our desires outwards, and because of its general character, which dilutes the blinding influence of our accidental and local circumstances.

Russell knew that logic has this ethical value and that ethics should be conducted logically: it is no accident that Russell's widely popular writings in ethics were preceded by *Principia Mathematica*.

Bibliography

Blackwell, Kenneth. 1985. *The Spinozistic Ethics of Bertrand Russell*. London: George Allen & Unwin Ltd.

Irvine, A. D. 1989. "Epistemic Logicism & Russell's Regressive Method." *Philosophical Studies*, 55(3), 303-7. Retrieved from https://www.jstor.org/stable/4320023

Monk, Ray. 2001. *Bertrand Russell: The Ghost of Madness 1921-1970*. London: Vintage.

Russell, Bertrand. 1912. *The Problems of Philosophy*. New York: Henry Holt and Company. Retrieved from https://archive.org/details/problemsofphilo00russuoft/mode/2up

Russell, Bertrand. 1914. *Our Knowledge of the External World: as a Field for Scientific Method in Philosophy*. Chicago: Open Court Publishing Company. Retrieved from https://archive.org/details/ourknowledgeofex00inruss/mode/2up

Russell, Bertrand. 1916. *Principles of Social Reconstruction*. London: George Allen & Unwin Ltd. Retrieved from https://archive.org/details/principlesofsoci0000russ

Russell, Betrand. 1917. "The Study of Mathematics." In *Mysticism and Logic, and Other Essays*. London: George Allen & Unwin Ltd. Retrieved from https://archive.org/details/mysticism00russuoft

Russell, Bertrand. 1919. *Proposed Roads to Freedom: Socialism, Anarchism and Syndicalism*. New York: Henry Holt and Company. Retrieved from https://archive.org/details/proposedroadstof00russuoft

Russell, Bertrand. 1921. "Philosophy for Laymen." In *Unpopular Essays*. London: George Allen and Unwin Ltd. Retrieved from https://archive.org/details/in.ernet.dli.2015.462628/mode/2up

Russell, Bertrand. 1925. *What I Believe*. London: Kegan Paul, Trench, Trubner & Co., Ltd. Retrieved from https://archive.org/details/whatibelieve0000russ/mode/2up

Russell, Bertrand. 1927. *An Outline of Philosophy*. London: George Allen & Unwin Ltd. Retrieved from https://archive.org/details/in.ernet.dli.2015.222952

Russell, Bertrand. 1929. *Marriage and Morals*. New York: Liveright Publishing Corporation. Retrieved from https://archive.org/details/marriagemorals00russ_0

Russell, Bertrand. 1935. *Religion and Science*. London: Thornton Butterworth Ltd. Retrieved from https://archive.org/details/in.ernet.dli.2015.52360

Russell, Bertrand. 1946. *History of Western Philosophy.* London: George Allen and Unwin Ltd. Retrieved from https://archive.org/details/TheHistoryOfWesternPhilosophy

Russell, Bertrand. 1954. *Human Society in Ethics and Politics.* London: George Allen & Unwin Ltd. Retrieved from https://archive.org/details/in.ernet.dli.2015.209076

Russell, Bertrand. 1968. *The Art of Philosophizing and Other Essays.* New York: Philosophical Library.

Russell, Bertrand. 1986. "Scientific Method in Philosophy." In *The Philosophy of Logical Atomism and Other Essays, 1914-19,* Ed. John G. Slater. Volume 8 of *The Collected Papers of Bertrand Russell.* London: Routledge. Retrieved from https://archive.org/details/mysticism00russuoft

Russell, Bertrand. 1992. "The Elements of Ethics." In *Logical and Philosophical Papers, 1909-13,* Ed. John G. Slater. Volume 6 of *The Collected Papers of Bertrand Russell.* New York: Routledge.

Russell, Bertrand. 2014. "The Regressive Method of Discovering the Premises of Mathematics." In *Toward Principia Mathematica, 1905-08,* Ed. Gregory H. Moore. Volume 5 of *The Collected Papers of Bertrand Russell.* New York: Routledge.

The Nobel Prize. 2020. *The Nobel Prize in Literature 1950.* April 16. Retrieved from Nobel Prize: https://www.nobelprize.org/prizes/literature/1950/summary/

BERTRAND RUSSELL'S LONG PURSUIT OF PEACE

Tony Simpson

> *"The nineteenth century was brought to its disastrous end by a conflict between industrial technique and political theory."*
>
> —*Freedom and Organization, 1814-1914*

RUSSELL SAW THE FIRST WORLD WAR AS A DIVIDING POINT. Life before 1914 retained hopes of peace and happiness. The horrors and mass slaughter of the 1914-18 war put paid to such hopes. But they also prompted Russell to attempt analyses of the causes of the war, in a series of books, as well as to volunteer for intense activism and work with the No-Conscription Fellowship. "He made a better administrator than he himself thought," was Jo Vellacott's assessment when Russell became Acting Chair of the NCF, alongside Catherine Marshall "who best knew what needed to be done," according to Vellacott. Russell's organisational and administrative skills were to serve him well throughout the rest of his long life of peace activism.

Three books, *Principles of Social Reconstruction, Political Ideals,* and *Roads to Freedom,* represent Russell's attempt to analyse the sources of war in human behaviour. They were written during the war years, and given initially as public lectures in the case of the first two. In January 1919, Russell prefaced *Roads to Freedom* thus: "The author has attempted to examine briefly the growth and scope of those pre-war doctrines [Socialism, Anarchism, and Syndicalism] which aimed at fundamental economic change. These doctrines are considered first historically, then critically, and it is urged that, while none can be accepted en bloc, all have something to contribute to the picture of the future society which we would wish to create."

The rise of fascism in Europe in the 1920s and 30s caused Russell to seek its sources and antidote. In "The Ancestry of Fascism" (1935) he wrote "while reason, being impersonal, makes universal co-operation possible, unreason, since it represents private passions, makes strife inevitable." This concern with "unreason'" preoccupied him for much the 1930s. Earlier, as the epigraph from *Freedom and Organization* indicates, he sought the causes of the First World War by tracing political change during the hundred years from 1814 to 1914. Looking ahead at the conclusion of this substantial work, he remarked: "It is not by pacifist sentiment, but by world-wide economic organisation, that civilized mankind is to be saved from collective suicide." It wasn't until 1940 that Russell publicly renounced pacifism, meaning the belief that war and violence are unjustifiable and that disputes should be settled by peaceful means. The prospect of another big war haunted him throughout the 1930s.

Russell spent much of the Second World War in the United States, where he had been teaching when war broke out in Europe in 1939. This caused him acute frustration as he watched from afar the Nazi advance across Europe, East and West. His approaches to the British Ambassador to the US, offering his services, were rebuffed. He had to sit it out until 1944, when he returned to Trinity College, Cambridge, to take up a fellowship and lectureship. "It heals the old wound of 1916," wrote Russell to his daughter, Kate. In 1916, Russell had been dismissed from Trinity, of which he had been a member since undergraduate days in the 1890s, following conviction under the Defence of the Realm Act for his opposition to conscription and the First World War.

"Russell was never more widely acclaimed as a public figure than in the years immediately after his return to England," writes Nicholas Griffin in *The Selected Letters of Bertrand Russell*, a sure and reliable guide to Russell's long and complex life. "Honours, financial security, public esteem, political respectability all came his way… for once, Russell found himself allied with the political establishment." Griffin summarises the next big development:

> Russell was cheered by the Labour landslide in the general election of 5 July [1945], but whatever optimism this generated was dispelled a month later when the first atomic bomb was exploded over Hiroshima … The use of nuclear weapons against Japan added a vast new dimension of horror to the world situation. It also transformed the remaining twenty-five years of Russell's life.

On September 1, 1945, Russell wrote to his friend Gamel Brenan: "I see very little hope for the world. There is no point in agreements not to use the atomic bomb, as they would not be kept. Russia is sure to learn soon how to make it. I think Stalin has inherited Hitler's ambition for world dictatorship. One must expect a war between USA and USSR, which will begin with the total destruction of London. I think the war will last 30 years, and leave a world without civilized people, from which everything will have to be built afresh—a process taking (say) 500 years."

By 1947, in his essay "Philosophy and Politics," Russell wrote that "war, in our scientific age, means, sooner or later, universal death." He likened what is now seen as the "Cold War" to "an epoch of wars of religion, but a religion is now called an 'ideology' ... Unfortunately the atomic bomb is a swifter exterminator than the stake." In these circumstances, the atomic bomb "cannot safely be allowed so long a run."

Russell's newly found international respectability was confirmed by the award of the Nobel Prize in Literature in 1950 "in recognition of his varied and significant writings in which he champions humanitarian ideals and freedom of thought."

In November 1952 in the Marshall Islands in the Pacific Ocean, the United States tested its first full-scale thermonuclear explosion, codename "Ivy Mike." Some 16 months later on March 1, 1954, at Bikini Atoll, the US exploded a "high-yield" bomb which, at the time, was the most powerful artificial explosion in history.

By now, Russell was writing short stories which conveyed the acute alarm of those nuclear-threatened Cold War years. They were published in collections entitled *Satan in the Suburbs, or Horrors Manufactured Here* and *Nightmares of Eminent Persons*, which he deemed "signposts to sanity."

Russell and Einstein

> *"He was not only a great scientist but a great man, a man whom it is good to have known and consoling to contemplate."*

WITH THESE WORDS, BERTRAND RUSSELL concluded his Preface to *Einstein on Peace*, first published in 1960. Down the years, Russell and Einstein had met from time to time, but they did not see much of each other except in the United States in 1943, while Russell was living in Princeton. Then they would meet weekly at Einstein's house to discuss "various matters in the philosophy of science". Wolfgang Pauli and Kurt Gödel also attended. "I found these informal discussions very illuminating and exceedingly valuable," said Russell.

Twelve years later, in February 1955 in London, Russell sent Einstein a proposal:

> In common with every other thinking person, I am profoundly disquieted by the armaments race in nuclear weapons. You have on various occasions given expression to feelings and opinions with which I am in close agreement. I think that eminent men of science ought to do something dramatic to bring home to the public and Governments the disasters that may occur. Do you think it would be possible to get, say, six men of the very highest scientific repute headed by yourself, to make a very solemn statement about the imperative necessity of avoiding war?

By this time, both the United States and the Soviet Union had the hydrogen bomb, and the US test at Bikini Atoll in the Pacific Ocean, in March 1954, had spread radioactive fall-out across wide areas, contaminating Japanese fishermen and their catch aboard the *Lucky Dragon* fishing boat.

EINSTEIN RESPONDED ENTHUSIASTICALLY, notwithstanding his failing health: "I agree with every word in your letter of February 11 ... This might be best achieved by a public declaration, signed by a small number, say, twelve persons, whose scientific attainments (scientific in the widest sense) have gained them international stature and whose testimony will not be blunted in its effectiveness by their political affiliations."

Russell replied promptly, agreeing with Einstein's suggestion to make sure of "two signatories in addition to yourself and me", and then send the draft appeal to selected persons. Russell wished to leave the choice of such persons to Einstein and his associates such as the physicist Niels Bohr "as you know the scientific world much better than I do." Russell's strong sense that he was an author and philosopher, not a scientist, was to help shape an enduring movement that soon became known simply as "Pugwash."

Einstein duly wrote to Bohr, suggesting he contact Russell directly, but hesitated about making wider contacts "because I am not clear about the role you intend them to play." Einstein continued, 'it seems to me that, to avoid any confusion, you should regard yourself as the dictator of the enterprise and give orders." He signed off, rather obligingly, "Awaiting orders."

"Don't frown like that!" was how Einstein began his letter to Bohr, "This is not about our old physics controversy, but about a matter on which we are in complete agreement." He explained that Russell sought to bring together a small group of renowned "scholars" to warn of the "perilous situation created by atomic weapons and the arms race." Then, with great precision, Einstein wrote: "Unless I miss Russell's purpose, he wants to go beyond a highlighting of the peril; he proposes to demand that the governments publicly acknowledge the necessity for renouncing any solution of problems by military means."

Einstein understood Russell's intention very well. Russell's reply of April 5, 1955, his last letter to Einstein, emphasised that scientists have, "and feel that they have," a special responsibility since their work has "unintentionally caused our present dangers." For this reason, Russell thought it better to approach only men of science and not those in other fields, such as Arnold Toynbee whom Einstein had mentioned. Widening the field would also make it much more difficult to "steer clear of politics."

Einstein died on April 18, 1955, but not before he'd written to Russell to say that he was "gladly willing to sign your excellent statement." Einstein also agreed to Russell's choice of prospective signers. This last letter from Einstein only reached Russell when he arrived in Paris by plane from Rome. During the flight, the pilot had announced the news of Einstein's death, and Russell felt "shattered," not least because his plan would fall through without Einstein as the scientist alongside the philosopher. As Russell remarked, signing the Appeal was one of the last acts of Einstein's public life.

Without Einstein, Russell clearly felt the need of another scientist's close collaboration and help. Some weeks after the Russell-Einstein Appeal was launched to widespread acclaim, in London in July 1955, Russell recruited Professor Joseph Rotblat at the Medical College of St Bartholomew's Hospital for what became a lifelong commitment: "When I began approaching scientists I had reason to expect Einstein's co-operation but this was diminished by his illness and ended by his death. I feel that further steps among scientists ought to be taken by scientists and that any further work by myself ought to be rather in the political field."

The medical physicist Rotblat "was brave enough to take the chair," in Russell's words, at the press conference to launch the Manifesto. They had first met in April 1954 at the BBC for a televised discussion about the hydrogen bomb. Russell was especially impressed by Rotblat's "detective" work uncovering the "dirty" bomb tested by the Americans at Bikini Atoll. Thus began an enduring collaboration which first alighted on Pugwash, Nova Scotia, in July 1957, as the venue for 22 mostly scientist participants from ten countries, including the US, USSR and China, to gather under the auspices of shared support for the objectives of the Russell-Einstein Manifesto.

Pugwash was the home of Cyrus Eaton, the Chicago-educated industrialist who paid the expenses of the initial conference, and the name has stuck. Sixty years on, the Pugwash Conferences on Science and World Affairs are held up as a beacon of hope in our difficult times. Joseph Rotblat personally nurtured the movement throughout his long life, for which he and Pugwash received the Nobel Peace Prize in 1995. In 2003, two years before his death aged 96, Rotblat urged Pugwash to "open up" and collaborate with others in alerting the public to the dangers of nuclear war in the context of President Bush's invasion of Iraq.

Now the world is faced with the coronavirus health pandemic and the climate change emergency, as well as escalating nuclear confrontation and proliferation. An aridity line spreads south across Africa's Sahel, south of the Sahara Desert, destroying the basic means of livelihood. People flee the affected countries where conflict often accompanies drought. More scientific imperatives compel action on a global scale. Shall we remember our humanity, and forget the rest?

Cuba and Beyond

> *"There lies before us, if we choose, continual progress in happiness, knowledge, and wisdom. Shall we, instead, choose death, because we cannot forget our quarrels? We appeal as human beings to human beings: Remember your humanity, and forget the rest..."*   Russell-Einstein Manifesto, 1955

PUGWASH SPRUNG INTO LIFE amidst large-scale atmospheric nuclear explosions, including hydrogen bomb tests at Christmas Island in the Pacific

Ocean, conducted by the British government in 1957. "Fall-out seemed something uncanny, unseen and frightening," wrote Peggy Duff in *Left, Left, Left*, her lively account of the origins and early years of the Campaign for Nuclear Disarmament (CND) in Britain. "The Christmas Island tests, because they were British tests, at last roused opinion in Britain." Meanwhile, in autumn 1957 the Labour Party rejected unilateral nuclear disarmament, contrary to the beliefs and preferences of many activists, and lost the subsequent general election in 1959. Britain was set on a foolish and legally questionable course, nuclear armed, which continues to this day.

Russell agreed to be President of CND when it was founded in early 1958, charged with others to mobilise a mass movement. So it was that there gathered the first Easter March to Aldermaston, 50 miles west of London, and site of the Atomic Weapons Research Establishment. It was largely organised by a small group known as the Direct Action Committee. In 1959, the marchers changed direction, starting in Aldermaston on Good Friday and, on Easter Monday, massing in London's Trafalgar Square for the final rally. But the march was the thing: a community drawn from all over Britain and beyond, which lives in the popular memory and continues to inspire spring-time odysseys in Germany and elsewhere.

One member of the Aldermaston community was Christopher Farley, who later came to work closely with Russell. He joined a young American, Ralph Schoenman, who was a student of Ralph Miliband at the London School of Economics and first met Russell in July 1960. Russell later wrote of Ralph in his *Autobiography* that "It was a temptation to turn to him to get things done" (Routledge Classics edition, 2010, p. 582). Ralph's proposal of mass civil disobedience, made to a conference of Youth CND in 1960, was narrowly defeated. He caught the mood of the time in proposing to Russell a Committee of 100, a hundred public signatories as the catalyst for mass non-violent resistance and civil disobedience to achieve nuclear disarmament by Britain. This would mean removal of US nuclear weapons including those on submarines, which were to be based at Holy Loch in Scotland. The Committee's first big demonstration was in February 1961, when Russell and Edith, his wife, with thousands of others sat down outside the Ministry of Defence in Whitehall to protest against the imminent servicing of US nuclear-armed submarines at Holy Loch. On this occasion, there were few if any arrests. Later, the authorities changed tactics and the police arrested thousands of people. In September 1961, Russell, Edith and others were imprisoned shortly before another weekend of demonstrations in London and Scotland, which had the effect of actually bolstering turnout. Russell's embrace of the Committee of 100 meant a public and quarrelsome break with Canon Collins, Chairman of CND, and Russell duly resigned as President. CND never had another.

Looking back on those years, Russell wrote in his *Autobiography,* "I continued my search, as I have done since, to find fresh approaches through which to try to sway public opinion, including governmental opinion." He continued, "By the summer of 1960 it seemed to me as if Pugwash and CND and the other methods that we had tried of informing the public had reached the limit of their effectiveness. It might be possible to so move the general public that it would demand en masse, and therefore irresistibly, the remaking of present governmental policies, here in Britain first and then elsewhere in the world" (Russell 2010, 578). So it was that he embraced mass civil disobedience and the Committee of 100.

Later, in 1965, Russell remarked during a filmed discussion that, though they were impressive and moving, not enough people had joined the sit-down demonstrations. Tens of thousands had, but hundreds of thousands were needed if there was to be any chance of shifting government opinion. Nevertheless, during the early 1960s, film and photographs of people sitting six deep on London's broad pavements caught the popular imagination around the world, particularly amongst the new generation.

Russell was a seasoned campaigner who had worked for half a century in diverse organisations seeking change such as the Union for Democratic Control and the No-Conscription Fellowship. He didn't stay longer than was useful to the cause. So it was that, in 1962, he took his distance from the Committee of 100. He was now spending more time in North Wales, after celebrating his 90th birthday in London in May that year.

"The last months of that year were taken up with the Cuban crisis and then with the Sino-Indian Border dispute," Russell later wrote. The seven-day Missile Crisis began on October 22, 1962, when the US announced that aerial surveillance of Cuba revealed construction of bases to house Soviet missiles which could strike the United States. America was to impose a naval blockade on Cuba to prevent delivery of further missiles. Some were already there. As Nicholas Griffin recounts in his introduction to the fiftieth anniversary edition of *Unarmed Victory* (2012), Russell's own account of the Crisis and his part in it, on October 22 Russell appealed to Khrushchev and Kennedy to put world peace above their rivalries, and the following day he issued statements to that effect to the British press.

> On the 24th, to Russell's surprise, Moscow Radio broadcast a long, and relatively conciliatory, reply from Khrushchev, who, while condemning American piracy and refusing to back down, none the less promised to avoid reckless action and, most importantly, proposed a summit conference to resolve the crisis. Russell replied with further telegrams urging Khrushchev to stop the Russian ships then heading towards the American blockade and urging Kennedy to accept Khrushchev's offer of negotiations. Kennedy, who seems to have been prone to alarming outbursts of petulance throughout the crisis, reacted furiously to Russell's message: "that son of a bitch", he said, could "go and soak his head." His public response was similarly uncompromising, but less intemperately phrased. (Brugioni, p. 405)

Unknown to Russell and the world, the Soviet ships carrying missiles to Cuba had already turned back, though the fate of the missiles already in Cuba still had to be decided. On October 26, Russell urged Khrushchev to remove the missiles. He also wrote to Fidel Castro, then Cuba's Prime Minister, urging him to renounce the missiles and accept UN inspection of their removal. On October 27, an American surveillance plane was shot down over Cuba and America issued a 48-hour ultimatum, placed its Strategic Air Command on full alert, and prepared to launch retaliatory strikes against Cuba to be followed by a full-scale invasion. The next day, Khrushchev agreed to remove the missiles if the US undertook not to invade Cuba. Thus, the crisis passed.

Later, Russell said that he did not consider he had "altered the course of history by one hair's-breadth," but his intervention provided an opportunity for Khrushchev to put the Soviet Union's case to the world. Averell Harriman, then an influential US diplomat, cited Khrushchev's letter to Russell as evidence that Russia did not intend to go to war over Cuba. The historian Arthur Schlesinger credited Harriman's intervention with encouraging Kennedy to keep diplomatic options open.

Meanwhile, Russell and his close collaborators (principally Edith, Farley and Schoenman) had already begun to think in terms of a "peace fund" to provide an established secretariat for Russell's wide-ranging work to buttress peace, human rights and social justice. In due course, in September 1963, Russell announced the formation of the Bertrand Russell Peace Foundation and a separate charity, the Atlantic Peace Foundation, to fund research. In January 1964, Russell, Edith, Farley, Schoenman and Charles R Ellis, another young American, signed and adopted the Constitution of the Bertrand Russell Peace Foundation, which stated that:

> *The Foundation is established to promote world peace and international disarmament; to persuade nations effectively to abandon warfare as an instrument of policy; and to develop, organise and manage international resistance to the threat of nuclear war.*

Bibliography

Brugioni, Dino A. 1992. *Eyeball to Eyeball: The Inside Story of the Cuban Missile Crisis.* New York: Random House.

Griffin, Nicholas. 2001. *The Selected Letters of Bertrand Russell: The Public Years, 1914-70.* London: Routledge.

Nathan, Otto & Norden, Heinz (editors). 1981. *Einstein on Peace.* New York: Avenel Books.

Russell, Bertrand. 1918. *Roads to Freedom.* London: George Allen & Unwin.

Russell, Bertrand. 1934. *Freedom and Organization, 1814-1914.* London: George Allen & Unwin.

Russell, Bertrand. 1935. *In Praise of Idleness*, for "The Ancestry of Fascism." London: George Allen & Unwin.

Russell, Bertrand. 1947. *Philosophy and Politics.* London: Cambridge University Press.

Russell, Bertrand. 1953. *Satan in the Suburbs, or Horrors Manufactured Here.* London: The Bodley Head.

Russell, Bertrand. 1954. *Nightmares of Eminent Persons.* London: The Bodley Head.

Russell, Bertrand. 2010. *Autobiography.* London: Routledge.

Russell, Bertrand. 2012. *Unarmed Victory.* Nottingham: Spokesman.

DID RUSSELL EXPERIENCE AN EPIPHANY IN 1911?

Alan Schwerin

> *"I wanted certainty in the kind of way in which people want religious faith."*
>
> —Russell, *Autobiography*

FOR MANY, THE EYES ARE THE WINDOW TO THE SOUL. But is there a gateway to the mysteries of the mind? Frustratingly elusive, the mind and its contents can, fortunately for us, be fathomed in a variety of ways. While many strands present themselves, arguably the most secure routes into the mind, especially that of the philosopher, are the rich philosophical fabrics that have been laced together by the thinker—texts both formal and informal. The hidden mysteries of the mind of the philosopher will unfold slowly to patient and persistent enquiries. As my paper will amply illustrate, we have much to gain from an investigation of the correspondence from one of the most prolific philosophers of the twentieth century: Bertrand Russell. While Russell's formal corpus is monumental, his informal correspondence is equally breathtaking, and revelatory.

Changing practically daily, the entries in the annotated catalogue of his correspondence in the Russell Archives at McMaster University listed 131,467 records by early December 2016. This fascinating resource offers a unique insight into the mind of Russell. More specifically, the correspondence generated by the philosopher from Monmouthshire and one of his lovers, Lady Ottoline Morrell, provides us with an invaluable inroad into Russell's philosophical thought precisely when his conception of philosophy and his commitment to certainty experiences a cataclysmic transformation. While Russell's views on philosophy change throughout his life, as has been well documented by numerous critics, my analysis and argument here suggest that 1911 saw an especially dramatic alteration in his conception of philosophy. This seismic shift in his thought is due in large measure to radical alterations in his commitment to certainty: a fundamental transformation—as I shall show—that is induced by an epiphany.

Now Russell is notorious for his numerous melodramatic reports about the changes in his thought and emotional state of mind. Take but one example. Russell's account—dare I say farcical account?—of his decision not to continue living with his wife Alys, allegedly made after a cycling trip in the English countryside, is arguably the most dramatic instance of this hyper attenuated way of characterizing his plight.[1] As he colorfully puts it in his *Autobiography*:

> I went out bicycling one afternoon, and suddenly, as I was riding along a country road, I realised that I no longer loved Alys. I had had no idea until this moment that my love for her was even lessening. The problems presented by this discovery were very grave… (Russell 1967, 237)

Really? While this report is arguably a little over the top, it surely does contain a kernel of truth: Russell has made a momentous decision, and he happened to make it while out on his bike.[2] Okay. So one needs to tread warily when characterizing Russell's situation in the dire terms that I am resorting to. Nevertheless, as I see it, the evidence is incontrovertible that Russell's change of heart on certainty in 1911 is dramatic and noteworthy:

---

[1] A second, equally dramatic report is the account of his emotional state of mind and the changes in his thinking on learning of the illness of Evelyn Whitehead, the wife of Russell's colleague, Alfred North Whitehead. This emotional transformation apparently induced a major alteration in Russell's views about the Boer War; initially a staunch supporter of the British imperialists in their escapades in the South African veld, Russell saw the world alright after a sobering encounter with the ailing Mrs. Whitehead. Within minutes, apparently, he dramatically switched allegiances to the pro-Boer movement;

> When we came home we found Mrs. Whitehead undergoing an usually severe bout of pain…Suddenly the ground seemed to give way beneath me, and I found myself in quite another region…At the end of those five minutes, I had become a completely different person. For a time, *a sort of mystic illumination possessed me*…Having been an Imperialist, I became during those five minutes a pro-Boer and a pacifist. (emphasis added; Russell 1951)

[2] A leading critic of Russell argues that "though Russell clearly massively exaggerates—as was his wont—the extent to which it was a sudden and unexpected revelation, there seems no reason to doubt that there was a bicycle ride and that there was a moment when he ceased to struggle against the facts and to admit to himself that he no longer loved Alys" (Ray Monk 1996, 145).

a major shift in his philosophical thought that has not received the attention it warrants from scholars. As I see it, the major components of the alteration in Russell's thought on certainty manifest themselves in one of his most famous texts: *The Problems of Philosophy*. Written over a relatively short span of a little more than seven weeks, this introductory text presents us with a dramatic account of philosophy that appears to vacillate on the role of certainty. While Russell initially embraces certainty in his philosophical investigations here, a strong case can be made—or so I shall argue below—that his views undergo a sea-change within the space of roughly forty-six thousand words.[3] The initial unqualified commitment to certainty in *The Problems of Philosophy* is ultimately replaced by an entirely different conception of philosophy that unequivocally embraces uncertainty. Let's consider the textual evidence for these suggestions. To begin with, consider the case for the proposal that Russell, early on in *The Problems of Philosophy*, is strongly committed to the view that philosophers are striving for certainty in their investigations.

Section One: An Unwavering Commitment to Certainty

REFERENCES TO CERTAINTY FEATURE PROMINENTLY in *The Problems of Philosophy*. As a matter of fact, the opening sections of the popular text are replete with allusions to certainty, beginning with the very first sentence: "Is there any knowledge in the world which is *so certain* that no reasonable man could doubt it?" (emphasis added; Russell 1971). Russell's modest analysis of some of the issues that concern philosophers opens on a dramatic note that sets the tone for the entire philosophical discussion that follows. But more than mere timbre is presented to the reader early in the book. In many respects, the opening stanza of *Problems* is even more significant than this as it does more than simply introduce the philosophical issues to his readers in a specific hue. From the outset, Russell draws on his conception of philosophy, with its emphasis on certainty, to guide, if not determine, the focus

---

[3] I have not counted the words in his text. However, in his August 7, 1911 letter to Murray, Russell says that he is sending "the greater part of my treatise for your shop-assistants, the rest will follow quickly...I think the total is about 46,000 words..."

of the investigation for the bulk[4] of the fifteen problems that constitute the shilling shocker.[5]

The question that *The Problems of Philosophy* leads with establishes a framework for the entire work. With Russell immediately drawing attention to the (alleged) role of certainty in our lives and activities, and by implication, to the lives of philosophers, he is laying a foundation for his analysis that is striking: while other issues are important in our lives, apparently it is the concern with certainty that is uppermost in our minds, and by implication, it is the search for certainly that is the single most important issue that motivates philosophers in their endeavors. As he sees it, this is "one of the most difficult" questions we can raise. Had we to consider this challenging question we would be "well launched on the study of philosophy—for philosophy is merely the attempt to answer such ultimate questions…" (Russell 1971, 1). But the answers that the philosopher proposes will emerge from a critical inquiry only if he[6] enquires into "all that makes such questions puzzling"—only then will profound, fundamental, rigorous and true answers emerge that are presumably free of the shortcomings that beset the questions and answers from the realm of the non-philosopher. That is to say, the philosopher's responses to the problematic questions that originate in our society-at-large will ultimately not be besmirched by the "vagueness and confusion that underlie our ordinary ideas" (*ibid.*). Untainted by the common ideas that are uncritically drawn on and used by the regular members

---

[4] While most of the text is dominated by Russell's predilection for certainty, the final chapter—that is strongly influenced by Lady Ottoline's spirituality—is a striking aberration in that it celebrates uncertainty, as I intend to show below.

[5] When did Russell first refer to *The Problems of Philosophy* as a shilling shocker? I can't be sure about this. He uses the term—actually an abbreviated version of the term—at an early stage in the project, in a letter to Lady Ottoline, when referring to Moore's contribution to Murray's series:

> Moore and I compared notes on *our respective S.S's* yesterday. He is making his just as difficult as his *Principia Ethica*—He has only one style and method, and can't alter for a different audience. He seems to be rather more behindhand with it than I am with mine. (emphasis added; Letter to Morrell 8 July, 1911)

Russell's use of the abbreviation "S.S" must surely be shorthand for "shilling shocker." As far as I can determine, he does not use this term where we would most expect him to do so—namely, when corresponding with his editor, Gilbert Murray.

[6] For convenience, I am using the words "he" and "his" to signify both male and female philosophers. The alternative strikes me as cumbersome.

of society, the contributions from the philosopher will be guided by his more philosophical insights and considered ideas—ideas that are robust and unfettered by the obstacles endemic to the thought of daily life. The outcome of this methodical investigation of the questions and ideas from the ordinary world is presumably highly desirable: namely, knowledge of the highest order. As Russell optimistically sees it—or at least, as he *appears to see it*—the philosopher's contribution reputably constitutes knowledge which is "*so certain* that no reasonable man could doubt it" (emphasis added; *ibid.*).[7]

All this suggests that Russell views the philosopher as a skilled laborer, willing and able to assist the reasonable members of society in their quest for a particular brand of knowledge: certain knowledge. And as the knowledge that is sought is not any type of knowledge, but knowledge *par excellence*—namely, indubitable knowledge—the contributions from the philosopher must be equally impeccable. As Russell sees it, the philosopher fortunately has the requisite tools to help produce this highly desired certain knowledge. The philosopher, as far as he is concerned, is well equipped to carry out this task as he possesses the requisite critical faculties—as well as an invaluable logical apparatus, as he will point out elsewhere—to provide helpful insights into the fundamental questions of society that require attention.[8] With his philosophical expertise and his refined logical notation, he is able to systematically explore the unexamined philosophical questions from the community that, unfortunately, are encumbered by vague and confused ordinary ideas. The task is to suggest more philosophically rigorous perspectives that are free of the defective ideas endemic to the views current in society-at-large. In the process, the outlook and puzzling questions that the non-philosopher is struggling with ought to dissolve, to be replaced by perspicacious and indubitable insights into the world and its problems.

---

[7] This qualification is important, as Russell never comes out and explicitly answers his opening question on the standing of the philosophers' response to the question. I am assuming that this is Russell's assessment of the contributions from the philosopher who answers the call for "knowledge…which is so certain that no reasonable man could doubt it." That is to say, the philosopher ought to be praised for his contributions—they are free of the defects that beset society-at-large and are welcomed for their surety.

[8] I am alluding here to the formal notation from *Principia Mathematica*—a symbolism designed by Whitehead and Russell, in large part, to assist philosophers in their attempts to clarify and more fundamentally grasp the issues endemic to the puzzles that bedevil ordinary citizens.

But is the search for certainty as pervasive as Russell intimates it is? Are non-philosophers and philosophers alike engaged in a joint enterprise, as Russell appears to assume they are? Are *both* parties dissatisfied with the knowledge that they currently possess and are they both intent on improving matters? That is to say, are the two sides ultimately striving for certainty? With the same level of fervor? Russell appears to think so. As he sees it, we are *all* searching for certainty and starting out from the same starting point:

> *In the search for certainty,* it is natural [for *both* parties] to begin with our present experiences, and in some sense, no doubt, knowledge is to be derived from them. (emphasis added; Russell 1971, 1)

This search for certainty is initiated by the realization, on the part of both philosophers and non-philosophers, that the assumptions that underlie our ordinary lives are problematic, requiring substantial effort on our part to produce an outcome that we can rely on—i.e. a set of beliefs that we can regard as certain:

> In daily life, *we assume as certain many things* which, on a closer scrutiny are found to be so full of apparent contradictions that only a great amount of thought enables us to know what it is that we really may believe. (emphasis added; Russell 1971, 1)

But what reasons are there for adopting this elevated perspective of the outlook of both parties? Why not simply let sleeping dogs lie? More importantly, what evidence does *Russell* present to his reader on these important questions? Take the first question: what reasons are there for assuming that the non-philosopher is actively searching for certainty, as the author of The Problems of Philosophy appears to intimate he is?

While the tendency towards inertia prevails in our non-philosophical lives, Russell clearly assumes that there are individuals in our society-at-large who are dissatisfied with the *status quo*—individuals who are moved to seek out different ideas that they can regard as certain. But the manner in which he substantiates this assumption of his is interesting. He draws attention to some of the shortcomings of the ordinary ideas from a *philosophical* perspective. That is to say, the philosopher, by virtue of his more refined philosophical perspective, is able to detect errors that the ordinary citizen overlooks. With his ordinary perspective the naïve non-philosopher is unable to notice the problems endemic to his outlook on "the problems."[9] After isolating a few of our common beliefs on the world around us and its contents—for instance, the view that we are able to perceive physical objects such as windows, buildings, tables, clouds, and the sun—Russell turns to our more fundamental beliefs. Two strike him as especially noteworthy: namely, the belief we have on the veracity of our senses and the belief that we, as ordinary citizens, can accurately describe what we sense:

> In daily life, *we assume as certain many things* which on a closer scrutiny, are found to be so full of apparent contradictions that only a great amount of thought enables us to know what it is that we really may believe. *In the search for certainty, it is natural to begin with our present experiences*, and in some sense, no doubt, knowledge is to be derived from them. But any statement as to what it is that our immediate experiences make us know is very likely to be wrong. (emphasis added; Russell 1971, 1)

But surely only *the philosophers* can identify these "apparent contradictions that only a great amount of thought enable us to know what it is that we really may believe." For the philosophers are trained to detect the contradictions—not the non-philosophers. Why would the latter group of members of society trouble themselves with infelicities in their ideas? Why in the world would they concern themselves with issues that exercise the members of the philosophical community? And if they do explore these philosophical issues, are they not *ipso facto* becoming more philosophical, if not turning into philosophers?

These are interesting remarks on the role of certainty in our regular, daily lives. Or should I say, the *presumed* role of certainty in our lives? Russell is clearly assuming that we—the royal "we" is telling here—not only believe in the existence of the physical objects that he confidently refers to,

---

[9] As Russell sees it, there are unnoticed problems lurking below the surface—but they manifest themselves only when the philosophical perspective is adopted. For this reason, some might suggest that for the non-philosopher, there actually is no problem to start with. The difficulties emerge only after the adoption of the philosophers' perspective. In short, claims about the existence of problems are relative to the outlook of the individuals involved.

he assumes we are also committed to the view that these beliefs are secure and immune from doubt. It is this additional component that strikes me as telling. As he boldly puts it, after his remarks on our beliefs in ordinary objects,

> *All this seems to be so evident* as to be hardly worth stating, except in answer to a man who doubts whether I know anything. Yet all this may be reasonably doubted, and all of it requires much careful discussion before we can be sure that we have stated it in a form that is *wholly true*. (ibid., 1, 2)

According to Russell, these inviolable beliefs that we willingly accept and act on in our daily lives are likely to remain unencumbered with invasive (epistemological) questions. But when confronted by an extreme sceptic—i.e. someone "who doubts whether I know anything"—this easy acceptance of the widely held beliefs of daily life becomes a source of much consternation, compelling us to engage in "much careful discussion before we can be sure that we have stated [our beliefs] in a form that is wholly true" (Russell 1971, 1-2).

All this suggests that in the opening section of his *The Problems of Philosophy* the philosopher is seen by Russell as a benign provocateur, willing to rouse regular citizens from their dogmatic slumbers with fundamental philosophical questions. Initially content with their unexamined ordinary ideas, these unsuspecting citizens soon realize that the philosopher has enticed them from the "high-road from plain common sense" and driven them into a strange and different world of "uncouth paradoxes, difficulties, and inconsistencies": namely, the philosophical world of the sceptic (Berkeley 2011, 152).[10] In short, the world of the ordinary citizen, that has served us well and that stood the test of time—its vague and confused ideas notwithstanding—is shown to be problematic and in need of refinement, if not replacement. This, unfortunately, is the price that has to be paid if we want certainty, for without the philosophers' perspective we will not "be *sure* that we have stated [our beliefs] in a form that is wholly true"(emphasis added; Russell 1971, 2).

This invasive conception of philosophy, with its commitment to certainty, contrasts strongly with Russell's later views of the philosopher and his

---

[10] I am alluding to George Berkeley's assessment of the impact of the philosopher on the unsuspecting ordinary citizen. In his *Treatise Concerning the Principles of Human Understanding* Berkeley bemoans the sinister outcomes of the questions philosophers direct at the contented members of society-at-large.

activities. As we shall see in the following section of my paper, the co-author of *Principia Mathematica* softens his conception of philosophy towards the end of his shilling shocker, ultimately adopting a more propitious view. For now the philosopher is viewed differently, engaged as he is in a quite different enterprise, encouraging others to add to, or to extend, their initial ordinary perspective. Russell's suggestion that the philosopher broaden his perspective—and presumably assist others to enlarge their perspectives as well—constitutes a major alteration in his understanding of the role of the philosopher in society. In proposing that individuals widen their conceptions of what is possible Russell is encouraging philosophers and regular citizens to be more creative and in the process to actively embrace *un*certainty. We need to consider this transformation in Russell's conception of philosophy.

Section Two: The Virtues of Uncertainty and the Epiphany

THE JOURNEY IS DEMANDING AND FRAUGHT WITH UNEXPECTED TURNS, but by the time the fifteenth and final chapter of Russell's shilling shocker emerges from the mists of philosophical angst the intrepid reader is likely to find the topic for consideration salutary: the value of philosophy. For surely, with the focus now on the non-technical issue of usefulness or utility—a consideration that the philosophically naïve shop assistant will certainly understand and be able to relate to—the investigation offers the prospect of welcome relief.[11] With the abstract excursions into idealism, induction, general principles and universals behind him, let alone the intricate investigations into

---

[11] It is important to remind ourselves that the project that originated in suggestions from Gilbert Murray started out with noble intentions: to introduce philosophy to a non-academic audience. Murray asked his colleague to write an introduction to philosophy that even relatively uneducated workers could understand. On September 19, 1910 Murray writes to Russell with an invocation to contribute to his series:

> You have got a message to the shop-assistants about philosophy, if you would only think it out. If you don't want to tell them what Mathematics is, can you not tell them what Philosophy is? You could do it with great detachment from the conventional schools, *and you could put all the main problems in their very lowest terms.* (emphasis added)

This suggestion from Murray that Russell can put "all the main problems in their very lowest terms" has been critically explored in my recent paper (Scherwin 2017).

truth and falsehood, with its elaborate analysis of statements on the beliefs of Desdemona and Cassio, the final chapter of *The Problems of Philosophy* must arrive not a moment too soon for the beleaguered neophyte. But this sense of relief is bound to be short-lived, to be replaced by puzzlement, if not concern, with Russell's concluding remarks on philosophy and its problems. For now the co-author of *Principia Mathematica* openly courts and promotes uncertainty in philosophy. Not only does Russell encourage the reader to consider uncertainty in philosophy and life in general, he explicitly invites the members of his audience to actively embrace and pursue uncertainty as a desirable end: "The value of philosophy is, in fact, to be sought largely in its very uncertainty" (Russell 1971, 91). This radical transformation in his thought calls for comment.

As we have seen, when Russell introduces his unsuspecting reader to the travails of philosophical thought he stresses the centrality of certainty, both in society-at-large and within the academy. According to him, while many problems occupy the minds of the members of both groups, there is one that is especially acute. This is an epistemological question on the status of our knowledge; namely, do we possess knowledge that can be viewed as certain? As he puts it, "Is there any knowledge in the world which is so certain that no reasonable man could doubt it?" (Russell 1971, 1). With this question as the guiding beacon for the entire enterprise that constitutes *The Problems of Philosophy*, Russell proceeds to outline a strategy for both parties to pursue. As I have pointed out earlier, Russell suggests that we begin with the evidence provided to us by the senses and look for positions that we can classify as certain:[12]

---

[12] Others have also gone down this path. René Descartes, for instance, in his search for certainty in *Meditations on First Philosophy* also opens his philosophical enquiry with the suggestion that we consider the contributions from the senses:

> What I have so far accepted as true par excellence, I have got either from the senses or by means of the senses. (Quoted in Scherwin 2011, 139)

As with Russell, Descartes' quest for certainty initially disappoints him. For Descartes, philosophy initially drives one towards malignant skepticism, with its forebodings on the senses and the possibility of an evil deceiver. And as with Russell, Descartes soon turns to his religious views to extricate him from his philosophically induced morass. While Descartes ultimately finds solace in his enquiry into his idea of God, Russell suggests that philosophical reflection can free the mind from the restrictive bonds of instinct: "The free intellect will see as God might see, without a *here* and *now,* without hope and fears, without the trammels of customary beliefs and traditional prejudices…" (emphasis in original; Russell 1971. 93).

> *In the search for certainty*, it is natural to begin with our present experiences, and in some sense, no doubt, knowledge is to be derived from them. (emphasis in the original; Russell 1971, 1)

So the analyses that follow these opening remarks from Russell presume that certainty is the ultimate objective of the enquiries. We are encouraged to welcome in the considered results of the philosophers' enquiries, as they will be precise, sophisticated answers that emerge from painstaking analysis and reflection on the foibles of our ordinary, allegedly defective ideas.[13] Most importantly, these clean and precise contributions from the philosophers are presumably contributions that we are all entitled to accept and to revel in, for they will be contributions that each one of us can be certain about. Surely the philosophers, who (apparently) are focused on important, fundamental questions, as the opening section of the text suggests is the case, are providing us with their elaborate philosophical contributions not because they view their work as inconsequential and of little value to society-at-large, but because they assume that the outcome of their efforts are of value? And it is the certainty of their results—a highly prized attribute of their contributions, in Russell's eyes—that presumably ensures that their efforts are worthwhile. Why then is Russell suddenly talking about uncertainty? Is this an implicit admission on his part that the philosophical problems that he has explored in the project—and for that matter, any other philosophical problems that he could have included in his journey—are difficult, and likely to yield counterintuitive results that shop assistants will not find valuable? More pointedly, is Russell's emphasis here on uncertainty—an emphasis that only emerges at the very end of his investigation into some of the leading problems of philosophy—an admission of failure on his part? Is his decision here to embrace and celebrate uncertainty in his philosophical investigations a tacit admission that the search for philosophical views that even shop assistants will regard as certain, is ultimately futile?

Perhaps. This uncompromising, deflationary interpretation of Russell's remarks on uncertainty appears to have some textual support. For Russell is the first to admit that the output from philosophers—and this must include him—is not held in high regard by society in general:

---

[13] If Russell, in the final chapter of his introduction to philosophy, is inviting uncertainty into the lives of his readers, both philosophical and non-philosophical, a pressing issue arises: What precisely do we do with the old, discredited views? To the best of my knowledge, Russell does not address this question in his primer into philosophy.

> [M]any men, under the influence of science or of practical affairs, are inclined to doubt whether philosophy is anything better than innocent but useless trifling, hair-splitting distinctions, and controversies on matters concerning which *knowledge is impossible.* (emphasis added; Russell 1971, 89)

When all is said and done, the philosopher appears to have little to offer society.[14] Apparently, nothing that they say can even be regarded as knowledge. And in that case, it follows that whatever emerges from the philosophers' deliberations *cannot be certain.* From both a scientific and practical perspective it seems then that their contributions, at best, can be classified as uncertain suggestions. Are we to conclude from all this that the results of the philosophers' investigations into the problems of daily life are ultimately to be classified as little more than useless perambulations?

For Russell, this defeatist conclusion is misplaced. We do not need to go this far in our assessment of the results of the investigations conducted by the philosopher. While the philosopher needs to concede that his contributions are modest, the contributions, nevertheless, *are valuable* in that they assist in the enlargement of the not-Self. As he sees it,

> ...true philosophic contemplation...finds its satisfaction in every enlargement of the not-Self, in everything that *magnifies the objects contemplated*, and thereby the subject contemplating...

---

[14] Russell will later bemoan the low estimation accorded his magnum opus, *Principia Mathematica*. Writing from Plas Penrhyn on June 9, 1963 to a Ms Hilton, thanking her for the complimentary copy of her recently completed book on logic, Russell thanks her for the compliments on his logic book:

> I am grateful for the nice things you say about *Principia Mathematica* and about me. The followers of Gödel had almost persuaded me that the twenty man-years spent on the *Principia* had been wasted and that the book had better been forgotten. It is a comfort to find that you do not take this view. (*Autobiography* 1975: 672)

In his view, not only was the work not appreciated, *Principia* did not have the audience it deserved. After all his efforts, along with those of his colleague Whitehead, Russell says this about the (sparse) reception accorded the book:

> I used to know of only six people who had read the later parts of the book. Three of these were Poles...the other three were Texans... (Russell 1956, 86)

While these are surely exaggerations, one wonders if there are elements of truth to Russell's remarks here.

> The mind, which has become accustomed to the freedom and impartiality of philosophic contemplation will preserve something of the same freedom and impartiality in the world of action and emotion. It will view its purposes and desires as parts of the whole...*Thus contemplation enlarges not only the objects of our thoughts, but also the objects of our actions and affections: it makes us citizens of the universe...*
> (emphasis added; Russell 1971, 93)

Russell has clearly undergone a paradigm shift in his conception of philosophy. There can be little doubt that the co-author of *Principia Mathematica* has acquired a new and profoundly different understanding of the outcome of philosophical investigations. And his newly acquired insight into the results of these fundamental investigations influences his views on the initial impetus for these enquiries. For it turns out that the questions that motivated the philosopher to explore the (allegedly vague and confused) ideas of ordinary citizens are unable to yield results that are certain. While both the philosopher and his non-philosophical companion are presumed to be looking for certainty, there, unfortunately, will always be unresolved issues that call for further investigation. In his letter to Morrell on December 13, 1911 Russell puts this succinctly:

> All the historic problems of philosophy seem to me either insoluble or soluble by methods which are not philosophical, but mathematical or scientific. The last word of philosophy on all of them seems to me to be that a priori any of the alternatives is possible... [P]hilosophy, it seems to me, can only say that all the arguments adduced on either side are fallacious, and that there is absolutely no evidence either way.

So the quest for definitive answers to our philosophical questions will not yield results that are sacrosanct: an outcome, as Russell sees it, that strongly suggests that the search for certainty in philosophy is futile. Is this to suggest that the exploration of the world of the philosopher is equally pointless? Not at all, intimates Russell.

The challenging journey into the philosophers' world is far from unproductive, as it ultimately engenders a radical transformation in the minds of the explorers. Initially desiring certainty, we ultimately find that our conceptions of what is possible are broadened by our philosophical endeavors, thus drawing us closer to our universe, and the people who populate it. How do we account for this dramatic transformation in Russell's views on the impact of philosophical enquiry? In a word, it appears that the conversion in his thought amounts to an epiphany. Let me elaborate.

My suggestion is that Russell has experienced an epiphany, or a quantum change in his conception of philosophy. The evidence strongly suggests that he has undergone a radical alteration in his philosophical thought that has been induced by his intimate association with the spiritually inclined Lady Ottoline Morrell. Epiphanies, as Miller and C'de Baca point out are

> ...quantum changes [that] are experienced as personal transformations whose hall marks are vividness, surprise, benevolence, and a conviction that the change is permanent. (Miller and C'de Baca 2001)

Many prominent intellectuals are thought to have experienced epiphanies in their lives. Perhaps the most famous epiphanies that have been documented and systematically studied are the radical transformations experienced by Dostoevsky and Tolstoy. The evidence suggests that both of these intense Russian writers experienced dramatic changes in their psyche, undergoing radical psychological transformations that amount to quantum changes in their respective outlooks on life. Their moving memoirs testify to these alterations.[15] In his correspondence to Lady Ottoline in 1911, Russell makes it clear that his outlook on philosophy, and on life in general, has similarly altered in a radical manner. As he sees it, his capacity for genuine empathy for others, his ability to see the world more clearly and his feelings for others have all been substantially increased. With his newly acquired heightened powers Russell is encouraged to adopt a dramatically new perspective on the role of philosophy in our lives. And as Russell sees it, these alterations are largely, if not exclusively, due to Lady Ottoline Morrell's influence on him.

In their voluminous correspondence references to the impact of Morrell's views on Russell's conception of philosophy are ubiquitous. Letters written by Russell during for the first year of their intense relationship—a relationship that would last twenty-eight years—contain numerous refer-

---

[15] In his "Epiphany in Autobiography: The Quantum Changes in Dostoevsky and Tolstoy" Martin Bidney spells out in detail the stages in the psychological transformation that the two great Russian writers experienced (Bidney 2004).

ences to her influence on his thinking. More specifically, the correspondence between Morrell and Russell often alludes to the transforming influence of Morrell on her lover from the department of philosophy from Cambridge University. What is especially significant is the fact that Russell explicitly acknowledges her influence as *The Problems of Philosophy* reaches its conclusion. That is to say, as the fifteenth, and final chapter on the virtue of uncertainty is being written and proofed, Russell makes it clear to Morrell that she has played a major role in the radical alteration in his thinking on fundamental matters. Here are but four of the most poignant passages from the substantial, emotionally charged correspondence produced by Russell during this period that makes reference to her influence:

- You don't know what a difficult thing it is for me to feel peace, yet with you I feel it completely. Generally I have such a reaching out after the infinite—such a blending of my own discontent with all the sorrows of the world and all the wretchedness of human life, that I feel existence itself inherently a curse, and unconsciousness the only real blessing…I never found a happiness before that filled me—pain filled me, but happiness always seemed to omit what was really most serious. Now that is all different and when I am with you no inmost recess remains unsatisfied—it is because of some quality of infinity in your love—making you call making you love [?] like God's. That is what raises it so far above what I could have imagined.
(Letter from Upper Wyche, July 10, 1911)

- It is not chiefly from vanity that I want to think well of the work I have been doing lately. It is chiefly because I want it to be a worthy outcome of our love, and a proof to you of the help you give me. It really is the truth, and not delusion, that my powers have expanded lately. I have more freedom, more mastery, more insight, more energy. If you had been the most eminent philosopher of the age, I could not have given you more of my mind than I have given. This last month, I have given you everything I have thought, and all my best thinking has been when I was with you.
(Letter from Ipsden, August 11, 1911)

- My darling, it is incredible how you have changed my life—it is all so much easier—before, I was always struggling and always falling short, and so filled with inward discords. Now it is utterly different. I feel I have so much to give to everyone—and I don't have any longer the restless longing to give that made me give too much and to the wrong people.
(Letter from Trinity, Wednesday October 18, 1911)

- I cannot tell you how amazingly you increase the fruitfulness of my thoughts; you help them to come to the surface and to clothe themselves in beauty, and you make me know what is dross and what is gold. This is so wonderful in our love, that with such immense happiness there is always the sense of pressing forward into new and fuller and wider vision.
(Letter from the train, 22 January 1912)

So Russell suggests that he has acquired a new vision, has more energy, that his (intellectual) powers have expanded lately and that he is now producing some of his best philosophy with Morrell. With the shilling shocker behind him, with its initial emphasis on certainty in philosophy Russell proudly proclaims that he has changed. This dramatic transformation that has been inaugurated by Morrell has ushered in a new Russell, with his newly found emphasis on creative uncertainty, a dramatic alteration that comes as a surprise to the aristocratic, self-centered and hard professor of philosophy. As he puts it, "it is incredible how you have changed my life—it is all so much easier—before, I was always struggling and always falling short, and so filled with inward discords. Now it is utterly different. I feel I have so much to give to everyone" (*ibid.*).

Morrell is clearly moved by Russell's remarks about her influence on his newly acquired views on philosophy. As the manuscript is making its way to the press, Morrell sends Russell a letter from Peppard Cottage, Henley-on-Thames that shows her delight in his transformed conception of philosophy:

> I wish you knew all the great happiness you give me when you say that you know *your powers have expanded*. It is difficult for me to tell but I should quite believe that they have and that you have broken through some wall and have *come out into a world of light and of possibilities and of visions*

> *that you were not in before* although you often saw into it, and had all the love of it in you and desire for it. (emphasis added; Letter from Peppard Cottage, August 12, 1911)

From the correspondence between Russell and Morrell we learn that Russell makes frequent references to the impact that his lover is having on his thoughts. As the shilling shocker takes shape, and especially after its completion, with its famous fifteenth chapter on uncertainty in the investigations conducted by philosophers, Russell informs Morrell about the sudden transformation and draws attention to her role in the changes in his conception of philosophy. His lover humbly acknowledges his overtures, and encourages him with the suggestion that his new philosophy will be well received. The reception of the transformed ideas from Russell, as Morrell sees it, will be superior to that accorded Spinoza, even with his "great vision":

> Yes, your...new work will be...less elusive and more applied to our present life [than that from Spinoza]. I believe it will have a very great effect on many people...[and] will lift them out into life and freedom and love and union with others and service. (*ibid.*)

With accolades like this it is no wonder that Morrell makes it clear that she looks forward to working through *The Problems of Philosophy*, especially the famous final chapter that celebrates uncertainty in philosophy: "I am impatient to hear your chapter. I hope you were able to write it all right yesterday" (*ibid.*).

While Morrell admits that she is not in the best position to judge whether or not Russell has actually broken through into a new vivid set of visions, she is clearly excited by the prospects, and keen to read first-hand about Russell's new conception of philosophy. Having spent the previous six months listening to and conversing with her philosophical mentor, with his unwavering commitment to certainty in philosophy, the thought that she will now be afforded the opportunity to explore a wide range of diverse, and more accessible ideas, from her newly energized philosopher who is extolling the virtues of uncertainty, proves intoxicating. The epiphany that Russell has experienced while completing his lonely excursion into the problems of philosophy for Gilbert Murray has not only liberated the co-author of *Principia Mathematica*, it has helped cement the evolving intense relationship between Russell and Lady Morrell.

Section Three: A Final Thought or Two

IN THE POSTSCRIPT TO HIS *AUTOBIOGRAPHY,* Russell points out to his readers that he did move away from his long-held commitment to certainty relatively early on in his career. After explaining that initially he "wanted, on the one hand, to find out whether anything could be known; and, on the other hand, to do whatever might be possible toward creating a happier world," Russell draws attention to the role certainty played in the "serious part of his life"[16] (Russell 1969, 326). While the quest for knowledge that is certain and the desire to create "a happier world," apparently motivated him in his youth, Russell suggests that it was his interest in and concern with the human condition that drove him from his preoccupation with certainty:

> Up to the age of thirty-eight I gave most of my energies to the first of these tasks. I was troubled by scepticism and unwillingly forced to the conclusion that most of what passes for knowledge is open to reasonable doubt. I wanted certainty in the kind of way in which people want religious faith. I thought that certainty is more likely to be found in mathematics than elsewhere…Then came the First World War, and my thoughts became concentrated on human misery and folly. (emphasis added; Russell 1969, 326-7)

As late as one year before his death Russell suggests that it was the First World War, with all its "human misery and folly," that drove him to adopt a conception of philosophy that celebrated uncertainty. This account of his dramatic transformation on the role of certainty in philosophy, however, does not appear to be consistent with the evidence. As I have attempted to show in my paper, an investigation of his evolving views on philosophy in *The Problems of Philosophy*, along with an exploration of the correspondence between Russell and Lady Ottoline Morrell around 1911, strongly suggests that Russell experienced a paradigm shift on philosophy

---

[16] What precisely does Russell mean with this phrase, "the serious part of my life"? He does not tell us. Given the role of certainty early on in his philosophical thought, it is highly probable, in my view, that Russell is at least alluding here to his academic activities at Cambridge and to the technical work he did immediately afterwards on "serious" matters i.e. work on problems that the academic philosophers would find interesting and worthy of comment and analysis, and that during this phase in his life Russell was taken with the search for certainty.

long before the war broke out. While the Great War might have intensified Russell's growing interest in the plight of humanity, as I see it, it was not his concerns with "human misery and folly" that drove him to relinquish his commitment to certainty. There can be little doubt that Russell experienced an epiphany a full three years before the outbreak of the First World War; namely, while putting the finishing touches to his shilling shocker. As my argument and analysis of the correspondence between Morrell and the aristocratic Cambridge philosopher suggests, Russell's 1911 work on his introduction to the problems of philosophy ultimately broadened his conception of philosophy and invited in uncertainty. Whether or not the exchanges with his lover, Lady Ottoline Morrell, played any role in the inauguration of the quantum changes experienced by Russell is another matter, calling for attention elsewhere.[17]

Bibliography

Bidney, Martin. 2004. "Epiphany in Autobiography: The Quantum Changes in Dostoevsky and Tolstoy." *Journal of Clinical Psychology* 60 (5): 471-80.

Miller and C'de Baca. 2001. *Quantum Change: When Epiphanies and Sudden Insights Transform Ordinary Lives.* New York: Guilford Press.

Monk, Ray. 1996. *Bertrand Russell: The Spirit of Solitude.* New York: Free Press.

Russell, Bertrand. 1959. *My Philosophical Development.* New York: Simon and Schuster.

Russell, Betrand. 1951. *Autobiography*. Boston: Unwin Paperbacks.

Russell, Bertrand. 1967. *The Autobiography of Bertrand Russell 1872-1914.* Boston: Little Brown and Company.

---

[17] An investigation of the correspondence between Morrell and Russell leads us to suspect that her spirituality provided a powerful stimulus for Russell's adoption of a more rounded, humane conception of philosophy. There can be little doubt that Russell's ultimate commitment to uncertainty in philosophy was influenced by his evolving views on the self – changes brought about by his emotional entanglement with Lady Ottoline Morrell in 1911. On this important factor in the development of Russell's thought, see Scherwin 1999.

Russell, Bertrand. 1969. *The Autobiography of Bertrand Russell 1944-1969.* New York: Simon and Schuster.

Russell, Bertrand. 1971. *The Problems of Philosophy.* London: Oxford University Press.

Russell, Bertrand. 2010. *Autobiography*. London: Routledge.

Schwerin, Alan. 1999. "A Lady, Her Philosopher and a Contradiction." *Russell* n.s. 19 (1) 5-28.

Schwerin, Alan. 2017. "Is Russell's Conclusion about the Table Coherent?" In *Bertrand Russell's Life and Legacy.* Ed. Peter Stone. Delaware: Vernon Press, pp. 107-35.

Schwerin, Alan. 2011. *Reason and Belief: Great Issues in Philosophy.* New York: Whittier.

CHOMSKY AND RUSSELL REVISITED

Peter Stone *

IN 1916, AN ANONYMOUSLY WRITTEN LEAFLET entitled *Two Years Hard Labour for Not Disobeying the Dictates of Conscience* was published in the UK. The leaflet told the story of Ernest Everett, a pacifist denied exemption from military service and court-martialed for his refusal to serve. The British government arrested several people for distributing this leaflet. Soon thereafter, a letter appeared in the *London Times* entitled "Adsum qui Feci," which roughly translates as, "Here I am, I did it" (Perkins 2002, 65-6). The letter's author identified himself as the author of the leaflet, and in effect challenged the authorities—if you're going after the distributors of that leaflet, come after me. The author of the letter was Bertrand Russell. For taking this courageous stand, Russell was prosecuted and fined £100. (More on this story can be found in chapter 8.)

In September 2001, Turkey's Aram Publishing Company put out a collection of translated essays by renowned linguist and political analyst Noam Chomsky. In one of the essays, Chomsky criticized the Turkish government for its treatment of its Kurdish minority. "The Kurds," Chomsky argued, "have been miserably oppressed throughout the whole history of the modern Turkish state," a condition that worsened considerably in 1984, when "the Turkish government launched a major war in the Southeast against the Kurdish population" (Chomsky 2001). By November, the Turkish government had charged the Istanbul-based publishing house's director, Fatih Tas, with publishing "propaganda against the indivisible unity of the country, nation, and State of the Republic of Turkey" (World Association of Newspapers and News Publishers 2002). When the publisher appeared in

---

* This is a revised and expanded version of a review essay originally published in the *Bertrand Russell Society Quarterly* 132-135 (2006-2007): 13-22.

court the following February for his trial, he was accompanied by—Noam Chomsky. Chomsky had flown to Turkey to be present at the trial. He argued before the court that he had written the remarks that generated the criminal charges, and so if the publisher of those remarks was facing trial, then so should he. The prosecution declined to press charges against Chomsky, and was embarrassed into dropping the charges against the publisher, who had been facing a one-year prison sentence (BBC News 2002; Bowcott 2002).

Chomsky's stance in support of Fatih Tas clearly has much in common with Russell's earlier stance in support of the antiwar activists who distributed his leaflet. Both Russell and Chomsky are deeply committed to justice. Both men have expressed this commitment vigorously throughout their long lives. (Russell died at the age of 97; Chomsky remains active at 91.) Moreover, they are not content to express this commitment only in costless ways. In particular, they are not willing to allow others struggling for justice to pay the price for this struggle while they remain unaffected. Rather, they have done whatever they could to stand in solidarity with those paying the price for justice, and if that stand can provide some measure of protection to those less privileged than themselves, so much the better.

The connection between Chomsky and Russell, however, is much more than one of simple similarity. Chomsky has long admired Russell, both for his intellectual achievements and for his political crusading. For years, a poster of Russell hung in Chomsky's office at the Massachusetts Institute of Technology, where Chomsky spent virtually all of his professional career (Achbar, ed. 1994, 17). And Chomsky's respect for Russell has not gone unnoticed; it led the Bertrand Russell Society to offer Chomsky Honorary Membership, an honor Chomsky has now held for almost 25 years.[1]

In light of all this, it makes sense to compare Russell and Chomsky, in hopes that the work of each may shed light on the other. There are many angles from which one could conduct such a comparison. Both men, for example, worked on many of the same political causes. Both actively opposed the Vietnam War (Russell 1967; Chomsky 1969, 2005a). Both have also been deeply concerned about the Israeli occupation of the West Bank,

---

[1] The Bylaws of the Bertrand Russell Society state that honorary membership may be offered, among other reasons, to someone who, "has acted in support of a cause or idea that Russell championed" or "exhibited qualities of character (such as moral courage) reminiscent of Russell" (Bertrand Russell Society 2019). Chomsky undoubtedly meets both criteria.

a cause which exercises Chomsky to this day (Chomsky 1974, 1999).[2] One could therefore compare their respective contributions to these causes. One could also consider causes on which Russell and Chomsky took contrasting positions. Russell, for example, helped create the Who Killed Kennedy Committee, which questioned the Warren Commission's investigation of John F. Kennedy's assassination. Chomsky, by contrast, takes no position on the various conspiracy theories regarding the Kennedy assassination; rather, he questions the importance of such theorizing, denying that the assassination had any deep and lasting impact upon U.S. foreign or domestic policy (Chomsky 1993).[3] And one could certainly consider their respective polemical contributions to various intellectual debates. One could, for example, compare Russell's critique of Nietzsche with Chomsky's critique of Foucault (Russell 1972, ch. XXV; Russell 1994; Chomsky and Foucault 2006). One could even examine the various graphic novels that have been written about both men (Cogswell 1996; Maher and Groves 1997; Robinson and Groves 1998; Doxiadis and Papadimitriou 2009; Wilson 2018).[4]

In this essay, I take a different approach. I consider the status of Russell and Chomsky as public intellectuals. This, I will argue, is a natural approach to take. Both Chomsky and Russell are leading intellectuals who earned their reputations through their work in highly technical fields. Both became radical critics of the existing social order, and made use of their professional reputations to help get their criticisms before a wider audience. But as a result, both Chomsky and Russell have had to face the accusation that they are nosing around in areas outside their areas of expertise.[5] Why should their criticisms be regarded as anything but mere carping? Is there something more to their ideas than that? In short, Russell and Chomsky may be highly successful public intellectuals, but do they deserve to be? Do they offer something of deep and lasting interest to the general public? And if so,

---

[2] Russell's last public statement was a condemnation of Israel's occupation of the territories it had seized during the 1967 Six-Day War. The statement was read at a conference on February 3, 1960—the day after Russell's death (Perkins, ed. 2002).
[3] Chomsky denies, for example, that the Vietnam War might have ended earlier if Kennedy had lived. It is a position he tenaciously defends to this day. Witness, for example, his exchange on the subject with James K. Galbraith in the *Boston Review* (Galbraith 2003; Chomsky and Galbraith 2003).
[4] I examine one of these graphic novels, which tells the story of Russell's co-authorship of *Principia Mathematica* (Doxiadis and Papadimitriou 2009), in chapter 13 of this book.
[5] See, e.g., Johnson (1988) and Posner (2003). For critiques of Johnson, see Griffin (1990-1991) and Hitchens (1993). For a critique of Posner, see Jacoby (2002).

what can be said about the nature of their respective contributions?

To answer this question, I shall examine three of Chomsky's books—*Problems of Knowledge and Freedom* (2003), *Chomsky on Anarchism* (2005), and *Government in Our Future* (2005). *Problems of Knowledge and Freedom* (hereafter *PKF*) is based on the first set of Russell Lectures, which Chomsky delivered at Cambridge University a year after Russell's death. It was originally published by Pantheon Books in 1971. *Chomsky on Anarchism* (hereafter *CA*) is a collection of Chomsky's essays and interviews. The collection was selected and edited by Barry Pateman, Associate Editor of the Emma Goldman Papers, who also introduces the work. The collection includes both well-known classic pieces by Chomsky (e.g., "Language and Freedom," "Notes on Anarchism") and more recent and lesser-known pieces (e.g., "Interview with Barry Pateman," "Interview with Ziga Vodovnik").[6] *Government in Our Future* (hereafter *GF*) is based on a talk given at the Poetry Center in New York City on February 16, 1970. The book contains the complete transcript of the lecture.[7] Together, these books shed a great deal of light as to how Chomsky approaches his task as public intellectual. I shall thus examine Chomsky's approach, as illustrated in these three books, and then compare it with that of Russell.

In these three works, Chomsky displays a keen awareness of what meaningful social criticism, as opposed to mere carping, requires. "Social action," he writes,

> must be animated by a vision of a future society, and by explicit judgments of value concerning the character of this future society. These judgments must derive from some concept of the nature of man, and one may seek empirical foundations by investigating man's nature as it is revealed by his behavior and his creations, material, intellectual, and social. (*CA*, 113-4)

Social criticism—or, for that matter, a defense of the status quo, or any kind of social action in between—thus rests ultimately upon some conception of

---

[6] This work should not be confused with the book *On Anarchism* (2014), a different collection of Chomsky's writings, although there is some overlap between the two works.
[7] For many years, the lecture was offered for sale on audio cassette in the Audio-Forum series offered by Jeffrey Norton Publishers (Madison, CT). The lecture has also been published by Seven Stories Press in its Open Media Series (2005), and the text can be downloaded for free at https://libcom.org/library/government-future-noam-chomsky. The original lecture can be heard (audio only) at numerous places on the web, e.g., https://www.youtube.com/watch?v=5uagjAtit7E.

human nature, a conception that "is usually tacit and inchoate, but it is always there, perhaps implicitly, whether one chooses to leave things as they are and cultivate one's garden, or to work for small changes, or for revolutionary ones" (*CA*, 190; see also 5-6). It is the development of a meaningful and defensible account of human nature—and through it the development of a compelling social vision—that distinguishes positive social criticism from merely negative hectoring.[8]

In all three of the books under consideration here, Chomsky lays out his vision of a better society along with the conception of human nature that he believes underlies it. The most concise statement of both the vision and the conception appears in *Government in Our Future*. In this book, Chomsky contrasts four visions of what government in the future might look like—classical liberal, libertarian socialist, state socialist, and state capitalist. The fourth of these is represented by the American political system of the 1960s, a considerably more enlightened time in American politics. The third of these, of course, is represented by the Soviet Union and its allies and satellites. Chomsky spends little time on these two visions except as foils for the other two, which attract considerably more of his attention and provide the focus for the book.

The classical liberal vision "asserts as its major idea an opposition to all but the most restricted and minimal forms of state intervention in personal and social life." This is essentially the well-known vision of the *laissez faire* state, widely associated today with libertarian capitalism. This vision, Chomsky notes, is "quite familiar" today, but "the reasoning that leads to it is less familiar and I think a good deal more important than the conclusion itself" (*GF*, 9). The libertarian socialist agrees with the classical liberal that "the functions of the state are repressive and that state action must be limited," but goes considerably further:

> The libertarian socialist goes on to insist that state power must be eliminated in favor of democratic organization of industrial society, with direct popular control over all insti-

---

[8] This position is accepted by many thoughtful individuals who would otherwise not agree much with either Russell or Chomsky. Consider the following quote from Jacques Derrida: "I cannot conceive of a radical critique which would not be ultimately motivated by some sort of affirmation, acknowledged or not" (Derrida 1984, 118). Derrida's approach, which Chomsky has dismissed as "infantile and ridiculous," could not be further from Chomsky's own (quoted in Rai 1995, 206 n. 49).

> tutions by those who participate in—as well as those who are directly affected by—the workings of these institutions. So one might imagine a system of workers' councils, consumers' councils, commune assemblies, regional federations, and so on, with the kind of representation that's direct and revocable, in the sense that representatives are directly answerable to and return directly to the well-defined and integrated social group for which they speak in some higher order organization—something obviously very different than our system of representation. (*ibid.*, 35-6)

Such a system is socialist in its demand for democratic[9] control of the economy, but libertarian in its refusal to entrust that control to any entity separate from those participating in that economy.[10]

    The core of Chomsky's argument regarding these four visions is twofold. First, the classical liberal and libertarian socialist visions share the same basic conception of human nature, with libertarian socialism doing the most justice to that conception in complex and technologically advanced societies such as our own. Second, the state socialist and state capitalist visions—represented by Russian revolutionary V.I. Lenin in the first case and U.S. Secretary of Defense Robert McNamara in the second—share fundamentally the same conception of human nature, a conception that is markedly inferior to, and less inspiring than, the conception underling libertarian socialism.

---

[9] Elsewhere, Chomsky speaks of the need for the democratization of social relations more generally:

> My feeling is that any interaction among human beings that is more than personal—meaning that takes institutional forms of one kind or another—in community, or workplace, family, larger society, whatever it may be, should be under direct control of its participants. So that would mean workers' councils in industry, popular democracy in communities, interaction between them, free associations in larger groups, up to organization of international society. (*CA*, 238)

[10] For Chomsky, according to Joshua Cohen and Joel Rogers, "the 'statelessness' of society is achieved neither by the abolition of coercion (the coercion-free system), nor by the multiplication of its authoritative dispensers (the dispersed-coercion system), but by the transcendence of the traditional division of labor in governance between specialized political institutions that rule, and the rest of a society subject to their rule" (Cohen and Rogers 1991, 13).

The conception of human nature that Chomsky sees underlying both classical liberalism and libertarian socialism is complex. Human beings have a natural need to control their own lives, an "instinct for freedom," as Bakunin famously put it (quoted in *CA*, 155). This need expresses itself individually, through the need for meaningful work, and collectively, through the need for democratic association. Or, as Chomsky puts it elsewhere, there is a "fundamental human need…for spontaneous initiative, creative work, solidarity, [and] pursuit of social justice (Chomsky 1987, 155; see also Marshall 1990-1991, 7-8). Healthy people leading healthy lives are free people, and free people both engage in creative work and relate to each other as equals. People are not free to the extent that they must obey the orders of others; when people relate to one another as master and servant, especially in the workplace, they are both alienated from their powers of creativity and denied the meaningful connection with others that democracy makes possible.

Chomsky assumes that both the individual need for meaningful work and the collective need for democratic association travel together, that both can be usefully subsumed under a single "instinct for freedom." This claim is not obvious; one can imagine, for example, an artist who expresses herself masterfully through her work but without any meaningful connection with others. But it is certainly true that many institutions frustrate both needs at once—witness the soul-deadening jobs within many corporate workplaces[11]—and so it is certainly reasonable to search for institutions that can satisfy both needs at once.

Before moving on, it should be noted that Chomsky does not claim to have proof that human beings have the instinct for freedom he attributes to them. He does, as we will see, believe that human beings clearly have some creative powers, and that any satisfactory conception of human nature must be able to defend them. But a truly scientific understanding of human nature—one adequate to provide conclusive foundations for politics—is far beyond us, and may always be so. Social criticism, of course, cannot wait around for such a scientific understanding, and so all of us have to make do with the most compelling conception of human nature we can devise here and now (Cohen and Rogers 1991, 6). It is in that spirit that Chomsky presents to us the classical liberal/libertarian socialist instinct for freedom.

---

[11] On the tyrannical nature of modern workplaces, see Anderson (2017).

To derive a vision of modern society from this conception of human nature requires some understanding of how society works, of how people acting in accordance with the conception will be affected by different forms of social organization. Here, Chomsky argues, classical liberalism did not so much go wrong as become outdated; social conditions changed, and with them changed the nature of the fundamental threat to human freedom. In days gone by, state power could reasonably be described as the gravest threat; in the modern era, private power poses just as big a threat, if not a bigger one. The classical liberal vision is thus antiquated, and requires updating. Chomsky's argument on this point is worth quoting at some length:

> To summarize, the first concept of the state that I want to establish as a point of reference is classical liberalism. Its doctrine is that state functions should be drastically limited. But this familiar characterization is a very superficial one. More deeply, the classical liberal view develops from a certain concept of human nature, one that stresses the importance of diversity and free creation, and therefore this view is in fundamental opposition to industrial capitalism with its wage slavery, its alienated labor, and its hierarchic and authoritarian principles of social and economic organization. At least in its ideal form, classical liberal thought is opposed to the concepts of possessive individualism, that are intrinsic to capitalist ideology. For this reason, classical liberal thought seeks to eliminate social fetters and replace them with social bonds, and not with competitive greed, predatory individualism, and not, of course, with corporate empires—state or private.

"Classical libertarian thought seems to me," he concludes, "to lead directly to libertarian socialism, or anarchism if you like, when combined with an understanding of industrial capitalism (22-3; see also *CA*, 149).[12]

---

[12] Cf. Joshua Cohen and Joel Rogers, who take Chomsky's social and political thought to be marked by the following two claims "(1) human beings have a 'moral nature' and a fundamental interest in autonomy; (2) these basic features of our nature support a libertarian socialist social ideal." They point out that Chomsky derives the following two further claims from them: "(3) the interest in autonomy and the moral nature of human beings help to explain certain important features of actual social systems, including for example the use of deception and force to sustain unjust conditions, as well as their historical evolution; and (4) these same features of human nature provide reasons for hope that the terms of social order will improve from a moral point of view" (Cohen and Rogers 1991, 6).

The collection *Chomsky on Anarchism* covers much of the same ground as *Government in the Future*. It does, however, stress two other points that are worth noting here. Both are implicit in *Government in the Future* but receive fuller expression in the later collection (alongside some of the social critique for which Chomsky is so well-known, most notably in his classic essay "Ideology and Liberal Scholarship"). First, Chomsky's argument depends on the assumption that human nature is not a *tabula rasa*, that is has certain fixed features that it brings to the table in interacting with the world. Second, the state and capitalism are not the only threats posed today to human freedom. Indeed, it is impossible to compile a list of possible threats that will be valid and relevant for all time. Rather, the conception of human nature that he endorses prescribes a method for formulating social vision, the results of which will change as social conditions change and as social knowledge advances. Chomsky relates both points together as follows:

> Looked at in this way, the empty organism view is conservative, in that it tends to legitimate structures of hierarchy and domination. At least in its Humboldtian version [Chomsky relies heavily on Wilhelm von Humboldt's work, especially his book *The Limits of State Action* (1993)], the classical liberal view, with its strong innatist roots, is radical in that, consistently pursued, it challenges the legitimacy of established coercive institutions. Such institutions face a heavy burden of proof: it must be shown that under existing conditions, perhaps because of some overriding consideration of deprivation or threat, some form of authority, hierarchy, and domination is justified, despite the prima facie case against it—a burden that can rarely be met. One can understand why there is such a persistent attack on Enlightenment ideals, with their fundamentally subversive convent. (*CA*, 174; see also *CA*, 178, 192; Cohen and Rogers 1991, 11)

The innatist view of human nature that Chomsky endorses has the implication that all threats to human freedom ought to be challenged and, if conditions permit, overcome.

Note that while in *Government in the Future* Chomsky more or less uses the terms "anarchism" and "libertarian socialism" interchangeably, in *Chomsky on Anarchism* he tends to restrict the latter to the specific social vision (especially the economic part) he has in mind for modern societies, while reserving the former term for the general method of challenging threats to human freedom that he recommends. Chomsky is thus both an anarchist and a libertarian socialist; the latter commitment depends heavily on his understanding of social conditions, whereas the former commitment depends only on his conception of human nature itself.

For Chomsky, then, human freedom—understood in terms of the anarchist vision of human nature—faces an open-ended list of potential threats. Different threats will prove more pressing at different times and places; indeed, at any given time and place, there will no doubt be threats that go unrecognized. In Chomsky's words,

> One might…argue…that at every stage of history our concern must be to dismantle those forms of authority and oppression that survive from an era when they might have been justified in terms of the need for security of survival or economic development, but that now contribute to—rather than alleviate—material and cultural deficit. If so, there will be no doctrine of social change fixed for the present and future, nor even, necessarily, a specific and unchanging concept of the goals towards which social change should tend (*CA*, 118-9).

The open-ended list of potential threats to human freedom does not obviate the need for a vision of a better world to undergird social critique. Because of that need, "at a particular time there is every reason to develop, insofar as our understanding permits, a specific realization of this definite trend in the historic development of mankind, appropriate to the tasks of the moment" (*ibid.*, 119)—to develop, in other words, the best picture one can of what a truly free society would look like, and to critique existing societies when they fail to realize the ideals underlying this picture.

According, to Chomsky, then, the defender of human freedom must be prepared to confront different threats at different times, all in the name of a vision of society in which those threats have been overcome. That vision is never set in stone, but evolves alongside the society which is to be judged by it. This fact has implications that Chomsky readily admits but that may seem counterintuitive from an anarchist perspective. Both the political and the economic system, for example, may pose threats to human freedom. In the present day and age, the former may represent the best way of containing the abuses of the latter. And so even an anarchist who ultimately wishes the dissolution of the state may oppose efforts to weaken the state here and now. Social welfare measures, health and safety measures, and environmental protections not only help weak and vulnerable people now;

they also place those people in a stronger position to fight for a better deal in the future. Chomsky defends this position, and refers to it (borrowing a line from the Argentinian labor movement) as "expanding the floor of the cage" (Chomsky 1997; see also Mitchell and Schoeffel 2002, 344-6). Only a simple-minded form of libertarianism, according to Chomsky, automatically equates less government with better government.[13]

How similar is Chomsky's social critique to that of Russell? And to what extent do they share the same conception of human nature? The answer to both questions is complicated, as can be gleaned from studying what Chomsky has to say about Russell. Chomsky greatly admires Russell, and discusses his ideas frequently (see, e.g., *CA*, 156, 194-5, 205). "To several generations, mine among them," he writes, "Russell has been an inspiring figure, in the problems he posed and the causes he championed, in his insights as well as what is left unfinished" (*PKF*, x). It is his concern with what Russell has left unfinished, or unsatisfactorily resolved, that motivates what Chomsky has to say about Russell. Chomsky does not approach Russell as an intellectual historian, determined to capture precisely what Russell had in mind. Rather, he approaches Russell as a source for intellectual inspiration, for ideas that may be of use in formulating his own positions.[14] Thus, the similarities between Chomsky's and Russell's ideas about human nature and social vision are there, but the differences are there as well.

Chomsky conducts his most systematic engagement with Russell's thought in his book *Problems of Knowledge and Freedom*. Based on the first set of Russell Lectures, which Chomsky delivered at Cambridge University a year after Russell's death, this book takes up the mature Russell's views on knowledge and freedom, with an eye to their relevance to contemporary

---

[13] Chomsky's low opinion of libertarian capitalism is well-known (see, e.g., Mitchell and Schoeffel, eds. 2002, 200). Note, however, that Chomsky's position on "expanding the floor of the cage" is far from universally held among self-professed anarchists. Indeed, his position has led some anarchists to deny that Chomsky qualifies as an anarchist (Marshall 1990-1991, 2). See Stone (2014) on the controversy.

[14] Chomsky takes this approach to the writings of others more generally. When it comes to the history of ideas, he describes himself as more of an "art lover" than an "art historian," less concerned with purity of tradition than with intellectual fruitfulness (Marshall 1990-1991, 3). More than most anarchists, for example, he has been happy to borrow liberally from a number of Marxist writers, notably Rosa Luxemburg and Anton Pannekoek. An interview with him thus appears in the recently republication of Pannekoek's *Workers Councils* (2003). Indeed, even with respect to anarchism he is content to describe himself as less of an "anarchist thinker" than a "derivative fellow traveler" (*CA*, 135).

concerns. While one of the lectures was devoted to questions of knowledge, and the other was devoted to questions of freedom, Chomsky perceives in Russell's writings on the two topics some unifying threads (*PKF*, x-xi). Chomsky draws out these threads, which not coincidentally relate Russell's conception of human nature and his social ideals to Chomsky's own.

Chomsky sees the mature Russell[15] as recognizing that pure empiricism alone could not account for the knowledge human beings obtain. Both prescientific knowledge, the knowledge people obtain naturally without scientific reflection, and the philosophical study of the relationship between knowledge and experience, suggest that there must be specific fixed cognitive mechanisms that influence knowledge acquisition. It cannot just be bald induction from experience plus generalized reasoning capacity, not least because the principle of induction itself, which is necessary to derive *anything* from experience, seems hard to ground in reason alone. In Russell's words, "Either, therefore, we know something independently of experience, or science is moonshine" (quoted in *PKF*, 4). Chomsky believes that this insight suggested the existence of a human nature, with certain fixed capacities that it used to derive working knowledge from a relatively information-poor environment (although he concedes that Russell might not have agreed with him on this).[16] Chomsky sees his own work on the nature of human language as providing insight into how one particular human capacity works; this insight might be used as a starting point for the study of other, less accessible human cognitive systems.

This view of human nature as having certain fixed capacities that determine how we are capable of interacting with the world has certain implications. It suggests, for example, that there might be limits to the kinds of knowledge that human beings can have. "We might say," Chomsky writes,

> that our mental constitution permits us to arrive at knowledge of the world insofar as our innate capacity to create theories happens to match some aspect of the structure of the world.

---

[15] Chomsky takes Russell's *Human Knowledge: Its Scope and Limits* (1948) as representative of Russell's final position on questions of epistemology, and relies heavily on this work in describing Russell's mature position on questions of knowledge.

[16] Chomsky quotes Russell as inquiring, "how comes it that human beings, whose contacts with the world are brief and personal and limited, are nevertheless able to know as much as they know" (quoted in *PKF*, 47). Chomsky subsequently dubs this question "Plato's problem" (Chomsky 1986).

> By exploring various faculties of the mind, we might, in principle, come to understand what theories are more readily accessible to us than others, or what potential theories are accessible to us at all, what forms of scientific knowledge can be attained, if the world is kind enough to have the required properties. Where it is not, we may be able to develop a kind of "intellectual technology"—say, a technique of prediction that will, for some reason, work within limits—but not to attain what might properly be called scientific understanding or common-sense knowledge. (*PKF*, 20)

There might, for example, be languages that from a purely logical standpoint do not seem more demanding to learn than English, but that the cognitive capacities of humans do not allow them to "pick up" as easily as virtually every American or British child learns English. Similar constraints might apply to other, nonlinguistic knowledge systems.

While there are thus many potential philosophical implications of the rejection of the *tabula rasa*,[17] it is the political implications that attract Chomsky's attention most clearly in *Problems of Knowledge and Freedom*. Chomsky sees Russell's admission of a fixed human nature, with certain definite capacities, as supportive of Russell's political vision. The political ideals that Russell held, according to Chomsky, cannot be sustained if human beings are as malleable as the *tabula rasa* conception of human nature is accurate. Why demand that the political system be molded to fit human needs, if human beings can be molded to fit the political system? The recognition that human nature is richer than that is the necessary foundation for any social vision based on human freedom, something that both Russell and Chomsky tried to construct.

As for Russell's own social vision and conception of human nature, they are remarkably similar to Chomsky's own. (I focus here on Chomsky's description of Russell's social vision; for more on that vision, see chapter 8

---

[17] One further philosophical implication worth noting is the potential reformulation of philosophical terms that this position might suggest. Thus, Chomsky suggests that the principles demonstrated by human knowledge patterns "are a priori for the species—they provide the framework for the interpretation of experience and the construction of specific forms of knowledge on the basis of experience—but are not necessary or even natural properties of all imaginable systems that might serve the functions of human language" (*PKF*, 44-5; see also 31). Needless to say, this use of the term "a priori" departs from standard philosophical usage, which employs it to distinguish knowledge immediately accessible to any rational being whatsoever.

of this volume.) With regard to the latter, Russell endorses the conception of human beings as free agents, beings whose natural development requires opportunities for both individual creativity and self-expression and egalitarian and democratic relationships with others. Chomsky describes this conception as "a humanistic conception of man, with due respect for man's intrinsic nature and the admirable form it might achieve" (*PKF*, 54). With regard to the former, Russell endorsed in such works as *Roads to Freedom* (1996) a form of social organization very much reminiscent of those advocated by anarchists such as Mikhail Bakunin and Peter Kropotkin. These two anarchist thinkers, writes Chomsky,

> had in mind a highly organized form of society, but a society that was organized on the basis of organic units, organic communities. And generally they meant by that the workplace and the neighborhood, and from those two basic units there could derive through federal arrangements a highly integrated kind of social organization, which might be national or even international in scope (*CA*, 133).

The social vision offered by Russell as appropriate to the modern age—grounded in Russell's "humanistic conception of man"—turns out to be strikingly similar to the libertarian socialism advocated by Chomsky, a social vision informed by a very similar conception of human nature.

Any attempt to assimilate Russell's political vision to that of Chomsky, however, must meet with two stumbling blocks. First, there is the matter of the rationalist model of human beings, in which people are born with certain cognitive abilities that do far more than simply compile data from the environment. Chomsky endorses this model, identifies elements of it in Russell, and links it to his vision of human beings as free creatures that require both creative self-expression and egalitarian social relations. But the link is not as clear as Chomsky would have it.[18] Granted, a conception of human beings as totally malleable could not support a vision of a free

---

[18] Others have questioned Chomsky's effort to derive enlightened political implications from rationalism, as well as nefarious implications from empiricism (e.g., Searle 1976; Williams 1976). More recently, Chris Knight has argued, from a Marxist perspective, that Chomsky's approach to language actively obstructs meaningful political activism (Knight 2016; see also Knight 2018a,b,c; 2019). Chomsky has strongly rejected Knight's argument (Chomsky 2019). For other responses to Knight, see Barsky (2016); Golumbia (2018); Harris (2018a,b); Levidow (2018); Newmayer (2018); Sperlich (2016, 2018); and Stone (2018).

society, or any other social vision for that matter. But the basic insight that people have inborn capacities of one sort or another could be developed in many different directions, some humane and enlightened, some not. It could be used, for example, to justify a patriarchal society on grounds that women are "built" differently than men, or a racist society on grounds that the white race is "naturally" superior to other races. (Needless to say, these are not hypothetical scenarios.)[19] Indeed, the unenlightened uses of the idea of a fixed human nature throughout history have arguably outnumbered the enlightened ones. It was recognition of this fact, I suspect, that led Russell himself to perceive a relationship between empiricism (i.e., a conception of human nature that attributed much more to social environment than to inborn capacity) and liberal democracy (Russell 1950). This fact does not demolish Chomsky's case, but it does suggest that the link between his philosophical work on language and the mind, and the conception of human nature Chomsky needs to sustain his libertarian socialism, is even more tentative than he may be ready to admit.[20]

Second, there is the matter of anarchism. As noted before, Chomsky's vision of the appropriate form of social organization for a modern industrial society is very similar to that advocated by Russell. But while Chomsky employs the term "anarchism" to describe his approach to social vision, Russell's relationship to the term is ambiguous. On the one hand, Russell once described anarchism as "the ultimate ideal to which society should approximate" (cited in *PKF*, 59-60; see also *CA*, 156). On the other hand, he perceived the social system he advocated—a decentralized, feder-

---

[19] Curiously, Chomsky has suggested there may be a relationship between *empiricism* and racism (Chomsky 1998, 130; see also Marshall 1990-1991, 9, n. 18).

[20] Chomsky is on firmer ground to link the possibility of creativity and self-expression with a mind fixed within certain limits. "The principles of mind," Chomsky writes,

> provide the scope as well as the limits of human creativity. Without such principles, scientific understanding and creative acts would not be possible. If all hypotheses are initially on a par, then no scientific understanding can possibly be achieved, since there will be no way to select among the vast array of theories compatible with our limited evidence and, by hypothesis, equally accessible to the mind. One who abandons all forms, all conditions and constraints, and merely acts in some random and entirely willful manner is surely not engaged in artistic creation, whatever else he may be doing (*PKF*, 49-50; see also Cohen and Rogers 1991, 7).

A completely unconstrained mind would have difficulty creating or learning anything. For further discussion of the link between constraints (self-imposed or otherwise) and creative expression, see Elster (2000, ch. III).

ated system of democratically-organized communities and workplaces—as an alternative to, and not an embodiment of, anarchism. He referred to this alternative, following G.D.H. Cole, as "guild socialism," as Chomsky acknowledges (*PKF*, 60).

Why might Russell take this stance regarding anarchism? Perhaps because he saw it as dispensing with the state and leaving nothing in its place—no proper "political" organization at all. He therefore perceives guild socialism—a system in which both workplaces and communities are organized—as superior to anarcho-syndicalism, which sees the need only for the former type of organization. But this may not be fair to anarchism, at least as Chomsky understands it. In a classic interview entitled "The Relevance of Anarcho-Syndicalism," for example, Chomsky describes that system as follows:

> Beginning with the two modes of immediate organization an control, namely organization and control in the workplace and in the community, one can imagine a network of workers' councils, and at a higher level, representation across the factories, or across branches of industry, or across crafts, and on to general assemblies of workers' councils that can be regional and national and international in character. And from another point of view one can project a system of governance that involves local assemblies—again federated regionally, dealing with regional issues, crossing crafts, industries, trades and so on, and again at the level of the nation or beyond, through federation and so on. (*CA*, 137)

It is difficult, if not impossible, to distinguish between anarcho-syndicalism, as articulated here, and guild socialism, as articulated by Russell. The difference may be more or less terminological; still, Russell's complex relationship to the word should make one pause before equating Russell's political position with that of an avowed anarchist like Chomsky.[21]

---

[21] To some extent, the word "socialism" played a role in Russell's thought similar to that played in Chomsky's thought by "anarchism"—designating less a particular social ideal and more an approach to formulating social ideals, an approach that must be informed by a proper understanding of social conditions. "Russell believed," Chomsky writes, "that 'socialism, like everything else that is vital, is rather a tendency than a strictly definable body of doctrine.' It should, therefore, undergo constant change as society evolves" (*PKF*, quoting Russell 1996). The parallel is not perfect, but it lends further credence to the idea that Chomsky and Russell simply understood (misunderstood?) anarchism in different ways.

Neither of these stumbling blocks, however, need prove fatal to Chomsky's endeavor. His goal, after all, is less to assimilate Russell's political position to his own than to identify political ideas in Russell's writings that may be of use to social critics today. These ideas have been developed by Chomsky is ways that would seem strange to Russell, and they certainly require further development in light of the questions and difficulties posed by them. In the end, however, these three books prove very instructive, and not simply for Chomsky fans. Anyone interested in understanding Russell the social critic would do well to consult these three books. In doing so, one might learn something about the ideals underlying Russell's social criticism. One might also learn something about which elements of those ideals might be worth preserving for use by today's social critics. And more than that, one will find a forceful defense of the importance of clearly articulated ideals to meaningful social criticism. And that is a lesson of which both Russell and Chomsky would approve.

Bibliography

Achbar, Mark, ed. 1994. *Manufacturing Consent: Noam Chomsky and the Media: The Companion Book to the Award-Winning Film by Peter Wintonick and Mark Achbar.* Montréal: Black Rose Books.

Anderson, Elizabeth. 2017. *Private Government: How Employers Rule Our Lives (and Why We Don't Talk about It).* Princeton: Princeton University Press.

Barsky, Robert F. 2016. Review of *Decoding Chomsky* by Chris Knight. *Moment*, September 15. https://momentmag.com/book-review-decoding-chomsky/.

BBC News. 2002. "Chomsky Publisher Cleared in Turkey." February 13. http://news.bbc.co.uk/2/hi/europe/1817598.stm.

Bertrand Russell Society. 2019. "Bylaws of the Bertrand Russell Society, Inc." June. https://bertrandrussellsociety.org/bylaws/.

Bowcott, Owen. 2002. "Chomsky Wins Case for Turkish Publisher: Istanbul Court Drops Charges after U.S. Author Flies in to Challenge Prosecution over Pro-Kurdish Essay." *The Guardian,* February 14. https://www.theguardian.com/world/2002/feb/14/books.pressandpublishing.

Chomsky, Noam. 1969. *American Power and the New Mandarins.* New York: Vintage Books.

Chomsky, Noam. 1974. *Peace in the Middle East? Reflections on Justice and Nationhood.* New York: Vintage Books.

Chomsky, Noam. 1986. *Knowledge of Language: Its Nature, Origin, and Use.* New York: Praeger.

Chomsky, Noam. 1987. "Language and Freedom." In *The Chomsky Reader*, ed. James Peck. New York: Pantheon.

Chomsky, Noam. 1993. *Rethinking Camelot: JFK, the Vietnam War, and U.S. Political Culture.* Boston: South End Press.

Chomsky, Noam. 1997. "Expanding the Floor of the Cage: Noam Chomsky Interviewed by David Barsamian." *Z Magazine*, April. https://chomsky.info/199704__/.

Chomsky, Noam. 1998. "Reflections on Language." In O*n Language: Chomsky's Classic Works Language and Responsibility and Reflections on Language in One Volume.* New York: The New Press.

Chomsky, Noam. 1999. *Fateful Triangle: The United States, Israel & the Palestinians.* Updated ed. Cambridge, MA: South End Press.

Chomsky, Noam. 2001. "Prospects for Peace in the Middle East." First Annual Maryse Mikhail Lecture, the University of Toledo, March 4. https://chomsky.info/20010304/.

Chomsky, Noam. 2003. *Problems of Knowledge and Freedom.* New York: The New Press.

Chomsky, Noam. 2005a. *At War with Asia.* Reprint ed. Oakland, CA: AK Press.

Chomsky, Noam. 2005b. *Chomsky on Anarchism,* ed. Barry Pateman. Oakland, CA: AK Press.

Chomsky, Noam. 2005c. *Government in the Future.* New York: Seven Stories Press.

Chomsky, Noam. 2014. *On Anarchism.* New York: The New Press.

Chomsky, Noam. 2019. "Replies and Commentary." In *The Responsibility of Intellectuals: Reflections by Noam Chomsky and Others after 50 Years*, eds. Nicholas Allott, Chris Knight, and Neil Smith. London: UCL Press. https://discovery.ucl.ac.uk/id/eprint/10080589/1/The-Responsibility-of-Intellectuals.pdf.

Chomsky, Noam and Foucault, Michel. 2006. *The Chomsky-Foucault Debate: On Human Nature.* New York: The New Press.

Chomsky, Noam and Galbraith, James K. 2003. "Letters from Chomsky and Galbraith on JFK and Vietnam." *Boston Review*, December 1 (online). http://bostonreview.net/world/chomsky-galbraith-letters-vietnam-jfk-kennedy.

Cogswell, David. 1996. *Chomsky for Beginners.* New York: Writers and Readers.

Cohen, Joshua and Rogers, Joel. 1991. "Knowledge, Morality and Hope: The Social Thought of Noam Chomsky." *New Left Review* 187 (May/June): 5-27.

Derrida, Jacques. 1984. "Dialogue with Jacques Derrida." *In Dialogues with Contemporary Continental Thinkers: The Phenomenological Heritage*, ed. Richard Kearney. Manchester: Manchester University Press.

Doxiadis, Apostolos and Papadimitriou, Christos H. 2009. *Logicomix: An Epic Search for Truth.* New York: Bloomsbury.

Elster, Jon. 2000. *Ulysses Unbound.* New York: Cambridge University Press.

Galbraith, James K. 2003. "Exit Strategy: In 1963, JFK Ordered a Complete Withdrawal from Vietnam." *Boston Review*, October/November (online September 1). http://bostonreview.net/us/galbraith-exit-strategy-vietnam

Golumbia, David. 2018. "The Chomskyan Revolution and the Politics of Linguistics." openDemocracy, September 25. https://www.opendemocracy.net/en/chomskyan-revolution-and-politics-of-linguistics/.

Griffin, Nicholas. 1990-1991. "Hacks & Thinkers." *Russell* n.s. 10 (2): 173-178.

Harris, Randy Allen. 2018a. "The History of a Science: Unreliable Narrators and How Science Moves on". openDemocracy, May 9. https://www.opendemocracy.net/en/history-of-science-unreliable-narrators-and-how-science-moves-on/.

Harris, Randy Allen. 2018b. "A Response to Wolfgang Sperlich on 'The Latter Day Critics of Noam Chomsky.'" openDemocracy, November 8. https://www.opendemocracy.net/en/response-to-wolfgang-sperlich-on-latter-day-critics-of-noam-chomsky/.

Hitchens, Christopher. 1993. "The Life of Johnson." In *For the Sake of Argument.* New York: Verso.

Jacoby, Russell. 2002. "Cornering the Market in Chutzpah." *Los Angeles Times*, January 27.

Johnson, Paul. 1988. *Intellectuals*. New York: Harper & Row.

Knight, Chris. 2016. *Decoding Chomsky: Science and Revolutionary Politics.* New Haven: Yale University Press.

Knight, Chris. 2018a. "Chomsky's Choice: How the Linguist's Early Military Work Led to a Life of Campaigning against the Military." openDemocracy, March 28. https://www.opendemocracy.net/en/chomsky-s-choice-how-noam-chomsky-s-early-military-work-led-to-life-of-campaigning-agai/.

Knight, Chris. 2018b. "Why Chomsky Felt 'Guilty Most of the Time:' War Research and Linguistics at MIT." openDemocracy, April 24. https://www.opendemocracy.net/en/why-chomsky-felt-guilty-most-of-time-war-research-and-linguistics-at-mit/.

Knight, Chris. 2018c. "Explaining Chomsky's Strange Science: A Reply to Randy Allen Harris." openDemocracy, September 6. https://www.opendemocracy.net/en/explaining-chomsky-s-strange-science-reply-to-randy-allen-harris/.

Knight, Chris. 2019. "Speaking Truth to Power—from within the Heart of the Empire." In *The Responsibility of Intellectuals: Reflections by Noam Chomsky and Others after 50 Years*, eds. Nicholas Allott, Chris Knight, and Neil Smith. London: UCL Press. https://discovery.ucl.ac.uk/id/eprint/10080589/1/The-Responsibility-of-Intellectuals.pdf.

Levidow, Les. 2018. "The Chomsky Paradox: The Responsibility of Intellectuals, Revisited." openDemocracy, September 6. https://www.opendemocracy.net/en/chomsky-paradox-responsibility-of-intellectuals-revisited/.

Maher, John and Groves, Judy. 1997. *Introducing Chomsky.* New York: Totem Books.

Marshall, Paul. 1990-1991. "Noam Chomsky's Anarchism." *Our Generation* 22 (Fall/Spring): 1-15.

Mitchell, Peter R. and Schoeffel, John, eds. 2002. *Understanding Power: The Indispensable Chomsky.* New York: The New Press.

Newmayer, Frederick J. 2018. "Chomsky's Linguistics and Military Funding: A Non-Issue." openDemocracy, April 15. https://www.opendemocracy.net/en/chomsky-and-needless-controversy-over-internalist-and-military-approaches-to-la/.

Pannekoek, Anton. 2003. *Workers Councils.* Oakland: AK Press, 2003.

Perkins, Ray, ed. 2002. *Yours Faithfully, Bertrand Russell: A Lifelong Fight for Peace, Justice and Truth in Letters to the Editor.* Chicago: Open Court.

Posner, Richard A. 2003. *Public Intellectuals: A Study of Decline.* Cambridge, MA: Harvard University Press.

Rai, Milan. 1995. *Chomsky's Politics.* London: Verso.

Robinson, Dave and Groves, Judy. 1998. *Introducing Bertrand Russell.* New York: Totem.

Russell, Bertrand. 1948. *Human Knowledge: Its Scope and Limits.* New York: Simon and Schuster.

Russell, Bertrand. 1950. "Philosophy and Politics." In *Unpopular Essays.* New York: Simon and Schuster.

Russell, Bertrand. 1967. *War Crimes in Vietnam.* New York: Monthly Review Press.

Russell, Bertrand. 1972. *A History of Western Philosophy.* New York: Simon and Schuster.

Russell, Bertrand. 1994. "The Ancestry of Fascism." In *In Praise of Idleness.* Reprint ed. London: Routledge.

Russell, Bertrand. 1996. *Roads to Freedom.* Reprint ed. New York: Routledge.

Searle, John. 1976. "The Rules of the Language Game." *Times Literary Supplement*, September 10.

Sperlich, Wolfgang. 2016. "A Review of *Decoding Chomsky* (2016) by Chris Knight." *Wolfgang B. Sperlich: Old but New* (blog), November 2. http://wolfgang-sperlich.blogspot.com/2016/11/a-review-of-decoding-chomsky-2016-by.html.

Sperlich, Wolfgang. 2018. "The Latter Day Critics of Noam Chomsky." openDemocracy, October 15. https://www.opendemocracy.net/en/latter-day-critics-of-noam-chomsky/.

Stone, Peter. 2014. "Anarchism." In *The Encyclopedia of Political Thought,* ed. Michael T. Gibbons. Oxford: Wiley-Blackwell.

Stone, Peter. 2018. Review of *Decoding Chomsky: Science and Revolutionary Politics* by Chris Knight. *Philosophy Now*, August/September. https://philosophynow.org/issues/127/Decoding_Chomsky_by_Chris_Knight.

Von Humboldt, Wilhelm. 1993. *The Limits of State Action.* Rev. ed. Indianapolis: Liberty Fund.

Williams, Bernard. 1976. "Where Chomsky Stands." *New York Review of Books*, November 11.

Wilson, Jeffrey. 2018. *The Instinct for Cooperation: A Graphic Novel Conversation with Noam Chomsky.* New York: Seven Stories Press.

World Association of Newspapers and News Publishers. 2002. "WAN Asks That Charges against Publisher and Editor Be Dropped." IFEX, February 12. https://ifex.org/wan-asks-that-charges-against-publisher-and-editor-be-dropped/.

"BUT THERE ARE ALWAYS EXCEPTIONS:"
AN INTERVIEW WITH NOAM CHOMSKY

Peter Stone

On May 13, 2020, I had the great pleasure of interviewing Noam Chomsky (online, of course). Chomsky has been an honorary member of the Bertrand Russell Society (BRS) for many years, and in 2020 was given the BRS Award. A recording of the interview was played publicly for the first time at the 2020 BRS Annual Meeting, also held online. This recording is available at https://bertrandrussellsociety.org/2020/06/25/noam-chomsky-interview/). Below is an annotated transcript of this interview. I am very grateful to Prof. Chomsky, for agreeing both to the interview and to its publication in this book; to Tim Madigan, for arranging the interview; and to David Blitz, for handling the technical side of the interview.

I should add that when Tim first requested the interview, Chomsky quickly replied as follows: "Hopeless schedule. Reduced to sending out form letters refusing the flood of interview requests. But there are always exceptions. This is certainly one." It is an honor and a privilege to see Chomsky make an exception for the BRS.

PETER STONE (PS): Hello, everyone, and welcome to a very special event for the Bertrand Russell Society. My name is Peter Stone. I'm a longtime member of the Russell Society, and I'm delighted to have with me today Professor Noam Chomsky. Professor Chomsky needs no introduction. I'll just mention here that he has been an honorary member of the Bertrand Russell Society for almost 30 years now and is also the recipient of the 2020 Bertrand Russell Society Award. Professor Chomsky, welcome.

NOAM CHOMSKY (NC): Thank you.

PS: You get interviewed about a vast array of topics—about the various wars of the United States, about the media, about Donald Trump, about all kinds of issues. But today we'd just like to talk to you a little bit about a different subject—about Bertrand Russell.

NC: Very good. If I was able to be at my office, which I can't get to now, you would see behind me a portrait of him.

PS: Oh, so you took it with you when you left MIT. I've seen the photographs of you with the picture.[1]

NC: It's the same one.

PS: Oh, lovely.

NC: I made sure to take that with me. And it's now on the same place in my new office.

PS: That's wonderful. That's definitely a collector's item. I've looked for the same poster. I haven't been able to find it.

NC: It also has a history. Some years back, there was an attack on my office. It was vandalized and things thrown down everywhere. And this poster was destroyed. I had to get a new one. I have a friend here—my dog—who wants me to pay attention to him, but nope.

PS: That's fine. I actually have one in my lap right now also.[2]

NC: OK.

PS: That's one of the joys of doing these things from home, I guess.

NC: Maybe they can talk to each other.

PS: So let's start to talk a little bit about Russell. I was looking at Robert Barsky's excellent biography of you. I was just looking at it again this past week and I came upon the fascinating line where he claims that your two

---

[1] In the documentary *Manufacturing Consent: Noam Chomsky and the Media* (1992), the poster of Russell can be seen in Chomsky's office. See also Achbar, ed. (1994, 17).
[2] I would like to thank Shaylee for sitting so quietly in my lap throughout the entire interview.

most important role models were the Dutch Marxist Anton Pannekoek and Bertrand Russell.[3] Do you think that's a fair thing to say?

NC: Well, I wouldn't exactly say that I had role models, but they were people I very much respected. Nobody's a role model, but there are people… people are complicated creatures, they have their own lives, achievements, flaws, and so on. But the important things that they did, which were major, were in fact things I respect and honor, and think we all should [do the same]. I can think of quite a few [such individuals]. I don't know why he picked those two.

PS: They're both, I guess, also men like you who managed to balance an interest in intellectual affairs and serious intellectual work—the life of the mind—and also a serious political commitment at the same time.

NC: Russell is an exemplar of that. Did fabulous work in philosophy, logic. Also very much involved in social and political issues and acted courageously as an activist. He was on the front lines in CND marches, strongly opposed the Vietnam war, despised by the elites in the United States—it's another credit to him. Bitter attacks on him—hard to believe when you re-read them. But much of his life was extremely admirable in both domains.

PS: I completely agree with you.

NC: One of the rare opponents of the First World War,[4] thrown out of his position at Trinity College [Cambridge], jailed…

PS: Very true. And managed to get arrested during the First World War and then also arrested again during the Cold War for his protests against the bomb in Britain.

NC: I remember a statement of his back in the late fifties, I guess, which often comes to mind. He was asked why he was wasting his time on CND demonstrations against the bomb when he could be doing things of lasting

---

[3] See Barsky (1997, 40). Pannekoek is best-known today, in radical circles, for his book *Workers' Councils,* originally published in English in 1948. Chomsky provided the introduction to a new edition of this book (Pannekoek 2003).

[4] For more on Russell's activism in the First World War, see the essay by John Lenz in this volume as well as my own "Russell the Political Activist."

importance in philosophy. He said, if we don't stop the bomb, nobody's going to be reading philosophy. That's a thought that often comes to my mind.

PS: He was definitely someone who had some sense of proportion, a sense about what really mattered throughout his life. I think. When did you first become acquainted with Russell and his work?

NC: When I was a high school student, I started reading some of his general works on philosophy, including his *History of Western Philosophy*, and got more and more interested. One of the important things, lucky things for me was that in the philosophical profession, his later work is mostly disregarded. Very little reference to it. But I happened to be studying with a superb philosopher, Nelson Goodman—one of the major 20th-century philosophers. He happened to respect Russell's later work, so he urged me to read *Human Knowledge, Inquiry into Meaning and Truth, Analysis of Matter*—things like that, which are very valuable, I think.

PS: Yes, I was thinking about *Human Knowledge*. I was rereading the Russell lectures that you gave at Cambridge on the anniversary of Russell's birth—the hundredth anniversary, I believe. They were published as the book *Problems of Knowledge and Freedom*,[5] [editor's note: originally published in 1971 and republished in 2003] which is a wonderful read. And you definitely take a reading of Russell in there that seemed a bit unconventional by the standards of the time when you gave those lectures. Is that fair?

NC: The lectures would have been about 1970, I guess. At the time we were deeply immersed in the devastation of Indochina, the worst war crime since the Second World War. The lectures were divided into Russell's interests in philosophy, knowledge, logic—that's the first part. The second part was his social and political concerns. And a lot of it was about the Vietnam War. Actually, there was an incident. The first lecture—this is in Trinity College [Cambridge]—the first lecture I was about halfway through when somebody ran up to the stage and told me, we have to get out, we have to get out of the building. There was a bomb threat, and they had to evacuate the building while they searched for the bomb. Luckily there was no bomb, but it made a little drama in the first lecture.

---

[5] See Chomsky (2003). I discuss this work extensively in my essay "Chomsky and Russell Revisited."

PS: Wow. Very turbulent times, I guess, for trying to be on a university…

NC: Oh yeah.

PS: In the Russell lectures, you talk about a topic that has been of great interest to you over the years, I know. It's what you call Plato's problem, the problem of how we come to know as much as we do given how little data we get from the world. Have you found Russell helpful in thinking about Plato's problem?

NC: He posed the problem in his typically eloquent way, which I quoted. I hate to imitate his words because he had it so perfect. It would reduce the impact. But he basically asked, how can it be we know so much when we have so little information. I called it Plato's problem, but I think that's fair. Well, it's a deep problem. My own particular professional concern with that problem happens to be with the knowledge of language. I think [it's] the most dramatic example of it and one of the few cases that can be studied in-depth with serious results and at many levels, ranging from the neurological to the behavioral. So yes, he posed the problem very well, and that's what he was doing. And I think he had important insights. The problem, of course, is millennia old, and we don't know much about it in many areas. We just know that it's a dramatic fact about humans which distinguishes us from the rest of the world. There's nothing even remotely analogous in the rest of the world. I mean, our two dogs know a lot of things, but they can't consider these questions.[6]

PS: What makes us so distinct and so unique in terms of what we're able to accomplish?

NC: Well, I think through the centuries people who've thought about this have concluded that it's probably the possession of language, and I think that's correct. I think there's good evidence to believe that whatever small event in evolutionary history provided us with the capacity for language opened the doors to creativity, to inquiry, to reflection, to achievement, to destruction—not always nice things—which are unique to the species. And in fact, there is no analog to human language in any other species. There

---

[6] This is unfortunately why our dogs were unable to start up their own conversation.

are a lot of efforts to try to find animal analogs, but if anything, they're extremely superficial.

And in fact, we see this in research. So it happens we know a lot about the human visual system—the neurology, how the different parts of the brain react, you know. How do we know it? By experimentation with other animals. You don't stick electrodes into the striate cortex of an infant, but rightly or wrongly we do it for cats. So we learn a lot about the visual system of other organisms, which happen to be very much like ours. So we therefore know a lot about our visual system. Can't do that for language. There's no organism that has anything remotely like it. So we're stuck, can't do that kind of…We can do lots of experiments with cats. Like we could raise a cat in darkness, let's say, or without pattern stimulation. We can see what happens to the visual system. You can imagine all sorts of experiments like that with language. Can't carry them out for ethical reasons. You want to understand the language? You can't do invasive experiments for ethical reasons. And therefore it's a very hard topic, the study of language, you know. You think of devious ways of trying to get information that you can get directly for other systems of the body by experimentation with animals. I mean, put aside the question of the ethics of experimentation with animals. That's a side question, but at least that's a way to approach it. The same with comparative evidence—you have it for other animals, you don't have it for humans. There's nothing comparable.

So we're a special thing in the world. Somehow, apparently, a couple hundred thousand years ago—roughly the time that *homo sapiens* appeared—a human language faculty appeared. We have some interesting ideas about what this might have been, but that's basically what happened. Not long after that period in evolutionary time—tens of thousands of years—not long after this, you start seeing the archeological evidence of complicated symbolic behavior. You go a couple of millennia beyond that—say, forty to fifty thousand years ago—you get the most amazing artistic achievements. I was lucky to be able to get into the Lascaux caves in southern France before they were closed off. It is utterly spectacular, way beyond anything you can see in the reproductions. It's claimed—I don't know if it's true—that when Picasso saw them, he said, we haven't learned anything in tens of thousands of years. That's probably twenty, thirty thousand years ago, but I know there's others back to forty, fifty thousand years.

So roughly speaking—remember, these are tiny moments in evolutionary history. These are seconds in evolutionary history. *Homo sapiens* appears. The faculty of language appears. Pretty soon you start getting complex symbolic activity. Before too long, it's amazing achievements and creativity. Then it goes on—not always for the good, as we know, but amazing achievements, unique in the animal world. Unique in history. It may soon come to an end. We do have the capacity to destroy ourselves. That's part of our achievement. We're now pursuing that. That may happen in a couple of generations. That's not at all impossible. That's the direction we're moving.

PS: It's a possibility. On the subject of language, did Russell have anything specifically to say that was influential to you in your thought?

NC: Well, Russell did very important work early in the 20th century on logic and language. So for example, his theory of descriptions is now a basic part of the work in natural language semantics that seeks to develop how our internal language systems assign meaning to utterances. Now that's a significant part. But his main interest was in something that was the main interest of practically everyone: a logically perfect language. You go back to Frege, for example, where a lot of the modern work begins. He assumed that language is an imperfect instrument. So we may use it for examples, but what we're interested in is a logically perfect language—ideas that actually go back to Leibniz, but were picked up in the 19th century, then developed. The same is true of the other major figures, Russell too. Alfred Tarski felt that language is just hopeless. You can construct contradictions in it. Rudolf Carnap, who I knew, couldn't understand why people even speak language, thought they ought to speak some logically perfect language. I could tell you more incidents about this. But the interest was in devising something that would be a perfect language without all the complications, difficulties of natural language, which is a natural organism. So natural organisms are not perfectly designed from an engineering point of view. Any engineer today could design something better than the human spine. Every one of us knows it's a very problematic system. It doesn't have to be that way. It has to do with its complicated evolutionary history, beginning apparently with a way to protect the nerve. It had nothing to do with holding the body up. But evolution goes on its own course, you know—takes the next step, doesn't look for a perfect design. If you think back in retrospect, you could maybe do it better.

Interestingly, language doesn't seem to be like that. The more we learn about language, the more it looks like it's in a way computationally perfect. Many of the deep—we're just learning about these things now. Doesn't look like it on the surface. It looks like a mess. But when you study it more deeply, make more discoveries about its fundamental nature, it turns out that large parts of it—maybe all—are computationally perfect. Can't do better. It uses the optimal computational possibilities. It is a computational system. No doubt about that. So it's based on computational principles. And it seems that when you look closely into notions like computational efficiency, it seems that in fundamental ways language developed that way. Now why isn't it a complicated mess like everything else? Probably the reason is that it developed almost instantaneously in evolutionary time and it hasn't changed. And so we know now, for example, by genomic analysis, that humans, *homo sapiens* began to separate roughly on the order of 150,000 years ago. Now that's not very long after *homo sapiens* appeared. So then in fact, as far as we know, all humans have the same language faculty. So it seems that it emerged in a brief period in evolutionary time, and hasn't changed. These are very short periods of time from an evolutionary point of view. So it looks roughly like that. And if that's the case, it could be that nature just found the simplest way, and it hasn't changed. There's some reason to believe that.

I mean, on the surface, languages seem extremely different. So listen to a foreign language, it sounds like just noise. So they seem to be very varied. But more and more we're discovering that those variations don't really have to do with language. They have to do with the way language is externalized in the sensory-motor system. So if you want a kind of an analogy, it's kind of like your laptop. Well, there's a program in your laptop which may be perfect, but when you send it to a printer, the printer may—it's the problem of sending it to a printer—may mess it up. Then you could send it to very different printers, which make it look very different, like different languages, but it's the same program in your laptop. It's increasingly looking like language may be something like that. It's controversial. Not many linguists would agree, but I think it's probably right.

PS: Yes, I think that's definitely controversial, as you say, but worth exploring, to be sure. We talked a little bit about Plato's problem. One of the other problems that you've talked about—and that Russell was also concerned about—is what you call Hume's problem: the problem in free societies of how so much inequality of power, how so much domination can take place. And I know for Russell, education was a critical part of the story.

NC: I think it's a large part of the story. Actually, Russell and John Dewey, who is another influential figure in my own life, both had important things to say about that. I mean, I was myself mostly immersed in the Deweyite tradition. In fact, I went to a Deweyite experimental school when I was 18 months old and stayed there until I was about 12. So it's a large part of my personal experience.[7] Then as a teacher I used Deweyite methods and so on. That's before I got interested in philosophy. I learned about Russell later on, and there are some similarities in their views. But I think that's important. Now I wouldn't say it's everything, but it's important. Educational programs can be designed in quite different ways.

Actually, this is discussed by another historical figure whose work I found extremely interesting in later years—before the Russell lectures, incidentally, I might have mentioned him. That's Wilhelm von Humboldt, a great linguist but also one of the founders of classical liberalism and the founder of the modern research university. There was a very interesting debate in the Enlightenment period about the nature of education. And there were kind of two polar opposites posed. The one used the model of pouring water into a vessel, and then the water is poured out of the vessel. The child is the vessel—you pour knowledge in and he pours it out on the test. Worst possible method of education, as they recognized. The kind that's used mostly. So in the United States—under the liberals, I should say—the educational system, [under] Obama and others, has been moved to what's called "teach to test." You have the teacher in the sixth grade pour a certain amount of information into the minds of the kids. They pass a test, and we all know from our own experience what happens. Two weeks later, you forgot what the course was about. Everybody's had that experience. That's the model that was derided during the Enlightenment.

The other model was essentially Humboldt's. The teacher's job is to lay out the string along which the student follows in his or her own way. So you have a kind of a structure, it's not just throw everything at the kid. There's a structure, some guidance, but the children are encouraged to learn and pursue their own ways of dealing with it. Learn how…you learn how to learn. Maybe you didn't get a lot of data at the end, but you know how to learn. Actually, one of the world's leading physicists at MIT used to open his

---

[7] The Deweyite school attended by Chomsky was called Oak Lane County Day School (Barsky 1997, 15-7). Interestingly, Russell spoke at Oak Lane a year or two before Chomsky began his attendance there (Ken Blackwell, personal correspondence, May 9, 2020).

freshmen physics classes. If a student asked him, what are we going to cover in this course, his answer was, it doesn't matter what we cover, it matters what you discover. You've got to learn how to learn and how to create. This can be done from kindergarten to high school.

In fact, there are now quite interesting science programs being developed to try to use the Humboldtian-Deweyite-Russellian method of education. So for example, to take one kindergarten program. Project begins with the teacher giving each one a shell. In the shell there are several objects: a bead, a stone, a seed, a couple of others. Then comes a task. The kids are supposed to figure out which one of these objects can grow. Then they have a meeting. Kids get together and they talk about what we can do to figure it out. And the teacher may intervene, you know, try to keep things going in the right direction. But finally they figure out some experiments, and they try the experiments. Sometimes they don't work, like most experiments. And finally they get experiments which begin to show some signs of germination. And finally they figure out it's the seed that can grow. After everybody understands that, the teacher comes around with a microscope. Cracks the seed. Each one can look into it, see the embryo, see what makes it grow. Now that's education. Telling the kids, here's the way it happens, learn it, memorize it, give it back in the test—that's not education. That's just training people to be regimented and obedient.

Well, those are two models. It can be done at any point. And I think Russell is correct. Education directed to creativity, independence, participation in a free community can change the way society evolves and is modified and changed by participants. It's not the only thing. Actually, experience can tell you a lot of the same things. The experience of…take my relatives, my extended family, back in the early thirties, unemployed immigrant working class. The experiment of participating in the emerging labor movement changed them a lot. That's very educational. Some didn't go to school, but they were educated, creative people through these experiences.

PS: The situations in which one can be thrust as one tries to struggle with the problems of the social and political world can cause one to learn very, very fast, I imagine.

NC: Well, the problems of the…there are, again, two different models of what politics is. There's a kind of an official doctrine promulgated by liberal intellectuals, conservatives, others. The official doctrine is, politics consists of pushing a lever every couple of years, and then going away and letting the smart guys run things. That's the kind of official model. There's another model, which says, politics consists of constant activism—constant—to try to change the world. Every once in a while, an event comes along called an election. You take 10 or 15 minutes to decide which lever to push. Then you go back to work. That's another model. Which of these models prevails will determine what kind of a world we live in.

PS: We're coming to the end of our time, but I know there's one definite question that the Russell Society members I'm sure would love to ask you. Did you ever meet Russell?

NC: Did I ever meet him? Never. Unfortunately not. We had one brief correspondence. It's in the Russell Archives at McMaster University. In 1966, a number of us were beginning to try to organize to go beyond protest, to direct resistance against the war. Involvement in draft resistance, tax resistance, other things, direct—what's called illegal activity. We didn't put it that way, but that's what it's called. So as we were organizing the group, I was designated to try to reach noted intellectual figures in the world to see if they would sign on. And the first person I wrote to, of course, was Russell. Got his agreement—strong agreement—by return mail. So it was the first one. You'll never guess who the second one was. Don't try. It was Rudolf Carnap.

PC: Rudolf Carnap again!

NC: He was quiet, but he was pretty radical. Thought the war was a horror. That's why I wrote to him.

PS: Excellent. Were you involved at all with the war crimes tribunal that Russell organized with Sartre?

NC: I was peripherally connected, actually not so much through Russell as through a close friend, Vladimir Dedijer, who was one of the leading figures. A Yugoslav partisan, former partisan activist, wonderful guy, he was a good friend. I was peripherally involved. Actually, I wrote the introduction to the volume that came out.[8] Tell you the honest truth, I wasn't a great

---

[8] The volume is Coates et al., eds. (1971).

enthusiast for the war crimes tribunals. I mean, I think they're very valuable, but there are some things about them that made me a little uncomfortable. For one thing, the outcome was preordained. It's not like…it's kind of like the Nuremberg trials. You know the judgment before they began. So I don't think they should be…I feel uncomfortable about the description as a tribunal. It's not as if we're going to look at the conflicting evidence and decide what's right. That's not what it's doing. They're very valuable, but I'd be a little happier with a different framework.

PS: Yes, there's a suggestion that perhaps…the framework suggests something a little bit different from what you actually get, I guess it sounds like.

NC: Although, you know, if you look at the history, it's not different. Take the Nuremberg Tribunal. Was there any doubt as to how it's going to come out? Was there any possibility that "Bomber" [Sir Arthur] Harris would be tried for destroying…for intense urban bombing, the bombing of civilian concentrations? It's only the British and the Americans who did that. But the tribunal was set up in advance with a principle: a German war criminal could plead innocence if he could show that the allies did the same thing. That's it. Actually, the German submarine commander, Commander Dönitz, argued in defense that the Americans did the same thing. Called as a witness Admiral Nimitz, an American admiral, who said, yeah, we also did those things. So he was therefore freed.[9] So what "war crime" meant was "crime you committed and we didn't." It's kind of a tribunal, but…

PS: No, I can see the parallels. Absolutely. I guess we should bring things to a close, but let me just by way of a final question—is there any part of Russell's legacy that you think is particularly important in the world right now that you'd like people to be paying attention to?

NC: Quite a lot, in both parts of his life. The intellectual world, in which I think he leaves very important ideas. In my own recent work, I've been using much of Russell's mostly unread work, like, for example, *The Analysis of Matter* and other publications from the 1920s. The other side of his life shows what an honorable human being can be like. Stand up for your principles, no matter who screams at you, who puts you in jail, stand up for them

---

[9] Admiral Dönitz, the Supreme Commander of the Navy of the Third Reich, was, however, found guilty on other charges and sentenced to ten years in prison.

because that's the way that leads to a better world.

PS: Wow. That's a very good note on which to end. And so on behalf of the Bertrand Russell Society, let me say I'm very grateful to have a chance to talk to you today. And I couldn't think of someone more deserving of the Russell Society's award this year. Thank you.

NC: Thank you very much.

Bibliography

Achbar, Mark, ed. 1994. *Manufacturing Consent: Noam Chomsky and the Media.* Montréal: Black Rose Books.

Barsky, Robert F. 1997. *Noam Chomsky: A Life of Dissent.* Cambridge, MA: MIT Press.

Chomsky, Noam. 2003. *Problems of Knowledge and Freedom.* New York: The New Press.

Coates, Ken; Limqueco, Peter; and Weiss, Peter, eds. 1971. *Prevent the Crime of Silence: Reports from the Sessions of the International War Crimes Tribunal, Founded by Bertrand Russell.* London: Allen Lane.

Pannekoek, Anton. 2003. *Workers' Councils.* Oakland, CA: AK Press.

ABOUT THE CONTRIBUTORS TO THIS VOLUME

DAVID BLITZ has been a faculty member at Central Connecticut State University since 1989. His areas of teaching and research are the history and philosophy of science, with special interest in theories of evolution and modern logic, as well as the work of Charles Darwin and Bertrand Russell. His book *Emergent Evolution: Qualitative Novelty and the Levels of Reality* was published in 1992 by Kluwer Academic Publishers. He is currently working on a monograph on Bertrand Russell's Philosophy of War and Peace. He is President of the Bertrand Russell Society.

NOAM CHOMSKY is one of the world's leading public intellectuals. He is currently Professor of Linguistics at the University of Arizona, which he joined in the fall of 2017. Previous to that he worked at the Massachusetts Institute of Technology from 1955

LANDON D. C. ELKIND is Izaak Walton Killam Postdoctoral Fellow in Philosophy at the University of Alberta. He earned his Ph.D. in Philosophy and M.S. in Mathematics from the University of Iowa in 2018. He is also the treasurer of the Bertrand Russell Society.

ROBERT HEINEMAN is Professor Emeritus of Political Science at Alfred University where he has been named Joseph Kruson Distinguished University Professor. He has authored or co-authored five books on public policy and on political thought and has served in elected and appointed positions at the national, state, and local levels of government.

JOHN LENZ is Associate Professor and former chair of the Department of Classics, and a member of the History and Culture Ph.D. program, at Drew University in Madison, NJ. A member of the Bertrand Russell Society since 1979, he served as President, 1994-98, and Chair, 2018-19. He was co-chair of the 4th Annual Harvard Conference on Public Intellectuals in 2013, and is immersed in a full-length study of Russell's thoughts about humanity and the future of the world.

TIM MADIGAN is Professor and Chair of Philosophy at St. John Fisher College in Rochester, NY. He is a Director and former President of the Bertrand Russell Society. He is the author, co-author, and editor of twenty books.

CARA ELIZABETH RICE is a Director of the Bertrand Russell Society, an independent scholar, and an educator. She has taught inner-city high school in Philadelphia and in a juvenile detention facility. Cara lives in central Pennsylvania with her daughter, Colette, and her husband, Chad Trainer, a co-contributor to this book.

MICHAEL RUSE is Lucyle T. Werkmeister Professor of Philosophy at Florida State University. He has been a philosophy professor for fifty years, first in Canada and now in the USA. Born in England into a Quaker family, he spent three Easters, beginning in 1960, on the Aldermaston March, protesting the atomic bomb. They ended in Trafalgar Square, and one of the speakers for the final one was a very aged Bertrand Russell, who gave a fiery speech denouncing the government, before he walked down Whitehall to Downing Street, the official home of the Prime Minister of Great Britain. There Russell sat on the pavement and got arrested, while Ruse was in Green Park kissing a girl he had met on the march.

ALAN SCHWERIN is Associate Professor of Philosophy at Monmouth University, and the former President of the Bertrand Russell Society. He is author and editor of several books, including *Russell Revisited: Critical Reflections on the Thought of Bertrand Russell* (Cambridge Scholars Press, 2008) and *Bertrand Russell on Nuclear War, Peace, and Language: Critical and Historical Essays* (Praeger, 2002).

TONY SIMPSON is Secretary of the Bertrand Russell Peace Foundation, and editor of *The Spokesman Journal*.

PETER STONE is an Associate Professor of Political Science at Trinity College Dublin. He is the author of *The Luck of the Draw: The Role of Lotteries in Decision Making* (Oxford University Press, 2011) and the editor of *Lotteries in Public Life: A Reader* (Imprint Academic, 2011). He has been a member of the Bertrand Russell Society for over 20 years, serves on its Board of Directors, and founded two of the Society's local chapters. He currently serves as President of the Political Studies Association of Ireland.

CHAD TRAINER is an independent scholar, former chair of the Bertrand Russell Society, and the Pennsylvania AFL-CIO's legislative director. He lives with his wife, Cara, and his daughter, Colette, in central Pennsylvania.

THOM WEIDLICH is a writer and former journalist who lives in New York City. His book, *Appointment Denied: The Inquisition of Bertrand Russell* (Prometheus Books), won the Bertrand Russell Society Book Award in 2001. He holds a bachelor's degree from the New School for Social Research and a master's degree in American history from Columbia University.

DAVID E. WHITE has completed a 40-year career of teaching philosophy, primarily at St. John Fisher College, Rochester, NY. He is a long-time member of and frequent presenter at meetings of the Bertrand Russell Society, and one of the organizers of the Bertrand Russell Set, a monthly meeting on Russell and related topics. White's stance is sufficiently wide that he can walk both sides of a freeway, devoting as much time and attention to Britain's greatest theologian, Bishop Butler, as to its greatest philosopher, Bertrand Russell.